P9-DIH-352

Urban Growth in the Age of Sectionalism

Urban Growth
in the Age of Sectionalism

Virginia, 1847–1861

DAVID R. GOLDFIELD

WITHDRAWN

Louisiana State University Press

Baton Rouge and London

for Barbara

HT
123.5
V5
G64

Copyright © 1977 by Louisiana State University Press
All rights reserved
Manufactured in the United States of America

Designer: Dwight Agner
Type face: VIP Baskerville
Typesetter: Moran Industries, Inc., Baton Rouge, Louisiana
Printer and binder: Kingsport Press, Kingsport, Tennessee

Publication of this book was assisted by the American Council of
Learned Societies under a grant from the Andrew W. Mellon Foundation.

LIBRARY OF CONGRESS CATALOGING IN PUBLICATION DATA

Goldfield, David R   1944–
   Urban growth in the age of sectionalism.

   Bibliography: p.
   Includes index.
   1. Cities and towns—Virginia—History. 2. Urbanization—
Virginia. 3. Virginia—Economic conditions. I. Title.
HT123.5.V5G64   301.36′3′09755   77–3514
ISBN 0–8071–0269–5

AUG 17 '78

Contents

Acknowledgments *ix*
Introduction *xi*

1 Redeemed, Regenerated, and Disenthralled *1*
2 The City-Builders *29*
3 Accommodation of Commerce and Labor *97*
4 Emergence of Local Government *139*
5 Cityhood *182*
6 Urban Virginia in an Urban Nation *226*
   Epilogue: The Renewed South *271*

APPENDICES

A Crosstabulation and the Computer *287*
B Virginia's Urban Leaders and Their Associational
   Activity *309*
C Classification of Occupations *311*

Bibliography *315*
Index *331*

Tables

1   Urban Population, 1840–1860   *xii*
2   Total Population States, 1840–1860   *xiii*
3   Activity Rate of Urban Leadership, 1847–1861   *33*
4   Occupation of Urban Leadership, 1850   *35*
5   Real Property Holding of Urban Leadership, 1850   *37*
6   Slave Ownership of Urban Leadership, 1850   *39*
7   Persistence and Priority of Urban Leadership, 1840–1860   *41*
8   Nativity of Urban Leadership, 1850   *42*
9   Age of Urban Leadership, 1850   *43*
10 Marital Status of Urban Leadership, 1850   *44*
11 Age of Wives of Urban Leaders, 1850   *45*
12 Number of Children of Urban Leaders, 1850   *46*
13 Age of Children of Urban Leaders, 1850   *47*
14 Boarders of Urban Leaders, 1850   *49*
15 Occupation by Richmond Study Group   *69*
16 Age by Richmond Study Group   *70*
17 Real Property by Richmond Study Group   *71*
18 Marital Status by Richmond Study Group   *72*
19 Age of Wives by Richmond Study Group   *73*
20 Number of Children by Richmond Study Group   *74*
21 Age of Youngest Child by Richmond Study Group   *75*
22 Age of Eldest Child by Richmond Study Group   *76*
23 Boarders by Richmond Study Group   *77*
24 Relative Boarders of Richmond Study Group   *78*
25 Family Boarders of Richmond Study Group   *79*
26 Occupational Boarders of Richmond Study Group   *80*
27 Servant Boarders of Richmond Study Group   *81*
28 Unknown Boarders of Richmond Study Group   *82*
29 Slave Ownership by Richmond Study Group   *83*
30 Male Slaves Owned by Richmond Study Group   *84*
31 Female Slaves Owned by Richmond Study Group   *85*
32 Persistence by Richmond Study Group   *86*
33 Nativity of Richmond Study Group   *87*
34 Share of Total Value of Exports of Principal Ports,
    1815–1860   *242*

Tables

35   Share of Total Value of Exports of Individual Ports, 1815–1860   243

36   Share of Total Value of Imports of Principal Ports, 1821–1860   244

37   Share of Total Value of Imports of Individual Cities, 1821–1860   245

38   Persistence by Occupation of Richmond Study Groups, 1850   289

39   Persistence of Age by Richmond Study Groups   290

40   Persistence by Real Property of Richmond Study Groups   291

41   Persistence by Marital Status of Richmond Study Groups   292

42   Persistence by Age of Wives of Richmond Study Groups   293

43   Persistence by Number of Children of Richmond Study Groups   294

44   Persistence by Age of Youngest Child of Richmond Study Groups   295

45   Persistence by Age of Eldest Child of Richmond Study Groups   296

46   Persistence by Boarders of Richmond Study Groups, 1850   297

47   Persistence by Relative Boarders of Richmond Study Groups, 1850   298

48   Persistence by Occupational Boarders of Richmond Study Groups, 1850   299

49   Persistence by Servant Boarders of Richmond Study Groups, 1850   300

50   Persistence by Family Boarders of Richmond Study Groups, 1850   301

51   Persistence by Unknown Boarders of Richmond Study Groups, 1850   302

52   Persistence by Slaves Owned by Richmond Study Groups, 1850   303

53   Persistence by Male Slaves Owned by Richmond Study Groups, 1850   304

54   Persistence by Female Slaves Owned by Richmond Study Groups, 1850   305

55   Persistence by Race of Richmond Study Groups, 1850   306

56   Persistence by Sex of Richmond Study Groups   307

57   Persistence by Nativity of Richmond Study Groups, 1850   308

Acknowledgments

ANY SCHOLARLY EFFORT is usually a joint production. In this case the supporting cast is legion. My debt to archival staff is great. They were not only helpful in unearthing pertinent manuscripts and newspapers, but they made me feel at home and pointed out the good, inexpensive restaurants and the best places to rest my strained eyes. The archivists at the Duke University Library, the Southern Historical Collection at the University of North Carolina at Chapel Hill, the Virginia Historical Society at Richmond, the Library of Congress, the University of Maryland Library, the C. W. Post College Library, and the Newman Library at Virginia Tech are all part of this book. The staffs at the Virginia State Library in Richmond and the Alderman Library at the University of Virginia deserve special mention because they are special people who went out of their way to provide me with important material and constantly encouraged my efforts. Louis Manarin of the Virginia State Library is to be praised for his efficient personnel, and Ann Stauffenberg and Michael Plunkett of the Alderman Library performed beyond the call of duty in making the research for this book easier to accomplish.

A research grant from C. W. Post College and computer time support from Virginia Tech facilitated the preparation of the book. I also received moral support and understanding at critical moments in the book's evolution from my bosses and friends, Leonard J. Simutis and Alan W. Steiss. Jacksie Dickerson, Louise Oliver, Christy Seaborn, and Patricia Wade all took turns squinting at my scrawl and still managed to do a first-rate job. Finally, colleagues Len Simutis and Thomas Watts helped me through the mysteries of SPSS and initiated a bond of friendship between myself and the computer.

The substance of this book is a product of considerable distillation over several years bridging my graduate years with my professional career. In the early years the inspiration of fine teachers and

Acknowledgments

scholars at Maryland, like Paul K. Conkin, David Grimsted, and David Sparks, helped me to both write and think more clearly. George H. Callcott, my mentor, turned my thoughts to Virginia, refined my skills, and gave up a good deal of his valuable time just to talk with me about southern history. His keen insights, which he shared freely, made a lasting impression on my historical consciousness. As the manuscript developed, its form and emphasis received valuable inputs from Charles B. Dew, Charles N. Glaab, and Grady McWhiney. Any shortcomings in the book are the result of my stubbornness—not of their recommendations.

Once I completed the manuscript, I was fortunate to come into partnership with another group of highly competent professionals. Lloyd Lyman, Les Phillabaum, and especially Beverly Jarrett of LSU Press have been accommodating and helpful at each stage in the production process. Their selection of Elizabeth Coccio to copyedit the manuscript was merely one example of their excellent judgment.

Last, but certainly not least, my parents and my wife Barbara are part of this book because they are so much a part of me. Barbara was not only a valuable research assistant, but she also prevailed through my moody moments. She inspired my writing and thinking by letting me know she would be there, stoking me with chicken soup, pasta, and encouragement at the end of the chapter. So, this book is dedicated to Barbara, my favorite Virginian of all.

David R. Goldfield

Introduction

OVER A GENERATION AGO, W. J. Cash quickly disabused his readers of the plantation ideal. Yet, Scarlett and Rhett continue to cavort through the pages of southern history, reinterpreted and scaled down perhaps, but essentially unchanged. Historian David L. Smiley remarked recently that writers still view the Old South as "planter, plantation, staple crop, and the Negro, all set in a rural scene." Southern ruralness and the region's antipathy to urbanization have been historical clichés. Eugene D. Genovese, for example, referred to southern antiurbanism as a "quasi-religious faith." The Old South, Genovese continued, was a "backward-looking society" dominated by slaveholders and their plantations. Raimondo Luraghi, in a provocative article comparing the southern Italian experience with the southern American experience, affirmed the Old South's "agrarian, backward status." Other historians have reasoned that southerners were self-evidently unsympathetic to urban growth because cities characterized the North. Northern cities, of course, harbored abolitionists, feminists, and other would-be traducers of southern civilization. To encourage urbanization in the South would be to create an environment conducive to the destruction of southern institutions.[1]

Some historians have begrudgingly admitted the existence of an urban South. They have, however, either dismissed the city's role in the region entirely or accorded it a subservient and ineffectual place. Actually, urban growth in all southern states, except for Louisiana and those states where figures were unavailable, outstripped the section's increase in general population between 1840 and 1860 (see tables 1 and 2). More specifically, scholars have

---

1. W. J. Cash, *The Mind of the South* (New York, 1941), vii–x; David L. Smiley, "The Quest for a Central Theme in Southern History," *South Atlantic Quarterly*, LXII (1972), 318; Eugene D. Genovese, *The World the Slaveholders Made: Two Essays in Interpretation* (New York, 1969), 123, 156; Raimondo Luraghi, "The Civil War and the Modernization of American Society," *Civil War History*, XVIII (1972), 236; see also Bayrd Still, *Urban America: A History with Documents* (Boston, 1974), 103–04.

Introduction

Table 1 Urban Population 1840–1860

	1840	1850	1860	1840–60%
COASTAL SOUTH[a]				
Alabama	12,672	35,179	48,901	
		177.6%	39.0%	285.9%
Florida	. . .	. . .	5,708	
Georgia	24,658	38,994	75,466	
		58.1	93.5	206.1
Louisiana	105,400	134,470	185,026	
		27.6	37.6	75.5
Maryland	113,912	188,045	233,300	
		65.1	24.1	104.8
North Carolina	13,310	21,109	24,554	
		58.6	16.3	84.5
South Carolina	33,601	49,045	48,574	
		46.0	−1.0	44.6
Virginia[b]	70,968	89,255	115,879	
		25.8	29.8	63.3
INTERIOR SOUTH[c]				
Arkansas	. . .	. . .	3,727	
Kentucky	30,948	73,804	120,624	
		138.5	63.4	289.8
Mississippi	3,612	10,723	20,689	
		196.9	92.9	472.8
Tennessee	6,929	21,983	46,541	
		217.3	111.7	571.7
Texas	. . .	7,665	26,615	
			247.2	247.2d
WESTERN VIRGINIA	7,885	11,435	20,077	
		45.0	75.6	154.6

SOURCE: Donald B. Dodd and Wynelle S. Dodd, *Historical Statistics of the South, 1790–1970* (University, Ala., 1973).
[a] States with a major gulf or ocean seaport.
[b] Excluding that region that now comprises West Virginia.
[c] States without a major gulf or ocean seaport.
[d] 1850–60 only.

Table 2 Total Population States, 1840–1860

	1840	1850	1860	1840–60%
COASTAL SOUTH				
Alabama	590,756	771,623	964,201	
		30.6	25.0	63.2
Florida	54,477	87,445	140,424	
		60.5	60.6	157.8
Georgia	691,392	906,185	1,057,286	
		31.1	16.7	52.9
Louisiana	352,411	517,762	708,002	
		46.9	36.7	100.9
Maryland	470,019	583,034	687,049	
		24.0	17.8	46.2
North Carolina	245,817	288,548	331,059	
		58.6	16.3	34.7
South Carolina	594,398	668,507	703,708	
		12.5	5.3	18.4
Virginia	1,025,227	1,119,348	1,219,630	
		9.2	9.0	19.0
INTERIOR SOUTH				
Arkansas	97,574	209,897	435,450	
		115.1	107.5	346.3
Kentucky	779,828	982,405	1,155,684	
		26.0	17.6	48.2
Mississippi	375,651	606,526	791,305	
		61.5	30.5	110.6
Tennessee	829,210	1,002,717	1,109,801	
		20.9	10.7	33.8
Texas	. . .	212,592	604,215	
			184.2	184.2
WESTERN VIRGINIA	224,537	302,313	376,688	
		34.6	24.6	67.8

SOURCE: Dodd and Dodd, *Historical Statistics of the South.*

emphasized the paucity and anemia of inferior towns in the Old South as evidence of the superficiality of southern urbanization.[2] Precisely the opposite was true: the most rapid rate of urbanization in the Old South occurred beyond the Appalachian region between 1840 and 1860. Memphis, an interior city, exhibited the rate of growth of 155%: the fastest of any southern city during the period. The emergence of Atlanta and Chattanooga and the steady development of Louisville attested to the health of interior settlements. Much of the lower Mississippi Valley was frontier well into the 1830s. The high percentages of the growth of the urban population reflected, in part, the newness of the region. There were, of course, no serious interior rivals to New Orleans, Richmond, or Baltimore. On the other hand New York, Boston, and Philadelphia overshadowed Pittsburgh, Cincinnati, and Chicago in the North. The dominance of coastal cities in both sections reflected more the commercial nature of the antebellum economy than any philosophical or economic disabilities prohibiting interior urban development.[3]

Writers acknowledging southern urbanization have pointed out the stunted nature of that development. Inadequate industrialization, one argument ran, rendered the South's cities little more than sleepy market towns reflecting the ideals of the surrounding countryside.[4] While it was accurate to belittle southern industrialization compared to the Northeast, this comparison was unfair since the Northeast was one of the most rapidly industrializing areas of the world at the time. The West also lacked industrial centers to match those of the Northeast, and in some industries the South's facilities were clearly superior.[5] Richmond contained the largest flour mill

2. Julius Rubin, "The Limits of Agricultural Progress in the Nineteenth-Century South," *Agricultural History*, XLIX (1975), 362–73.

3. Statistical references helpful to students of the urban South include the compendiums of the U.S. Census (1850 to 1870 for the antebellum era); "Progress of the Population in the United States," *Hunt's Merchants' Magazine and Commercial Review*, XXXII (1855), 191–95 (this periodical will hereafter be cited as *Hunt's*); and Donald B. Dodd and Wynelle S. Dodd, *Historical Statistics of the South, 1790–1970* (University, Ala., 1973).

4. Luraghi, "Civil War and Modernization," 237.

5. Stanley L. Engerman, "A Reconsideration of Southern Economic Growth, 1770–

in the nation in 1860 and manufactured more tobacco than any other city in the world. Augusta's textile complex earned that city the title Lowell of the South. Wheeling glass achieved a national reputation, and its iron industry, for a time, rivaled Pittsburgh's.[6] The ability of the South to mount a war effort of four years' duration was testimony to the fact that an industrial potential existed prior to the Civil War.

Industrialization and urbanization are not synonymous. Francis Cabot Lowell took great pains to maintain a pastoral atmosphere in his industrial villages. Similarly, South Carolina industrialist William Gregg and Alabama textile entrepreneur Daniel Pratt viewed cities as inappropriate environments for industry.[7] Much of the South's industry was, in fact, small-scale, rural, and often plantation based—a fact that tended to depress southern industrial statistics. It is unclear whether industry is even essential for urban growth. Cincinnati, for example, achieved hegemony in the West over its industrial rival, Pittsburgh, by developing its commerce, not its manufacturing.[8]

A final argument advanced by historians to minimize the effect of southern urban civilization emphasizes the pervasiveness of a rural ideal that smothered urban progress.[9] This rural-mindedness, though, was not a distinctly southern phenomenon. Prominent northerners excoriated the evils of urban civilization and extolled the benefits of pastoral life just as passionately as their southern

1860," *Agricultural History*, XLIX (1975), 343–61. See also Richard C. Wade, "An Agenda for Urban History," in George A. Billias and Gerald N. Grob (eds.), *American History: Retrospect and Prospect* (New York, 1971), 392.

6. Richmond *Daily Dispatch*, September 22, 1859; Wheeling *Argus*, quoted in Richmond *Enquirer*, September 16, 1853; Joseph C. Robert, *The Tobacco Kingdom: Plantation, Market and Factory in Virginia and North Carolina, 1800–1860* (Durham, 1938); Richard W. Griffin, "The Origins of the Industrial Revolution in Georgia: Cotton Textiles, 1810–1865," *Georgia Historical Quarterly*, XLII (1958), 355–75.

7. Clement Eaton, *The Growth of Southern Civilization, 1790–1860* (New York, 1961), 173; Randall Miller, "Daniel Pratt's Industrial Urbanism: The Cotton Mill Town in Antebellum Alabama," *Alabama Historical Quarterly*, XXXIV (1972), 5–35.

8. See Richard C. Wade, *The Urban Frontier: The Rise of Western Cities, 1790–1830* (Cambridge, Mass., 1959).

9. See Eugene D. Genovese, *The Political Economy of Slavery* (New York, 1965), 24–25, 91, 158; Still, *Urban America*, 103–104.

counterparts. If, as some have charged, southern city dwellers poured profits into country homes and farms, there is no evidence that northern merchants and bankers did not long equally hard for a country estate. Northern reverence for rural quietude seemed to have little impact upon urban growth in the region. In fact, mid-nineteenth-century Americans generally possessed ambivalent attitudes toward both urban and rural living that enabled them to build great cities and to write romantic literature exalting country life without apparent self-contradiction. To hold that love of nature and rural virtues were antagonistic to urbanization is to establish a dichotomy that was not always clear to contemporaries.[10]

Implied and often explicit in the discussion on southern ruralness is that southerners, captured by visions of moonlight and magnolias, invested heavily in slaves and land and left urban enterprises languishing.[11] Southern rural investors, however, evidently understood that growing cities ultimately redounded to the benefit of their farms. Their investments did not stop at the city line because neither did their economic interests. Inventories of planters' estates indicated that well-to-do scions of the soil placed their profits in a variety of schemes during the 1850s when both capital and investment opportunities were relatively abundant in the region. Internal improvements and industrial firms, bank stock, and city bonds as well as land and labor attracted planters' money.[12]

Between 1850 and 1860, southern railroad mileage, constructed primarily with local capital, quadrupled while northern mileage (including that of western states), often aided by foreign capital, tripled. Industrial investments in the South increased by 64% dur-

10. See Morton White and Lucia White, *The Intellectual versus the City: From Thomas Jefferson to Frank Lloyd Wright* (Cambridge, Mass., 1962).

11. See Genovese, *Political Economy of Slavery*, 171–73, 186, 246; and Luraghi, "Civil War and Modernization," 230–49.

12. See, for example, Jeremiah C. Harris Diary (MS in Duke University), November 28, 1859; "Inventory and Appraisement of the Estate of William Massie, 1862," (MS in William Massie Notebooks, Duke University); "Meetings of Stockholders of the Alexandria, Loudoun, and Hampshire Railroad Company," Alexandria *Gazette*, September 8, 1858; and "Annual Meeting of the Stockholders of the Orange and Alexandria Railroad," Alexandria *Gazette*, October 23, 1857. See also Fred Bateman, James Foust, and Thomas Weiss, "The Participation of Planters in Manufacturing in the Antebellum South," *Agricultural History*, XLVIII (1974), 277–97.

ing this period, compared with an increase of 83% for the more heavily industrialized northern states. Southern bank capital also compared favorably with northern financial institutions. A survey of bank capital in twenty-eight cities just prior to the southern railroad boom in 1848 revealed that banks in twelve southern cities possessed capital amounting to $56,000,000, while in sixteen northern cities bank capital totaled $80,000,000. New York and Boston alone, though, accounted for more than half of the northern total ($45,000,000). Since planters held the bulk of investment capital in the South, it was not surprising that such enterprises benefited from rural largesse.[13]

The competition for the rural investment dollar was all the more severe as southern agriculture revived during the 1850s. Financing additional land and labor promised a profitable return; indeed more profitable, some scholars have asserted, than comparable enterprises anywhere in the Union. The wonder is that, considering the return from agriculture, planter capital found its way into such a broad spectrum of economic activities.[14]

Patriotism as well as profits motivated agriculturists to enhance the urban economic base. Southern rhetoric during the period between the Mexican War and the firing on Fort Sumter demonstrated an increasing appreciation for the efficacy of urban growth as a response to northern economic and political power. J. D. B. DeBow, an indefatigable spokesman for the urban South, achieved his greatest fame, and his *Review* its greatest circulation, during the decade prior to the Civil War.[15] George Fitzhugh, a leading proponent of planter society, also encouraged urban development as a means to sectional strength:

13. U. S. Bureau of Census, *Compendium of the Eighth Census: 1860. Mortality and Miscellaneous* (Washington, D.C., 1861), IV, 331; *Compendium of the Ninth Census: 1870* (Washington, D.C., 1871), 789–99; "Bank Capital of Cities in the United States," *Hunt's*, XVIII (1848), 326.

14. Robert W. Fogel and Stanley L. Engerman, *Time on the Cross: The Economics of American Negro Slavery* (Boston, 1974), 247–57. On the revival of southern agriculture in the 1850s see Lewis C. Gray, *History of Agriculture in the Southern United States* (2 vols.; Washington, D.C., 1933), especially vol. II; and Kathleen Bruce, "Virginia Agriculture Decline to 1860: A Fallacy," *Agricultural History*, VI (1932), 3–13.

15. See Otis C. Skipper, *J. D. B. DeBow: Magazinist of the Old South* (Athens, Ga., 1958), 123–30.

Towns and villages . . . afford respectable occupations in the mechanic arts, commerce, manufactures, and the professions. . . . They sustain good schools, which a sparse country neighborhood never can. They furnish places and opportunities for association and rational enjoyment to the neighborhood around. They support good ministers and churches. . . . Rivers and roads without towns, are mere facilities offered to agriculture to carry off the crops, to exhaust the soil, and to remove the inhabitants.[16]

Neither DeBow nor Fitzhugh were voices in the southern wilderness. Their writings were read widely and their calls for urban growth drew sympathetic responses throughout the antebellum South. Within the past decade, urban biographies of Natchez, New Orleans, and Houston; monographs dealing with various aspects of southern urban life; and a spate of articles have attested to this fact and have begun to redress the imbalance in southern historiography.[17]

These scholarly efforts and the general surge in urban history have underscored the fact that nineteenth-century cities possessed influence far greater than their small number warranted. They were crucibles of change in a changing society. This is not surprising. Richard Hildreth, marveling at the rapid pace of urbanization in what still was a predominantly rural society, observed that America's cities "are the central points from which knowledge, enterprise, and civilization stream out upon the surrounding country."[18] From Hildreth's vantage point (mid-nineteenth-century America) the urban phenomenon must have been truly impressive. The years between 1820 and 1860 witnessed the most rapid rate of growth of cities in American history. The decade between 1840 and

16. George Fitzhugh, *Sociology for the South; or, The Failure of Free Society* (New York, 1854), 136.

17. See, for example, Blaine A. Brownell and David R. Goldfield, *The City in Southern History: The Growth of Urban Civilization in the South* (Port Washington, N.Y., 1976); D. Clayton James, *Antebellum Natchez* (Baton Rouge, 1968); David G. McComb, *Houston: The Bayou City* (Austin, 1969); Merl E. Reed, *New Orleans and the Railroads: The Struggle for Commercial Empire* (Baton Rouge, 1966); Kenneth W. Wheeler, *To Wear a City's Crown: The Beginnings of Urban Growth in Texas* (Cambridge, Mass., 1968); Blaine A. Brownell, "Urbanization in the South: A Unique Experience?" *Mississippi Quarterly*, XXVI (1973), 105–20; Leonard P. Curry, "Urbanization and Urbanism in the Old South: A Comparative View," *Journal of Southern History*, XL (1974), 43–60; and Lyle W. Dorsett and Arthur H. Shaffer, "Was the Antebellum South Antiurban? A Suggestion," *Journal of Southern History*, XXXVIII (1972), 93–100.

18. Richard Hildreth, *Despotism in America: An Inquiry into the Nature, Results, and Legal Basis of the Slave-Holding Systems in the United States* (Boston, 1854), 139.

1850 showed the largest increase in urban population.[19] The South participated in the unprecedented urban growth, but mere numbers do not reveal the influence of southern cities. While population is an index of urban growth, it is not the only barometer of urbanization. Nineteenth-century Tokyo possessed more than three million residents but could hardly be called a city in the modern sense of extensive commercial connections, internal organization, urban services, and civic pride. Historians have begun to address themselves to the question of urbanization since it was such a pervasive phenomenon in the nineteenth century. Although a satisfactory model of urban growth has yet to appear, writers have isolated several factors crucial to the process of urbanization.

Scholars have employed two general measures of urbanization: quantitative and qualitative.[20] The quantitative measure includes two indicators of urbanization. The first is the development of an economic superstructure consisting of transportation facilities, industry, and export trade. The second quantitative index measures the increase in population, area, and wealth, which is usually triggered by the impact of the economic superstructure. The differentiation and segregation of urban functions is an important manifestation of the quantitative growth indexes. Some quantitative indicators are more important than others. Industry and population are not necessarily indicative of modern urban civilization. Transportation links with the countryside and with other cities, on the other hand, liberate "island communities" and enable them to establish regional relationships crucial to the process of urbanization.

The qualitative measure also consists of two indicators. First, there is the organization of urban life. The quantitative aspects of growth require the evolution of an urban leadership and a com-

19. In addition to the statistical aids cited in n. 3, see Wade, "Agenda for Urban History," 391.

20. For some recent attempts at explaining urbanization see Richard D. Brown, "The Emergence of Urban Society in Rural Massachusetts, 1760–1820," *Journal of American History*, LXI (1974), 29–51; Curry, "Urbanization and Urbanism," 43–60; and Peter G. Goheen, "Industrialization and the Growth of Cities in Nineteenth-Century America," *American Studies*, XIV (1973), 49–65.

munications system. Together, they must rationalize the urban economic and political system. Urban consciousness is the second indicator of qualitative growth. It is the most intangible but one of the most important of all measures. Urban consciousness is both a feeling of uniqueness and a sense of civic pride. It is not only an indicator of growth but, in a sense, marks its fulfillment.

Since George Rogers Taylor's exhaustive study of the transportation revolution in nineteenth-century America, scholars have viewed the railroad as an important catalyst in the compound of cityhood. The railroad increased the accessibility of the city to the hinterland and vice versa. In making commercial agriculture more feasible, the railroad accelerated prosperity in the countryside and ultimately in the market town. Prosperity generated capital, and capital promoted growth. The railroad was also one of the earliest forms of corporate enterprise. It thus provided entrepreneurs with corporate experience—often at the expense of public and private stockholders—which proved valuable for later corporate endeavors. Finally, the railroad helped to transform local economies into a regional and eventually a national economy. The formation of a national economy was a major theme in antebellum America.[21]

The economic superstructure led by the railroad generated advances in population, area, and wealth. A modern, differentiated city began to emerge. The diversification of the urban economy created a labor-class consciousness. The hazy lines of distinction between employer and employee, characteristic of the colonial period, began to harden with the appearance of larger mercantile and industrial establishments. Further, residence and work became differentiated. As the city expanded spatially, the central business district evolved as just that: a business district with few residential areas. Although zoning codes did not appear in American cities until the twentieth century, segregated land use was common by the end of the antebellum era.[22]

21. See George Rogers Taylor, *The Transportation Revolution, 1815–1860* (New York, 1951), Chap. 17; and see also Douglass C. North, *The Economic Growth of the United States, 1790–1860* (New York, 1961), Chap. 9, 193–94.
22. See Sam Bass Warner, Jr., *The Private City: Philadelphia in Three Periods of Its Growth* (Philadelphia, 1968).

The emergence of an identifiable, cohesive leadership to rationalize the city's quantitative growth is another indicator of cityhood. Technology and natural advantages were virtually useless without the existence of entrepreneurial skill to parlay them into effective forces for the promotion of urban growth. From the rise of the port of New York to the development of frontier settlements, the role of the civic booster was essential to success. The entrepreneur possessed not only the requisite skills and capital, but through collective leadership in most phases of urban life, he personally directed urban development. Urban leaders organized urban, and ultimately, regional growth. Voluntary associations of leaders facilitated and rationalized the process. More efficient marketing procedures, organized charity relief, and cooperative action on projects designed to improve urban life were some of the accomplishments of urban leadership.[23]

Improved communications was another qualitative index of urban growth. Besides the improvement of the mail service and the introduction of the telegraph—both of which facilitated business transactions—the development of the urban press was an important ally to city-building. The press was essential to leaders' efforts to organize the city. In antebellum America the urban press was primarily a political weapon. Toward the end of the period, however, the political press came increasingly under the influence of local leaders and began to emphasize local development. Further, nonpartisan newspapers appeared (they were called penny presses) that dedicated their columns to the promotion of their city's interests. The urban press disseminated price and market information, functioned as the city's major advertising medium, and served as both creator and defender of the city's image. The Norfolk *Southern Argus*, a leader in the new wave of urban journalism that occurred after 1847, stated an axiom of the day when it observed, "The mighty influence of this silent teacher [the press], pouring its lessons every day into the minds of men, it is impossible to estimate."[24]

23. On the influence of leadership on urban growth see Wade, *Urban Frontier*, 203–10.
24. Norfolk *Southern Argus*, December 29, 1853.

The rise of local government to translate the expressions of the press and the goals of the leaders into policy was a significant development in the urbanization process. Local government was unimportant in early nineteenth-century America. Urban growth and the leaders' awareness of the efficacy of government involvement in the process of growth assured a broader role for urban government than it had ever experienced. A range of urban services from police and fire protection to street lighting and relief for the poor enabled city dwellers to cope with urbanization and, in turn, spurred further growth. Finally, the new powers of taxation—a benefit of charter amendments—imposed local government on the community as an important financial force.[25]

The development of urban consciousness was central to urban growth. Urban consciousness, or civic pride, cut across all indexes of urbanization. Demands for railroads, the differentiation of urban life, civic boosterism, the press, and the increased role of local government were all manifestations of urban consciousness. Civic pride represented a belief that the city was a distinct environment that was somehow different from the countryside and shared a commonality with cities elsewhere. Antebellum southern social critic Daniel R. Hundley observed that "nearly all classes of residents in the Southern cities differ in no essential particulars from the same classes in other cities anywhere else in the Union." Urban historian Richard C. Wade concurred with Hundley's observation in noting that urban centers were more like each other than their respective countrysides. Wade concluded that cities muted regional differences and were thus a nationalizing force.[26]

If urbanization was a nationalizing force, it contravened another major theme of nineteenth-century America: sectionalism. The apparent contradiction between the two themes as well as the reluctance of scholars to recognize southern urban growth have inhibited a study of the relationship between these two movements.

25. See Charles N. Glaab and A. Theodore Brown, *A History of Urban America* (New York, 1967), Chap. 7.
26. Daniel R. Hundley, *Social Relations in Our Southern States* (New York, 1860), 258; and Wade, "Agenda for Urban History," 393. See also Carl Abbott, "Civic Pride in Chicago, 1844–1860," *Journal of the Illinois State Historical Society*, LXIII (1970), 421.

In the Old South there was a connection between sectional feeling and urban growth. Articles exploiting and explaining the growing sectional crisis appeared alongside articles devoted to subjects promoting urban growth in the press and in magazines. It was not long before contributors and editors combined the two themes and championed the cause of cities as a response to sectionalism. J. D. B. DeBow related the themes of urban ascendancy and sectionalism time and again. DeBow believed that the South's port cities—Baltimore, Richmond, Charleston, Savannah, Mobile, and New Orleans—would break the stranglehold of New York on the nation's commerce and deliver the South from northern¯dependence. George Fitzhugh similarly urged that southern cities take up the cudgels for the South to release the region from the avaricious and threatening grasp of the North. "The South," Fitzhugh wrote earnestly, "must build up cities, towns, and villages, establish more schools and colleges, educate the poor, construct internal improvements, and carry on her own commerce." On a somewhat smaller scale, though equally urgent, the Richmond *Enquirer* claimed that developing Virginia's cities would save the South from the "indellible brand of degradation the North is trying to affix."[27]

The reasoning of these and other southern writers seemed to be that urban growth would help to strengthen the South and ameliorate sectional antagonism. The South's continued dependence invited northern economic and political aggression and depressed the section. Cities as repositories of labor, capital, expertise, railroads, industry, and mercantile establishments would enable the South to compete on a more equal basis with the North. The region's interests and institutions could thus be safeguarded. Just as New York, Boston, and Philadelphia came to characterize the economic and political leadership of the North, so the South's cities would fill a similar role for her.[28]

The example of northern cities provided southerners with awesome models for urban growth. Southern cities, of course, would

27. "Commercial, Agricultural, and Intellectual Independence of the South," *DeBow's Review*, XXIX (1860), 466–88; Fitzhugh, *Sociology*, 158; Richmond *Enquirer*, February 27, 1854.

28. See George Fitzhugh, *Cannibals All! or, Slaves without Masters* (New York, 1857), 59.

possess all of the majesty and none of the social problems that beset the urban North. The dreams of majesty, though, usually overcame concern about the quality of urban life. Americans had canonized the pursuit of prosperity in the four decades preceding the Civil War, and the city seemed to be the working symbol of this American dream. The South shared the vision, and at no time was it stronger than in the 1850s. It was not surprising that the South looked to its cities for the fulfillment of that dream.

The northern urban empire had been built, to a great extent, on the trade of the West. The West held a seemingly limitless bounty, and a share of its trade was a major objective in the southern blueprint for urban growth and sectional equilibrium. Ever since John C. Calhoun and Robert Y. Hayne had successfully promoted a railroad from Charleston to up-country Hamburg, South Carolina, in 1833, southerners had cast covetous eyes upon the western trade. When a group led by Hayne secured a charter for a railroad to Cincinnati, the South Carolina senator pronounced, "The South and the West—we have published the banns—if anyone knows ought why these two should not be joined together, let him speak now, or forever after hold his peace." As for Charleston, Hayne was equally sanguine: "The far and fertile West will pour her inexhaustible treasures into our lap." The wedding announcement was premature. A decade later, under darkening clouds, J. D. B. DeBow placed the South's task in its proper economic perspective: "A contest has been going on between North and South . . . for wealth and commerce of the great valley of the Mississippi. We must meet our Northern competitors . . . with corresponding weapons."[29] The southern city was at the point of the spear.

The contest outlined by DeBow was a difficult one for the South to undertake for at least two reasons. First, southern cities entered the contest belatedly and had to mount a massive effort in a short period of time (1847 to 1861), defying the laws of trade. The patterns of trade by the end of the Mexican War were unmistakably

29. Charleston *Courier*, August 31, 1836; "Contests for the Trade of the Mississippi Valley," *DeBow's Review*, III (1847), 98.

West to Northeast.[30] New Orleans, the urban bellwether of southern prosperity, enjoyed the return of cotton prosperity in the
1850s. Produce from the Ohio River and upper Mississippi river
valleys, however, declined drastically as the railroad overshadowed
the Mississippi River as a major commercial artery. Second, southerners overestimated the capacity of their cities to secure western
trade in their uneven rivalry with northern urban centers. Besides
railroads, financial, factoring, industrial, and direct trade linkages
were essential to generate commerce. The capital, energy, and
expertise that went into creating these linkages were prodigious.
Moreover, these relationships could not appear spontaneously.
New York, for example, had been working assiduously since the
end of the War of 1812 to erect a commercial superstructure to
accommodate and to attract western trade. Even by 1847 New
York's economic leadership was not a monopoly.[31]

Southerners like DeBow and Fitzhugh were aware that their
section and, more particularly, their cities entered the competition
for commercial empire at a considerable disadvantage. It was essential, however, that the South make the challenge. They and
other southerners believed that "pecuniary and commercial
supremacy" were the real objectives behind the North's strident
sectional and anti-slavery rhetoric.[32] If the South, through its cities,
would launch a successful economic offensive, the North would
respect its southern neighbors as economic equals and seek to
cultivate trade, not enemies. Nothing less than the Union was at
stake. "Give us [southern cities] the trade of the West," the
Richmond *Enquirer* promised, "and we will pacify the nation."[33]

If some southerners linked urbanization with sectionalism, most
historians have not. One persistent interpretation in the origins of
the Civil War emphasizes the distinction between the agrarian,

30. See Louis B. Schmidt, "Internal Commerce and the Development of the National
Economy Before 1860," *Journal of Political Economy*, XLVII (1939), 798–822.
31. See Thomas C. Cochran, "The Business Revolution," *American Historical Review*,
LXXIX (1974), 1449–66.
32. Portsmouth *Daily Pilot*, August 17, 1850. See also speech of Senator R. M. T. Hunter
in U.S. Senate, quoted in Richmond *Enquirer*, April 5, 1850.
33. Richmond *Enquirer*, August 28, 1855. See also John R. Tucker to M. R. H. Garnett,
January 1, 1846, in Charles F. Mercer Papers, Virginia State Library, Richmond, Va.

"quasi-colonial" South and the urban, industrial North and the inevitable clash of these two different "nationalities."[34] This ignores the presence of an urban South as well as a rural North, not to mention the overwhelmingly-agrarian West. In addition, the Beardian proponents and their present-day disciples assume that contemporaries perceived themselves and their section as either rural or urban and that there existed a natural animosity between the two. As I have noted earlier, Americans often blurred the differences between city and country. Their experience, in fact, confirmed the compatability between rural and urban enterprise. As the Norfolk *Southern Argus* observed, "Their [city and country] interests are often one in the same."[35]

As cities grew and prospered throughout the nation, their agricultural hinterlands developed accordingly. The agrarian South, like the agrarian West and North, moved into the orbit of its respective urban market centers. Farmers supported the efforts of their cities to extend the urban commercial network beyond sectional borders. In short, as there was a similarity between the urban South and cities elsewhere, so there was little difference between market-oriented farms in the Old South and similar units in the North and West. Even conceding that the South was agrarian (and what section was not in 1860?), the section's agriculture was intimately bound to urban development, just as it was in the rest of the nation's farms and cities.[36] Thus, any interpretation that presumes the antagonism of urban and rural environments contradicts the experience of antebellum America.

The dominance of slavery and the slaveholder in southern society is a corollary to the agrarian thesis.[37] The argument assumes an

34. See James C. Hite and Ellen J. Hall, "The Reactionary Evolution of Economic Thought in Antebellum Virginia," *Virginia Magazine of History and Biography*, LXXX (1972), 476–88; and Luraghi, "Civil War and Modernization," 234–36. See also Eric Foner, *Free Soil, Free Labor, Free Men: The Ideology of the Republican Party Before the Civil War* (New York, 1970).

35. Norfolk *Southern Argus*, June 16, 1854.

36. On the mutual dependence of city and hinterland, see Michael P. Conzen, *Frontier Farming in an Urban Shadow* (Madison, Wisc., 1971); Robert R. Dykstra, *The Cattle Towns* (New York, 1968); and Wheeler, *To Wear A City's Crown*.

37. See Genovese, *Political Economy of Slavery*; Eric Foner, "The Causes of the Civil War:

identity between slavery and the farm. An interpretation relying on the importance of slavery in the sectional equation should include a discussion of urban slavery. The city and slavery proved congenial to each other. Increasing use of slave labor in urban pursuits sounded not the death knell for the institution but rather portended a renaissance. Urban slavery demonstrated the flexibility of the institution and the ability of the slave to learn and adapt to new techniques. In a competition against northern cities, slave labor was an important commodity. Slaves manned factories, built railroads and canals, unloaded and loaded produce, and performed other peculiarly urban tasks as southern cities utilized their section's resources to save their section and to achieve prosperity.[38] Slavery was indeed an important element in propelling the nation to civil war. It was important because the South, and southern cities in particular, viewed the demise of the institution as the end to dreams of prosperity and urban growth, and hence of achieving sectional equilibrium. Slavery thus would strengthen the commonality between the sections while its destruction would create a backward colonial, and poverty-stricken region.

Similarly, there is no denying the influence of slaveholders in determining the direction of the South to secession. Slaveholders were dominant figures in the Old South, just as property-holders were influential everywhere. Further, slaveholding was more widespread in the South than real property-holding was in the North. The portrait of a small, exclusive slaveholding aristocracy does not comport with statistics on slave ownership. About one-quarter of the adult white householders in the South owned slaves; in the cities it was usually more than one-third. Even these figures underestimate the ubiquity of the institution in the city, because numerous urban residents hired slaves. Though technically not slave-

---

Recent Interpretations and New Directions," *Civil War History*, XX (1974), 197–214; and Sheldon Hackney, "The South as a Counterculture," *American Scholar*, XLII (1973), 283–93.

38. See Robert S. Starobin, *Industrial Slavery in the Old South* (New York, 1969); Charles B. Dew, "Disciplining Slave Ironworkers in the Antebellum South: Coercion, Conciliation, and Accommodation," *American Historical Review*, LXXIX (1974), 393–418; and Clement Eaton, "Slave-Hiring in the Upper South: A Step Toward Freedom," *Mississippi Valley Historical Review*, XLVI (1960), 633–78. *Cf.* Richard C. Wade, *Slavery in the Cities: The South, 1820–1860* (New York, 1964).

holders, these citizens were intimately bound with and dependent on the institution for their personal prosperity. Slavery and slaveholding were as characteristic of the city as it was of the countryside, and perhaps even more so. Interpretations emphasizing the rural "pre-bourgeois" aspects of slave and master omit a richer side of the "peculiar institution."[39]

Historians have spent careers searching for the ethereal quality that made and makes the South distinctive. These probers agree that southern experience varied sharply from the overall American experience.[40] Yet without discounting the importance of such oft-mentioned unique characteristics—dominance of agrarian society, slavery, and slaveholders' philosophy—there exists some evidence to propose a different view. These distinctions contributed to an urbanizing process that moved the Old South toward greater similarity with the North. Charles G. Sellers, Jr., stated the case succinctly when he observed that "the traditional emphasis on the South's differences is wrong historically." As the Civil War approached, southerners may well have been simply "other Americans."[41]

Viewing the coming of the Civil War as a conflict between sections becoming more similar to each other seems more common-sensical than to depict the decade and a half prior to Sumter as a cold war between two nationalities. It was, after all, a brothers' war. The ferocity of the war was due, in part, to the close relationship of the sections. Both sections had similar objectives as manifested in the goals of their respective cities. There could be only one victor in the economic contest, and each section saw the other as a threat to the fulfillment of a common goal.[42]

39. See Otto Olsen, "Historians and the Extent of Slave Ownership in the Southern United States," *Civil War History*, XVIII (1972), 101–16.

40. Some of the more recent forays into the search for southern identity are Hackney, "South as a Counterculture," 283–93; Michael C. O'Brien, "C. Vann Woodward and the Burden of Southern Liberalism," *American Historical Review*, LXXVIII (1973), 589–604; Smiley, "Quest for a Central Theme," 307–25; and George B. Tindall, "Beyond the Mainstream: The Ethnic Southerners," *Journal of Southern History*, XL (1974), 3–18.

41. Hennig Cohen, review of Grady McWhiney, *Southerners and Other Americans*, in *American Historical Review*, LXXIX (1974) 582–83.

42. See Still, *Urban America*, 114–16.

The role of the cities was crucial because it was within the urban milieu that the programs to reach sectional success were formulated and carried out. A study of the urban response to sectionalism could be fruitful on three levels. First, the absence or appearance of the indexes of urbanization in southern cities can be a convenient method for measuring not only the urban response to sectionalism in the South but also the extent and nature of urban growth compared with the North. If urbanization—a major theme of nineteenth-century American life—reputedly neutralized sectional differences, cities in both sections should share some common features. Second, the role and function of southern cities within a regional context must be discerned if the agrarian-dominated interpretations of the Old South are to be seriously challenged. Conceivably, southern cities could have been isolated way stations amid a vast sea of farms and plantations. Finally, on the national level, it would be interesting to test out an urban hypothesis on the coming of the Civil War. Most interpretations have emphasized the section's differences, and none have focused attention on the cities.

Urban Virginia is a good point of departure for such an inquiry. Virginia was not the most urbanized state in the South, nor did it contain the section's largest cities. Hence, Virginia's cities were not mutations of the larger southern environment, any more so than, say, Connecticut's cities were atypical of the northern environment. Further, Virginia was the largest slaveholding state in the nation on the eve of the Civil War. If slavery and cities were indeed compatible, and if slavery were not a significant point of distinction, Virginia would be a fair testing ground. Also, Virginia, in a sense, was both a microcosm of the Old South and of the nation as a whole. The four sections of Virginia—Tidewater, once the center of the South's greatest glory; the Piedmont, with its resurrected tobacco culture creating an agricultural pattern similar to the Deep South; the Valley, a common geographical link running from Pennsylvania through Georgia that was the heartland of southern yeomanry; and the trans-Allegheny region, Virginia's hill country that resembled eastern Tennessee and northern Alabama considerably more than neighboring parts of the Old Dominion—corresponded to the geographical division of the South as a whole. The disruption of Virginia mirrored the disintegration of the Union. Finally, if the agrarian ideal of the Old South could ever be said to have a historic lineage, its birthplace was Virginia. The study of the response of urban centers to sectionalism in a state with such a background should prove a rigorous test for any hypothesis relating to southern urbanization and the coming of the Civil War.

Urban Growth in the Age of Sectionalism

If you could not accept the past and its burden there was no future, for without one there cannot be the other, and if you could accept the past you might hope for the future, for only out of the past can you make the future.

Robert Penn Warren, *All the King's Men*

Redeemed, Regenerated, and Disenthralled

THE JAMES RIVER meanders quietly, though never inconspicuously, through the heart of Virginia. Wrapped up in its rivulets from Jamestown to Williamburg and on to Richmond is the history of a nation: a peculiarly urban course for a river known for its pastoral beauty. The ambivalent James River country presents an appearance that is "both stirringly sad and wonderfully giddy."[1] The lazy James can and has transformed into a deadly torrent. For Virginians gazing out over the crooked river and watching the storm clouds of sectional strife gather on the horizon, the river's course seemed to trace their glorious past and their miserable present and stress their feeling of helplessness over where the next bend would take them.

The decades between the end of the War of 1812 and the Mexican War were bitter years for Virginians. Virginia, the Mother of Presidents, became the mother of states as her young sons and daughters quit their ancestral home for more fertile lands of opportunity to the West and the South. Agricultural prices dropped steadily, and by the mid-1840s they had plummeted to record depths. A bushel of wheat, for example, that sold for $1.42 in 1812, went for $.83 in 1844.[2] Virginia's cities regressed as well. Norfolk and Alexandria, once buoyed by the sound of sail luffing in the breeze, now heard only the mournful wail of the gull—a faint echo of the past. Williamsburg was in disrepair and the College of William and Mary, educator of the new nation's leaders, became a struggling relic of the past. Richmond, Lynchburg, and Petersburg

1. For a beautiful portrait of the James River country see Walter McQuade, "Spring in Virginia: An Appreciation," New York *Times*, February 11, 1973, Sec. 10, p. 1.
2. Arthur G. Peterson, *Historical Study of Prices Received by Producers of Farm Products in Virginia, 1801–1927*, (Blacksburg, Va., 1929), 168, 205–15 (this is Technical Bulletin 37 prepared by the Virginia Agricultural Station at Virginia Polytechnic Institute). See also Avery O. Craven, *Soil Exhaustion as a Factor in the Agricultural History of Virginia and Maryland* (Urbana, Ill., 1926).

seemed content to spend their days in dusty oblivion; as commerce was a chimera, and industrial output, (what little there was) scarcely had a market beyond the town line.

Stagnation replaced growth. Of sixty-two cities with a population of more than 10,000 in 1850, only four cities, New Orleans; Springfield and Salem, Massachusetts; and Smithfield, Rhode Island; experienced increases in population that were less than those of the three Virginia cities of Norfolk, Richmond, and Petersburg. Wheeling, Virginia's only other city with more than 10,000 residents, barely outdistanced four other cities. Commerce, like people, trickled into Virginia's cities over an internal improvements network that ranked seventh in the nation in mileage by 1847. It was a poor showing for the largest state east of the Mississippi. Exports declined as well, reflecting the agricultural malaise. The coastwise tobacco trade from Richmond and Norfolk to New York declined from 1,754 hogsheads in 1834—the first year that such records were kept in New York—to 180 hogsheads in 1845.[3]

As the Old Dominion stumbled, her citizens fell to quarrelling amongst themselves. Since the 1820's western and eastern Virginians had been engaged in a bitter verbal combat concerning representation and taxation. The compromise Constitution of 1830 had proved unacceptable to westerners and by 1850 rancor was deep in both sections, and talk of secession was common in western counties.[4] An incensed western political leader shared the rhetoric of rebellion with his constituents: "This spurious aristocracy [Tidewater leadership] under the croakings of 'taxation upon the slaves of Eastern Virginia,' has . . . brought Virginia nearly upon the verge of ruin." An easterner returned the sentiment by declaring that western Virginians would "go against the slaves and the slavemaster with more rancor and bitterness than was ever belched

3. "Progress of the Population," 191–95; "Railroads of the United States," *Hunt's*, XXVIII (1853), 110–15; "Tobacco Trade and Inspections at New York," *Hunt's*, XXX (1854), 354–55.
4. See Charles H. Ambler, *Sectionalism in Virginia, 1776–1861* (Glendale, Cal., 1910); and A. A. Rogers, "Constitutional Democracy in Ante-Bellum Virginia," *William and Mary Quarterly*, 2nd ser., XVI (1936), 399–407.

forth by the most rancorous fanatic."[5] This mutual distrust compounded the state's political and economic regression.

The entire state of Virginia, it seemed, had tumbled into a morass of poverty and division that was virtually inextricable. Virginians, like most southerners, had a keen sense of history which made their present predicament even more irksome. The past threatened to become a fixation as Virginians buried their contemporary difficulties beneath a plethora of cavaliers, Washingtons, and Henrys. Contemporary fiction never moved past 1800.[6] A widely read history of Virginia by William R. Howison, published in 1848, ended in 1788.[7] Not coincidentally, a group of prominent Virginians formed the Virginia Historical Society in 1847 to formalize and organize what was already a state-wide passion for the study of the past. Virginians reminded each other that the Old Dominion was once "first in point of wealth and political power," and that "we once swayed the councils of the Union."[8] Yet they seemed transfixed by these reminders of glory as if the nightmare of the present would eventually end with Washington president and Jefferson and Marshall occupying leading roles in national affairs.

Reality told otherwise. Sheared of economic prosperity, the Old Dominion watched feebly as its once awesome political power ebbed westward and northward beyond her borders. Virginia had once sent twenty-two representatives to Congress. By 1850, that number had declined to thirteen—an indication of the stagnation enveloping the state.[9] The great figures of Virginia's halcyon days had departed and with them the state's national luster. "Virginia," a Norfolk resident observed sadly, "has greatly descended . . . in the

5. Speech of Samuel Staples quoted in Lynchburg *Virginian*, August 25, 1851; Samuel Claiborne to Robert T. Hubard, July 31, 1850, in Hubard Family Papers, Alderman Library, University of Virginia.

6. See Joseph L. King, Jr., *Dr. George William Bagby: A Study of Virginia Literature, 1850–1880* (New York, 1927); and William R. Taylor, *Cavalier and Yankee: The Old South and American National Character* (New York, 1961).

7. William R. Howison, *Virginia: Her History and Resources* (New York, 1848).

8. Richmond *Enquirer*, December 24, 1847; May 28, 1850.

9. *Ibid.*, October 12, 1852.

scale of political power." Impoverished and impotent, the Old Dominion drifted in the backwaters of American civilization. "We suffer badly enough," was one appraisal of the plight of Virginia.[10]

The Mexican War and the ensuing sectional crisis placed Virginia's status into bold relief. It began a period of analysis and self-appraisal.[11] Before action there must be understanding. The first task was to place the past in its proper perspective. History must be a teacher and not a shackle. Henry A. Wise, an ardent urban booster who was soon to be Governor, put the matter plainly in 1850 and startled his audience at the annual Virginia Historical Society meeting: "No more of the past glories of Virginia.... Labor, action, self-devotion to work... should employ every mind." A Norfolk writer agreed: "We deal too much by far with the dead." George Fitzhugh similarly urged his fellow Virginians to forego the abstractions of the past for concrete accomplishments.[12]

Some Virginians considered slavery to be the greatest abstraction of the past. They charged that it was an outmoded and a debilitating institution in a modern society. William R. Howison was a leading proponent of this theory. Howison asked, "Why is it that Virginia, the oldest of the States, rich in resources, and rich in great intellects . . . fails to attain the prosperity which her sources place within her reach? . . . The most important cause unfavorably affecting Virginia . . . is the existence of *slavery* within her bounds."[13] The argument was not new in Virginia. Governor Thomas Mann Randolph had advanced a similar proposition a generation before Howison's book appeared and a decade prior to the famous debates over slavery and its proposed abolition.[14] However, the ap-

10. Norfolk *Southern Argus*, November 4, 1851; Charles W. Dabney to Robert L. Dabney, March 19, 1846, in Charles W. Dabney Papers, Southern Historical Collection, University of North Carolina.

11. See J. Stephen Knight, Jr., "Discontent, Disunity, and Dissent in the Antebellum South: Virginia as a Test Case, 1844–1846," *Virginia Magazine of History and Biography*, LXXVIII (1970), 437–50.

12. Speech by Henry A. Wise, quoted in Richmond *Enquirer*, January 18, 1850; Norfolk *Southern Argus*, November 24, 1853; Fitzhugh, *Sociology*, 188–89.

13. William R. Howison, "Virginia: Her History and Resources," *Hunt's*, XXI (1849), 185–87.

14. Governor Thomas Mann Randolph, "Annual Message to the General Assembly," in Richmond *Enquirer*, December 5, 1820.

pearance of Howison's argument and others as well at a time of
sectional tension demonstrated that Virginians, albeit a small
minority, could discuss the subject openly and were genuinely
concerned about the severity of their current condition.

There was more general agreement on another aspect of the past
that had become the albatross of the present: Virginia's involvement in national affairs to the neglect of her own. While Jefferson,
Madison, Marshall, and Randolph dominated the national stage,
Virginia was being reduced to a bit player. A survey of the governor's annual messages from 1820 to 1846 revealed that national
politics dominated every message except two. In 1820, Governor
Thomas Mann Randolph, concerned about Virginia's decline since
the turn of the century compounded by a postwar depression,
suggested a program of rehabilitation to the legislature headed by a
recommendation that slavery be abolished. The legislature received the message politely and did nothing. In 1836, the governor's message concentrated on the state's perennial agricultural
and banking woes and suggested the development of internal
improvements, manufacturing, and public education as panaceas
for the state's sagging economy. The message scarcely mentioned
federal politics. Alas, the deliverer of the address was as unique as
the message itself. Lieutenant Governor Wyndham Robertson, a
Richmond businessman who was too young to be lulled by dreams
of the past, prepared the message since the governor had resigned
several weeks earlier. Robertson's precocious plea found few sympathetic ears in the legislature. Virginia was not ready to listen to
new voices.[15]

The growing threat of sectionalism awakened Virginians to the
fact that they no longer possessed the means to play the game of
federal politics. One year after Thomas Ritchie, Virginia's last
living link with its glorious political past, resigned as editor of the
Richmond *Enquirer,* the new editors struck the following warning:
"We . . . find our power gone, and our influence on the wane, at a
time when both are of vital importance to our prosperity, if not to

15. *Ibid.*; Governor Wyndham Robertson, "Annual Message to the General Assembly,"
in Richmond *Enquirer,* December 6, 1836.

our safety. As other States accumulate the means of material greatness, and glide past us on the road to wealth and empire, we slight the warnings of dull statistics, and drive lazily along the field of ancient customs, or stop the *plough*, to speed the politician."[16] Others agreed readily that attention to national affairs had abetted Virginia's backwardness.[17] Worse still, in the words of one Richmond resident, "Our mad pursuit of political honor has impoverished our State and rendered us dependent on a hostile North. We must turn our energies to agriculture, manufacturing, and commerce."[18]

In addition to questioning the efficacy of ruminating in the "twaddle of federal politics," the sentiment in Virginia betrayed a sense of anxiety over her own weakness in an era of sectionalism.[19] Suspicion of the North and growing fear of her power, though not new themes in Virginia rhetoric, became commonplace and incessant in the years following the Mexican War. Virginia had indeed awakened, only the nightmare was not over; apparently it was just beginning. James A. Seddon, a Richmond political leader, declared that the North's numerical majority and increasing role in the federal government was "the worst form of despotism." Troubled by the North's power and belligerancy, the *Enquirer* warned that the "North has it in her power to enslave or destroy the Union." The Lynchburg *Virginian* agreed that the South was virtually helpless before the northern giant.[20]

Most Virginians, though, did not present such a gloomy prospect. They were concerned, though, that somehow, through the years of inertia, their state and their section had fallen behind and that the Union was no longer a compact of equals. Still avowing faith in the federal government and its institutions, Virginians

16. Richmond *Enquirer*, December 29, 1852.

17. Charles W. Dabney to Robert L. Dabney, July 7, 1845, in Charles W. Dabney Papers, Southern Historical Collection, University of North Carolina; Richmond *Whig*, September 3, 1852. See also "Virginia Iron and Steel," *American Railroad Journal*, XX (1847), 593–94.

18. John P. Little, *Richmond: The Capital of Virginia* (Richmond, 1851), 252.

19. Richmond *Daily Dispatch*, October 18, 1853.

20. Speech of James A. Seddon in U.S. House of Representatives, August 13, 1850, quoted in Richmond *Enquirer*, September 24, 1850; Richmond *Enquirer*, January 31, 1851; Lynchburg *Virginian*, November 10, 1854.

viewed with alarm the growing dominance of the North in the national arena and the potential for the perversion of those institutions. Virginians believed that "perfect equality between the States of the Union is the corner stone . . . of American liberty."[21] Hence there existed a serious danger if the North sought to "exclude the South from an equal participation in the Union."[22] Virginians recalled the experience of their illustrious forebears not so much to becloud contemporary problems as to illuminate their seriousness. Analogies with the American Revolution, more specifically with how the changing nature of the British Empire after 1763 altered the delicate balance between colony and mother country, became commonplace.[23] Like the American colonies, antebellum Virginians sought "to maintain things as they are; not the Union of the vulture and the lamb—but a league between equals."[24]

The greatest imbalance was the North's economic superiority over the South. Northern political superiority was not yet manifest in federal circles and could be viewed as a potential threat rather than as a present danger. It was an era of rapid urbanization, bitter economic rivalry, and the beginnings of industrialization. The age of the common man bowed before the age of materialism. It was not surprising, therefore, that the Old Dominion should translate the impending sectional crisis and her own impoverished condition into a case of the North's economic dominance. Particularly ominous was the federal government's partnership in producing this dominance. A Richmond resident charged that "the federal government by an iniquitous system of taxation and expenditure has despoiled the South for the benefit of the North." Virginia senator

21. "Proceedings of Public Meeting at Louisa Court House," in Richmond *Enquirer*, February 15, 1850. See also speech of R. M. T. Hunter in U.S. Senate, February 24, 1854, quoted in Richmond *Enquirer*, March 7, 1854; "Letter from the Hon. H. A. Wise to the National Democratic Meeting," in Richmond *Enquirer*, November 6, 1855; and Theodore Dwight Bozeman, "Joseph Le Conte: Organic Science and a 'Sociology for the South,'" *Journal of Southern History*, XXXIX (1973), 565–82.

22. Portsmouth *Daily Pilot*, January 28, 1850.

23. Richmond *Enquirer*, January 25, 1850, December 6, 1850. See also John [Barbarossa] Scott, *The Lost Principle; or, The Sectional Equilibrium: How It Was Created—How Destroyed—How It May Be Restored* (Richmond, 1860).

24. Speech of John S. Millson in U.S. House of Representatives, February 21, 26, 1850, quoted in Norfolk and Portsmouth *Herald*, March 5, 1850.

R. M. T. Hunter agreed that "an increasing population, addition of new States and Territories, and greatly extended commercial relations have unavoidably enlarged executive patronage and augmented federal disbursements for the benefit of the North." The monetary wealth accruing so conveniently to the North would then be used, agriculturist Edmund Ruffin feared, "to corrupt and enslave the South." The North's economic advantages were not only evidenced by monetary windfalls, but, complained a Richmond merchant, "millions have been lavished by the Federal Government to build marble palaces for the comfort of the wealthy merchants of Philadelphia, Boston, and New York."[25]

Besides monetary gains and "marble palaces," northern advantages under the federal system included a burgeoning commerce and a vibrant urban life. "Under the tonnage duty," the Richmond *Whig* observed, betraying a sense of envy as well as indignation, "they [the North] have built up a commerce which excels that of any other nation; under the protective system their cities are thronged with artisans and merchants; under the prestige of American powers, and the protection of the American flag, their ships roam the world without passports." Implied in the *Whig*'s review of northern attributes was that the South, or at least Virginia, should adapt to the prevailing economic climate and imitate northern success in order to redress sectional balance. If Virginia hoped to attain equality with northern states, it must dedicate itself to "energy and enterprise, not the lullaby song of self-glorification."[26]

Concern over the North's growing economic dominance and the increasing awareness of their own weaknesses prompted Virginians to formulate responses that would secure sectional equilibrium

25. For examples of such thinking see R. M. T. Hunter to Shelton F. Leake, c. 1857, in Charles H. Ambler (ed.), *Correspondence of Robert M. T. Hunter, 1826–1876*, in *Annual Report of the American Historical Association, 1916* (Washington, D.C., 1918), vol. II, 256–61; Richmond *Enquirer*, March 8, 1850, April 23, 1850; Richmond *Enquirer*, July 18, 1854; Robert T. Hubard to R. M. T. Hunter, November 25, 1856, in R. M. T. Hunter Papers, Alderman Library, University of Virginia; Letter by "A Virginian" [Edmund Ruffin] in Richmond *Enquirer*, April 2, 1850; and Richmond *Enquirer*, November 26, 1850. See also Robert R. Russel, "Southern Secessionists Per Se and the Crisis of 1850," in Robert R. Russel (ed.), *Critical Studies in Antebellum Sectionalism* (Westport, Conn., 1972), 75–86.

26. Richmond *Whig*, January 3, 1851; Reverend A. B. Van Zandt, *The Claims of Virginia upon Her Educated Sons* (Petersburg, 1854), 18.

and economic independence. As the Lynchburg *Virginian* reasoned, "Viriginia can regain her pristine greatness only by emancipating herself from her commercial dependence."[27] The specific avenues of progress to be followed by Virginians were already well marked by the North, especially by northern cities. Nineteenth-century cities borrowed from each other freely. Newer cities in the Midwest strove to duplicate the amenities of urban life back East. The construction of anything from a railroad to a street-lighting system was likely to trigger a wave of similar responses across the urban nation. Imitation was one major aspect in creating an integrated urban network and in developing a community of cities irrespective of section.[28]

Internal improvements, especially railroads, received the highest priority in Virginia after 1847. The railroad was the medium of commercial prosperity in mid-nineteenth-century America. "In sleepless and indefatigable competition," the Baltimore *American* declared, "success is best secured by transportation."[29] The railroad's most obvious impact, improved access to market, thrilled urban and rural residents alike and ensured cooperation of both sectors in building iron links to the West. Increased agricultural production, greater inventory for merchants, increased value of real estate, and cheaper transportation were among the mutual benefits arriving with the first locomotive.[30] "Around all these Southern cities," George Fitzhugh predicted of the advent of the railroads, "the country will become rich [and] there will be increased property values in town and country." Fitzhugh concluded by observing that "rapid intercommunication is the distinguishing feature of modern progress."[31]

On a more ethereal level, the railroad assumed the status of a

27. Lynchburg *Virginian*, October 19, 1848.
28. On the proclivities of cities to imitate each other see Julius Rubin, *Canal or Railroad: Imitation and Innovation in Response to the Erie Canal in Philadelphia, Baltimore, and Boston* (Philadelphia, 1961); Wade, *Urban Frontier*, 314–21.
29. Baltimore *American*, quoted in Alexandria *Gazette*, May 9, 1859.
30. See B. M. Jones, *Railroads: Considered in Regard to their Effects upon the Value of Land in Increasing Production, Cheapening Transportation, Preventing Emigration and Investments for Capital* (Richmond, 1860); see also Reed, *New Orleans and the Railroads*, 4.
31. Fitzhugh, *Sociology*, 141–42.

demigod with the ability to leap rivers and abolitionists in a single bound. Senator Charles Sumner of Massachusetts, who frequently discerned divine purpose in the course of daily living, wrote in 1852, "Where railroads are not, civilization cannot be. . . . Under God, the railroad and the schoolmaster are the two chief agents of human improvement." A Presbyterian minister from New York went even further. He saw railroads as "the evolution of divine purposes of Christianity and the coming reign of Christ." Virginians looked for more immediate though equally grandiose results from the railroad. The Richmond *Enquirer* stated confidently that railroads "will kill abolition in Congress." On another occasion the editors promised readers, "Internal improvements connecting the Atlantic with the teeming storehouses of the West" would allow Virginia "to command justice at the hands of the other sections of the confederacy." A Petersburg newspaper concluded that the railroad "is better calculated to make Southern people independent of Northern busy-bodies than any other scheme."[32] Small wonder that communities and states embraced this iron messiah enthusiastically.

The best indication of zealous faith in railroads was the facility with which the Virginia legislature pledged millions of dollars for railroads following the Mexican War. Funding internal improvements was not a new endeavor for legislators in 1847. The James River and Kanawha Canal—"the Erie of Virginia"—had been receiving sporadic appropriations since the 1830s. Between 1830 and 1846, the general assembly chartered eight steam railroads. All of these, however, were small affairs that were little more than coal railroads, and most never went beyond the paper stage. Lawmakers rarely accorded major projects, except for the canal, sufficient consideration.[33] The Richmond and Danville Railroad, for exam-

---

32. Charles Sumner, "Influence of Railroads," *Hunt's*, XXVI (1852), 506–07; "Moral View of Railroads," *Hunt's*, XXVII (1852), 173; Richmond *Enquirer*, August 28, 1855; Richmond *Enquirer*, June 28, 1850; Petersburg *News*, quoted in Richmond *Enquirer*, January 21, 1851; see also Richmond *Whig*, January 25, 1850.

33. For the progress of Virginia internal improvements prior to 1847 see W. Asbury Christian, *Richmond: Her Past and Present* (Richmond, 1912), 134; Wayland F. Dunaway, *History of the James River and Kanawha Company* (New York, 1922); John V. Horner and P. B. Windfree, Jr. (eds.), *The Saga of a City: Lynchburg, Virginia, 1786–1936* (Lynchburg, 1936),

ple, an important line designed to facilitate the cultivation and marketing of a once-dominant staple crop-(tobacco)-waited fifteen years before the assembly granted it a charter in 1847.[34] In that year, when lawmakers essayed their first halting steps toward constructing transportation lines to the West, public and press alike urged caution and warned against "pecuniary profligacy."[35]

In subsequent sessions in the late 1840s and early 1850s, the state lavished millions on railroads. Governor John B. Floyd's annual message of 1849 was the first such message in more than a decade that dealt substantially with internal improvements. During the 1850–51 and 1851–52 sessions the assembly funded fifteen railroad projects for $2,300,000 and $2,600,000 respectively—more than five times the amount appropriated by any previous session.[36] The Virginia Board of Public Works, in its 1851 report, marveled at the changed attitude abroad in the state: "Probably no state in the Union has in a few years so radically changed its policy upon the subject of internal improvement as Virginia. The revolution in public opinion has been almost complete."[37]

The commercial avalanche that would inevitably rain down upon Virginia's cities as a result of the railroads required an outlet. Unless Virginians could develop direct trade with Europe, their winning of the West would be a Pyrrhic victory. The task confronting Virginians was difficult for two reasons. First, the Old Dominion had to establish regularly scheduled commerce between her cities and European markets. Second, her cities also had to assume the services performed by northern market centers. The dependence of Virginia upon northern ports made fulfillment of these

28–32; Robert F. Hunter, "The Turnpike Movement in Virginia, 1816–1860," *Virginia Magazine of History and Biography*, LXIX (1961), 278–89.

34. Malcolm C. Clark, "The First Quarter-Century of the Richmond and Danville Railroad, 1847–1871" (M.A. thesis, George Washington University, 1959).

35. Richmond *Enquirer*, December 7, 1847; see also *Fincastle Democrat*, March 27, 1847; speech of Thomas H. Daniel of Prince George County in Virginia Senate, February 18, 1848, printed in Richmond *Enquirer*, April 4, 1848; "Virginia Iron and Steel," 593–94.

36. Richmond *Enquirer*, March 29, 1850, and April 18, 1851; see also Isaac F. Boughter, "Internal Improvements in Northwestern Virginia: A Study of State Policy Prior to the Civil War" (Ph.D. dissertation, University of Pittsburgh, 1930), 254–66.

37. Virginia Board of Public Works, *Thirty-Sixth Annual Report* (1851), iii (hereinafter cited as 36 BPW 1851).

objectives difficult. Virginia was once the first commercial state in the Union, lamented the Richmond *Enquirer*, "Now we import through Boston and New York; let us recover."[38] In 1790 the commerce of Virginia and New York was roughly equal. Sixty years later the value of Virginia's imports had declined by nearly 85%, while exports remained stationary. The value of New York's imports meanwhile increased by sixteen times the 1790 figure, and the city's exports jumped to $52,713,000, or fifty times greater than they were at the time of Washington's inauguration. New York's figures represented one-third of the total value of the nation's exports and three-fifths of the nation's imports.[39]

New York's commercial superiority was especially galling because Virginia and other southern states were subsidizing this hegemony. Southerners paid for the services provided by New York merchants, bankers, and factors. "We are but the slave colonies of the North," complained De Bow in an article urging direct trade for southern ports. A Norfolk legislator calculated that this tribute from Virginia amounted to nearly $9,000,000 annually, not including commissions paid to banks for buying drafts. This loss not only helped to "build up northern cities in commerce, wealth, and power," but understandably served to dampen any motivation to develop a hinterland trade, since western commerce would eventually terminate in the coastwise trade to New York. William M. Burwell, a Virginia civic booster and railroad promotor, stated the problem in an article in *DeBow's Review* in 1852: "The export and import trade of Virginia is now taxed with transport coastwise; it is burthened with charges of Northern merchants." The Old Dominion's dependent situation prompted the following query from a Wheeling journalist: "Why shall we be obliged to do business for the benefit of Northern ports alone?"[40] The establishment of direct trade from a Virginia port could be the only response.

38. Richmond *Enquirer*, May 28, 1850.
39. "Proceedings of the Southern Rights Association," in *ibid.*, March 4, 1851; see also Robert G. Albion, *The Rise of New York Port [1815–1860]* (New York, 1939), 389, 391, 410.
40. "Commercial Agriculture and Intellectual Independence of the South," 466; speech of Simeon Wheeler in Virginia House of Delegates, quoted in Richmond *Enquirer*, December 10, 1852; William M. Burwell, "Virginia Commercial Convention," *DeBow's Review*, XII (1852), 32; Wheeling *Daily Intelligencer*, December 10, 1852.

Virginians imbued direct trade with almost the same prowess they assigned to railroads. Commercial independence from the North was the key aspect of the direct trade movement. The rhetoric of sectionalism meshed easily with calls for direct trade. Virginia's board of public works viewed direct trade as a means of "securing our political independence." A Norfolk resident believed that direct trade would "act as a charm upon the pernicious fangs of abolitionism." Direct trade was a patriotic movement in the tradition of Virginia's illustrious past. A writer in *DeBow's Review* predicted that the establishment of direct trade with Europe from Norfolk would secure the Old Dominion's "commercial independence, just as Virginia secured her civil and religious freedoms during the Revolution." Of more immediate concern, some Virginians believed that their own export commerce would stimulate capital investment in Virginia, as it had done in northern market centers. Eventually the program would transform Virginia into "the Excelsior State of the Union."[41]

Manufacturing was another aspect of southern dependence on the North. Virginians not only sent their produce northward, but ships returned with manufactured products. Only the capital remained behind. "These Northern gentlemen," the Richmond *Enquirer* noted in 1850, "have grown too fat at our expense. . . . We should establish manufactures of every kind within our own limits." In a similar vein another Richmonder observed that "no people are independent who are compelled to rely upon others for industry." As with direct trade, sectional feeling was inherent in the manufacturing program: "Home reliance and home production are the most effective checks against abolition assaults."[42] Although the connection between city-building and manufacturing was unclear, the city possessed important incentives for industry. The city offered capital, labor, expertise, and linkages not ordinarily available in rural areas.

41. 36 BPW 1851, x; Norfolk *Day Book*, December 31, 1857; "Foreign Trade of Virginia and the South," *DeBow's Review*, XIII (1852), 503; Richmond *Enquirer*, November 4, 1859; Richmond *Enquirer*, November 23, 1852.

42. Richmond *Enquirer*, February 1, 1850; Richmond *Whig*, December 17, 1850; Richmond *Enquirer*, January 28, 1851.

There certainly was room for improvement in Virginia's urban industry. In the fall of 1850 a mining and manufacturing convention assembled in Richmond to assess the state's industrial condition. They reported blast furnaces working at a quarter of their capacity, the abandonment of two of the state's four rolling mills, and the closing of two textile mills for a variety of reasons (including lack of capital), transportation difficulties, managerial ineptness, and insufficient raw material. Only the grain and tobacco-processing industries seemed to be holding their own.[43] Further, legislators did not apply their generosity to privately owned industry. The legislature could, of course, grant tax privileges to home-based industries, as the Southern Rights Association urged, but direct appropriation was out of the question. There was also the sticky subject of the tariff. Virginia opposition to the tariff was not synonymous with opposition to industry. Some of the most vociferous opponents of the tariff were manufacturers themselves. Processing industries feared that high tariffs would depress the agricultural sector to a degree that would deleteriously affect these industries.[44] In short, development of manufacturing presented Virginians with numerous obstacles.

Manufacturing, nevertheless, was an essential link in the drive toward economic independence. Cities with manufacturing facilities paid farmers higher prices for their produce. Higher prices would allow Virginia's markets to compete successfully with northern centers, while at the same time encouraging increased cultivation of staple crops. The bonanza on the farm then would eventually redound to the benefit of the cities in the form of increased commerce. Second, a city without heavier industry could not hope to develop a lucrative reciprocal trade. Railroads could not exist with produce flowing eastward only, regardless of volume. Home manufacturers could supply farmers with everything from ploughs to musical instruments. If cities wanted to avoid becoming mere carriers for northern manufactured goods, entrepreneurs

43. "Committees' Reports to the Miners and Manufacturers Convention," Richmond *Whig*, December 17, 1850.
44. See Wade, *Urban Frontier*, 180.

would have to establish foundries, shoe factories, and glassworks. The ability to initiate urban industrial enterprises thus affected the success of both internal improvements and direct-trade projects.[45]

The chemistry of the national economy in the nineteenth century was like a compound. It was impossible to isolate or to remove one element without destroying the economy. Manufacturing, for example, attracted produce, helped railroads, and provided cargo for direct trade. It would be futile to construct elaborate rail networks to the West only to have western produce pile up on docks because of an absence of a shipbuilding facility; or, worst yet, have the commerce for which Virginians spent so dearly be "whipped to the North."[46] Without railroads, however, it was doubtful whether Virginia's cities would become commercial and manufacturing centers.[47] A more maddening thought was that railroads and industry required coal for operation; but there would be no coal until the construction of rail lines to the western Virginia coal beds.[48] Each program depended on fulfillment of the other programs which in turn required the success of each program.

Compounding the complexity of the integrated economy was the fact that the response of Virginians to the sectional crisis was not uniform. Some Virginians remained hostile to spending of any sort at any level of government, others maintained an indifferent attitude toward northern economic supremacy, and a few never overcame the inertia of the 1830s and forties. It is impossible to estimate the size of these nonbelievers, because they were, for the most part, the silent Virginians. Occasionally a letter might have appeared in the press, or perusal of a manuscript collection can uncover these sentiments expressed more in innuendo than in explicit terms.[49] The drumbeating urban press was not likely to

45. See Norfolk *Southern Argus*, June 19, 1850.
46. Alexandria *Virginia Sentinel*, September 17, 1853; see also Burwell, "Virginia Commercial Convention," 30–41.
47. See Alexandria *Gazette*, February 7, 1854.
48. Richmond *Enquirer*, January 7, 1851; see also "Iron Ore in Virginia for Iron Manufactures," *Hunt's*, XXXI (1854), 768; Otis K. Rice, "Coal Mining in the Kanawha Valley to 1861: A View of Industrialization in the Old South," *Journal of Southern History*, XXXI (1965), 393–416.
49. See Benjamin Johnson Barbour, "Address to the Literary Societies of Virginia Military Institute," *Southern Literary Messenger*, XX (1854), 513–28.

devote much space to slackers. Public spirit, togetherness, and enterprise were indigenous to the cities. The response of urban Virginia to the sectional crisis and more particularly their response to the faith placed in them by citizens throughout the state would determine the success or failure of Virginia's attempt to secure economic independence and sectional equality.

Virginians looked to their cities in the time of sectional crisis. The final report of the Virginia Mercantile Convention, assembled in Richmond in 1851, placed the role of Virginia's cities in a historical perspective: "Virginia's cities are entering a competition, the consequences of which are similar to those of the American Revolution." The Richmond *Daily Dispatch*, projecting an influence beyond the Old Dominion, outlined the consequences of urbanization clearly: "Building up Virginia's cities will save the South from an indellible brand of degradation." The Virginia Board of Public Works echoed these words by predicting that prosperity for Virginia's cities meant "freedom from commercial vassalage" for the state.[50] The cities were to be Virginia's weapons against the growing power and influence of the North.

Urban Virginia presented a physical appearance that was hardly calculated to inspire the confidence of fellow Virginians. Like most of urban America, the Old Dominion's cities were small—more towns than cities. They were not cosmopolitan centers, but, rather, secondary market towns. A walk through urban Virginia would leave a visitor covered with dust (assuming it had not rained recently) and impressed at how the rural countryside seemed to melt into the urban setting, virtually overtaking the latter. On a hot summer afternoon the visitor would be likely to find himself alone except for annoying swarms of flies and mosquitoes that seemed to congregate at every street corner like leading citizens. For entertainment the traveler might find low comedy or equally tasteless musical performances delivered with enthusiasm if not with skill.

50. "Report of the Virginia Mercantile Convention," in Richmond *Enquirer*, September 16, 1851; Richmond *Daily Dispatch*, February 27, 1851; "Report of the Board of Public Works to the General Assembly," in Alexandria *Gazette*, February 7, 1854.

Otherwise, he might be content with watching the dust accumulate on an empty wagon. This was urban Virginia in the 1840s.

For all its apparent backwardness, urban Virginia concealed the raw materials of progress. Once the cloud of depression lifted, life stirred anew. Richmond was the Old Dominion's largest city in 1850 with a population of 27,500. William Byrd laid out the town in 1737, and five years later it had been incorporated. The growth of the James River community accelerated after it was named the capital of the state in 1779. Richmond received a new charter and city status in 1842. Visually, it was one of the loveliest capitals in the Union. The neoclassic capitol dominated the city. Hovering around the capitol, like so many supplicants to its ancient power, were lesser government buildings and two Protestant churches. At the bottom of the hill stretched Main Street, Richmond's major business artery. Richmond's hilly terrain presented some problems to tired pedestrians, especially in the hot, humid summer months. From the tops of these hills, though, residents and visitors alike could enjoy a picnic at lovely Hollywood Cemetery and watch the James wind its way through the green hills. Already, however, the effluvia from the proliferating tobacco factories and iron foundries interrupted the pastoral scene and reminded Richmonders that their city's destiny lay in the smoke and smell of industry rather than in the verdant hills. Activity at the James River wharves had increased in recent years, and the railroad was beginning to spread its iron arms of progress out into the countryside.[51]

Norfolk, the state's second largest city in 1850, with 14,300 inhabitants, typified the decline of the Old Dominion. The city on the Chesapeake possessed probably the finest natural harbor south of New York; yet it carried on only a moderate coastwise trade. Norfolk's immediate hinterland was a swamp, and until transportation facilities transcended the countryside the city's trade would be

51. See Julia L. Noyes Journal (Typescript in Julia L. N. Loveland Papers, Duke University), April 5, 1855; S. D. Whittle to his wife, November 10, 1852, in Lewis Neale Whittle Papers, Southern Historical Collection, University of North Carolina; "Richmond, Virginia," *Hunt's*, XX (1849), 52–55; Christian, *Richmond*, 166–77; Emory M. Thomas, *The Confederate State of Richmond* (Austin, 1971), 16, 17.

meager. In the colonial and early national periods, though, a lucrative trade with the West Indies enabled Norfolk to achieve considerable prosperity. The War of 1812 ended the era of economic growth. In 1845, the borough of Norfolk received a new charter and city status. Citizens hoped that the new designation portended a new era for the unfortunate seaport.[52]

Petersburg, twenty-three miles south of Richmond and destined to come increasingly under the capital city's shadow, had a population of 14,000 in 1850. Situated on a gradually sloping hill above the Appomattox River, it shared the picturesque setting of its larger urban neighbor to the north. William Byrd, in fact, planned the city simultaneously with Richmond. Petersburg possessed excellent water power and looked forward to industrial development.[53]

Wheeling, at the extreme northwestern corner of the state, passed the early decades of the nineteenth century struggling unsuccessfully with Pittsburgh for commercial supremacy at the head of the Ohio River. In 1850 it claimed 11,400 inhabitants. Befitting its position on the Virginia frontier, Wheeling was settled later than other Virginia cities (in 1769). It commanded a good view of the river 400 feet above the bank. The city attained its initial phase of growth as a result of the completion of the Cumberland road to the Ohio River in 1818. Wheeling achieved city status in 1836. The city had long been known for the rich coal deposits in the adjacent countryside. By 1850 Wheeling possessed more heavy industry than any other city in the state. Just as the Cumberland road had inaugurated an era of growth, so the completion of the Baltimore and Ohio Railroad to Wheeling in 1853 introduced a period of prosperity to the city.[54]

52. See George E. Waring, Jr., *Report on the Social Statistics of Cities; Part II, The Southern and Western States* (Washington, D.C., 1887), 65–70; Thomas Jefferson Wertenbaker, *Norfolk, Historic Southern Port* (Durham, 1931); Peter C. Stewart, "The Commercial History of Hampton Roads, Virginia, 1815–1860" (Ph.D. dissertation, University of Virginia, 1967), 47–48.

53. See Waring, *Social Statistics of Cities*, 71–74; Edward A. Wyatt, IV, "Rise of Industry in Ante-Bellum Petersburg," *William and Mary Quarterly*, 2nd ser., XVII (1937), 1–36.

54. See Wheeling *Argus*, quoted in Richmond *Enquirer*, September 16, 1853; Waring,

Alexandria was probably the oldest of Virginia's extant cities, having been discovered by Captain John Smith in 1608. The city lay slightly above the Potomac River. Like Norfolk, Alexandria had enjoyed an era of prosperity in the late eighteenth and early nineteenth centuries only to have the events leading up to the War of 1812 paralyze her commerce. Alexandria's decline was accelerated by cession to the District of Columbia in 1823. Congress cared little about developing a fringe of the capital. In 1846, after years of appeals, Alexandria was retroceded to Virginia and attained city status in 1852. In 1850 the city included 8,700 people.[55]

Lynchburg, with a population of 8,000 in 1850, began as a trading depot under the direction of John Lynch in 1786. Wooded country surrounded the settlement, and the James River stretched alongside it, just before it cut through the Blue Ridge Mountains. It was perhaps the most difficult city to traverse because of its abrupt grades. Lynchburg also became a city in 1852.[56]

Virginia's cities shared certain characteristics which in terms of nineteenth-century urban growth theory presaged an era of urbanization. Geographic determinism was an axiom in predicting urban development. The countryside surrounding Richmond, Alexandria, Lynchburg, and Petersburg was potentially as bountiful as the Hudson River and Mohawk River valleys of New York. J. D. B. De Bow, in advancing Norfolk's natural harbor as the South's great Atlantic port, emphasized the city's temperate climate, her fine harbor, and her position midway between North and South.[57] Further, Virginia's cities enjoyed natural transportation advantages. A major reason why goods, investment capital, and people poured into cities like Saint Louis, Cincinnati, Baltimore, Philadelphia, and New York was that these centers were breaks in transportation, which is a prerequisite to commercial development.

Social Statistics of Cities, 87–92; Clifford M. Lewis, "The Wheeling Suspension Bridge," *West Virginia History*, XXXIII (1972), 203–33.

55. See Mary G. Powell, *The History of Old Alexandria, Virginia* (Richmond, 1928); Waring, *Social Statistics of Cities*, 55–59.

56. See Jeremiah C. Harris Diary, June 4, 1856 (MS in Jeremiah C. Harris Diaries, Duke University); W. Asbury Christian, *Lynchburg and Its People* (Lynchburg, 1900), 145–54; Horner and Windfree, *Lynchburg*, 27; Waring, *Social Statistics of Cities*, 60–64.

57. "Foreign Trade of Virginia and the South," 493–503.

Wherever goods must shift from one form of transport to another, a significant current of commerce will develop.[58] Richmond on the fall line, Alexandria on the Potomac, and Norfolk with easy access to the Chesapeake Bay and the Atlantic presented good prospects for a break in transportation once rail and canal lines penetrated the interior.

Virginia's position midway between North and South was another geographic attribute advanced by optimistic urban residents. This strategic position gives Virginia's eastern cities equal proximity to the Ohio and Mississippi River valleys. Specifically, rail lines connecting Richmond with Memphis on the Mississippi or with Cincinnati on the Ohio River would provide a more direct route to those centers than the links running from New York, Philadelphia, or Baltimore.[59] The Old Dominion's temperate climate was a final geographic factor that favored her in the competition for western goods. While northern rivers and canals froze for a good portion of the winter and while railroad schedules remained uncertain with the threat of icing and heavy snows, Virginia's relatively mild winters rendered such unfortunate disruptions to a nation's commerce unlikely.[60] Viewing Virginia's geographic advantages and the seemingly infinite bounty of the West, William M. Burwell wondered aloud if striving for merely a portion of that trade was understating the potential for his state's cities: "Nature tells us to stretch out our hands and grasp nearly the WHOLE of it."[61]

This faith in geography might seem naive or even foolish, but in the context of the era it was plausible. William Gilpin's rendition of geographer Alexander von Humboldt's isothermal zodiac—a beneficent climatic zone where great urban civilizations evolved—was more elaborate and theoretical than the rather pedestrian geog-

58. For an exposition of location theory see Goheen, "Industrialization and Cities in Nineteenth-Century America," 49–65; J. Christopher Schnell and Patrick E. McLear, "Why the Cities Grew: A Historiographical Essay on Western Urban Growth, 1850–1880," *Bulletin of the Missouri Historical Society*, XXVII (1972), 162–77; see also Wade, *Urban Frontier*, 327–30.
59. William M. Burwell, "Address on the Commercial Future of Virginia," in Richmond *Enquirer*, July 4, 1851.
60. "Foreign Trade of Virginia and the South," 493–503.
61. William M. Burwell, quoted in Richmond *Enquirer*, February 19, 1858.

raphy pieced together by Virginians, but it was not any more sound. The "inevitable" great metropolis of Independence, Missouri, hardly developed according to Gilpin's master plan. S. H. Goodin's thesis of commercial "gravitation" appeared first in 1851 to explain how Ohio Valley cities would ultimately and inexorably gravitate to Cincinnati's orbit.[62] There were other equally esoteric theories, but the feature that was common to all was the centrality of geography to urban growth. Virginians avidly read such publications as *Harper's, De Bow's Review,* and *Hunt's Merchants' Magazine* where these theories appeared. In comparison with other cities, Virginia's cities were well situated. The fact that northern cities had already attained the trappings of economic power did not discourage urban Virginians, but rather it spurred them to do for their section what "New York did for the North."[63]

Urban Virginians did not rest on their geographic laurels. The stakes of sectional power were too high to take growth and prosperity for granted. Just as the assembly plunged heavily into railroad subscription, so did the cities. Prior to 1847, corporation charters prohibited urban subscriptions to internal improvements extending beyond city limits. The gradual return of prosperity, a railroad fever, and the sectional crisis produced enabling legislation. By 1852 urban Virginia could appropriate funds directly to railroads, canals, and turnpikes. Virginia's cities abandoned their traditional conservative financial stance and followed the assembly's example. In April 1850 the people of Alexandria voted 501 to 7 to subscribe $150,000 to the Manassas Gap Railroad; in December, by a "close" vote of 409 to 170, Richmonders approved an appropriation of $100,000 for the Virginia and Tennessee Railroad—a railroad that did not run even through or near the city; in September 1851, Norfolk citizens voted 440 to 23 to incur a debt of $200,000 to their city to help construct a railroad to North Carolina; and the citizens of Wheeling agreed, 332 to 18, to subscribe $250,000 worth of stock in the Cincinnati, Marietta, and Hempfield Railroad Com-

62. See Glaab and Brown, *A History of Urban America,* 75–79; J. Christopher Schnell, and Katherine B. Clinton, "The New West: Themes in Nineteenth-Century Urban Promotion, 1815–1880," *Bulletin of the Missouri Historical Society,* XXX (1974), 75–88.
63. "Foreign Trade of Virginia and the South," 501.

pany in June 1852. In no city was the voter turnout below 15% of the usual vote for city officials.[64] The Virginia Board of Public Works noticed the more generous attitude of the cities: "The people are themselves voting directly for liberal subscriptions, by counties, cities and towns, in every quarter of the commonwealth." The Richmond *Enquirer* termed the new urban awareness "a wonderful revolution."[65]

The lopsided urban referendums revealed, if nothing else, that city residents were confident that internal improvements would fulfill the most saccharine promotional propaganda. There was good cause for such optimism. In 1851 the Virginia Board of Public Works published a comprehensive internal improvement plan for Virginia (see map in fig. 1). The proposal divided Virginia and neighboring states in the Ohio and Mississippi valleys into four commercial regions with a Virginia city as the hub of each sector. The southern commercial sector, with rail lines emanating from Richmond and Norfolk, encompassed the rich tobacco- and grain-growing region of southern Virginia and western North and South Carolina. The southwestern corridor, whose headquarters was Lynchburg, protruded into Tennessee to capture the cotton trade of the lower Mississippi. The central sector, with Richmond and Alexandria its primary urban centers, traversed the heart of Virginia to tap the trade of the Shenandoah and Ohio valleys. Finally, the northwestern commercial area reached into Virginia's coal beds and beyond to the mineral wealth of the Great Lakes region. Covington and Wheeling were the two key cities in this region.[66]

The board believed that the completion of this elaborate scheme would fulfill the state's two major objectives of urban growth and sectional equilibrium. "Then our cities . . . will at once become receptacles of a trade and commerce which will attract capital and population. They will be cities, not in name merely, but in all the

64. Alexandria *Gazette*, April 19, 1850; Norfolk *Southern Argus*, September 30, 1851; Richmond *Enquirer*, December 13, 1850; Wheeling *Argus*, quoted in Richmond *Enquirer*, June 2, 1852.
65. 36 BPW 1851, iii; Richmond *Enquirer*, February 25, 1853.
66. 36 BPW 1851, viii.

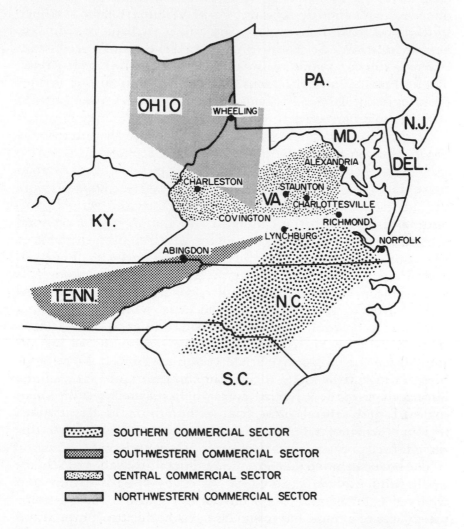

Fig. 1 Virginia's Commercial Sectors, 1851 (based on BPW 1851, viii)

elements to give them manufacturing and commercial consequence. We may then look forward to a freedom from the vassalage
to which we have been so long subjected." William M. Burwell,
writing in *DeBow's Review* in 1852, echoed the board's prediction:
"Completion of Virginia's railroads will result in the rapid increase
of our cities . . . and the South will be restored to her former
position in the Union."[67] Thus Virginians linked urban growth
and sectional harmony.

In turn, Virginia's cities identified closely with the internal improvements emanating from their particular sector. An Alexandria merchant averred that his city would be "made" by a railroad
to the Valley. The proposed Virginia and Tennessee Railroad from
Lynchburg drew a similar reaction in that interior town: "Lynchburg is destined to become a market for the West."[68] Richmond
residents had carried on a love affair with the unfinished James
River and Kanawha Canal for more than half a century. The canal
was destined to terminate at Covington beyond the mountains
where the Covington and Ohio Railroad would provide Richmond
with a direct water-rail link with the Ohio. Samuel Mordecai, a
venerable Richmonder, summarized the feelings of his fellow citizens when he noted that "the progress of Richmond and of the
James River Canal are so intimately connected that it is due to the
one to notice the other." Richmond citizens expressed a similar
intimacy toward the Virginia Central Railroad which was the major
project for the central commercial sector: "the work [is] identified
with her [Richmond] in all conceivable interests." A week later the
same source predicted that after the road's completion "Richmond
shall be one terminus of a great continental trunk of railroad, by
which cars loaded in St. Louis may be brought to her own
wharves. . . . Richmond shall have a due portion of that trade,
which, in a few years, has raised New York, Boston, Philadelphia,
and Baltimore to the magnitude, wealth and proportions of the
greatest and oldest towns in Europe." Lynchburg, Norfolk, and

67. 38 BPW 1853–54, xxi; Burwell, "Virginia Commercial Convention," 34.
68. Letter from "A Merchant," in Alexandria *Gazette*, September 29, 1848; Lynchburg
Virginia, August 19, 1850.

Wheeling launched similar predictions concerning the impact of their internal improvement lines to the West on their city's growth.[69]

Urban Virginia entered the contest for direct trade with equal enthusiasm and confidence. On July 4, 1850, Norfolk called the first statewide convention on direct trade in the history of Virginia. The date was not coincidental. A neighboring Portsmouth journal declared that "July 4, 1850 will be as important to the South as 1776."[70] Several months later, a group of Richmond merchants formed the Southern Rights Association to lobby for legislative appropriations for a direct line of steamers between a Virginia city and England. Their recommendations included improving harbor facilities in the state's river ports and dredging the tortuous James River near Richmond. Some of the more radical members of the association submitted proposals to effect nonintercourse with the North. The majority of the mercantile community, though, were neither willing nor able to cut the commercial umbilical cord just yet.[71]

In another direct trade convention in Norfolk, convened a year after the initial meeting, emphasis shifted to the encouragement of shipbuilding and the training of home-based factors.[72] In 1852 Richmond responded to the resolutions by appropriating $250,000 to dredge the James River channel. Although a trans-Atlantic port on the relatively shallow James transcended reality, Richmond merchants believed that energy and enterprise would overcome natural obstacles. In an age when fabulous riches and vast populations seemed within the grasp of every urban frontier outpost, Richmond's hopes were perhaps not so farfetched. Finally, Norfolk merchants facing the perennial if somewhat unlikely

69. Samuel Mordecai, *Virginia, Especially Richmond in By-Gone Days; Being Reminiscences and Last Words of an Old Citizen* (Richmond, 1860), 297–301; Richmond *Enquirer*, May 17, 1853; Richmond *Enquirer*, May 24, 1853; Lynchburg *Virginian*, August 19, 1850; Norfolk *Southern Argus*, September 29, 1851; Wheeling *Daily Intelligencer*, January 31, 1853.
70. Portsmouth *Daily Pilot*, July 8, 1850.
71. "Memorial to the Virginia General Assembly" (MS in Central Southern Rights Association of Virginia Papers, Virginia Historical Society, Richmond, Va.), February 14, 1851; Richmond *Enquirer*, December 10, 1850.
72. Richmond *Enquirer*, October 17, 1851.

challenge from a river port dispatched Dr. Francis Mallory to Belgium to meet with parties who would be interested in establishing a direct steamship line.[73]

The growing awareness throughout the state of the efficacy of manufacturing allowed urban Virginia to proceed with industrialization in a climate that was philosophically conducive to such development. Despite the absence of both an industrial tradition and state subsidies, urban leaders admonished fellow citizens to support local industry with capital and patronage. A Norfolk resident urged his neighbors to "never send abroad for an article we can manufacture." Assiduous attention to manufacturing was "one plain, common-sense way to build up a city," asserted another Norfolk citizen. Civic boosters never questioned the relationship between urbanization, sectional harmony, and industry. As one leader stated, the connection "is so obvious." Richmond's water power and the proximity of natural resources led to encouraging indications that the capital city would be in the vanguard of urban industry. "Ought Richmond not to be one of the greatest manufacturing cities in the Union?" asked the Richmond *Daily Dispatch*.[74] Since industrial investment was a private affair, the press and leading citizens could do little but cheer the opening and expansion of manufacturing enterprises.[75] Nevertheless, the favorable and extensive publicity as well as the explicit allusions to southern patriotism inspired investment. As the Lynchburg *Virginian* observed, "The mere encouragement of manufacturing in the South will attract the attention of the speculator, and him with his laborers hither."[76]

Optimism blossomed over the rutted streets and wooden roofs of Virginia's cities. Confidence dissipated gloom and inertia as urban Virginia flexed the muscles of economic potential. After years of

73. *Ibid.*, January 9, 1852, March 1, 1853; Norfolk *Southern Argus*, February 3, 1852.
74. Norfolk *Southern Argus*, August 30, 1849; Norfolk *Southern Argus*, May 15, 1849; Norfolk *Southern Argus*, September 19, 1849; Richmond *Daily Dispatch*, July 28, 1853; see also "Richmond, Virginia" 52.
75. See Wheeling *Daily Intelligencer*, September 28, 1853.
76. Lynchburg *Virginian*, June 20, 1850.

neglect, both self-inflicted and imposed, the city moved to stage center. Stardom was assured. "The Almighty designed that we should have this [western] trade," proclaimed a Petersburg journal. Alexandria was more secular but equally as confident: "There is no town in Virginia whose future promises to be more brilliant and successful . . . than Alexandria." Norfolk exclaimed, "Behold a new town and a new people! . . . Who can set bounds to the destiny of such a sea-port as Norfolk?" Richmond saw its inevitable growth as a phenomenon of sectional import: "We can and will build up our beautiful city to the benefit of the South." A Wheeling journal, after reviewing the city's growth potential, stated matter-of-factly, "There are few cities in the Union offering greater inducements for profitable investment . . . than the city of Wheeling."[77]

The new era of optimism pervaded the state. Even the old and bitter divisiveness between eastern and western Virginia temporarily melted under the influence of the reform Constitution of 1851. The new constitution established universal white male suffrage, increased the representation of cities in the assembly, and, most important, equalized representation between the eastern and western portions of the state.[78] Now Virginia would know "no north, no south, no east, no west."[79] The new constitution joined the pattern of change and energy that had worn away the cloak of depression and stagnation. The Richmond *Whig* rejoiced, "A new brighter era is evidently at hand." In western Virginia, a Charlestown journal clasped hands with the east: "Virginia is entering upon a new era, and old manners, customs and things must give place to the progressive spirit of the age." A fresh start, a rebirth, thrilled Virginians to action: "A new era has dawned upon Virginia . . . and we shall make it a new starting point," a Norfolk editor pledged.

77. Petersburg *News*, quoted in Richmond *Enquirer*, January 21, 1851; Alexandria *Gazette*, quoted in Richmond *Enquirer*, September 27, 1853; Norfolk and Portsmouth *Herald*, February 18, 1854; Richmond *Daily Dispatch*, March 18, 1859; Wheeling *Daily Intelligencer*, November 27, 1852.

78. S., "The New Constitution," *Southern Literary Messenger*, XVIII (1852), 116–22; see also, Chilton Williamson, *American Suffrage: From Property to Democracy, 1760–1860* (Princeton, 1960), 229.

79. 38 BPW 1853, xxi.

Indeed, as the Norfolk *American Beacon* declared, "progress has become the motto of our people."[80]

The effervescence of the new era contrasted sharply with the sullen omnipresence of sectional conflict. Yet sectionalism had awakened the Old Dominion. The state responded with a variety of economic programs designed to secure economic independence and sectional equilibrium. Urban Virginia—the focal point of economic regeneration—eagerly took up the banner to save the South and the Union. Natural advantages, enterprise, and the example of northern cities convinced urban Virginia that success lay in the near future. The sounds of progress echoed on the wharves and in the streets: "Our principal orator . . . will be Steam, and the railroad, the factory, and the river our field of debate." The day was drawing closer "when Virginia . . . is to be redeemed, regenerated, and disenthralled."[81]

80. Richmond *Whig*, October 31, 1854; Charlestown *Spirit of Jefferson*, September 30, 1851; Norfolk *American Beacon*, November 4, 1851; Norfolk *American Beacon*, August 20, 1853.

81. Richmond *Daily Dispatch*, October 18, 1853; Charlestown *Spirit of Jefferson*, quoted in Richmond *Enquirer*, August 15, 1851.

The City-Builders   2

THE REDEMPTION of the Old Dominion rested on the accomplishments of her cities. Whether urban Virginia succeeded in restoring economic prosperity and sectional equality or not, the cities themselves would change. The processes of urbanization would alter urban life considerably. The extent of urbanization, as well as the quality of life produced by growth, depended on the role of urban leadership.

The nineteenth century was the halcyon era for the urban booster. Through his efforts, the insularity of individual cities transformed into an urban network. The civic leader articulated the needs of his city and directed implementation of programs designed to promote wealth and progress. On the frontier, the urban booster led the effort to carve urban civilization out of the wilderness. In established communities he defended against grasping rivals, organized the city, and set it on a course of continued growth. He was, in short, a city-builder.[1]

Historians have only recently recognized the central role of the city-builder in the process of urbanization. Massive institutional and technological changes have generally dwarfed the role of individual enterprise in urban growth, though it was the entrepreneur who directed and rationalized these changes. Untapped sources such as the manuscript census, city directories, and tax lists have facilitated the discovery of the city-builders who rarely left papers or diaries to guide historians through their lives. Finally, quantitative techniques have enabled historians to collate and correlate large amounts of data concerning these elites. A pattern of elitism has emerged from the study of urban leaders in diverse cities. The boosters were mature, stable members of the community who were typically family men and property holders. They were not the

1. On the importance of the city-builder to urban growth see, for example, Charles N. Glaab, *Kansas City and the Railroads* (Madison, Wisc., 1962); Wade, *Urban Frontier*; Wheeler, *To Wear a City's Crown*; and Schnell and McLear, "Why the Cities Grew," 162–77.

wealthiest members of their respective cities, but they were usually among the top 15% in property ownership. They held occupations of fairly high status. The most common characteristic of urban elites in mid-nineteenth-century America was their ubiquity. They formed an interlocking directorate to control most aspects of urban life from government to business to church to charity. Virginia's urban leadership conformed to the general pattern.[2]

Despite the wealth of scholarship lavished on antebellum urban elites, southern cities have yet to receive the benefit of such study. Yet allusions in the literature to southern urban leaders have indicated that they were no different from northern boosters. They, like their northern counterparts, "hoped to see in their region," one scholar has suggested, "the establishment of a happy, prosperous, and essentially bourgeois society."[3] Indeed, as Clement Eaton has observed, some prominent southern civic leaders, like New Orleans railroad promoter James Robb, were northerners.[4] Studies of southern urban leaders could prove fruitful from another standpoint. They were among the most organized, the most articulate, and the most enterprising voices in their section before the Civil War. In such a capacity they framed the South's political goals in economic terms and provided direction for the renaissance of the 1850s. Southern urban elites, in advocating programs for economic independence and urban growth, set the tone for their section following the Mexican War. Southern patriots such as New Orleans publicist J. D. B. De Bow and Richmond industrialist Joseph R. Anderson disseminated progressive thought throughout Dixie. In short, understanding antebellum

2. See, for example, Michael H. Frisch, "The Community Elite and the Emergence of Urban Politics: Springfield, Massachusetts, 1840–1880," in Stephen Thernstrom and Richard Sennett, *Nineteenth-Century Cities: Essays in the New Urban History* (New Haven, 1969), 77–96; Walter S. Glazer, "Participation and Power—Voluntary Associations and the Functional Organization of Cincinnati in 1840," *Historical Methods Newsletter*, V (1972), 151–68; Frederic C. Jaher, "Nineteenth-Century Elites in Boston and New York," *Journal of Social History*, VI (1972), 32–77; and Edward Pessen, "Who Governed the Nation's Cities in the 'Era of the Common Man,'" *Political Science Quarterly*, LXXXVII (1972), 591–614. See also Lawrence Stone, "Prosopography," *Daedalus*, C (1971), 46–89.

3. Knight, "Discontent in the Antebellum South," 455.

4. Eaton, *Growth of Southern Civilization*, 242–43.

southern urban leadership is essential to grasping the essence of the South before Sumter.

Identifying Virginia's urban elite is quite simple because, like leaders elsewhere, they were highly visible. Visibility has been a primary criterion for selecting urban leaders and it includes attendance at important civic meetings, membership in voluntary associations, participation in local government and service on the boards of internal improvement companies and banks. These distinctions are not sufficient by themselves to identify a selective group of individuals who influenced urban life. These persons must occupy positions of leadership in these activities to qualify for entrance into the urban elite. Thus, it is not enough to be superintendent of police; the individual must be a member of the city council. Similarly, it is not sufficient to be merely a member of the board of trade; the merchant must be on the executive committee to attain urban leadership.[5] The individual also must hold an important position in two activities to qualify as an urban leader. These rather rigid parameters restricted the size of the elite group. In the three Virginia cities that I chose for this study—Richmond, Alexandria, and Norfolk—the leadership represented roughly 2% of the total number of households in their respective cities. The selectivity of the leadership list ensured at least some comparability between visibility and power.[6]

The characteristics of Virginia's urban elite did not differ markedly from city to city, but they did indicate some divergence reflecting the distinct nature of each city under study. In Richmond, analysis of visibility and leadership between 1847 and 1861 generated sixty-five civic leaders (1.8% of the total heads of households).

5. See Glazer, "Participation and Power," 151–68.
6. The sources that I used in the leadership and random sample analyses included Seventh Census of Virginia: 1850. Free Inhabitants, II, XI, XVIII; Slave Schedule, I, IV, IX; Eighth Census of Virginia: 1860, Free Inhabitants, I, XII, XIX; Slave Schedule I, IV, V; John Boyd, *Boyd's Washington and Georgetown Directory, 1860* (Washington, D.C., 1860); James Butters, *Butters' Richmond Directory, 1855* (Richmond, 1855); William S. Forrest, *The Norfolk Directory for 1851–52* (Norfolk, 1851); William L. Montague, *Richmond Directory and Business Advertiser for 1852* (Baltimore, 1852); and S. Bassett French, "Biographical Sketches" (MS in Virginia State Library). In addition to the directories, the urban press for each city proved invaluable in discerning leadership.

Prospective leaders were scrutinized for participation in at least two of ten activities. Employing the index of associational activity developed by Walter S. Glazer in a study of Cincinnati elites, I determined that 46.2% of Richmond's leaders were minimum activists; that is, they assumed leadership positions in two activities. Those who held important positions in three or four activities numbered 38.5%; they were moderate activists. Finally, 15.4% of the leaders were maximum activists. These men were the elite of the elite.[7] They influenced the most important aspects of community life. They participated as leaders in five or more activities. None of Richmond's leaders was involved in all ten activities. Such a feat would have required super-human energy, perseverence, wealth, and dedication. Joseph R. Anderson, whose Tredegar Iron Works became one of the leading examples of southern urban industrial enterprise before the Civil War, participated in eight activities. A brief account of Anderson's role in Richmond society is not only a tribute to him, but an example of the opportunities and options available in antebellum southern cities (see table 3).

Joseph R. Anderson, born on the western Virginia frontier, transformed a struggling iron foundry into one of the nation's most prolific iron works. Despite the energy required to run a successful industrial operation, Anderson plunged into Richmond activities almost at the point of his accession of Tredegar in 1841. By the time he was forty in 1853, Anderson was director of the Richmond branch of the Farmers' Bank of Virginia, a major stockholder in two internal improvement companies, trustee of the Tredegar Free School, and Richmond's representative to the Virginia House of Delegates. He was also a prominent member of Saint Paul's Episcopal Church. Later in the decade, he won a seat on the Richmond City Council and became an executive of the Richmond Board of Trade. Anderson's path crossed virtually every phase of urban life: business, government, finance, and religion.[8]

7. Glazer, "Participation and Power," 151–68.
8. Seventh Census of Virginia: 1850, Free Inhabitants, IV, 793; French, "Biographical Sketches," 262; Richmond *Daily Dispatch*, January 19, 1859, April 7, 1860; Richmond

Table 3 Activity Rate of Urban Leadership, 1847–1861

Study Group	N %	Minimum Activists N %	Moderate Activists N %	Maximum Activists N %
Richmond	65	30	25	10
	100.0	46.2	38.5	15.4
Norfolk	56	18	28	10
	100.0	32.1	50.0	17.9
Alexandria	44	15	19	10
	100.0	34.1	43.2	22.7

Anderson was the most active but by no means atypical example of Richmond's elite. More than half the leadership held prominent positions in at least three or more activities. Although most did not contribute as much to the city as Anderson, some were pioneers in their respective vocations. They generated at least as much growth and prosperity as the master of Tredegar. James A. Cowardin, a Richmond leader, inaugurated the Richmond *Daily Dispatch* in 1850. The *Dispatch* was a nonpartisan penny press dedicated to furthering the interests of the city. Cowardin, like Anderson, came from western Virginia. He helped to found the Virginia Mechanics' Institute, which was a combination of school, public library, and lyceum.[9] Hugh W. Fry, offspring of a prominent Virginia family, came to the city from Fredericksburg in 1832. By 1850 he was operating Richmond's leading commission house. He was a founder of the board of trade, the Richmond Savings Institution, the Belle Isle Nail Works, a cotton factory, and he ran a steamship line to New York City.[10] R. B. Haxall operated one of the nation's largest milling concerns in Richmond. He was a founder of

---

Enquirer, November 30, 1849, and April 30, 1858. See also Charles B. Dew, *Ironmaker to the Confederacy: Joseph R. Anderson and the Tredegar Iron Works* (New Haven, 1966).

9. Butters, *Directory, 1855*, 200; Richmond *Daily Dispatch*, September 23, 1860; Richmond *Enquirer*, August 15, 1851.

10. Montague, *Richmond Directory*, 1852, 157; French, "Biographical Sketches," 207; Richmond *Enquirer*, June 13, 1854, and April 10, 1855.

both the Richmond Board of Trade and the Grain and Cotton Exchange. Haxall was also a leader in the Episcopal Church and initiated several insurance enterprises in Richmond.[11] Finally, James Thomas, Jr., came to Richmond from Lynchburg and opened a tobacco factory that was to become known throughout the country. He financed several Baptist institutions in the city.[12] Richmond's leaders shared the imagination and enterprise of their contemporaries elsewhere. They were the modern men of Virginia's urban renaissance.

Collectively, Richmond's civic boosters were as impressive as they were individually. As expected, merchants, industrialists, and professionals dominated the city's elite (see table 4). I extracted the occupations of fifty-nine of Richmond's sixty-five leaders (90.8%) from the 1850 manuscript census for Virginia and from city directories. Employing the occupational categories devised by Peter R. Knights in *Plain People of Boston*, I found that 59.3% of the civic leaders held proprietary occupations that included bank president, railroad executive, industrialist, merchant, and important government official; 27.1% held professional jobs such as lawyer, physician, and editor.[13] Thus, 86.4% of Richmond's elite held positions in the two highest occupational categories. Only 11.9% were classified as petty proprietors (owning less than $1000 in property), and only one was employed in a service occupation. This occupational homogeneity exceeded the pattern discerned by Glazer for Cincinnati in 1840. In that study, Glazer's maximum activists, who represented less than 2.0% of the total male householders (a more select group than the Richmond leaders) placed a little more than two-thirds of their number in the two high-status categories.[14]

The occupations of Richmond leaders indicated a broader base of leadership than existed in many antebellum cities. Of the fifty-

11. Butters, *Directory, 1855*, 95; French, "Biographical Sketches," 239; Richmond *Enquirer*, January 17, 1854.
12. Montague, *Richmond Directory*, 1852, 122; French, "Biographical Sketches," 260; Richmond *Enquirer*, May 27, 1853.
13. Peter R. Knights, *The Plain People of Boston, 1830–1860: A Study in City Growth* (New York, 1971), Appendix E.
14. Glazer, "Participation and Power," 151–68.

Table 4 Occupation of Urban Leadership, 1850

Study Group	N %	Un- skilled	Semi- skilled and Service	Petty Propri- etors	Skilled	Clerical and Sales	Semi- Profes- sional	Propri- etors	Profes- sional	Gentle- men[a] or Unlisted
Richmond	59	0	1	7	0	0	0	35	16	0
	100.0	0.0	1.7	11.9	0.0	0.0	0.0	59.3	27.1	0.0
Norfolk	54	0	0	3	0	5	0	29	12	5
	100.0	0.0	0.0	5.6	0.0	9.3	0.0	53.7	22.2	9.3
Alexandria	43	0	0	3	1	1	0	30	5	3
	100.0	0.0	0.0	7.0	2.3	2.3	0.0	69.8	11.6	7.0
Richmond Random Sample	373	29	19	69	65	14	3	48	19	107
	100.0	7.8	5.1	18.5	17.4	3.8	0.8	12.9	5.1	28.7

[a] No "gentlemen" among random sample; no unlisted occupations among leadership groups.

one individuals in high-status occupations, merchants comprised nearly one-third of this group. There were also seventeen professionals, eleven industrialists, three bankers and one railroad executive. This configuration reflected the healthy diversity of the city's economy. The leaders' occupations also demonstrated that the major segments of the economy were well represented. Historians have characterized the early nineteenth-century city as dominated by a mercantile elite. Richmond had evidently passed through that stage of urbanization by 1850. While merchants formed an important part of the city's leadership, new groups such as industrialists, professionals, and bankers joined the mercantile old guard.[15] The economic diversity of the leadership ensured a broad coalition in business, society, and above all in government. Twenty-five leaders (38.5%) were members of the city council at some time between 1847 and 1861. The increasing role of urban government in the late antebellum city attracted business leaders interested in rationalizing their city's growth.

In addition to occupation, property-holding is another variable that successfully characterized the urban elite. In the urban milieu, acquisition of real estate rather than possession of personal property was a symbol of status and prosperity. Real property was, as Clyde Griffen observed in his demographic study of nineteenth-century Poughkeepsie, the most visible evidence of success.[16] Ownership of land was and is a common American penchant that permeates urban and rural society alike. Indeed, it is perhaps stronger in the city because land is usually more valuable and less available. The percentage of Richmond's elite who held real property with a median value of $15,000 numbered 71.7% (see table 5). Few leaders held vast estates. Only two of the forty-three propertied boosters possessed holdings valued at more than $100,000 which was the usual benchmark figure of wealth in mid-

15. See David T. Gilchrist (ed.), *The Growth of the Seaport Cities, 1790–1825* (Charlottesville, Va., 1967); and Michael H. Frisch, *Town into City: Springfield, Massachusetts and the Meaning of Community, 1840–1880* (Cambridge, Mass.,1972).

16. Clyde Griffen, "Workers Divided: The Effect of Craft and Ethnic Differences in Poughkeepsie, New York 1850–1880," in Stephen Thernstrom and Richard Sennett (eds.), *Nineteenth-Century Cities: Essays in the New Urban History* (New Haven, 1969), 59.

Table 5 Real Property Holding of Urban Leadership, 1850

Study Group	N %	N$50–$6500	$6501–$99,999	$100,000+	$\bar{X}$ ($)[b]	s ($)[c]	Median ($)[d]
Richmond	43 100.0 (or 71.7% of total leadership)[a]	13 30.2	28 65.1	2 4.7	28,390	37,153	14,898
Norfolk	41 100.0 (or 75.9% of total leadership)	14 34.1	27 65.9	0 0.0	17,306	19,873	11,775
Alexandria	38 100.0 (or 88.4% of total leadership)	13 34.2	24 63.2	1 2.6	20,621	25,397	11,000
Richmond Random Sample	89 100.0 (or 23.9% of total sample)	62 69.7	26 29.2	1 1.1	8,456	18,791	3,208

[a] Total leadership refers to those leaders listed in 1850 census; Richmond, 60; Norfolk, 54; Alexandria, 43.
[b] Mean to nearest dollar.
[c] Standard deviation to nearest dollar.
[d] Median to nearest dollar.

nineteenth-century America. There were only four leaders among the twenty wealthiest Richmonders in 1850, indicating that great wealth and leadership were not necessarily synonymous. Since studies of elites have included personal property as part of property holding, direct comparison is not possible. Implications from Glazer's study indicate that the real estate holdings of Cincinnati leaders comported with those from Richmond in terms of holders versus nonholders.[17] Since some northern cities like Philadelphia and New York harbored considerably more wealth than Richmond, elites in those cities would have found a median of $15,000 a relatively small holding.

Analyzing the wealth of the leadership in a southern city, the question of slaveholding must inevitably occur. Slaves were included under personal property for tax purposes, but obviously their acquisition carried more import than the purchase of a pocket watch. Like real property, slaves represented tangible evidence of success. Urban southerners were not antagonistic to slave ownership any more or less than rural southerners. In an urban environment, slaveholdings, of necessity, had to be smaller. Occasionally, city dwellers owned a considerable complement of slaves. Industrialists and wealthy merchants required increasing amounts of labor and the institution of slavery supplied an important portion of such needs. The percentage of leaders who were discovered by the 1850 census to be slaveholders came to 83.3% (see table 6). The median slaveholding was six, and more than two-thirds of the slaveholders possessed less than nine slaves. A few civic boosters had slaveholdings that rivaled plantation forces. Five leaders owned more than twenty slaves; two of them possessed over ninety bondsmen. Male slaves outnumbered female slaves by more than two to one, reflecting the importance of large male slave work forces in Richmond's growing industries. It was almost certain that if a leader possessed more than ten slaves, he operated a large-scale mercantile house or a factory; hence the dominance of male labor. D. Clayton James's study of Natchez suggests that slaveholding was even more prominent among the elite of the Mississippi River port

17. Glazer, "Participation and Power," 151–68.

Table 6 Slave Ownership of Urban Leadership, 1850

Study Group	N %	1–4 Slaves	5–8 Slaves	9–19 Slaves	20+ Slaves	Total Males	Total Females	$\bar{X}$	s	Median
Richmond	50 100.0 (or 83.3% of total leadership)	19 38.0	16 32.0	10 20.0	5 10.0	390 68.1	183 32.0	11	19	6
Norfolk	46 100.0 (or 88.5% of total leadership)	15 32.6	18 39.1	8 17.4	5 10.9	180 48.4	192 51.6	8	6	6
Alexandria	30 100.0 (or 69.8% of total leadership)	23 76.7	4 13.3	3 10.0	0 0.0	41 35.3	75 64.7	4	3	3
Richmond Random Sample	152 100.0 (or 40.8% of total random sample)	102 67.1	38 25.0	8 5.3	4 2.6	284 40.7	413 59.3	5	11	3

than in Richmond.[18] Nevertheless, with more than three-quarters of Richmond's leadership owning slaves, those Virginians who were sensitive about the subject of slavery need not have had any worries concerning the orthodoxy of those who guided the destiny of the capital city.

Besides being a prosperous elite, Richmond's civic leaders were a stable group as well. Persistence and priority have assumed great significance in recent studies of antebellum urban populations.[19] Persistence refers to an individual's residence within the city *after* a given year. Priority signifies a person's residence within the city *prior* to a given year. Both measures are indicators of the stability of a population group. Of the sixty Richmond leaders located in the 1850 manuscript census, fifty-three (88.3%) were present in the city for the 1840 census or the 1860 census or both (see table 7). There were 38.3% who remained in the city during the entire twenty-year period; 11.7% were transients or leaders who resided in the city for less than ten years. Walter S. Glazer characterized his Cincinnati activists as mature, experienced, and stable. In Glazer's study of 1840, 38.9% of the city's leaders had been living in Cincinnati eleven years earlier.[20] The priority rate for Richmond's leadership was 51.7% The difference in priority percentages probably stemmed from the fact that Cincinnati was a newer city where elites would naturally be less established. Also, the Richmond base census year was 1850, ten years later than Glazer's census. Clyde Griffen's study of Poughkeepsie, though not an analysis of elites, can be helpful for comparative purposes. The persistence rate of native property owners—the closest category in Griffen's study to Richmond's elite—was 49.0% between 1850 and 1860. Richmond leadership during the same decade persisted at the rate of 75.0%. The only group in Griffen's sample that approached this figure was the merchants at 59.0%.[21] It is conceivable, of course, that the Poughkeepsie sample, if pared down to activists only, could yield as high a rate of persistence as Richmond's. Nevertheless, with over

18. James, *Antebellum Natchez*, 129.
19. See Knights, *Plain People of Boston*, 57–64.
20. Glazer, "Participation and Power," 156.
21. Griffen, "Workers Divided," 62.

Table 7 Persistence and Priority of Urban Leadership, 1840–1860

Study Group	N %	Persistence[a] 1850–1860	Priority 1840–1850	Transiency	Permanence[b]
Richmond	60	45	31	7	23
	100.0	75.0	51.7	11.7	38.3
Norfolk	54	36	17	12	11
	100.0	66.7	31.5	22.2	20.4
Alexandria	43	30	23	6	16
	100.0	71.4	54.8	16.7	38.1
Richmond	373	128	89	200	43
Random Sample	100.0	34.3	23.9	53.6	11.5

[a] Including permanent residents.
[b] Those individuals who remained in their respective cities throughout the twenty-year period.

half of the leaders persisting between 1840 and 1850, and three-quarters persisting in the next decade, Richmond civic boosters were becoming an entrenched elite with a significant stake in the community's fortunes. Richmond's leaders were typically not new arrivals, though many were born elsewhere; their roots in the city were deep, and in a section where tradition and stability were essential aspects of the social liturgy, the elite's persistence added to their respect and confidence.

The leaders were not only established members of the community, but their lineage was typically Virginian. Of the fifty-nine civic boosters for whom place of birth could be found, 88.1% were born in the Old Dominion, 8.5% were born in various northern states, one in another southern state, and one in Scotland (see table 8). Thus, not only were Richmond's elite overwhelmingly native born, they were predominantly indigenous to Virginia as well. Glazer's study of Cincinnati revealed a similar pattern of native dominance: 78.1% of Glazer's group were native born compared with 98.3% for Richmond. Immigration was a larger factor in Cincinnati than in Richmond, and, once again, Cincinnati was a newer city with fewer number of native born than Richmond.[22] In his study of

22. Glazer, "Participation and Power," 156.

Table 8 Nativity of Urban Leadership, 1850

Study Group	N %	Virginia	Southern States	Northern States	Ireland	British Isles	Germany	Other [a]
Richmond	59	52	1	5	0	1	0	0
	100.0	88.1	1.7	8.5	0.0	1.7	0.0	0.0
Norfolk	53	37	8	4	1	2	1	0
	100.0	69.8	15.1	7.5	1.9	3.8	1.9	0.0
Alexandria	42	32	5	3	0	2	0	0
	100.0	76.2	11.9	7.1	0.0	4.8	0.0	0.0
Richmond Random Sample	372	260	19	21	26	16	23	7
	100.0	69.9	5.1	5.6	7.0	4.3	6.2	1.9

[a] Includes France, West Indies, Holland, Italy, and Switzerland.

Table 9 Age of Urban Leadership, 1850

Study Group	N %	Under 30	30–49	50+	$\overline{X}$	s	Median
Richmond	53	6	36	11	41	9	40
	100.00	11.3	67.9	20.8			
Norfolk	53	6	35	11	40	10	40
	100.0	11.5	67.3	21.2			
Alexandria	42	2	26	14	46	11	46
	100.00	4.8	61.9	33.3			
Richmond	373	92	208	73	39	12	37
Random Sample	100.0	24.7	55.8	19.6			

Poughkeepsie, Griffen did not give a specific breakdown of nativity for leaders, but he stated that the city's elite was "overwhelmingly" native born.[23]

The age of Richmond's leaders reflected further the stability and maturity of the group. The median age was forty (see table 9). Only six of the fifty-three leaders for whom data on age was found were under thirty in 1850, yet only eleven were fifty years of age or older. In short, these civic leaders were in their prime years: they were mature yet energetic enough to direct economic programs and to cope with the changes inspired by urban growth. Glazer discovered that none of his Cincinnati elite was under thirty, while most were over forty.[24] These figures correspond to the findings in Richmond and join them in emphasizing the maturity of leadership groups in nineteenth-century cities.

The family life of the Richmond activists was a final indicator of the stability of the city's elite group. The family played a central role in nineteenth-century society, particularly in the South. George Fitzhugh wrote that family life was essential to the physical and mental well-being of the southerner: "Love and veneration for the family is with us not only a principle, but probably a prejudice."[25]

23. Griffen, "Workers Divided," 62.
24. Glazer, "Participation and Power," 158–59.
25. Fitzhugh, *Cannibals All!*, 192.

Table 10 Marital Status of Urban Leadership, 1850

Study Group	N %	Unmarried	Married	Widow or Widower
Richmond	49	9	39	1
	100.0	18.4	79.6	2.0
Norfolk	52	8	40	4
	100.0	15.4	76.9	7.7
Alexandria	42	2	36	4
	100.0	4.8	85.7	9.5
Richmond	358	74	217	67
Random Sample	100.0	20.7	60.6	18.7

In cities the families provided stability and security in an environment that threatened to engulf both. Historians have begun to realize the importance of the family to any discussion about American society.[26] In the antebellum South, however, little has been written beyond the clichés of the domineering, sexually promiscuous male, and the long-suffering, ever-pregnant female.[27] In the urban South a husband could doubtless hide his infidelity to a greater degree than on the isolated plantation. Clues to this particular aspect of family life are therefore scarce in the urban environment. Other evidence of family life tends to support the view that the southern urban home differed very little from life at northern hearths.

Marriage was typical of Richmond's elite. Of the forty-nine leaders for whom marital status could be found in 1850, 79.6% were married, 18.4% were single, and one was a widower (see table 10). Wives were typically five years younger than their husband, usually thirty-five years old (see table 11). One-third of them were thirty or younger and only four were over fifty. Marriage, at least for the male, was a sign of settling down, an indication of a less frivolous

26. See Tamara K. Hareven, "The Historical Study of the Family in Urban Society," *Journal of Urban History*, 1 (1975), 259–65.
27. See Anne Firor Scott, "Women's Perspective on the Patriarchy in the 1850s," *Journal of American History*, LXI (1974), 52–64.

Table 11 Age of Wives of Urban Leaders, 1850

Study Group	N %	30 or Less	31–50	Over 50	$\bar{X}$	s	Median
Richmond	39	13	22	4	36	9	35
	100.0	33.3	56.4	10.3			
Norfolk	40	11	26	3	36	10	34
	100.0	27.5	65.0	7.5			
Alexandria	36	8	22	6	39	11	38
	100.0	22.2	61.1	16.8			
Richmond	217	100	97	20	34	10	32
	100.0	46.1	44.7	9.2			

outlook on life. Marriage also provided an avenue of upward mobility for an ambitious businessman. Kinship ties, though less important in the city, still counted for something in nineteenth-century America. Edward Pessen, for example, noted the reoccurrence of certain family names on lists of the elite in northern cities for generation after generation.[28]

The configuration of the household revealed a familiar pattern. Spatial limitations as well as less rigorous labor requirements tended to keep family size in southern cities comparable with family size in the urban North. Thirty-seven of the forty-nine leaders for whom information on marital status was available had children, that is, almost the same number of leaders who were married (see table 12). Thus, children and marriage were virtually synonymous. Leaders and their wives typically had four children ranging in age from three years old for the average youngest child to fourteen years of age for the average eldest child (see table 13). Children of these families tended to stay in the home longer than those who belonged to the rest of urban society. More than one-third of the children of the elite were eighteen years of age or older and still under their parents' roofs. Large nuclear families were rare. Only four leaders were fathers to more than seven children. The households of Richmond's elite, though, were rarely limited to

28. Pessen, "Who Governed," 591–614.

Table 12 Number of Children of Urban Leaders, 1850

Study Group	N %	1–2[a]	3–6	7+	$\overline{X}$	s	Median
Richmond	37	12	21	4	4	2	4
	100.0	32.4	56.8	10.8			
	(or 75.5% of leadership)[b]						
Norfolk	42	14	20	8	4	3	4
	100.0	33.3	47.6	19.0			
	(or 80.8% of leadership)						
Alexandria	37	11	17	9	4	3	4
	100.0	29.7	45.9	24.3			
	(or 84.1% of leadership)						
Richmond	234	119	96	19	3	3	2
Random Sample	100.0	50.9	41.0	8.1			
	(or 65.4% of sample)						

[a] Age in years.
[b] Leadership refers to those for whom marital status was discerned: Richmond, 49; Norfolk, 52; Alexandria, 42; Richmond sample, 358.

the nuclear family. The average household size was seven, which meant that boarders were part of the leaders' households.

Boarders were commonplace in mid-nineteenth-century urban households, North and South. An established household was an excellent staging area from which a newcomer could launch a career. The urban family acted as his surrogate family, providing him with a modicum of stability in the new urban environment. Sometimes apprentices would share their masters' dwellings in the days before industry obviated this kind of relationship. Relatives who boarded added stability to the nuclear family, and those families who could afford servants (certainly the urban leaders qualified) sometimes kept them in the household. Finally, boarders were a part of the urban household scene out of a purely logistical necessity. Housing construction could not keep pace with the increases in population and business. In the era before multiple family dwellings became feasible, if not desirable, construction techniques prohibited a rapid rise in housing. Thus, urban families

Table 13 Age of Children of Urban Leaders, 1850

Study Group	Youngest							Eldest						
	N %	1[a]	2–3	4+	X̄	s	Median	N %	1–8	9–17	18+	X̄	s	Median
Richmond	37	9	10	18	6	6	3	37	11	13	13	14	8	14
	100.0	24.3	27.0	48.6				100.0	29.7	35.1	35.1			
Norfolk	42	14	9	19	5	6	3	42	11	16	15	15	9	15
	100.0	33.3	21.4	45.2				100.0	26.2	38.1	35.7			
Alexandria	37	10	5	22	7	8	4	37	10	9	18	16	9	17
	100.0	27.0	13.5	59.5				100.0	27.0	24.3	48.6			
Richmond Random Sample	234	78	47	109	6	6	3	234	97	80	57	12	8	10
	100.0	33.3	20.1	46.6				100.0	41.5	34.2	24.4			

[a] Includes infants less than one year old.

became temporary and in some cases permanent repositories for a rather substantial population.[29]

Richmond's elite households usually possessed at least one or two boarders: thirty-five of the sixty leaders included boarders in their households (see table 14). The most typical category of boarder residing in the elite household was the relative. The extended family included relatives as well as the families of sons and daughters. More than half of those activists who had boarders residing with them included family and relatives in their households. Servants were present in 40.0% of the households that had boarders. It is interesting to note that despite the existing institution of slavery, many elite families obviously opted for free servants. It would be incorrect to conclude, however, that leaders had an aversion to slave ownership, since many leaders owned slaves. The scarcity of labor simply forced families to seek other elements of the work force. Other types of boarders included those whose status I was not able to ascertain accurately.

Despite their diverse vocational interests, the Richmond leadership was a homogeneous group. Most held property and were slaveholders; they were part of the same generation; the boosters typically came from stable household arrangements with a wife, children, and a boarder or two. They were native born and were established residents of the city. In these characteristics, the Richmond leadership did not differ significantly from activists in other cities. There were, of course, some differences in degree rather than in kind. No two cities presented the same economic or demographic base; hence the difference in elites. Even other Virginia cities deviated from the Richmond example.

In Norfolk, fifty-six leaders (2.5% of the heads of households in the city) emerged from a study of visibility and leadership. Of the fifty-four leaders for whom occupations were discerned in 1850, 53.7% were proprietors; 22.2% were professionals; 5.6% were petty proprietors; 9.3% listed themselves as "gentlemen," a

29. John Modell and Tamara K. Hareven, "Urbanization and the Malleable Household: Examination of Boarding and Lodging in American Families," *Journal of Marriage and the Family*, XXXV (1973), 467–79.

Table 14 Boarders of Urban Leaders, 1850

Study Group		Number							Type			
	N %	1	2–4	5+	$\bar{X}$	s	Median	N %	Family	Servant	Occupa-tional	Unknown
Richmond	35	16	14	5	3	4	2	35	19	14	7	10
	100.0	45.7	40.0	14.3				100.0	54.3	40.0	20.0	28.6
	(or 58.3% of leadership)[a]											
Norfolk	35	10	21	4	3	2	2	35	16	9	7	21
	100.0	28.6	60.0	11.4				100.0	45.7	25.7	20.0	60.0
	(or 67.3% of leadership)											
Alexandria	29	12	16	1	2	2	2	29	11	10	5	9
	100.0	41.4	55.2	3.4				100.0	37.9	34.5	17.2	31.0
	(or 67.4% of leadership)											
Richmond Random Sample	181	74	71	36	3	3	2	181	75	23	32	99
	100.0	40.9	39.2	19.9				100.0	41.4	12.7	17.7	54.7
	(or 48.5% of sample)											

[a] Leadership refers to those leaders for household data were found: Richmond, 60; Norfolk, 52; Alexandria, 43; Richmond Sample, 373.

euphemism for retired. Thus, 75.9% of Norfolk's activists held the high status proprietary of professional occupations, compared with 86.4% for Richmond's boosters. Presumably, those identifying themselves as "gentlemen" in the Norfolk group held those positions of high status prior to retirement. If they are included in the proprietary and professional group, the percentage becomes 85.2%, or nearly identical to that of the Richmond elite.

The occupational similarity between the Richmond and Norfolk groups ends when the high-status positions are broken down into specific occupations. The broad base of business leadership evinced by Richmond's elite was absent from Norfolk's leadership. Norfolk's economic base was predominantly commercial. Of the forty-one individuals who were either proprietors or professionals, twenty-five (61.0%) were merchants, eleven (26.8%) were professionals, and only three leaders (7.3%) were bankers. There were no industrialists among Norfolk's elite. This was not surprising since there were no large-scale processing industries in the city as there were in Richmond. The largest single group in Richmond's elite, the merchants, accounted for less than one-third of the high-status occupations. Thus, the occupations of Norfolk's boosters did not necessarily indicate the exclusivity of the leadership as much as they reflected the mercantile character of Norfolk's economy and society.

Despite the relative homogeneity in occupation, Norfolk's leaders cut as wide a swath through the city as did their Richmond brethren. In fact, they were on the average more energetic in community affairs than were Richmond leaders. Less than one-third could be classified as minimum activists; one-half were moderate activists; and 17.9% were maximum activists. Participation in government was also more widespread among Norfolk's elite than in Richmond's. Forty Norfolk leaders were members of the city council between 1847 and 1861, and two of those forty held the office of mayor. Thus, Norfolk leaders were almost twice as likely to be involved in city government as were the Richmond group. The rate of turnover of high-government officials in Richmond was considerably lower than it was in Norfolk. Reelection of city councilmen was common in the capital city. Among the twenty-five Richmond civic leaders who served on the city council after 1847, only one failed at a reelection attempt. Mayor Joseph Mayo, a civic leader himself, served in his office from 1853 to 1866, despite having to face the electorate every year. Before that he was the city attorney for thirty years. In Norfolk, the leaders were relatively newer to the city. Public office-holding was less secure, particularly during the Know Nothing imbroglio in the middle of the decade.

If Richmond could boast of its urban patriots, so could Norfolk. No leader participated in all ten activites that we have established as our criterion, but two were involved in seven of them. Henry Irwin, just thirty years old in 1850, was Norfolk's counterpart to Joseph R. Anderson. Irwin was a commission merchant who established the Norfolk Board of Trade. During the 1850s his activities included being director of the Farmers' Bank in Norfolk, president of the Merchants' and Mechanics' Exchange, and an officer in the Norfolk County Agricultural Society (where he doubtless effected numerous contacts for his mercantile business). Irwin also organized and managed a hotel and a steamship company. Finally, Irwin was active in charity affairs. He organized the New Orleans Relief Committee when yellow fever struck that city in 1853.[30]

Charles Reid was another Norfolk leader whose energy infused most phases of urban life. Reid, a longtime Norfolk resident, was one of the oldest members of the elite at fifty years of age in 1850. Yet he not only maintained his vigor but increased his activity during the 1850s. In 1849 he became director of the Farmers' Bank branch in Norfolk, and assumed the leadership of the charitable Norfolk Association for the Improvement of the Condition of the Poor as well. The following year he was a principal investor and director of the Norfolk and Petersburg Railroad Company. In 1851 he was elected to the city council and assumed the directorship of another bank. The next year he founded a savings institution. In 1854 he helped to found the Norfolk Board of Trade, and

30. Eighth Census of Virginia: 1860, Free Inhabitants, XIX, 288; Forrest, *Norfolk Directory, 1851–52*; Norfolk *Southern Argus*, August 30, 1853, June 9, 1854, June 26, 1857, and January 20, 1859.

in the following year he organized an insurance company. By 1856 he was a member of the city council again, vice president of the board of trade, president of an insurance company, and director of two banks—all positions that he retained until the end of the decade. In addition to his activities, he was one of the city's leading commission merchants.[31]

The wealth of Norfolk's elite reflected the commercial nature of the economy, which is to say that wealth was accumulated in smaller amounts there than in Richmond. The median real property holding for Norfolk's leaders was $12,000, compared with $15,000 in Richmond. Property holding was a bit more widespread in Norfolk, however, with forty-one out of the fifty-four leaders (75.9%) listed in the 1850 census owning real property compared with 71.7% of Richmond's elite. None of the leaders held real estate valued at more than $100,000. Only two members of the Norfolk elite were among the twenty wealthiest residents in 1850—a pattern that followed Richmond's. These two leaders were the only boosters who possessed more than $50,000 in real estate. Neither Irwin or Reid were among the top property holders.

Slaveholding was also slightly more common among Norfolk's leaders than among Richmond's activists. Of the fifty-two leaders located in the 1850 census, 88.5% owned slaves. As in Richmond, the median slaveholding was six slaves, and 71.7% of the slaveholders possessed fewer than nine slaves. Female slaves outnumbered male slaves slightly, indicating a smaller industrial base. Total slaveholdings were not prodigious primarily because of the absence of large industry. The largest single slaveholding was thirty-one, compared with ninety-two for one Richmond leader.

Norfolk's elite exhibited a pattern of stability that mirrored the condition of Richmond's leaders. Of the fifty-four activists located in the 1850 census, forty-two (77.8%) had been in the city for at least ten years or had begun a residence that was to last another decade or both. This is a little lower than Richmond's combined

31. Seventh Census of Virginia: 1850, Free Inhabitants, XVIII, 64; Forrest, *Norfolk Directory, 1851–52*, 90; Norfolk *Southern Argus*, January 20, 1849, May 26, 1851, June 9, 1854, April 26, 1855, and June 26, 1857.

persistence and priority figure of 88.3%. The longevity of Norfolk's leaders was also less than that of leaders in Richmond. The activists who remained in the city for the entire twenty-year period-numbered 21.2%. Further, the elite class in Norfolk was newer to the city than the one in Richmond. Less than one-third of the leaders had established residences in Norfolk by 1840. Finally, the rate of transiency was higher than in Richmond. This would explain, partially at least, the rapid turnover in political office.

Norfolk leaders were newcomers and their places of birth were more diverse than those of Richmond's elite. The percentage of the boosters who were Virginia born was 69.8% compared with 88.1% in the Richmond group. Norfolk, a seaport easily accessible from Maryland and North Carolina, attracted people from these states, and 15.1% of the leaders came from the adjacent states. Northern states provided 7.5% of the leaders, and 7.6% were of foreign birth: one from Ireland, one from Germany, and two from Scotland. Thus, as befitted a coastal port, Norfolk's leadership was more ethnically and religiously diverse than Richmond's elite. Although the Norfolk leadership was newer to the city, they were as mature as the Richmond group. Forty was the median age. The Norfolk leaders who were under thirty or were fifty or over matched the Richmond elite in the same age groups.

The stability of the leaders' family lives matched their maturity and nativity patterns. The typical Norfolk leader was married (76.9% compared with 79.6% in Richmond). 15.4% were single, and 7.7% were widowers. This comported with the marital status of Richmond's elite. The booster's wife was, on the average, six years younger than himself, with a median age of thirty-four. One-quarter of the wives were thirty years of age or younger, and only three were over fifty. Children and marriage were also as closely related in Norfolk as in Richmond. The leaders who fathered children totaled 80.8%, or 100% of those who were married, plus two widowers. The usual number of children in a leader's household was four, with the youngest child being typically three years old and the eldest fifteen. Nearly one-fifth of the leaders who had children had more than six, or almost twice the figure for

Richmond's leaders. The children tended to remain in the home as long as they did in Richmond. These figures are similar to the family profile of Richmond's leaders.

Family size indicated that boarders were common fixtures of elite family life. The median size of a household was seven. The percentage of the leaders' households that included boarders came to 67.3% (slightly more than Richmond's 58.3%) and 88.6% of those households having boarders had four or less, the same as in Richmond. The extended family accounted for the typical boarder situation in leaders' homes. Servants appeared in one-quarter of the homes, which was less than the 40.0% for Richmond's elite. One-fifth of the homes included occupational boarders and nearly two-thirds housed boarders whose status I was not able to discover. The latter figure represented a significant departure from the Richmond pattern. It resulted from a severe housing shortage and a larger transient population common to a seaport. These unknown boarders were taken in by the leader probably as much because of custom and civic duty as for the income in either money or services.

Norfolk's leadership was the same stable, mature, and propertied type of group who directed Richmond's fortunes. The differences, and they were minor, resulted primarily from the city's commercial base and geographic location. The leaders were ubiquitous in a variety of community functions, and their investment interests stretched beyond the borders of their city in the form of steamship lines and railroads. As in Richmond, Norfolk leaders were crucial in breaking the insularity of an isolated and stagnant community and in promoting the state's economic regeneration.

Alexandria, like Richmond, was a river port, and like Norfolk it had ready access to contiguous states. Forty-four Alexandrians (2.1% of the heads of households) achieved leadership status between 1847 and 1861. As expected, proprietary and professional occupations were the dominant ones in the elite group. Of the forty-three leaders whose occupations were discerned, 69.8% were proprietors and 11.6% were professionals. Other leaders were scattered fairly evenly through the other occupational categories. Thus, 81.4% of the city's leaders were involved in high-status occupations similar to the occupational configuration of both Richmond and Norfolk (including "gentlemen"). If "gentlemen" were added to these occupations, the figure would be an impressive 88.4%, or higher than any other urban elite.

On a more specific level, merchants dominated Alexandria's elite as they had in Norfolk. Merchants accounted for twenty-five (71.4%) of the thirty-five leaders with high-status occupations; professionals represented 20.0%; bankers, 2.9%; and manufacturers, 5.7% of the proprietary and professional group. The occupational pattern corresponded to the commercial orientation of the city. Even the two industrialists—one a cabinetmaker, the other a brickmaker—represented more traditional manufacturing enterprises.

Alexandria's leaders, individually and collectively, had a broad impact on urban society. One-third of Alexandria's boosters were classified as minimum-level activists, and 43.2% of the elite held leadership positions in three or four major activities. Both figures fell between those in the indexes of activity of Richmond and Norfolk. The highest percentage among the three cities (22.7%) were maximum activists. Thus, a large proportion of leaders monopolized most of the city's activities. One reason for this was that family ties were more crucial in Alexandria than they were elsewhere. There were six sets of two brothers among the elite plus the father of one of the brother sets. Of the thirteen leaders in this group, seven were moderate activists and five were maximum activists.

Befitting the family nature of the leadership, fewer boosters 40.9% participated in politics in Alexandria, and they remained in office for longer periods of time than Norfolk's elite did. The figure is actually lower than it appears to be because Alexandria's elite tended to be involved in more activities per person than any other urban leadership group. For example, 59.1% of the city's leaders were officers of at least one bank and 53.6% assumed leadership positions in at least one internal improvement company. Alexandria, one of the older cities in the state, just up river from the ancestral homes of the Old Dominion's greatest families, was not an international port with the accompanying diversity of population like Norfolk was. The city on the Potomac also lacked the economic diversity and the influx of new leadership that characterized Richmond.

The benefits of family name evidently did not dull the enterprise of some of the city's more active leaders. George D. Fowle, whose brother, William H., and father, William, provided two generations of leadership to the city, became involved in a wide range of activities during the 1850s despite his youth (he was twenty-eight years old in 1850). Fowle helped to organize the Alexandria Library Association in 1852 and the Potomac Insurance Company in 1854; these were two activities that characterized leaders' attempts to improve the quality of life in the era of urban growth. Fowle was also director of the Alexandria Water Company and became vice president of the corn exchange, one of the city's new commodity exchanges. Finally, the energetic young merchant was elected to a term on the city council.[32] William N. McVeigh, whose brother James was also a member of the city's leadership, was another maximum activist participating in financial and charitable institutions as director of the Bank of the Old Dominion and the Female Orphan Asylum respectively. McVeigh was also one of the founders of the city's first major voluntary mercantile association, the Alexandria Board of Trade. His other activities included directorships of the Alexandria Water Company, the Alexandria Canal Company, and the Potomac Insurance Company. In his spare time, McVeigh was one of the most prominent merchants in the city.[33]

Lewis McKenzie was the most energetic leader in Alexandria. He assumed prominent roles in eight out of a possible ten activities. His interests were eclectic. He was president of the Alexandria, Lou-

32. Seventh Census of Virginia: 1850, Free Inhabitants, II, 724; Boyd, *Washington & Georgetown Directory*, 1860, 195; Alexandria *Gazette*, April 26, 1852, May 2, 1855, February 8, 1854, October 2, 1956, and January 9, 1857.
33. Seventh Census of Virginia: 1850, Free Inhabitants, II, 688; Boyd, *Washington and Georgetown Directory, 1860*, 195; Alexandria *Gazette*, January 12, 1853, and January 9, 1857; Powell, *Alexandria*, 327.

doun, and Hampshire Railroad while at the same time he owned a large portion of stock in the Orange and Alexandria Railroad Company. His interest in city improvements included a directorship of the Alexandria Gas Works, a vice presidency on the board of trade, and membership on the city council. In the field of charity, McKenzie donated liberally to and was an officer of the Female Orphan Asylum. Interestingly enough, he ran only a modest commission house and was among the lower quarter of the leadership in real property holding. McKenzie was a booster dedicated to directing his city and his state to urban maturity and prosperity.[34]

The family orientation of Alexandria's leadership probably made it a more exclusive group than those of other cities. Property-holding statistics support this view, since of the forty-three leaders on whom data could be found in the 1850 census, 88.4% owned real estate. This exceeded the percentage of elite property holding in Norfolk and Richmond. The median property holding of $11,000, however, was lower than those in either of the two other cities. Four leaders possessed holdings valued at $70,000 or more, including one with an estate worth $100,000. These individuals were among the twenty wealthiest individuals in the city. The most active leaders—Fowle, McVeigh, and McKenzie—were not among this wealthy group.

Slaveholding was slightly less common among the Alexandria leadership than among the elite in other cities. Alexandria was, after all, a border city. Nevertheless 69.8% of the leaders whom I located in the 1850 census owned slaves, a remarkably high figure considering the location of the city. It was another indication of the exclusivity of the leadership, since less than one-seventh of all the heads of households in the city possessed slaves. Slaveholdings were typically smaller in Alexandria than in Norfolk and Richmond, with 3 being the median size. Of the slaveholders, 90.0% possessed 8 or fewer slaves, while only two owned more than 10. With such relatively small slaveholdings, it was not surprising

34. Seventh Census of Virginia: 1850. Free Inhabitants, II, 674; Alexandria *Gazette*, March 8, 1849, January 12, 1853, April 19, 1854, September 23, 1857; Powell, *Old Alexandria*, 327.

that female slaves predominated. While twenty-eight of the thirty slaveholders owned female slaves, only twenty-one owned any male slaves. Of the 116 slaves owned by Alexandria's elite, 64.7% were female. Without a significant industrial base, and with proximity to free territory, it was understandable that most slaves toiled in some domestic capacity.

The priority and persistence rates of the city's boosters reflected the closely-knit nature of the group. Thirty-seven (86.0%) of the forty-three leaders located in the 1850 census were either priority residents or would become persisters in the city. The rate was similar to Richmond's 88.3% and higher than Norfolk's 77.8% combined priority and persistence figures. Alexandria's leaders who remained in the city for the entire twenty-year period numbered 38.1%, 16.7% had established residences by 1840 but were gone by 1860, and one-third were not in the city in 1840 but remained there throughout the 1850s. Thus, more than half of Alexandria's leaders were established residents in the city by 1850—a greater stability than in either Norfolk or Richmond. The transiency rate of Alexandria's boosters was lower compared with Norfolk but slightly higher than in Richmond.

Despite the fact that Alexandria was a border city, the activists were predominantly Virginia born, which was another indication of the homogeneity and stability of the leadership. The percentage of leaders born in the Old Dominion exceeded that of the Norfolk group but was less than that of the Richmond group. Five Alexandria leaders came from contiguous states, three from the North, and two were immigrants from the British Isles. Considering the fact that Alexandria was part of the District of Columbia for almost a generation, the preponderance of Virginians among the elite is all the more impressive.

The persistence and nativity figures indicated a stable, indigenous leadership. Alexandria's activists were also older than the groups in Richmond and in Norfolk. The median age was forty-six. Only two leaders were under thirty years of age—a third less than either Richmond or Norfolk. On the other hand, one-third of Alexandria's elite was fifty years old or over—more than one-

and-a-half times the figures for Richmond and Norfolk. Family patterns in Alexandria were also indicative of a more entrenched, mature leadership than existed in other cities with 85.7% of the leaders married, 9.5% widowers, and only two single. The percentage of married leaders in Alexandria was higher than that in either Richmond or Norfolk. Marriage and fatherhood once again were linked together, with thirty-four of the married and three of the widowers having children in their households. Thus, 84.1% of the leaders—the highest percentage of the three cities—fathered children.

The household configuration of Alexandria's boosters was similar to the patterns in other cities. There were typically four children in an elite household, with the youngest child being usually four years old and the eldest seventeen, or slightly older than the children in either Richmond or Norfolk. Alexandria's leaders and their wives tended to have more children than the elite groups in other cities: almost one-quarter of the elite families had more than six children. Wives tended to be older, as might be expected, than in other cities. Their median age was thirty-eight. The age span of eight years between husband and wife was somewhat larger but still comparable to other cities. One-fifth of the wives were thirty or under, and one-sixth were over fifty, both figures reflecting the greater maturity of their husbands.

Household size in Alexandria did not vary much from that in other cities. The typical elite household held between six or seven people. Considering the larger number of children, there were obviously fewer boarders than in other cities. Actually, about the same number of activist's households included boarders as in other cities; but nearly two-thirds of the households held one or two boarders, and only one leader housed more than four boarders. Of the twenty-nine households possessing boarders, 37.9% included an extended family arrangement and 34.5% of the boarders in these households were servants. Occupational boarders lived in 17.2% of the households, and 31.0% of the boarders could not be identified.

The nature of Virginia's elite varied from city to city because of the variance of the cities themselves. Nevertheless, maturity, wealth, stability, and homogeneity were general characteristics possessed by leaders regardless of the urban environment. Virginia's urban leaders were not the wealthiest men in their communities, but they were rich in energy and enterprise. There was a strong connection between leadership and associational activity. Voluntary associations were essential to the urbanizing process because they rationalized growth and enabled leaders to manage their city with greater efficiency. Of course, protection and furtherance of their own particular business interests were primary goals of the urban elite. They sincerely believed, however, as Robert R. Dykstra observed in his study of Kansas cattle towns, that what profited business profited all.[35]

Fitting urban Virginia's elite into a national pattern illustrates the different stages of urbanization in the three Old Dominion cities. Robert A. Dahl, in a study of political elites, erected a model of urban political development. The three cycles posited by Dahl included a patrician oligarchy that gave way to new entrepreneurs who in turn were usurped by immigrants and the lower class. Richmond leadership corresponded to the second stage of urbanization by 1850, and probably Norfolk did as well. Alexandria more closely resembled the patrician oligarchy but was more than likely in a transitional period by 1850. None of the cities in Virginia, if in the nation, had passed on to the third stage of development by 1850.[36] Perhaps Michael B. Katz's characterization of Hamilton, Ontario, was most appropriate to urban Virginia in the same time period. Katz depicted Hamilton as "poised between the pre-modern and industrial eras and [having] characteristics of each." Virginia's cities, at least as evidenced by the interest and activities of their leaders, were on the verge of modern cityhood.[37] Comparing Virginia's urban leadership with similar groups elsewhere, similar

35. Dykstra, *The Cattle Towns*, 356.
36. Robert A. Dahl, *Who Governs: Democracy and Power in an American City* (New Haven, 1961), 11.
37. Michael B. Katz, "Social Structure in Hamilton, Ontario," in Thernstrom and Sennett (eds.), *Nineteenth-Century Cities*, 209–44. See also Frisch, *Town into City*; and Robert A. McCaughey, "From Town to City: Boston in the 1820s," *Political Science Quarterly*, LXXXVIII (1973), 191–213.

attributes emerge. A relatively small group of boosters throughout the urban nation dominated and directed urban life.

The problem with some studies of the elite, however, is that the leaders are analyzed in a vacuum. In order to appreciate the exclusivity of an elite, some attempt should be made to compare the privileged group with the rest of the urban population. Accordingly, a random sample of 10% of the heads of households in Richmond in 1850 provided a basis for comparing Richmond's leaders with their fellow citizens.[38] It was not surprising that a different pattern of stability, maturity, and wealth emerged; but the divergence between elite and the urban "plain folk" was not as great as might be expected.

The occupational pattern of the random sample offered the first distinction between the rest of the population and the leadership. Of the 373 households covered in the sample, 18.0% were included in the proprietary and professional occupational categories. On the other hand, only 12.9% of the sample could be included in the unskilled and semiskilled categories. The largest representation occurred in the middling occupations: the petty proprietors, clerical and sales personnel, skilled craftsmen, and semiprofessionals. The occupational data, however, are misleading. More than a quarter of the subjects of the sample listed no occupations at all. It is inconceivable that in a city where labor shortages were chronic, this large a proportion of the sample should be unemployed. Actually, 24.6% of the household heads were women, and the census typically listed no occupation for them. A portion of those without occupations formed part of the transient, floating population that every growing city included. These were persons who were often between jobs or were temporary laborers. Finally, suspicion of census takers' motives was likely to be greater among the general population than among the more educated leadership. Silence, even hostility, greeted some of the takers' queries.[39] The members

38. This is a representative sample from which generalizations for the entire population may be made. See Knights, *Plain People of Boston*, Appendix D.

39. On the use and limitations of the federal census and city directories, see Robert G. Barrows, "The Manuscript Federal Census: Source for a 'New' Local History," *Indiana Magazine of History*, LXIX (1973), 181–92. See also Knights, *Plain People of Boston*, 3–10.

in the sample who were without occupations should probably be listed with those in low-status positions. Even so, with better than a sixth of the sample in high-status occupations, and two-fifths in middling positions, the occupational gap between leaders and citizens was not vast.

Richmond's elite were three times more likely to hold property than the rest of the household heads were. Less than a quarter of the sample were property holders. This is a relatively large figure when compared with those of northern cities. Pessen implied in his studies of leadership that real-property ownership among the general urban population was considerably less than 10%[40] Glazer put the figure right at 10% for Cincinnati householders in 1840. He arrived at the figure by sampling only male household heads.[41] If he had included women, it doubtless would have been less. The property in slaves is even more impressive for Richmond. Attesting to the fact that urban life was not iminical to slavery, 40.8% of the sample owned at least one slave, which far exceeded property ownership among citizens in any northern city. The median slaveholding—3—was less than the median of the leaders, and 92.1% of the slave owners possessed fewer than 9 slaves. Only 2.6% owned more than 20 slaves. Considering the small slaveholdings in the sample, it is not surprising that female slaves dominated the total number of slaves: 95.4% of the slaveholders owned female slaves, while only 54.6% owned male slaves. Female slaves outnumbered male slaves 413 to 284.

The relatively prosperous standards of occupation, property and slaveholding upheld by the Richmond sample was all the more remarkable because 17.4% of the sample were free blacks and 24.6% of the group were women (including black women), neither of whom was likely to hold slaves or real estate. No blacks and two mulattoes were involved in high-status occupations, which accounted for 1.7% of the proprietary and professional job holders. White female household heads accounted for only one proprietary and professional occupation. Removing the sixty-five blacks and

40. Pessen, "Who Governed," 591–614.
41. Glazer, "Participation and Power," 156.

the fifty-four white women from the random sample, and the two mulatto and one white female household head from the high-status occupations, the result was that a quarter of the city's white male household heads (25.1%) were in either proprietary or professional occupations.

Since property holding defines occupation in part, the relatively high level of membership in high-status occupations predicts a strong incidence of real-property ownership among the Richmond sample. Only six blacks and mulattoes owned real estate in the sample. Seven white female householders were property holders. Omitting both blacks (including mulattoes) and white women from the sample and the thirteen blacks and white female property holders from the ranks of the propertied, 29.8% of the white male heads of households owned real property, compared with 23.8% of the sample. Real-property ownership in the city usually meant home ownership. More than a quarter of the white male householders in the sample, therefore, probably owned their own dwellings, which would have been a large percentage in any city.

Slaveholding was another indicator of material wealth. Nine blacks and sixteen white women owned slaves. Following the same procedure of elimination employed for occupation and property holding, 50.2% of the white male householders owned slaves. Thus, one-half of the white householders held a direct stake in the "peculiar institution."

It is interesting to observe that in the categories pertaining most directly to wealth—occupation, property ownership, and slaveholding—the white female sample members generally fared little better than the black householders. Thus, 3.2% of the black householders were in high-status occupations compared with 1.9% of the white women. There were proportionately only slightly more women than blacks who owned real estate (13.0% to 9.2%). White women, as expected, held a greater advantage in slaveholding, but the disparity between women and blacks was not overwhelming (29.6% to 13.8%.) The figures are less a tribute to the relative mobility enjoyed by free blacks in a slave city than to the generally depressed status of single and widowed women.

If scholars have uncovered a low incidence of property accumulation among antebellum urban populations, they have also discerned a low level of persistence in nonelite groups. Recent studies have demonstrated that such measures of stability as persistence and priority decline in direct correlation with a decrease in income level and occupational status. Clyde Griffen's analysis of Poughkeepsie's work force indicated that a persistence rate of one-third was a median rate for the entire sample.[42] Peter Knights' Boston sample taken from household heads experienced a persistence rate of roughly 40% at ten-year intervals, compared with 30% to 38% for Philadelphia and only 20% for Rochester between 1850 and 1860.[43] The residential behavior of Richmond's sample corresponded more with the smaller city of Poughkeepsie than with Boston. Slightly more than one-third of the 1850 sample persisted to 1860. The rate for the leadership was more than twice as high. More than one-half of the sample were transients compared with only 11.7% of the elite. Priority rates were two times and permanence was three times more common among the elite as among the sample. Griffen's emphasis on occupation and property holding as determinants of persistence seems to apply to Richmond as well as to Poughkeepsie.

Persistence and/or priority were low among blacks and white women. Thirty-four white women (63.0% compared with 53.6% for the whole sample) were transients. This figure probably exaggerated their transiency, however, since marriage or remarriage altered their identifying last name. Among blacks, transiency was at 62.5%. Following the standard procedure of elimination, the transiency rate of the white male-dominated households was only slightly lower (49.4%). Although a divergence in residential mobility existed between the sample and the elite (and the adjusted sample as well), the persistence and priority rates for the Richmond random sample indicate a pattern of stability approaching and even exceeding the configuration in some northern cities. The

42. Griffen, "Workers Divided," 57. See also Clyde Griffen, "Occupational Mobility in Nineteenth-Century America," *Journal of Social History*, V (1972) 310–30.
43. Knights, *Plain People of Boston*, 103.

more widespread distribution of property and the relatively high level of skill of the population accounted for the relative stability of the sample.

The pattern of relative stability extended to nativity. More than two-thirds of the sample were born in the Old Dominion and another 10.7% were born in other states. Foreign born, however, accounted for nearly one-fifth of the sample, deviating markedly from the elite group. The Irish were the largest contingent, the Germans were next, followed by a scattering of Scots and English. All other groups were a fraction of 1%. Black heads of households were all native born; indeed, all were born in the Old Dominion. Four white women were foreign born. Eliminating these groups from statistics of nativity, 27.1% of the white male householders were foreign born.

Although they were a minority, the presence of immigrants lent a more cosmopolitan atmosphere to the city and provided another element of diversity that complicated the rationalization of urban growth by the civic leaders. Their skills and labor would find useful employment in the decade ahead as the Old Dominion sought to regain its economic prominence. Immigration to and immigrants in antebellum southern cities have received only cursory attention from scholars.[44] The role, impact, and lifestyle of the foreign born, as well as their commonality with or distinction from their ethnic brethren in northern cities, would seem to be a beneficial line of inquiry to pursue in understanding the urbanizing process in the Old South.

There was less difference between the sample and the Richmond elite in another indicator of stability: age. The median age of the sample was thirty-seven compared with forty for the leadership. Although a sample member was twice as likely to be under thirty than a leader, the majority of sample members fell into the middle-age category as did the leadership. Finally, there was no difference in the percentage of age fifty or over between sample and elite. Race and sex apparently had little or no impact on the age

44. See Eli N. Evans, *The Provincials: A Personal History of Jews in the South* (New York, 1973); and Earl F. Niehaus, *The Irish in New Orleans, 1800–1860* (Baton Rouge, 1965).

of the sample. One potentially interesting aspect of race and age, however, was the preponderance of mulattoes in the younger age group. Further study of mulatto urban demography might imply an increase in miscegenation toward the end of the antebellum period or a tendency on the part of younger mulattoes to escape the ostracism of the rural districts for the grudging tolerance of the city.

Family patterns provided an index of stability as well as an insight into urban lifestyles. Marriage characterized the random sample as well as the leadership. The percentage of single individuals in both groups was relatively the same. There was a difference in the number of single spouses with 18.7% of the random sample falling under the status of widow or widower compared with only 2.0% of the elite. The higher figure for the sample resulted primarily from the fact that women were included in that group. More than two-thirds (69.9%) of the women household heads were widows (or 86.6% of the total number of single spouses). Eliminating these women results in a percentage of 2.5%, or almost the same as that of the leadership group. Thus, Richmond's elite did not exhibit a marital pattern significantly distinctive from the rest of the white male householders.

Marriage and children were apparently synonymous among the sample householders as well as among the elite. Women heads of households tended to have children at the same rate as households headed by males (59.4%). For black heads of households parentage was slightly lower at 50.0%. Richmond householders generally had fewer children than the elite, which was a function of greater infant mortality and the average younger age of the sample householders. The typical household head had two children. The sample house-holders rarely had more than six children. The median age of the sample members' wives, though lower at age thirty-two than that of the wives of leaders, exhibited the same five-year gap between wife and husband. As expected, nearly one-half of the women in the sample were thirty years of age or younger, compared to only one-third of the activists' wives, though roughly the same percentage were over fifty in both groups. Black wives did not differ from the rest of the sample with nearly half under thirty years of age, and 10.3% over fifty. The youngest child was typically three years old and the eldest was slightly more than ten, the latter figure being four years less than the median age for the eldest child of the Richmond leadership. Considering the slight age differential between household heads and activists, this was not unusual. The average household size was also smaller (four among the sample compared with seven for the leadership), indicating that the nuclear family was more common among the sample population. The dwellings of sample members were likely to be smaller than those of the elite. Boarders, therefore, were less likely to inhabit sample households. Nevertheless, nearly one-half of the sample households included boarders, which was only slightly less than the figure for the leadership.

While the sample households typically included boarders, the nature of these inhabitants provided one of the few real differences in family patterns between elite and sample. The extended family was the most common boarder situation for both the sample and the leadership. Occupational boarders were equally as common in both groups. The two greatest distinctions, however, were in the presence of servant boarders and in the number of unknown boarders. Only 12.7% of the sample who housed boarders possessed servant boarders, while 40.0% of the elite households held servant boarders. Twice as many sample members as leaders included boarders in their households whose status it was not possible to determine. The relatively high percentage of boarders who did not match the boarder categories signifies perhaps that boarders were less often an integral part of the family (that is, servants, apprentices, and relatives) in the general population than in the homes of leaders. It could indicate, further, that the income-producing function of the boarder system was more important in the homes of sample members.

Race and sex did not have a strong impact on household size and composition. The households headed by women included 81.4% (six persons or less) compared with 89.6% for the entire sample. For blacks the figure was 86.9%. Households headed by white women possessed boarders at about the same frequency as the general sample (45.1%). Black households were less likely to harbor boarders (37.5%). Of those women who included boarders in their households, the extended family showed the most common boarder pattern (39.0%, or roughly comparable to the sample). Servant boarders resided in 12.2% of the households, once again similar to the sample; and there were no occupational boarders, reflecting the fact that few women were involved in occupations that would necessitate such a living arrangement. Boarders who could not be categorized were present in 68.3% of the white female-dominated households that had boarders. The greater frequency of such boarders in households led by women probably reflected the fact that nearly two-thirds of the sample's women householders were widows. Boarders represented necessary income to that hard-pressed group. Black households that included boarders exhibited similar patterns to the general sample. Thus, 38.5% of the black householders with boarders included extended family members, 19.2% included occupational boarders, no boarders were servants, and 53.8% of the black households included boarders whose status could not be discerned.

Simple crosstabulation (comparison) of the wealth and stability variables with the sample and leadership groups indicated two things (see tables 15 to 33). First, crosstabulation, through the chi square statistic, reveals whether a relationship exists, that is, if it is significant. Second, through a contingency coefficient, it is possible to relate whether the dependence is strong or weak.[45] The reference that indicated the strongest relationship between the study groups and a wealth or stability variable was with occupation. The occupational categories were collapsed to some degree in order to minimize the number of empty cells. Further, the unlisted category was removed because many of the unlisted probably belong in some other job category: proprietary and professional for the elite and unskilled and semiskilled for the sample. Also, since the

45. In this study, dependence means that there is a major difference between the sample and the leadership study groups (see Appendix A for discussion of computer program involved here).

Table 15 Occupation by Richmond Study Group

Count Column % Total %	Sample	Leaders	Total
Unskilled	29 11.0 9.0	0 0.0 0.0	29
Semiskilled and Service	19 7.2 5.9	1 1.7 0.3	20
Petty Proprietor	69 26.1 21.4	7 12.1 2.2	76
Skilled[a]	80 30.3 24.8	0 0.0 0.0	80
Proprietor [b]	67 25.4 20.8	50 86.2 15.5	117
Column	264	58	322
TOTAL	82.0	18.0	100.0

NOTES: Chi square = 78.65044 with 4 degrees of freedom.
Significance = 0.0000.
Contingency coefficient = 0.44307.
[a] Includes clerical and sales, and semiprofessional categories.
[b] Includes professional category.

Table 16 Age by Richmond Study Group

Count Column % Total %	Sample	Leaders	Total
17–32	136	9	145
	36.5	17.0	
	31.9	2.1	
33–44	124	23	147
	33.2	43.4	
	29.1	5.4	
45+	113	21	134
	30.3	39.6	
	26.5	4.9	
Column	373	53	426
TOTAL	87.6	12.4	100.0

NOTES: Chi square = 7.84332 with 2 degrees of freedom.
Significance = 0.0198.
Contingency coefficient = 0.13446.

Table 17 Real Property by Richmond Study Group

Count *Column %* *Total %*	*Sample*	*Leaders*	*Total*
Non-property holders	284 76.1 65.4	18 29.5 4.1	302
$25–$6500	62 16.6 14.3	13 21.3 3.0	75
$6500+	27 7.2 6.2	30 49.2 6.9	57
Column	373	61	434
TOTAL	85.9	14.1	100.0

NOTES: Chi square = 87.26906 with 2 degrees of freedom.
Significance = 0.0000.
Contingency coefficient = 0.40917.

Table 18 Marital Status by Richmond Study Group

Count Column % Total %	Sample	Leaders	Total
Unmarried	74 20.7 18.2	9 18.4 2.2	83
Married	217 60.6 53.3	39 79.6 9.6	256
Widow or Widower	67 18.7 16.5	1 2.0 0.2	68
Column	358	49	407
TOTAL	88.0	12.0	100.0

NOTES: Chi square = 9.75228 with 2 degrees of freedom.
Significance = 0.0076.
Contingency coefficient = 0.15297.

Table 19 Age of Wives by Richmond Study Group

Count *Column %* *Total %*	*Sample*	*Leaders*	*Total*
17–29	89 41.0 34.8	10 25.6 3.9	99
30–38	62 28.6 24.2	15 38.5 5.9	77
39+	66 30.4 25.8	14 35.9 5.5	80
Column	2.7	39	256
TOTAL	84.8	15.2	100.0

NOTES: Chi square = 3.41326 with 2 degrees of freedom.
Significance = 0.1815.
Contingency coefficient = 0.11471.

Table 20 Number of Children by Richmond Study Group

Count Column % Total %	Sample	Leaders	Total
No Children	139 37.3 32.0	24 39.3 5.5	163
1–2	118 31.6 27.2	12 19.7 2.8	130
3+	116 31.1 26.7	25 41.0 5.8	141
Column	373	61	434
TOTAL	85.9	14.1	100.0

NOTES: Chi square = 4.14184 with 2 degrees of freedom.
Significance = 0.1261.
Contingency coefficient = 0.09723.

Table 21 Age of Youngest Child by Richmond Study Group

Count *Column %* *Total %*	*Sample*	*Leaders*	*Total*
1–3	124	19	143
	53.0	51.4	
	45.8	7.0	
4+	110	18	128
	47.0	48.6	
	40.6	6.6	
Column	234	37	271
TOTAL	86.3	13.7	100.0

NOTES: Corrected chi square = 0.00007 with 1 degree of freedom.
Significance = 0.9932.
Contingency coefficient = 0.00052.

Table 22 Age of Eldest Child by Richmond Study Group

Count Column % Total %	Sample	Leaders	Total
1–8	96 41.0 35.4	11 29.7 4.1	107
9–16	75 32.1 27.7	10 27.0 3.7	85
17+	63 26.9 23.2	16 43.2 5.9	79
Column	234	37	271
TOTAL	86.3	13.7	100.0

NOTE: Chi square = 4.20863 with 2 degrees of freedom.
Significance = 0.1219.
Contingency coefficient = 0.12366.

Table 23 Boarders by Richmond Study Group

Count Column % Total %	Sample	Leaders	Total
No	191	26	217
Boarders	51.2	42.6	
	44.0	6.0	
Boarders	182	35	217
	48.8	57.4	
	41.9	8.1	
Column	373	61	434
TOTAL	85.9	14.1	100.0

NOTES: Corrected chi square = 1.22076 with 1 degree of freedom.
Significance = 0.2692.
Contingency coefficient = 0.05296.

Table 24 Relative Boarders of Richmond Study Group

Count Column % Total %	Sample	Leaders	Total
No Relative Boarders	346 92.8 79.7	51 83.6 11.8	397
Relative Boarders	27 7.2 6.2	10 16.4 2.3	37
Column	373	61	434
TOTAL	85.9	14.1	100.0

NOTES: Corrected chi square = 4.52149 with 1 degree of freedom.
Significance = 0.0335.
Contingency coefficient = 0.10154.
For the purpose of crosstabulation analysis, the extended family boarders were divided into relative boarders (e.g., parent, brother, or sister of household head) and family boarders (e.g., son's family). This table and the following one indicate that neither of these was a significant aspect of distinction between study groups.

Table 25 Family Boarders of Richmond Study Group

Count Column % Total %	Sample	Leaders	Total
No	325	52	377
Family	87.1	85.2	
Boarders	74.9	12.0	
Family	48	9	57
Boarders	12.9	14.8	
	11.1	2.1	
Column	373	61	434
TOTAL	85.9	14.1	100.0

NOTES: Corrected chi square = 0.03989 with 1 degree of freedom.
Significance = 0.8417.
Contingency coefficient = 0.00959.

Table 26 Occupational Boarders of Richmond Study Group

Count Column % Total %	Sample	Leaders	Total
No	341	54	395
Occupational	91.4	88.5	
Boarders —	78.6	12.4	
Occupational	32	7	39
Boarders	8.6	11.5	
	7.4	1.6	
Column	373	61	434
TOTAL	85.9	14.1	100.0

NOTES: Corrected chi square = 0.24190 with 1 degree of freedom.
Significance = 0.6228.
Contingency coefficient = 0.02360.

Table 27 Servant Boarders of Richmond Study Group

Count Column % Total %	Sample	Leaders	Total
No	350	47	397
Servant	93.8	77.0	
Boarders	80.6	10.8	
Servant	23	14	37
Boarders	6.2	23.0	
	5.3	3.2	
Column	373	61	434
TOTAL	85.9	14.1	100.0

NOTES: Corrected chi square = 16.84790 with 1 degree of freedom.
Significance = 0.0000.
Contingency coefficient = 0.19331.

Table 28 Unknown Boarders of Richmond Study Group

Count Column % Total %	Sample	Leader	Total
No	273	51	324
Unknown	73.2	83.6	
Boarders	62.9	11.8	
Unknown	100	10	110
Boarders	26.8	16.4	
	23.0	2.3	
Column	373	61	434
TOTAL	85.9	14.1	100.0

NOTES: Corrected chi square = 2.48085 with 1 degree of freedom.
Significance = 0.1152.
Contingency coefficient =0.07539.

Table 29 Slave Ownership by Richmond Study Group

Count *Column %* *Total %*	*Sample*	*Leaders*	*Total*
No Slaves	220 59.0 50.7	11 18.0 2.5	231
Slave Owners	153 41.0 35.3	50 82.0 11.5	203
Column TOTAL	373 85.9	61 14.1	434 100.0

NOTES: Corrected chi square = 33.68416 with 1 degree of freedom.
Significance = 0.0000.
Contingency coefficient = 0.26837.

Table 30 Male Slaves Owned by Richmond Study Group

Count *Column %* *Total %*	*Sample*	*Leaders*	*Total*
No	290	17	307
Male	77.7	27.9	
Slaves	66.8	3.9	
Male	83	44	127
Slave	22.3	72.1	
Owners	19.1	10.1	
Column	373	61	434
TOTAL	85.9	14.1	100.0

NOTES: Corrected chi square = 60.62549 with 1 degree of freedom.
Significance = 0.0000.
Contingency coefficient = 0.35010.

Table 31 Female Slaves Owned by Richmond Study Group

Count *Column %* *Total %*	*Sample*	*Leaders*	*Total*
No Female Slaves	228 61.1 52.5	20 32.8 4.6	248
Female Slave Owners	145 38.9 33.4	41 67.2 9.4	186
Column	373	61	434
TOTAL	85.9	14.1	100.0

NOTES: Corrected chi square = 16.05467 with 1 degree of freedom.
Significance = 0.0001.
Contingency coefficient = 0.18887.

Table 32 Persistence by Richmond Study Group

Count Column % Total %	Sample	Leaders	Total
Transiency	199	8	207
	53.4	13.3	
	46.0	1.8	
Persistence	131	29	160
or Priority	35.1	48.3	
	30.3	6.7	
Permanence	43	23	66
	11.5	38.3	
	9.9	5.3	
Column	373	60	433
TOTAL	86.1	13.9	100.0

NOTES: Chi square = 44.12012 with 2 degrees of freedom.
Significance = 0.0000.
Contingency coefficient = 0.30409.

Table 33 Nativity of Richmond Study Group

Count Column % Total %	Sample	Leaders	Total
Virginia	260	52	312
	69.7	88.1	
	60.2	12.0	
Southern States	19	1	20
	5.1	1.7	
	4.4	0.2	
Northern States	21	5	26
	5.6	8.5	
	4.9	1.2	
Foreign-Born	73	1	74
	19.6	1.7	
	16.9	0.2	
Column	373	59	432
TOTAL	86.3	13.7	100.0

NOTES: Chi square = 13.85537 with 3 degrees of freedom.
Significance = 0.0031.
Contingency coefficient = 0.17628.

categories are primarily arranged according to levels of skill and wealth, the unlisted category would be incongruous and would generate a chi square that is too high. The relationship was highly significant as the chi square indicates. A contingency coefficient of .44 indicated a strong relationship. With such a large number of cases, any contingency coefficient over .40 would reveal a strong dependence between study group and selected variable. Real property holding, ownership of male slaves, and persistence were the only other variables above .30, which is probably the lowest coefficient that could show a strong dependence in this particular study.[46] Occupation and real property were the two primary indicators of wealth, and they were, in turn, the most important determinants of persistence. Generally, large slaveholding and substantial proprietary operations were associated with ownership of male slaves. That too, therefore, was an index of wealth. In wealth, Richmond's activists stood above but not far apart from their fellow citizens.

The family patterns of both groups were similar in a number of areas including marital status, the relationship between marriage and children, ages of spouse and children, and the presence of boarders. Further, households headed by white women and blacks did not deviate from the prevailing family relationships in their city. This could be portentous in reassessing the role of free blacks in southern cities. Compared with other cities, Richmond's leadership could not be characterized as an oligarchy.

A final test remains to analyze the relationship between the two study groups. This was to determine which group, among those who persisted until 1860,—the elite or the sample—achieved the greatest economic mobility during the decade. Occupation, property holding, and slave ownership are the measures of economic mobility for this study. There were 128 persisters in the random sample: those who remained in the city between 1850 and 1860, or 34.3% of the sample householders. Their economic status in 1850

46. This is my standard. After consultation with colleagues who work with such statistics, the consensus was that .3 was a fair cutoff point for this analysis.

was, of course, higher than the nonpersisting sample members. Thirty-five of the 128 sample persisters (27.3%) held professional or proprietary positions in 1850, compared with 12.7% of the rest of the sample. Virtually the same percentage of persisters (12.5%) held unskilled or semiskilled jobs as the nonpersisters (13.1%). The sample persisters also participated in the middling occupations about as often as the rest of the group (43.7% to 38.7%). Fewer persisters, however, failed to receive an employment listing than the sample group (16.4% to 35.5%). These figures indicated that temporary employment or unemployment was less characteristic of the persisters. Property holding was more common among persisters in 1850, with 38.3% of them owning real estate compared with 15.9% of the remaining sample group. Finally, 59.4% of the sample persisters held slaves, while 31.0% of the nonpersisting sample owned them. Thus, although the occupational distinctions between sample persisters and sample nonpersisters were not significant in most categories, the persisters possessed a clear advantage in the ownership of property.

The sample persisters were more similar to the nonpersisters in terms of stability and family life. The sample persisters were only slightly older (thirty-eight being the median age) than the rest of the sample (with the median age equaling thirty-seven). Place of birth apparently had little impact on the persistence of the sample group. The persisters who were born in the Old Dominion amounted to 67.2% compared with 70.9% of the nonpersisters; and 20.3% of the persisters were foreign born compared with 19.9% of the remaining sample. The statistics depicting family patterns revealed a greater divergence between the groups than those depicting nativity. Marriage characterized the persisters slightly more than the entire group (68.3% to 56.0%). The persisters with children (68.7%) outnumbered by a small margin the nonpersisters with children (59.6%). A majority of the persisters' households included boarders (53.9%), compared with 45.7% of the nonpersisters who housed boarders. Relatives were the most common boarders in both persister and nonpersister households (36.2% and 43.8% respectively). Occupational boarders were present in greater numbers in persisters' homes than in nonpersisters' homes (26.1% and 12.5% respectively); while fewer boarders with undetermined status resided in persisters' homes (47.8% and 59.8% respectively). The greater affluence of the persisters probably accounted for the increase in servants and the decline in the number of boarders who would have been present primarily for income that they might generate.

Race and sex of the persisters emphasized the white male, as might be expected. The degree, however was not spectacular. The persisters included twelve blacks and mulattoes (10.4%) compared with 20.9% of the nonpersisters. Women persisters represented 18.8% of the persisting sample, compared with 27.5% of the nonpersisters. Thus, free blacks were not necessarily a highly mobile and invisible group in the city, and neither marriage nor remarriage was an automatic condition for single or widowed women.

The sample persisters differed from their nonpersisting fellow citizens primarily in wealth. The persisting leaders, on the other hand, tended to be less well-off than the nonpersisting elite. Three-quarters of Richmond's leaders were persisters which was more than double the persistence rate of the random sample. Persisting boosters who held high-status occupations came to 83.8% compared with 93.3% of the fifteen nonpersisting leaders. Petty proprietors included 14.0% of the persisters, and there was one (2.3%) semiskilled persister. The nonpersisters included only one petty proprietor (6.7%) and none in the semiskilled category. Property holding was similar among both groups (72.7% for the persisters to 73.3% for the nonpersisters). The median property holding however, increased to $23,000 for the nonpersisters from $15,000 for the persisting leaders. Conversely, 88.6% of the persisting leaders held slaves, compared with 73.3% of the nonpersisters. The median slaveholding, however, remained at six for the persisters but increased to ten for the nonpersisters. Generally, the nonpersisters exhibited greater wealth and status than the persisting leaders. This situation may have been due to a number of factors. First, a sample size of fifteen is probably too small a one from which to draw meaningful conclusions. Second, it is also possible that, as far as persistence is concerned, the *size* of a slaveholding or property holding is not as important as the fact of *owning* slaves and property. Third, eight of fifteen nonpersisters were priority residents. That is, they had established residence in the city at least a decade prior to 1850. All of them held slaves and real property. Finally, it is possible that nonpersistence may have resulted from death rather than from geographic mobility. The median age of the persisters was thirty-nine, compared with forty for the nonpersisters who could count more than two-thirds of their number in the over-fifty age category in 1850.

Stability and family patterns elicited smaller differences between the persisting and nonpersisting leaders. Both groups were over-whelmingly Virginia born: 88.6% for both persisters and nonpersisters. There were no persisters and one nonpersister of foreign birth. Marital status was virtually the same for both groups: 81.1% for the persisters and 75.0% for the nonpersisters. Nearly two-thirds (65.9%) of the persisters fathered children, compared with 75.5% of the nonpersisters. Both groups tended to have from three to four children. Wives of persisters were typically ten years younger (thirty-four years of age) than the wives of non-persisters (forty-four years of age). Boarders were present in an equal ratio in both groups: 59.1% for persisting leaders and 60.0% for nonpersisters. The extended family and servant boarders still predominated. Persisters' households that included family boarders numbered 53.8%, and 39.1% held servants. Both figures are almost identical to those describing the nonpersisters (55.5% and 44.4%). Occupational boarders were present in 23.1% of the persisters' households and in only one nonpersister's household; 26.9% of the persisters had boarders who could not be categorized, compared with 33.3% for nonpersisters in the same situation.

Having achieved an economic profile of the persisters from both groups in 1850, as well as an insight into family patterns, it is appropriate to define the status of one relative to the other in 1860. The sample persisters tended to increase their occupational status during the decade. The diversified economy of the city and the prosperity of the 1850s doubtless provided opportunities for upward mobility. The sample persisters who held proprietary or professional positions numbered 41.5% compared with 27.3% of the persisters who had done so a decade earlier. The percentage of sample persisters in the unskilled and semiskilled categories remained roughly the same: 14.1% in 1860 and 12.5% in 1850. The middling occupations experienced a decline from 43.7% to 26.6%. The figures are consistent with the occupational configuration of a city undergoing urbanization and industrialization. Studies have demonstrated that artisans and petty proprietors are the most prominent occupational casualties of such processes.[47] In 1850, 35.1% of the sample persisters were artisans or petty proprietors. In 1860 that figure declined to 21.9%. Almost all those who left these occupations moved into the proprietary category. Without an occupational analysis of the entire population, though, it is not possible to confirm the hypothesis that these two occupational categories were depleted by urban growth.

Property holding increased as well among the sample persisters, though not as evidently as occupational mobility. In 1860, 45.3% of the group held property compared with 38.3% a decade earlier. Slaveholding statistics paralled those of property holding, with 45.3% of the sample persisters holding slaves. This signified a decline in slaveholding; since 59.4% of the persisters had been slave owners in 1850. The decline in slaveholding reflected both the rapid inflation of slave prices during the 1850s and the increasing popularity of slave hiring. Sample persisters were not abandoning slavery, but rather slave ownership.

The sample persisters achieved a measure of upward economic mobility during the 1850s. This was not unusual, because an individual's decision to remain in a city very often was a function of his economic status. Upwardly mobile people tended to persist (see tables 38 to 57 in Appendix A). The important question, though, is whether the sample persisters advanced as quickly as the elite persisters. It has been a maxim of urban growth that wealth be-

47. See Griffen, "Occupational Mobility," 310–30. See also Sam Bass Warner, Jr., "If All the World Were Philadelphia: A Scaffolding for Urban History, 1774–1930," *American Historical Review*, LXXIV (1968), 26–43.

comes more concentrated and that economic division becomes wider.[48]

The persisting leaders held high-status occupations with greater frequency in 1860 than they had in 1850. The percentage of the elite persisters who were involved in professional or proprietary activity was 87.2%, compared with 83.8% in 1850. The increase in occupational status among the leaders was not so great as it was among the sample persisters. At that high level, however, it would not be expected that any index of wealth could attain or even approach 100%. There was a sharp drop in the middling occupations (14.0% to 2.1%), while the percentage of leaders in the semi-skilled category remained the same. The number of property holders among activist persisters also increased to 83.0%, up from 72.7%. The leaders outdistanced the sample group's rise in property holding. Moreover, while the median property holding for the sample increased from $5,650 in 1850 to $7,750 in 1860, it rose for the persisting leaders from $14,765 in 1850 to $26,250 in 1860. Thus, although the sample persisters added a few more property holders to their ranks during the 1850s, the size of their holdings did not increase appreciably. The boosters who persisted included several more property holders in their group and nearly doubled their median holdings besides. Finally, real property accumulation proceeded to the point where several of the leaders (21.5%) amassed property in excess of $100,000, while 7.7% held real estate valued at more than a quarter of a million dollars. In 1850 only one persisting leader had achieved $100,000. The sample persisters on the other hand also included one individual with real property valued at over $100,000 in 1850, and the same individual but no others in 1860. Thus, not only did more leaders own more property, but the size of some of their holdings attained impressive levels while the sample persisters possessed virtually the same amount of property.

The slaveholding pattern of the persisting leaders resembled

48. See Edward Pessen, "The Egalitarian Myth and the American Social Reality: Wealth, Mobility, and Equality in the 'Era of the Common Man,'" *American Historical Review*, LXXVI (1971), 989–1034.

that of the sample persisters. Slaveholding declined slightly—though not so much as among the sample group—from 88.6% to 85.1% of the leaders. The median slaveholding remained the same at six. Although the exorbitant prices for slaves toward the end of the decade affected the leadership less than the sample, it was evident that the prominence of slave hiring cut into slaveholding statistics. Thirty-three of the forty slaveholding leaders (82.5%) either hired slaves, hired them out, or both. Six of the seven nonslaveholders hired slaves. Thus, of all the persisting elite, only one did not own or hire a slave in 1860.

The 1850s were prosperous years for the city of Richmond. While it would be erroneous to conclude that all elements of the population shared equally in the bonanza, the distribution of wealth in the capital city was more equitable than in northern communities. These findings correspond to the arguments advanced by Frank L. Owsley a generation ago in his research on yeoman farmers in the Old South. Owsley contended that the southern yeomanry was a true middle class that achieved considerable prosperity during the 1850s.[49] The "plain folk" in Richmond seemed to conform to this generalization. Though scholars have subsequently pilloried Owsley's thesis, similar studies conducted on urban subjects could lend some new support to the thesis. With new quantitative techniques and procedures at their disposal, historians should be able to avoid the methodological problems that beset Owsley.

This is not to deny that the Richmond leaders tended to get richer faster than even the persisting nonleaders. This was to be expected, though. Richmond's boosters possessed the energy and the important positions in the business and government communities in 1850. It was not difficult to parlay these advantages into a substantial accumulation of wealth and status. Moreover, their familiarity with the city (38.3% were residents for at least twenty years by 1860) as well as their knowledge of the mechanisms of a

49. Frank L. Owsley, *Plain Folk of the Old South* (Baton Rouge, 1950); Frank L. Owsley and Harriet C. Owsley, "The Economic Basis of Society in the Late Antebellum South," *Journal of Southern History*, VI (1940), 24–26; and Frank L. Owsley, "The Fundamental Causes of the Civil War: Egocentric Sectionalism," *Journal of Southern History*, VII (1941), 3–18.

modern urban economy enabled the leaders to pursue their personal and citywide objectives in an intelligent manner. Finally, the Richmond activists were organization men. They formed a fairly cohesive group. This did not imply that the rest of Richmond's population was an unorganized mass. They were joining too. However, a few nonleaders enjoyed such a broad commonality through a variety of associations. This cohesion did not appear suddenly in 1847. There were urban leaders in the city since its founding. Through the 1850s, however, an identifiable, compact elite emerged who were imbued with the American desire for organization and efficiency. Urban leadership was not new, but rather the manifestations which it took were novel.

The profiles of leadership in three Virginia cities as well as the comparative analysis in the state's largest city provide an insight into the type of urban society that existed in the Old Dominion. As the state poised for what its citizens believed would be a momentous economic boom, an energetic, ecumenical leadership inhabited the cities. If Richmond represented the best and biggest example of civic leadership, then Virginians could indeed be sanguine about their future. Accumulation of wealth distinguished Richmond's activists. Their sensitivity to the needs of their city and fellow citizens must have been great, however. They shared basic social values with the rest of the population. The patterns of family life seemed similar throughout the city, regardless of income level. The family was the great value giver in nineteenth-century America. The commonality of family configuration ensured, in part at least, that leaders and citizens alike would share basic assumptions about their society. Although it was not possible to obtain the religious affiliation of a meaningful number of elites, much less the random sample, evidence indicated that religious values formed another common bond among all Richmonders. If some of the more prominent leaders attended Saint Paul's Episcopal Church on Sundays, there were boosters who were members of Baptist, Presbyterian, and Catholic congregations as well. Churchgoing was a weekly ritual for most citizens. Their common faith in religion was an important reason for the optimism that pervaded urban society in the 1850s. Finally, Richmond seemed to be an open society for at least white males. The advent of universal white male suffrage in 1851 added to the equitable nature of Richmond society. The absence of vast accumulations of wealth as well as of yawning chasms in the white social structure was calculated to provide a broad base of support for the projects of the new era.

VIRGINIA'S URBAN LEADERS were well qualified to direct their cities and their state to prosperity. Their broad range of activities demonstrated civic responsibility. The leaders' variety of economic contacts and interests indicated an awareness of the complexities of a modern urban economy. They realized that in the national urban competition, railroads, direct trade, and manufacturing facilities represented the promise, not the fulfillment, of economic prosperity. In order to transform opportunity into success, civic leaders organized their cities. In planning for urban growth, they were moving their communities to cityhood and their state to respectability.

1

The first task of the leadership was to secure a broad rural clientele composed of country merchants and commercial agriculturists. Customers meant commerce, and commerce was a key to sectional equilibrium. Urban entrepreneurs fanned out into the hinterland in person and through the media to establish commercial relationships with rural clients. In an era when personal contact was still an important aspect of economic relations, agricultural societies provided an excellent opportunity to promote both a business transaction and a city.

The Virginia State Agricultural Society, formed in February 1850, dedicated itself to promoting scientific, market-oriented cultivation. The society and local groups that it inspired received heavy urban support from the beginning.[1] The progressive, scientific agriculturists were precisely the individuals whom urban businessmen sought in order to develop a commercial empire. Urban merchants and manufacturers would profit not only from

1. Richmond *Enquirer*, March 1, 1850, and February 21, 1851; "Virginia State Agricultural Convention," *Southern Planter*, XII (March, 1852), 81–82. See also David R. Goldfield, "Urban-Rural Relations in the Old South: The Example of Virginia," *Journal of Urban History*, II (1976), 146–68.

the farmer's bounty, but from a reciprocal trade of fertilizers, agricultural implements, and provisions as well. William H. Richardson, a Richmond merchant and civic leader, understood the necessity of an urban-rural connection and became one of the leading supporters of the state society. In 1856, the society elected him to the office of vice president. In his tireless efforts to educate farmers (no Virginian except for Edmund Ruffin worked more diligently toward that end) he convinced his city to support the society's struggle for existence in the early 1850s. Richmond responded by placing more members in the society than any other county or city in the state.[2]

The society rewarded Richmond's support by agreeing to hold its first annual fair in that city in 1853. In return, the city council appropriated $10,000 to defray expenses. It proved to be a wise investment. Merchants looked forward to the event to contact clients, to pass their cards to prospective customers, and to display their wares. Manufacturers enjoyed the opportunity presented by the fair to demonstrate the latest agricultural implements, to provide samples of flour and tobacco, and to show off manufactured items like glassware and kitchen utensils that no progressive country merchant would fail to stock or no modern housewife would fail to buy. Farmers thronged the fair to take advantage of an extensive urban market. They displayed their produce and stock and purchased necessities and frills for the family back home.[3]

The fair was a lucrative enterprise for all concerned. One source estimated that Richmond grossed $300,000 from the event—a substantial return on its initial investment. The state society raised approximately $10,000 annually from the fair.[4] Urban merchants found it a profitable endeavor as well. Rural visitors, spurred by the holiday mood and encouraged by persuasive advertisements, di-

2. Richmond *Enquirer*, February 20, 1852, and April 11, 1856.
3. *Ibid.*, November 4, 1853; Nathaniel F. Cabell, "Some Fragments of an Intended Report on the Post-Revolutionary History of Agriculture in Virginia" (MS in Nathaniel F. Cabell Papers, Virginia State Library), c. 1860; Kathleen Bruce, *Virginia Iron Manufacture in the Slave Era, 1800–1860*, (New York, 1951), 305–19; Sydney Penn, "Agricultural Organization in Ante-Bellum Virginia" (MS thesis, University of Virginia, 1935).
4. "First Annual Show of the Virginia State Agricultural Society," *American Agriculturist*, XII (1853), 136.

vested themselves of a considerable amount of currency for omnibus rides, canes, concerts, dry goods, jewelry, and the like. Micajah Woods, a farmer near Charlottesville, attended the fair in Richmond in 1856 and recorded the following expenses: omnibus fare, $1.50; bill at Exchange Hotel for three nights, including meals, $6.62; one hat, $5.00; newspapers, $.20; one cane, $.57; entrance fee at Mechanics Institute,—$.25; "segars, apples & co.," $.60; and church donation, $.15. The total was $14.87. This figure did not include railroad transportation to the fair or other incidentals that Woods might have deemed discretionary to omit from his account. Nevertheless, it was a profitable three days for farmer Woods. He sold four pigs and a beef cow at the fair and won $81 in premiums as well. His total income from the fair amounted to $191. When the first fair closed in 1853, the Richmond City Council immediately donated $5,000 toward the next one.[5]

The mutual benefits of the state fair inspired other cities and counties to form agricultural societies and stage regional fairs at market centers. Norfolk, Wheeling, Lynchburg, and Alexandria became annual sites for county or regional exhibitions. Urban leaders in these communities found it imperative to join these organizations whether they knew the difference between a seeder and a plough or not. Local government cooperated by appropriating land and money to the local society. By the end of the 1850s, the state fair and several regional exhibitions had become institutionalized in urban Virginia.[6]

The profits—both immediate and long range—reaped by Richmond rankled other cities. Civic leaders elsewhere were eager to provide their merchants and manufacturers with a profitable forum like the state fair. In 1858, after severe pressure from rival sites as well as an attractive financial arrangement, the society designated Petersburg as the site for the annual fair. Richmond

5. Woods-Belmont Farm Journal (MS in Woods-Belmont Farm Journals, Alderman Library, University of Virginia), 1854–61, 3–10; Richmond *Daily Dispatch*, November 7, 1853.

6. Alexandria *Gazette*, October 5, 1859; Lynchburg *Virginian*, October 20, 1858; Norfolk *Southern Argus*, August 16, 1853; Wheeling *Daily Intelligencer*, September 2, 1852.

leaders, upset at the loss in revenue, but more concerned with the ultimate affect of the fair's removal on commercial contacts, seceded from the state organization. They formed, together with neighboring societies opposed to the transfer of the fair, the Virginia Central Agricultural Society. The primary motive of this rump group was not to spread the gospel of scientific agriculture, but rather to facilitate commercial relations and profits. This became obvious, if it was not already apparent, when the first business of the new society was the implementation of a plan to hold a rival state fair. It was ironic, but perhaps indicative of the importance of cities in the Virginia economy, that urban rivalry threw the state's agriculturists into two warring camps. In 1860 the state fair returned to Richmond, and the central society dissolved.[7]

The odyssey of the state fair demonstrated that urban businessmen could not depend upon a yearly event to secure rural patronage. Most Virginia cities, after all, participated only peripherally in the state society. A more dependable, more frequent line to the countryside was necessary. The urban press qualified on both accounts. As an organ edited usually by a civic leader, it was a reliable medium for purveying the economic messages of the urban leadership. Second, most urban journals were triweekly and even daily newspapers. Their frequent appearance ensured a constant barrage of alluring advertisements and positive propaganda. The urban press proved to be an effective tool for encouraging and rationalizing urbanization.[8]

The urban press was both a creation of urbanization and an urbanizing force itself. From 1847 to 1861, Virginia's city newspapers underwent significant changes to facilitate the process of urbanization. Like most journals of the period, Virginia's newspapers were affiliated with the major political parties. Their format was stereotypical with an emphasis on national news usually culled

7. Richmond *Enquirer*, April 30, 1858; "Report of the Virginia Central Agricultural Society," *Southern Planter*, XX (1860), 756.

8. On the role of the urban press in promoting urban growth, see, for example, Dykstra, *Cattle Towns*, 149; Wade, *Urban Frontier*, 130–32; Wheeler, *To Wear a City's Crown*, 23; Abbott, "Civic Pride in Chicago," 399–421; and Schnell and McLear, "Why the Cities Grew," 162–66.

from party organs in Washington. The drive for economic independence altered the emphasis of city newspapers in Virginia. News of state and local economic policies, city news, and self-aggrandizing editorials began to appear frequently for the first time in the late 1840s.[9] The Norfolk *Southern Argus* and the Richmond *Daily Dispatch* typified the new wave of urban journalism. The *Argus,* although associated with the Democratic party, soft-pedaled politics and dedicated itself instead to "keeping pace with the growing city." Founded appropriately in 1847, the *Argus* fulfilled its promise in the ensuing years "to contribute to the wants and stimulate to active enterprise our commercial community."[10] Within three years after its inception, the *Argus* achieved the widest circulation in the area.

The rise of James A. Cowardin's Richmond *Daily Dispatch* was even more spectacular than the *Argus*'s success. It illustrated both the growing maturity of Richmond and the popularity of the new urban journalism. Cowardin, a young civic leader, inaugurated the state's first daily penny press in Richmond in 1850. Popular penny presses were just beginning to have an impact in northern cities. The *Dispatch* was a nonpartisan journal and its focus on city affairs quickly found a receptive audience. Businessmen discovered its format of summaries and short articles rather than long political discourses especially amenable. Subscribers read the paper at breakfast, and by the time they finished their coffee they had ingested a range of subjects from current prices to notices of stockholders' meetings.[11] Though Cowardin operated virtually under the nose of Thomas Ritchie's venerable and nationally renowned Richmond *Enquirer,* the *Dispatch* soon outdistanced its more traditional rival. By 1860 Cowardin's journal had attained a circulation of 18,000 in the city. The energetic editor attributed his success to a new urban spirit spurred by the state's economic revival.

9. Lester J. Cappon, *Virginia Newspapers, 1821–1935* (New York, 1936), 3–15.
10. Norfolk *Southern Argus*, December 19, 1848.
11. Cappon, *Virginia Newspapers*, 10–13.

The active and persevering character of the time in which we live demanded a paper in keeping with its spirit. People have not the leisure they once had—they cannot now take a paper and read it through, advertisements, editorials, the political essays of "Lycurgus" and "Cato," while waiting for a customer. They must do their reading at breakfast and the day must be devoted to business. The days of leisure are certainly gone.[12]

In an era when the press was the primary communicative medium, it was important that local entrepreneurs should have access to an accommodating journal. As cities grew, so did information. Business depended on the effective organization of information from notices of local prices and economic conditions to descriptions of regional crop failures and national economic trends. Effective reception and interpretation of such information facilitated commercial relations and the flow of commerce.[13] The success of the *Argus* and the *Dispatch* initiated changes in other publications as they sought to provide their readers with the necessary information to conduct business intelligently.

In 1852, Wheeling welcomed its first daily, urban-oriented press, the *Intelligencer*. From the outset, the *Intelligencer* devoted several columns to apprising its readers of events throughout the city. That same year, the Lynchburg *Virginian*, which had begun publication three decades earlier, inaugurated a daily edition that included a section devoted to "city items." The editors reasoned that "the people of this section of the country have a right to expect a more frequent . . . account of the affairs of the world to keep pace with the spirit of the times and increasing importance of Lynchburg." Other urban journals followed in creating columns or sections of special interest to city dwellers. Even the Richmond *Enquirer*, the most fiercely political of Virginia's urban press, initiated a feature on city news "in obedience to our friends who seem to think the growing importance of our city and the spirit of the times demand it."[14]

Besides keeping local citizens informed and aware of important

12. Richmond *Daily Dispatch*, October 20, 1860.
13. On the relationship between rational information systems and urban growth, see Cochran, "The Business Revolution," 1460.
14. Wheeling *Daily Intelligencer*, August 24, 1852; Lynchburg *Virginian*, August 10, 1852; Richmond *Enquirer*, July 8, 1853. See also Norfolk *Southern Argus*, July 11, 1853.

economic developments, the modern press served as an effective liaison with the countryside. The urban press enjoyed a wide circulation, especially in rural districts. Farmers' inventories often included subscriptions to two or three city journals.[15] By 1860, most urban presses published a weekly summary edition for rural subscribers.[16] Commercial agriculturists were as interested in price current lists and proceedings of stockholders' meetings as urban businessmen. A receptive and wide audience awaited a talented urban editor to regale them with the benefits of trading and shopping at his city.

The urban editor promoted his city to country readers. The editor had a keen sense of his missionary activities and frequently reminded people of his services. The Wheeling *Daily Intelligencer* lectured its city subscribers on the importance of the urban press: "Abroad, it [the newspaper] is regarded as our oracle, and speaks volumes for, or against us. In its business features may be discerned the indications of our prosperity. It is the . . . chronicler of our advancement." Although in some of its more jingoistic moments the urban press represented less an "oracle" than a propaganda sheet, most urban editors took their responsibility as news broadcasters seriously. As the Lynchburg *Republican* asserted, "There is nothing which points with surer index to the character of a city and its people than the quality and appearance of its newspaper press."[17] In attempting to attract commerce to the city, though, the urban press occasionally sacrificed quality for drumbeating. Thus, Norfolk was "one of the very best corn markets in the country"; Alexandria produced flour "of the highest grade"; and Lynchburg was unequivocally "the best market for the sale of fine manufacturing tobacco in the world."[18] Editors usually followed these state-

15. B. J. Barbour, "Post Office a/c" (MS in James Barbour Papers, Alderman Library, University of Virginia), January 18, 1855; John W. Gilliam, "a/c with Thomas Jones, 1845" (MS in Gilliam Family Papers, Alderman Library, University of Virginia); Thomas Taylor to John Rutherfoord, December 12, 1853, in John Rutherfoord Papers, Duke University.

16. Alexandria *Gazette*, February 12, 1853; Norfolk *Southern Argus*, November 3, 1852; Richmond *Daily Dispatch*, August 10, 1855.

17. Wheeling *Daily Intelligencer*, July 28, 1854; Lynchburg *Virginian*, October 16, 1858.

18. Norfolk *Southern Argus*, February 10, 1854; Alexandria *Virginia Sentinel*, quoted in Richmond *Enquirer*, October 3, 1854; Lynchburg *Virginian*, June 12, 1856.

ments with a salesman's pitch: "Let our friends from the country try this market, and they will be satisfied that they can purchase their supplies here as advantageously as they can by going abroad."[19]

Advertising augmented the urban editor's entreaties to the countryside. Advertising was a mutually beneficial activity for businessman and editor. The press received revenue and the entrepreneur attained widespread circulation and contact with farmers and country merchants. Advertising columns were the yellow pages for nineteenth-century country residents. The editors of the Lynchburg *Virginian*, although probably hankering for additional advertising profits, exhibited good business sense when they observed, "If anything is wanted, a newspaper is consulted to ascertain where it may most conveniently be procured. Those who advertise have an immense advantage over those who do not." Urban entrepreneurs followed this advice and sought space in the press avidly. The *Virginian's* prosyletizing efforts were so successful that it introduced smaller type in its advertising columns to accommodate the crush of requests.[20]

As the railroad stretched across the countryside, business advertisement went along. Urban entrepreneurs, in addition to employing the columns of their city journals to display their cards, began advertising in hinterland presses. By 1860 newspapers in the far reaches of the state, and in the rural districts of North Carolina and Tennessee, carried business cards of urban Virginians. Old Dominion merchants promised "speedy transmission" of goods to country stores; "prompt and careful attention" to farmers' produce; the "highest prices" paid; and a familiar mercantile lure, "convenient financial arrangements."[21] Business advertising in country presses was a welcome revenue source for financially pressed editors. As a result, urban merchants not only received exposure through their ads, but rural editors praised the merchant's city as a market for local farmers and country merchants. It was an accepted quid pro

19. Alexandria *Gazette*, September 8, 1852.
20. Lynchburg *Virginian*, May 5, 1855; Lynchburg *Virginian*, October 1, 1855.
21. Danville *Appeal*, July 18, 1860; Salem *Weekly Register*, February 1, 1855, July 20, 1860. See also Richmond *Daily Dispatch*, September 14, 1859.

quo of the period: advertising revenue for the country press, free publicity for the market center. The Rockingham *Register*, a popular advertising medium for Alexandria businessmen, reported to country merchants that "there is no need of any of our Valley merchants going beyond Alexandria to purchase supplies." Another Valley newspaper that received patronage from Richmonders advised its readers that "pride of state interests . . . should prompt us of the Valley to trade with Richmond, and Richmond to trade with us."[22] Advertising was another example of the cooperation of urban and rural Virginia in the contest for economic independence.

The press, regardless of location, facilitated commercial relations. The urban press served as a clearinghouse for business and city news, as a promoter of urban interests to the countryside, and as a medium through which local entrepreneurs could achieve contact with potential rural clients. "Not all other influences combined," the Norfolk *Southern Argus* asserted correctly if somewhat boastfully, "can compare with or stand against it [the press]."[23]

The influence of the press and the businessmen's own personal contacts attracted customers and commerce. Editors and businessmen could talk or write a farmer's produce to town, but that was not enough. Words were not sufficient to attract a lasting commerce. Urban leaders, in planning for urban growth, concentrated on improving their cities' marketing facilities to accommodate rural merchants and farmers. The goal was to retain country patronage. Appropriate marketing facilities not only ensured commerce but aided other enterprises as well. As a Richmond merchant noted, "Facilities will develop business . . . and capital will find an investment in foundries, mills and mines, heretofore unthought of."[24]

Attractive warehouse and market house accommodations were essential to the retention of commerce. As tobacco cultivation was revived in the 1850s, urban Virginia sought to improve old or to

22. Rockingham *Register*, quoted in Alexandria *Gazette*, March 21, 1857; Staunton *Messenger*, quoted in Richmond *Enquirer*, September 21, 1853.
23. Norfolk *Southern Argus*, December 29, 1853.
24. Richmond *Daily Dispatch*, June 15, 1855.

erect new tobacco warehouses. A damp, ill-ventilated warehouse could ruin a tobacco crop. Lynchburg tobacconists renovated Lynch's Warehouse—the largest in the city—in 1855 to ensure "dry conditions" for the sensitive crop. Alexandria merchants feared a loss of the tobacco trade to Washington, D.C. and Baltimore unless they constructed an appropriate warehouse to "accommodate increased production of the crop" in neighboring counties. War intervened before the city's business leaders could fulfill their purpose, and Alexandria failed to develop as an important tobacco market.[25]

A decaying, inclement market house provided inadequate, unsanitary conditions for a farmer's produce. Norfolk businessmen began clamoring for a new market house "like Northern cities have" as early as 1848. An elaborate iron market house, not completed until 1860, provided "shelter from the elements" for produce and wares as well as for customers and local businessmen. Under its vast roof, merchants conducted a weekly fair for the benefit of themselves and country visitors. The iron market house became a goal for urban leaders. Its construction signified a progressive mercantile community whose primary concern was their customers' goods. When Wheeling was constructing its iron market house, a group of residents complained about the disruption to traffic and the noise resulting from its erection. The *Intelligencer* dismissed the charges: "They have not the right to complain; the evils complained of being necessary to a very necessary improvement which will more than compensate for all present inconvenience."[26] It was a new era, and individual perturbation relented before community welfare.

Just as businessmen expressed anxiety over appropriate accommodations for their customers' produce, they were also concerned about comfortable facilities for the customers themselves. The longer a farmer or a country merchant tarried in the city, the more

25. Lynchburg *Virginian*, October 2, 1852; Alexandria *Gazette*, September 16, 1858.
26. Norfolk *Southern Argus*, December 18, 1848, March 26, 1860; Wheeling *Daily Intelligencer*, October 2, 1852.

opportunities there would be for business transactions. A well-appointed hotel was a prerequisite for urban growth and commercial prosperity. The absence of such a facility was, in the word of one Norfolk resident, "humiliating." The concerned Norfolk citizen cited New York's Astor House as an example of the value of a first-class hotel to a business community.[27] Though most communities possessed few illusions of rivaling the famous New York inn, they sought to provide comfortable surroundings for their prospective clients and visitors. Richmond, as state capital and convention center, possessed four first-class hotels that provided private rooms, meals, and valet services: the Ballard House, the Exchange Hotel, the Spotswood Hotel, and the American Hotel. The Exchange was the city's most elegant hotel. New owners remodeled it in the late 1840s to accommodate the city's growing importance as a market center. Its French chandeliers and English broadlooms rivaled, according to residents, the appointments of the Astor House.[28]

If other Virginia cities lacked Richmond's potential, they matched her pretension in hotel construction. Alexandria refurbished its two major hotels, the Mansion House and the City Hotel, as trade and visitors came to the city. One satisfied farmer in 1849 classified the Mansion House "among the best hotels in the United States." Five year later, however, city leaders felt that growth demanded an additional "large and commodious HOTEL . . . so that our customers have the best accommodations that can be afforded." Norfolk entrepreneurs were more dissatisfied with the hotel situation in their city. The problem became acute when some visitors to a regional agricultural fair in the fall of 1858 were forced to seek lodging in private homes due to lack of suitable accommodations. Residents soon opened subscription books to erect a "first class hotel," and within a week they had raised $10,000. Lynchburg

27. Norfolk *Southern Argus*, March 27, 1851.
28. Richard Irby, "Recollection of Men, Places, and Events, 1845–1900" (MS in Richard Irby Papers, Alderman Library, University of Virginia); Christian, *Richmond*, 209.

also entered the modern hotel era when a wealthy resident refitted an old hotel and reopened it as the Norvell House in 1853. The Norvell became a popular watering place for visiting tobacco planters in the 1850s.[29]

However luxurious the hotel accommodations may have been, rural visitors who could transact their business in one day would return home that same night unless the city provided them with appropriate diversions not readily available in the countryside. An Alexandria merchant, in 1854, lamented the demise of regular stage productions in that city and suggested a resurrection of the theater because "we want inducements for strangers to stop here. . . . Had the Theatre been preserved, we should have had a theatrical season here every year, which would have been an inducement to strangers to stop here." Three years later a farmer raised a similar plaint: "You should have a well-conducted Theatre in Alexandria. . . . but very few will leave the comfortable sitting room of the Mansion House or the City Hotel . . . to travel round to the Concert rooms to be regaled with the stale slight [sic] of hand tricks or the singing of fifth-rate Ethiopian Minstrels. . . . What you want are inducements in your own town for people to stay there." In the fall of 1859 Alexandria at last resurrected its theater, which had been gone for more than two decades. A delighted farmer from a neighboring county recalled that Alexandria "used to be as dull as the d———l after night—no amusement—nothing to do—no where to go. . . . Now that some of your enterprising citizens have established a Theatre, do pray keep it—you'll see the benefits in a very little while." In Richmond there were also theater performances with occasional concert treats such as black pianist Blind Tom, and Jenny Lind.[30] The general level of entertainment in other Virginia cities, however, was most similar to "fifth-rate Ethiopian Minstrels." Legitimate theater never became popular in

29. Alexandria *Gazette*, January 1, 1849; Alexandria *Gazette*, March 23, 1854; Norfolk *Southern Argus*, November 6, 1858; Christian, *Lynchburg*, 158.

30. Letter from "A Merchant," Alexandria *Gazette*, March 23, 1854; letter from "A Farmer," Alexandria *Gazette*, January 3, 1857; Alexandria *Gazette*, October 11, 1859; Thomas, *Confederate State of Richmond*, 30.

the urban South, though most Old South cities presented passable concert and theatrical performances.[31]

While visitors were enjoying the comfort of a warm fire at a sumptuous lodge, or the warm laughter of a lively comedy, urban leaders were concocting other measures to facilitate the business relationship. The city directory was a published locator file for the benefit of residents and visitors alike. City directories not only facilitated the process of locating businessmen, they provided an opportunity to organize the city's population between the covers of one readily accessible book. It is true that not all or even most of a city's residents found their way into the directory, but comprehensiveness was not the goal of the publication. The directory was a businessman's guide to other businessmen.[32] In addition to names and addresses, city directories often proudly displayed the social and commercial organizations of the city, as well as a list of hotels and newspapers, which were things a visitor would find useful. The Alexandria *Gazette* noted that directories were as important as advertising and market facilities in lubricating the commercial relationship: "Such an enterprize [the directory] has been carried out in every city of the Union, and has proved a great convenience to every one transacting business."[33]

The publication of directories related directly to urban growth. They were superfluous in a city where commerce and visitors were occasional interlopers on an otherwise tranquil scene and where trees and grass grew, but ledgers did not. As urban economies and lifestyles grew more complex, directories became effective planning tools. Richmond, for example, published a directory in 1819, but it was a very modest affair. Another directory appeared in 1845; but not until 1852 did its publication become a biennial event. Norfolk issued its first directory amid a fanfare of publicity in 1849 and revised it four times during the next decade. Wheeling waited until 1856 to publish its first directory. It was an enterprise that "is very much needed at this time, and should be encouraged

31. See Eaton, *Growth of Southern Civilization*, 261–64.
32. See Knights, *Plain People of Boston*, 7.
33. Alexandria *Gazette*, June 12, 1860.

by our business men." Lynchburg prepared a directory for the first time in 1859.[34] As with most other economic planning devices, the directory produced a chain reaction throughout urban Virginia. When one city published a volume, others invariably followed. It became another artifact of a progressive, growing city.

A movement to number dwellings and stores and to properly label streets and lanes often accompanied the publication of a directory. Once again, numbering and labeling were unnecessary in the small, familiar urban milieu before the 1840s. As the city expanded spatially, residence and business became differentiated, and its geography grew more complex. Businessmen did not wish to subject clients and other visitors to the adventure of locating an unnumbered residence or a commercial establishment. Considerable agitation from leading merchants as well as the examples of Alexandria and Norfolk caused Richmond to finally number its houses and commercial establishments in 1859.[35] As the tedious process of numbering began in Lynchburg, an editor predicted that the project "will afford great facilities to strangers in seeking out places of business."[36] The house number and the street name, like the directory, made the city a more efficient place in which to carry on the business of business.

The fairs; the new urban press; the shiny, sturdy iron market houses; the splendid hotels and theaters; and the attempt to make the suddenly unfamiliar city more familiar again attracted and maintained commerce. The rural clientele was secure from foreign predators for the time being. Virginia's urban leaders, however, moved in circles that extended far beyond the horizon of the immediate hinterland. The transportation revolution as well as commercial prosperity meant that Virginia's cities would no longer be secondary market centers isolated from the regional and national economies. Greater responsibility accompanied this

34. Montague, *Richmond Directory, 1852*, Introduction; Norfolk *Southern Argus*, September 5, 1849; Forrest, *Norfolk Directory, 1851–52*; Wheeling *Daily Intelligencer*, June 23, 1856; Lynchburg *Virginian*, June 13, 1859.

35. Christian, *Richmond*, 198. See also Alexandria *Gazette*, October 12, 1854; and Norfolk *Southern Argus*, November 2, 1849.

36. Lynchburg, *Virginian*, June 13, 1859.

broadened perspective. Business decisions now had not only local but regional and even national implications. Kinship ties no longer sufficed to guide the city in an organized manner. The point of reference was no longer the countryside, but the "commercial, agricultural world."[37] Individual businessmen were powerless either to direct their city's economic progress or to rationalize urban growth itself. The best fairs, the most commodious market houses, and the most helpful directories were group activities. Urban entrepreneurs, acting in concert, developed regulations and procedures to effect the free flow of commerce and to facilitate the entrance of urban Virginia into an urban nation.

Virginia's civic leaders were joiners. This was the American passion. As one foreign traveler observed, "These people [Americans] associate as easily as they breathe."[38] Voluntary associations were important to the process of urbanization. As a city grew, these associations enabled leaders to plan the development of their city with greater system. Associations indicated both the presence of an active, identifiable leadership and their own awareness of themselves as urban leaders.[39]

The establishment of a board of trade, which was the predecessor of the modern chamber of commerce, was an early goal of city-builders. The function of the board was twofold: to provide an interchange of opinions and information and to formulate commercial regulations. Most boards initiated reading rooms or libraries where the latest issues of *Hunt's Merchants' Magazine* and *DeBow's Review* were displayed. It was important for urban Virginia's cosmopolitan businessmen to be aware of developments in other cities. Just as urban activists knew the interior accouterments of the Astor House even if they had never been there, they were apprised of activities of other urban entrepreneurs as well. The board of trade facilitated urban Virginia's entrance into the community of cities. Finally, urban merchants and manufacturers dis-

37. Charles W. Dabney to Robert L. Dabney, March 29, 1853, in Dabney Papers.
38. Quoted in Jonathan Lurie, "Private Associations, Internal Regulation and Progressivism: The Chicago Board of Trade, 1880–1923, as a Case Study," *American Journal of Legal History*, XVI (1972), 215.
39. See Glazer, "Participation and Power," 151–68.

covered that the competition engendered by free enterprise was not an efficient means of conducting business. It led to price wars, financial insolvency, and ill feeling among members of the business community. The board of trade, by setting rules and fixing prices, removed insecurity from the market place thus crystallizing business and business sentiment and channeling them in a more orderly fashion.

Richmond became the first Virginia city to organize a board of trade. The pressures of increased commerce, growth, and contact with regional and national economies occurred earlier in the capital city than elsewhere. In June 1854, a group of Richmond merchants organized an association to "arbitrate all disputed accounts and contracts, and all controversies of a mercantile character." As commerce and competition advanced in Richmond, the litigious nature of the mercantile population threatened to disrupt the free flow of commerce. By providing for binding arbitration and also by fixing prices of commodities, Richmond's leaders introduced more order into business transactions. In addition to self-regulation, the board recommended programs to the city council and to the state legislature. Indeed, some Richmonders believed the board to be a third legislative unit that was even more powerful and representative of the business community than the city council.[40] In 1859, for example, the board marshalled sentiment that favored deepening the James River channel so that large vessels could arrive and depart from Richmond. This proposal had been discussed for at least two decades but had never received the organized support that the board provided. The board presented their petition to the council, and the latter body agreed to grant $30,000 worth of city bonds to defray the costs of improving the James River.[41]

The board of trade movement, as with other urban improvements, proved contagious. Alexandria and Norfolk merchants established similar associations within weeks of the inauguration of the Richmond association. Merchant William H. Fowle and railroad president Lewis McKenzie (who were both civic leaders) or-

40. Richmond *Enquirer*, June 9, 1854.
41. Richmond *Daily Dispatch*, March 18, 1859.

ganized the Alexandria Board of Trade with similar goals and activities as those of the Richmond board. The Alexandria group perceived one of their purposes to be educating the public on the "facts of modern commerce." This was not merely a public-service effort on the part of the newly-formed board. It was an attempt to organize public opinion behind the board's endeavors. Norfolk business leaders organized a board along the lines of existing groups in Alexandria and Richmond. In 1857, the board rallied the city from the torpor that had followed in the wake of a devastating yellow-fever epidemic two years earlier. The members restated the needs of the city and formed the Seaboard Towing and Transportation Company to improve trade between Lynchburg and Norfolk. Within a year, business activity returned to the zest and level of the period prior to the epidemic. Wheeling finally entered the list of cities with boards of trade by organizing an association in March 1860. The major goal of the group was to "establish a uniformity of prices for all articles and place all dealers on an equal footing." Wheeling merchants discovered what other urban Virginians had recognized for some time: security and order were more economical and productive than free enterprise.[42]

In connection with controlling their city's economic growth, businessmen formed more specialized organizations. These associations dealt with specific problems resulting from a widening circle of commercial intercourse. Exchanges, organized to regulate the buying and selling of a certain commodity, were becoming widespread in mid-century cities. Virginia's cities followed the national urban pattern. Corn, a prominent commodity in Virginia's market centers, attracted the attention of entrepreneurs in Alexandria following the establishment of the board of trade in 1854. A group of merchants formed the corn exchange to regulate the buying and selling of that crop. They announced that they would purchase the farmer's crop only by weight, with one bushel to equal fifty-six pounds, rather than by relying on sale by the measure of one bushel. Alexandria merchants had discovered that one bushel var-

42. Alexandria *Gazette*, April 19, 1854; Norfolk *Southern Argus*, June 9, 1854, and July 16, 1857; Wheeling *Daily Intelligencer*, March 2, 1860.

ied in weight, depending on the particular farmer's conception of that measure. In earlier times, this haphazard practice sufficed. In the new era, however, precision was important, especially when Alexandria merchants sold the corn in northern cities. Sale by weight would inject uniformity into the corn trade and bring the city in line with northern cities where sale by weight was a common practice. Four years later, however, the corn exchange reversed its policy and returned to sale by measure. Corn receipts had fallen off drastically as farmers, preferring the leeway of the inaccurate bushel, turned to neighboring Virginia and Maryland cities where sale by measure prevailed. It was a Hobson's choice for Alexandria merchants. Sale by weight increased the coastwise trade with northern cities but decreased the flow of corn to Alexandria, while sale by measure had the reverse effect.[43] The situation underscored the difficulty of economic decision making in a national economy.

Norfolk merchants confronted the weight-measure controversy with similar results. The merchants organized a corn exchange in 1854. As in Alexandria, they required the selling of corn by weight, "that being the standard in New York." Although Norfolk merchants professed the new regulation to be in the farmer's interest by encouraging him to raise better and heavier grades of corn, the move was clearly self-serving. The merchants hoped to attract direct trade with England and to increase profits at home by not being "forced to sell under current market rates." Unfortunately, farmers found more amenable outlets for their corn, and Norfolk's dreams of a European connection never materialized. Three years later Norfolk returned to selling corn by a bushel measure that rarely exceeded fifty-two pounds.[44]

Tobacco was even more vital to the Virginia economy than corn. It was not surprising, therefore, to see that crop come under the scrutiny of merchants' and manufacturers' associations. Richmond was the hub of the Virginia tobacco trade. The Panic of 1857 that closed Richmond's tobacco factories and threw thousands of workers into the ranks of the unemployed provided the impetus for the

43. Alexandria *Gazette*, June 22, 1854; Alexandria *Gazette*, February 11, 1858.
44. Norfolk *Southern Argus*, May 4, 1854; Norfolk *Southern Argus*, May 28, 1857.

formation of the tobacco exchange. The depression touched off by the panic drew an embittered but constructive response from Virginia's hard-hit tobacco merchants and manufacturers.

The cause of the delirium in Virginia's tobacco community was relatively simple: almost all of the New York tobacco houses defaulted on their obligations to Virginia tobacco manufacturers. Richmond alone lost one million dollars overnight.[45] To rectify the situation, Richmond tobacconists called a convention to assemble in the capital city in December 1857. The 100 manufacturers who attended adopted resolutions designed both to rationalize the tobacco trade within Virginia and to establish new ground rules in dealing with New York factors. The credit system received the greatest attention of the manufacturers. Urban Virginia merchants sold their tobacco on a long-term credit system. They collected their debt from New York factors between eight to twelve months after the initial transaction. New York merchants and factors, on the other hand, extended only short-term credit (usually four months) to their debtors. This situation resulted in two phenomena, both of which were detrimental to Virginia's urban economy. First, New York businessmen could call up debts before Virginia tobacconists could, therefore placing a great strain on the financial resources of the manufacturer. Second, when hard-pressed New York factors purchased manufactured tobacco on the usual long-term credit arrangement, they sometimes dumped the tobacco on the market immediately at a price below normal level. This action depressed the market and the profits for the manufacturer. To compound the problem, some of these factors went bankrupt periodically, leaving the Virginia manufacturer with a worthless long-term note. The manufacturers resolved, therefore, to limit their credits on the sale of tobacco to four months. This regulation went into effect July 1, 1858.

The manufacturers adopted other marketing measures to cope with the rational selling and buying of their commodity. When manufacturers sold their product to northern markets they nor-

45. Richmond *Enquirer*, October 20, 1857; "Banking at the South with Reference to New York City," *Hunt's*, XLII (1860), 312–23.

mally gave factors an allowance of one to five pounds per package to make up for weight or quality deficiencies. The concession was "a source of immense loss to the manufacturers," and the convention discontinued it. Northern factors were not the only obstacles to a smooth and profitable tobacco trade. Some western manufacturers represented their tobacco as manufactured in Richmond or Lynchburg and stamped their packages accordingly. Virginia's manufacturers, unimpressed by this backhanded tribute to the quality of their product, urged Congress to make such trickery a felony.[46] Unfortunately, Congress failed to consider this measure and charlatan tobacco continued to find its way to New York.

The final procedure for rationalizing the tobacco trade was the establishment in May 1858 of a tobacco exchange in Richmond. In addition to enforcing the resolutions passed at the manufacturers' convention six months earlier, the exchange instituted another major reform. It provided that all buying and selling of tobacco was to be done by sample and at the exchange. This meant an end to auction sales at the various warehouses throughout Richmond. By creating a monopoly on sales, the tobacco buyers and merchants could get a uniform price and regulate other procedures of the trade. In monopolizing the sales, the merchants were cornering the trade by eliminating the multitude of inspectors at the various warehouses and removing an extra step in the sales process as well. With the commission merchant dealing directly with the planter, greater profits and regularity would result.[47]

The convention and the exchange demonstrated the degree of cooperation between manufacturers and merchants. Farmers resented this combination. Once again, organizing businessmen found themselves caught between the exigencies of a national market and the necessity of pleasing their local clients. "Corporations have no souls," stormed one farmer, "and this 'Exchange Association' is governed only by the dictates of its own interests." Another farmer condemned "*coercive* measures entered into by a

46. Richmond *Daily Dispatch*, December 8, 1857; Joseph C. Robert, *The Tobacco Kingdom*, 228–34.
47. Richmond *Enquirer*, May 26, 1858.

combination."[48] For Richmond's tobacco merchants and manufacturers the reforms induced by "combination" were essential to survival in a competitive national economy. Virginia could never hope to confront the North on a basis of equality in a sectional conflict if her cities failed to establish a more equal economic relationship with northern cities. In this instance, the exchange prevailed.

The Panic of 1857 not only inspired reforms in the tobacco trade but stimulated similar rationalization in other sectors of the urban economy. The short-term credit system proved a popular innovation with urban merchants, even if their rural customers chafed under the new regulations. The logic of short credit was compelling. "In Philadelphia, New York, and Boston," an Alexandria merchant explained, invoking the trinity of American urbanization, "the short credit system is most rigidly adhered to, and its beneficial effects evidenced in the prosperity of trade and the wealth of the merchants." For a merchant purchasing imported goods in New York on a four-month credit and selling those items in Virginia on an eight-month credit, the inconvenience was obvious. Alexandria adopted the short-credit system with the accompaniment of anguished cries from rural customers in the fall of 1857. Several months later, Wheeling, "in the wake of similar charges in Northern cities," went to the short-credit system.[49]

Daily it seemed, urban businessmen were entering into permanent unions to achieve economic equality in the urban nation. The reaction from the countryside was fierce, and in some instances caused a reversal in urban policy. In other cases, seething submission characterized the rural position best. The clash was inevitable. Country residents had been accustomed to doing business with individuals. Now, it seemed, impersonal organizations directed commercial affairs and surrounded these transactions with a wreath of regulations that the urban businessman framed solely for his own benefit. As urban Virginians came to regard their environment as unique with its own special problems, rural uneasiness

48. *Ibid.*, June 11, 1858.
49. Alexandria *Gazette*, September 10, 1857; Wheeling *Daily Intelligencer*, July 10, 1858.

increased. The transition to a modern urban economy with frequent commercial contacts throughout the urban nation was a difficult process for the countryside to understand and for the city leaders to implement. On the one hand, businessmen were devising programs to secure country patronage; and on the other hand, another set of policies was alienating a portion of the rural clientele. The goal of the associations, though, was to facilitate commercial relationships with all sectors of the economy. Despite temporary discomfort, farmers and country merchants would ultimately benefit from the new system.

Urban leaders attempted to adapt both their city and their business methods to the increased flow of commerce from the countryside and to the expansion of commercial relations with other cities. Successful planning in these areas ensured rapid and orderly urban growth. Businessmen, often acting in association with each other, consciously selected plans to achieve this end. Commerce was the bedrock of the urban economy but not the entire foundation. Labor was the oil of the urban economy. An effective labor system was as important to urban growth as commerce was. In fact, the extent of growth and, hence, sectional equality depended upon the sufficiency and reliability of the urban labor force.

2

Civic activists were aware of the centrality of labor to their plans for growth and prosperity. One railroad promoter confided to a friend that "a laboring population is indispensable to the development of the resources of Virginia. Production and wealth are dependent upon it." A Richmond editor went even further: "labor . . . is the foundation of all national greatness."[50] Accordingly, urban businessmen attempted to accommodate the urban labor system to the exigencies of growth. Labor accommodation sprang not so much from conscious, organized, policy making as from a groping attempt by individual entrepreneurs to solve a chronic labor short-

50. John Coles Rutherfoord Diary (MS in Virginia Historical Society), November 20, 1857; Richmond *Whig*, April 27, 1858.

age. Once they discovered the solution, they attempted to codify and rationalize it, just as they had done with commerce.

The labor shortage that confronted urban Virginia complicated plans for urban growth and prosperity. The deficiency resulted from two features of the state's economy: one new, the other old. First, the projects of the new era from railroads to factories made strapping demands on Virginia's labor supply. Second, the return of cotton prosperity to the Deep South revived a lucrative domestic slave trade for Virginia that removed considerable numbers of able-bodied workers from the labor pool. Since labor was a finite resource, urban leaders would have to secure the maximum efficiency out of a relatively small labor force.

Progress on internal improvements and in manufacturing enterprises depended upon a continuous labor supply. As the James River and Kanawha Canal Company expanded its works from the construction of wharves in Richmond to the completion of the canal to Covington, labor requirements tripled.[51] The insatiable desire of railroad companies for labor led some foremen to impress slaves without their masters' consent. Yet, as one executive explained, without such measures construction could be delayed for as much as a year.[52] The permanent maintenance and operating crews of railroads, exclusive of construction gangs, consisted of 300 men.[53] Burgeoning urban industries such as Richmond's Tredegar and Belle Isle foundries required hundreds of operatives to keep up with the orders from their growing network of customers.[54] Major tobacco factories in Richmond and Lynchburg required a work force of at least 150 laborers.[55] Companies, local governments, and individuals crowded the columns of the urban press advertising for labor in the early 1850s. A half-decade earlier,

51. 40 BPW 1857–58, "Report of the James River and Kanawha Company," 1857, n.p.

52. Virginia, House of Delegates, *Journal of the House of Delegates, 1850–51* (Richmond, 1850), 84; 38 BPW 1853–54, "Report of the Virginia and Tennessee Railroad Company," 579–80.

53. 41 BPW 1859–60, "Report of the Virginia Central Railroad Company," 144.

54. "Forge Wages to Negro a/c" (MS in Tredegar Journals, Virginia State Library), 1850, 1852; Richmond *Daily Dispatch*, September 14, 1859, and February 9, 1860.

55. Robert, *Tobacco Kingdom*, 198.

newspapers had barely filled a column with such announcements.[56] Without labor, the cadence of the hammer, the whir of the machine, and the groan of drays, docks, and loading platforms under the weight of western commerce would be stilled.

The prodigious need of urban Virginia for labor arose at a time when the domestic slave trade snatched thousands of slaves to the cotton South. The trade had begun in post-Revolutionary days when Virginia's cities were decaying, and when injudicious cultivation transformed Tidewater farmland to parchment. Simultaneously, the lower South burst into a cotton bonanza requiring immediate infusions of labor.[57] The business was profitable. British traveler James F. W. Johnston, figuring on an exodus of 15,000 slaves in 1850, calculated that Virginians received at least $4,500,000 from the traffic—more than income from the sale of cotton and tobacco combined. Johnston used the very conservative estimate of $300 for the value of a prime field hand in his calculations.[58]

Urban and rural Virginians shared in the profits of the domestic slave trade, so it enjoyed broad support. Richmond and Alexandria were important slave markets, much like New Orleans and Natchez in the cotton South.[59] Extensive slave traders such as Pulliam & Slade and the Omohundro brothers made Richmond the center of the traffic. By 1860 the Omohundros were paying Virginia farmers $1,500 for a prime field hand and managing a $100 profit on every sale of such a slave to the Gulf states.[60] As transportation links between the capital and the hinterland improved, rural buyers and sellers from as far as southwest Virginia sent agents or went themselves to Richmond to buy and to sell slaves.[61]

56. See, for example, Richmond *Daily Dispatch*, January 3, 1853; Richmond *Enquirer*, January 4, 1850, and January 15, 1851.
57. See Harold D. Woodman (ed.), *Slavery and the Southern Economy: Sources and Readings* (New York, 1966), 4–8.
58. James F. W. Johnston, *Notes on North America; Agricultural, Economical and Social* (2 vols.; Boston, 1851), II, 356.
59. See Frederic Bancroft, *Slave-Trading in the Old South* (Baltimore, 1931), 96.
60. Silas and R. F. Omohundro Accounts, 1857–63 (MS in Omohundro Brothers Papers, Alderman Library, University of Virginia), January 3–April 27, 1860.
61. Pulliam & Slade, "Bill of Sale" (MS in Harris-Brady Papers, Alderman Library, University of Virginia), February 7, 1850.

With greater profits, the trade increased during the 1850s. By mid-decade approximately 20,000 slaves were leaving the Old Dominion annually through the domestic slave trade.[62] One estimate claimed that Richmond's handle in the traffic doubled between 1847 and 1857.[63] An anomalous situation seemed to be developing. Just as urban Virginia's labor needs increased, the domestic slave trade extracted more slaves than ever before. It remained to be seen whether this ambivalence could be resolved.

In the meantime, the domestic trade depleted the labor supply at an alarming rate. "Every slave that is sold to go out of the State," warned the Norfolk *Southern Argus,* "diminishes the amount of production in the State." The concern was not peculiarly urban. As agricultural prosperity returned to Virginia, farmers wondered about their sources of labor as well. Hill Carter, a tobacco planter, lamented that the domestic slave trade "has taken off both our wealth and population, and retarded the improvement of Virginia."[64] The prospects for the future labor supply were dimmer still, even if the interstate traffic ceased immediately. By 1859, the annual loss of slaves to the Deep South exceeded the natural increase of slaves.[65] Though there were more slaves in Virginia in 1860 than in 1850, the rate of increase during the decade was the smallest since 1790. More important, there was a decided imbalance in the distribution of age. In the 1850s there were fewer young slaves (under ten years of age) and more older slaves (over fifty years of age) than at any time in Virginia since 1820. Though Virginia possessed 73,000 more slaves than Mississippi in 1860, the Old Dominion had 2,000 fewer slaves in the twenty-to-thirty-year-old age category and nearly 20,000 more in the over-fifty age group.[66] Thus, Virginia's slave population would be increasingly less able to provide productive labor.

62. Norfolk *Southern Argus*, April 27, 1857.
63. Maury Bros. to Samuel Mordecai, May 4, 1857, in Mordecai Family Papers, Southern Historical Collection, University of North Carolina.
64. Norfolk *Southern Argus*, April 27, 1857; Hill Carter, "Address Delivered before the Virginia Central Agricultural Society," *Southern Planter,* XX (1860), 272.
65. Edmund Ruffin, "The Effects of High Prices of Slaves," *Southern Planter,* XIX (1859), 472–77.
66. Bureau of Census, *Eighth Census: 1860 Population*, I 268–69, 512–13.

The labor demands of urban growth projects combined with the domestic slave trade to produce a severe labor shortage in Virginia. "Labor is daily becoming more scarce amongst us," the Norfolk *Southern Argus* charged, "and if this drain is to continue, our State will suffer serious inconvenience in commanding the means necessary to carry on the various schemes of public and private enterprise." On another occasion, the *Argus* pleaded, "We need all the labor we now have and more." The situation was much the same in Alexandria: "Laborers are very scarce and in much demand here." Farmers also complained about labor shortages and the necessity to curtail production (which in turn curtailed shipments to the market center). Edmund Ruffin, the state's leading advocate of market-oriented, scientific agriculture, lamented the "general *home want* for labor." The Richmond *Whig* summarized the situation in the Old Dominion: "The cry of a scarcity of labor is heard on all sides."[67]

Scarcity helped to send the price of labor skyrocketing. Inflation proved burdensome on farmers and industrialists who desired to expand their operations; on modest urban merchants who could not afford a capital outlay of more than $1,000; and on internal improvement contractors whose labor bills threatened to erode dividends, profits, and even solvency. In the 1840s it was possible to buy a young adult male slave for $500 to $600. In the early 1850s slave prices rose slightly to $700 to $800. By 1860, $1,500 was a common figure for a healthy young adult male—the type of slave whom most prospective buyers desired. The price boost for slaves far outstripped the slight inflationary trend of prices throughout the Virginia economy during the 1850s.[68] Even if an individual could afford to purchase a slave at these inflated prices, few slaves

67. Norfolk *Southern Argus*, November 9, 1853; Norfolk *Southern Argus*, April 27, 1857; Alexandria *Gazette*, March 25, 1853; Ruffin, "High Prices of Slaves," 474; Richmond *Whig*, April 22, 1858.

68. Pulliam & Slade to James Brady, June 23, 1846, October 30, 1850, in Harris-Brady Papers; Omohundro Accounts, 1857–63, in Omohundro Brothers Papers. The consumer price index remained relatively stable throughout the 1850s. See U.S. Bureau of Census, *Historical Statistics of the United States: Colonial Times to 1957* (Washington, D.C., 1960), 127.

could be found anyway. Charles W. Dabney probably exaggerated when he noted in 1851 that "the supply of slaves for sale is totally exhausted," but it probably seemed that way to labor-starved Virginians.[69] Wages for nonslave labor spiraled upward as well. Urban wages consistently exceeded the nonfarm average wages in the 1850s. As early as 1848, urban mechanics earned $1 a day, whereas laborers throughout the nation did not attain that figure until 1860.[70]

The nature of employment in a modern city compounded the labor shortage. There were relatively few workers in the urban South who were familiar with factory routine, the workings of machinery, and the processes of production. Even so-called unskilled labor had to adapt to more disciplined working conditions and to new labor techniques and tools. One of the earliest attempts of urban Virginians to ameliorate the labor shortage was focused, therefore, on training their young white male population. Through vocational education, these youngsters would become familiar with contemporary factory life and the use of machinery. In 1851, a need was expressed in Norfolk for a manual labor school for indigent boys. Three years later a group of Norfolk business leaders organized such a school. The trade-school concept had the additional advantage of social control. No longer, the *Argus* predicted, would these children "run wild through our streets." There is no evidence that the school ever attained a substantial enrollment. The Virginia Mechanics Institute in Richmond, however, enjoyed a statewide reputation and carried on a wide variety of activities as a vocational institution. The institute, formed in 1853, held an annual fair that exhibited student projects. The institute's night school was a unique feature educating over 160 adults in the rudiments of mechanical arts. Richmond's donation of a lot and building worth $20,000 to place the institute in new quarters for the 1857 academic year testified to the school's success in rendering

69. Charles W. Dabney to Robert L. Dabney, August 22, 1851, in Dabney Papers.
70. Stanley Lebergott, "Wage Trends, 1800–1900" *Trends in the American Economy in the Nineteenth Century* (Princeton, 1960), 462–63.

white boys "useful citizens in times to come."[71] Similar educational facilities existed in Alexandria, Lynchburg, and Wheeling.

Trade schools were investments in the future; contemporary labor requirements demanded a more immediate response. Urban Virginians studied northern cities assiduously. One conclusion they reached was that northern labor was underclothed, underfed, and unappreciated. Virginia, on the other hand, had secure employment and abundant, cheap land for the prospective northern refugee.[72] As to the danger of courting the enemy in such a flagrant manner, one urban editor reprimanded doubters, "We cannot but think that many of our people are quite too sensitive on the subject of Southern institutions."[73] Virginians believed that the state's economic prosperity would secure and maintain all of her institutions, and labor was essential to that prosperity.

Several urban Virginians established an agency in New York to relate the benefits of the Old Dominion to potential emigrés, and they placed advertisements in several widely read journals.[74] There was a small influx of northern farmers in the Northern Neck and lower Valley regions of Virginia in the 1850s, as well as the celebrated pilgrimage of abolitionist Eli Thayer later in the decade. Their number, however, could not have been enough to engage idle lands or to release a significant number of slaves for use in other sections of the economy. The trickle of northerners into Virginia's cities provided some necessary technical, mechanical, and even journalistic skills but could hardly be called a laboring class.[75] Urban entrepreneurs pressed on for other, more realistic solutions to the labor problem.

Urban journals observed the good habits of foreign immigrants periodically and recommended Virginia as an appropriate place for their settlement. Though there was no organized effort to

71. Norfolk *Southern Argus*, June 17, 1851, and June 28, 1854; Richmond *Daily Dispatch*, February 6, 1857, and January 7, 1859.
72. Lynchburg *Virginian*, June 20, 1850; Richmond *Enquirer*, February 5, 1856; "Cheap Virginia Lands," *American Agriculturist*, X (1851), 192.
73. Norfolk *Southern Argus*, April 22, 1857.
74. "Northern Agency for the Sale of Land," *Southern Planter*, X (1950), 17–19.
75. Gray, *History of Agriculture*, II, 919; See Fletcher Green, *The Role of the Yankee in the Old South* (Athens, Ga., 1972).

attract Europeans, foreigners, especially German and Irish, provided an increasing number of urban services by 1860. They taught, performed domestic work, engaged in tailoring, built railroads, and toiled in factories.[76] A Richmond writer, recommending European immigration to bolster the city's strained labor supply, termed such an influx "the greatest benefactor of the human family." Richmond was proud of its foreign-born population and noticed and applauded the arrival of immigrants.[77] Foreigners accounted for more than one-quarter of the white male householders in the capital city. In the Richmond free-labor force, immigrants comprised 65% of the laborers and 47% of the craftsmen.[78] For other Virginia cities, however, foreigners were a distinct minority in both the population and the work force. Besides, employers in enterprises such as railroad construction and tobacco manufacturing preferred other types of labor.

The white urban woman entered the labor force in appreciable numbers for the first time in the 1850s. James Thomas, Jr., Richmond's largest tobacco manufacturer and a prominent civic booster, probably began the trend in the middle of the decade. He employed white women in the preparation of chewing tobacco for the presses—an operation which blacks had performed previously. The practice spread to other factories in Richmond and Petersburg. A proprietor in the latter city erected a dormitory similar to buildings in Lowell, Massachusetts, for his women operatives. Reports from travelers and factory owners indicated that the women provided efficient and competent labor.[79]

Other Virginia cities found work for willing young women as well. The Mount Vernon Cotton Factory in Alexandria employed 150 "industrious females," paying wages ranging from $12 to $17 a month. The latter figure was just slightly below the national average (which included wages for male labor) for such work. The Alexandria *Gazette* claimed that the production per hand at the

76. See Eighth Census of Virginia: 1860. Free Inhabitants, I, XII, XIX.
77. Richmond *Daily Dispatch*, February 5, 1856; Richmond *Enquirer*, October 17, 1856.
78. Herbert G. Gutman, "The World Two Cliometricians Made: A Review Essay of F + E = T/C," *Journal of Negro History*, LX (1975), 101.
79. "White Girls in Tobacco Factories," *Hunt's*, XL (1859), 522–23.

cotton factory surpassed that of Lowell. In Norfolk, merchants employed women in their counting rooms, to the satisfaction of both. The *Argus* was so enthusiastic about female labor that it recommended women workers to all employers. Not only would this help to alleviate the labor shortage to some degree, but it would also cure one of the city's major ills—prostitution.[80] The Civil War intervened before an empirical study could confirm the *Argus's* logic. Women successfully provided labor in a number of occupations, albeit mostly menial, during the decade before Sumter. In 1860, the employment of white women in urban Virginia had ceased to be a novelty, but it was by no means widespread. The vast majority of working women were still seamstresses and domestics.[81] For heavier labor tasks on railroads and in city streets and factories, American society was unprepared for white women workers. The great contribution of female labor on southern textile mills would not occur until the era of the New South.

Convict lease, another ubiquitous though considerably more infamous labor system of the New South, similarly had roots as an alternative form of labor in antebellum urban Virginia. The labor system was an example of the resourcefulness of labor-starved entrepreneurs. The first appearance of convict lease occurred during the depression winter of 1857–58. The legislature authorized convict lease as an alternative punishment to sale and transportation beyond the state for convicted slave felons. Governor John Letcher, in his annual message in December 1859, related that in less than two years of operation, the state had received a flurry of bids from internal improvement contractors and had leased hundreds of black convicts for an average of $175 per hire while turning the penitentiary into a profit-making institution. The governor, seeing an opportunity to enhance the sagging state treasury as well as to bolster the labor supply, successfully urged the legislature to extend the provisions of the law to white felons as well. By 1860 the convict lease system had become an accepted

80. Alexandria *Gazette*, May 6, 1852, and March 2, 1854; Norfolk *Southern Argus*, March 17, 1854, October 28, 1859.
81. See Eighth Census of Virginia: 1860. Free Inhabitants I, XII, XIX.

penal solution to a labor problem.[82] It came too late, however, to assess its impact on the labor supply of the state.

The free black population represented a growing and virtually untapped labor source. Free blacks increased at a faster rate than the slave population (7% to 4%) in the 1850s.[83] The proverbial wretchedness of the free black, North and South, attested to the attitude of society toward him.[84] Urban businessmen shared the general abhorrence of Virginia society for the free black. The exigencies of the labor crisis in urban Virginia, however, resulted in grudging acceptance of and even enthusiasm for the free blacks' presence in the labor market.

Free blacks were an anomaly in southern society. They were relegated to a sort of racial purgatory between free white and black slave; yet they were much closer to the latter. Especially since the Nat Turner uprising in 1831, southerners viewed free blacks as dangerous to the security of their society. With the explosion of the sectional crisis following the Mexican War, southern animus toward free blacks reached a new ferocity. At the same time, massive immigration and civil disturbance in the North were depressing the condition of northern urban blacks.[85] Virginia's response was twofold: to press for the ultimate removal of the free black population from Virginia and to enact legislation bringing free blacks closer in status to their slave brethren. The first response failed and the second achieved fruition only to be selectively ignored by urban Virginians. In both cases the influence of the labor shortage loomed large.

82. House of Delegates, "Governor's Message to the General Assembly, December 13, 1859," *House of Delegates, 1859–60*, Document Number 1, 44; "Governor's Message to the General Assembly, January 7, 1861," *House of Delegates, 1861*, Document Number 1, xxxiv; "Communication from the Governor of the State Relative to Reprieves and Pardons," *House of Delegates, 1861*, Document Number 3, 5–6.
83. Bureau of Census, *Seventh Census: 1850*, 256–57; *Eighth Census: 1860. Population*, I, 516–18.
84. See Luther P. Jackson, *Free Negro Labor and Property Holding in Virginia, 1830–1860* (New York, 1942); and Leon F. Litwack, *North of Slavery: The Negroes in the Free States, 1790–1860* (Chicago, 1961).
85. See David M. Katzman, *Before the Ghetto: Black Detroit in the Nineteenth Century* (Urbana, Ill., 1973), 44, 47, 121–22, and Donnie D. Bellamy, "Free Blacks in Antebellum Missouri, 1820–1860," *Missouri Historical Review*, LXVII (1973), 198–225.

Virginians agitating for removal of free blacks focused attention on the nuisance and danger of that class to the larger society. Some legislators depicted free blacks as a profligate, base, and conniving group.[86] Although opponents to removal of free blacks often mentioned humanitarian reasons, they stressed the benefit of the class to Virginia's economy. A Wheeling journal reasoned, "Remove free negroes and the State comes down one more peg in the down hill progress which she has made for the last half-century." The Charlottesville *Advocate* agreed, adding that "Virginia cannot afford to lose any portion of her laboring population." "They are not a bad class," pleaded a Richmond editor, "their labor is needed."[87] The defense of free blacks was not strictly an urban one. Tidewater farmers in particular depended on free black farm hands and fought their removal. Indeed, to remove 53,000 people from the Old Dominion at a time when a scarcity of labor threatened to stall urban growth and sectional harmony would "produce great inconvenience."[88] The opponents to the removal of free blacks in the cities and countryside were successful with their arguments.

The fear of labor depletion also proved effective to curtail what little freedom free blacks possessed. The aim of proponents of such laws was to extend the same control over the free blacks that existed over slaves. Just as the Black Codes following the Civil War were an attempt, in one sense, to control labor and to ensure stability in the labor force, so, too, laws restricting free black mobility in antebellum Virginia relieved the tight labor situation to some degree. George Fitzhugh's answer in "What Shall be Done with the Free Negroes?" was the introduction of peonage, which was exactly the New South's solution. Fitzhugh based his plan on the unreliability and high mobility of free black labor. He recommended slave labor because, among other reasons, such labor was relatively easy to control. In *Sociology for the South,* Fitzhugh repeated the theme of

86. Virginia House of Delegates, *House Journal, 1850–51* (Richmond, 1851), 41, 54; *House Journal, 1853–54* (Richmond, 1854), 55, 83, 132, 216.

87. Wheeling *Daily Intelligencer,* February 16, 1858; Charlottesville *Advocate,* quoted in Wheeling *Daily Intelligencer,* February 16, 1858; Richmond *Daily Dispatch,* February 14, 1853.

88. Speech of Edwin Mapp in House of Delegates, quoted in Richmond *Whig,* March 22, 1853; Ira Berlin, *Slaves without Masters: The Free Negro in the Antebellum South* (New York, 1974), 238.

the necessity for a controlled labor force: "No association, no efficient combination of labor can be effected till men give up their liberty of action and subject themselves to a common despotic head or ruler. This is slavery."[89]

The selective enforcement of antebellum free black laws suggested that labor control was a primary motivation in Virginia. For example, urban authorities rigorously applied the law providing for forced labor as punishment for misdemeanors. By mid-decade the chain gang, formed primarily of free blacks, was a common appearance on city streets in Virginia. The gang performed such valuable tasks as street repairing, bridge building, and wharf maintenance.[90] On the other hand, Lynchburg tobacco factory owners ignored the free black curfew law with impunity and without remonstrance.[91] Further, laws requiring employers of black help to ascertain positively the status of their hands, whether they were slave or free, were openly violated with approval from the press. The Norfolk *Southern Argus* warned that "full enforcement of such a law will act seriously detrimental to the thriving prospects of our city." There is no evidence that the authorities ever hauled in an employer who was in violation of these laws.[92] Finally, all Virginia cities systematically ignored state law requiring manumitted slaves to leave the Old Dominion within the first twelve months of their freedom.[93]

Aversion to free blacks modified considerably as their labor proved valuable. Skilled free blacks in Richmond, for example, functioned as barbers, carpenters, plasterers, blacksmiths, bricklayers, and shoemakers. Though whites prevented freedmen from advancing much beyond these occupations, the contribution of free black labor to a growing city was important.[94] Advertise-

89. George Fitzhugh, "What Shall be Done with the Free Negroes," in *Sociology*, 259–91; Fitzhugh, *Sociology*, 61.
90. Lynchburg *Virginian*, February 23, 1853; Richmond *Daily Dispatch*, January 23, 1857; Wheeling *Daily Intelligencer*, March 25, 1858.
91. Lynchburg *Virginian*, April 29, 1852.
92. Norfolk *Southern Argus*, July 25, 1853. See also Richmond *Daily Dispatch*, July 13, 1860.
93. Berlin, *Slaves without Masters*, 147.
94. *Ibid.*, 238.

ments for labor often called for black and white applicants even though white laborers were opposed to integrated employment.[95] Testimonials from urban and rural employers depicted the free black as quite the opposite of the shiftless individual his detractors portrayed him to be. An official of the Covington and Ohio Railroad preferred hiring free blacks rather than white laborers because the former were "more docile, less expensive, and less prone to riot." The Lynchburg *Virginian* depicted the free black as "industrious," "quiet," and "better and more tractable in their menial capacities than the correlative class (white or colored) in any nonslaveholding state in the Union."[96]

Still, Virginians possessed an ambivalent attitude toward free blacks. Labor necessities aside, it was not a work force that could be counted on as permanent. The North's economic supremacy in the context of sectional animosity understandably made Virginians protective of their primary labor system—slavery. Northern and European immigrants, white female labor, convict lease, the chain gang, and free black labor contributed some relief to the chronic labor shortage. None of these labor systems, however, provided the flexibility, mobility, efficiency, and profitability that the institution of slavery did. Virginia's urban entrepreneurs not only would discover all of these attributes in the institution, they would give to slavery a new vigor.

Urban businessmen, together with rural partners, adapted slave labor to urban growth and economic expansion. Slave hiring was the system that effected the transformation of slavery to a profitable urban institution. The system strengthened the urban economy, the institution of slavery, and the sometimes wobbly bond of trust between urban and rural Virginians.

Slave hiring was not a new labor system. Virginians had begun hiring slaves in the colonial period in a variety of employment ranging from agricultural labor to skilled positions in iron foundries.[97] Although there were numerous complaints about both the

95. Richmond *Daily Dispatch*, August 19, 1853.
96. 39 BPW 1855, cxx; Lynchburg *Virginian*, February 23, 1853.
97. See S. Sydney Bradford, "The Negro Ironworker in Antebellum Virginia," *Journal of Southern History*, XXV (1959), 194–206.

treatment of slaves and the dangers of allowing a slave to hire his own time and accept wages, the system persisted throughout the antebellum period. Following the Mexican War, however, slave hiring became a pervasive and profitable institution at a magnitude not approached by earlier versions of the system. The major impetus was the employment opportunity in Virginia's cities generated by the projects and activities related to the new era.

The attraction of slave hiring to entrepreneurs was its flexibility. For a growing commercial or industrial concern, slave hiring had the advantage of obviating a substantial investment in a labor force. Considering the price of slaves in the 1850s, slave hiring involved an important saving. As British traveler Robert Russell observed, "were they [the hired slaves] to be bought it would require too much capital to carry on business."[98] Slave hiring also had the advantage of establishing a temporary relationship. The system proved efficacious for the completion of internal improvement projects which typically experienced heavy and slack periods of construction and maintenance and for farmers who found hiring a large work force or even a few extra hands to be necessary only around harvest time. Parties to hiring bonds could frame them from one day to one year.[99]

The attributes of slave hiring resulted in its widespread utilization following the Mexican War. Advertisements of companies seeking to employ slaves proliferated, while they had hardly existed before 1847.[100] During the 1850s, Virginia tobacco manufacturers hired 164% more blacks than they had in the previous decade, leading Robert Russell to conclude after a tour of Richmond factories that "all" operatives were hired slaves. The iron industry also practiced slave hiring extensively. Richmond's Tredegar Iron Works shifted to employing rather than purchasing its work force in the 1850s. Internal improvement contractors hired slaves almost exclusively. Between 1854 and 1856 the James

98. Robert Russell, *North America: Its Agriculture and Climate* (Edinburgh, 1857), 152.
99. Charles W. Dabney to Robert L. Dabney, January 8, 1846, Dabney Papers; E. Meldahl, "Letter for the *American Agriculturist*," *American Agriculturist*, XIII (1854), 345.
100. Advertisements in Richmond *Daily Dispatch*, January 1, 1853; Richmond *Enquirer*, January 1, 1835, January 2, 1840, and December 31, 1852.

River and Kanawha Company employed over 300 slaves as masons, quarrymen, carpenters, laborers, and even put them on patrols. In 1860 the Virginia Central Railroad employed nearly 300 black laborers on their road. Though the company gave most slaves menial tasks, the railroad relied on slave labor for the relatively skilled jobs of firemen, brakemen, and boilermakers.[101]

There seemed few tasks that could not benefit from the work of a hired slave. Newspaper advertisements represented a catalog of urban employment: waitresses, cooks, washers, cotton factory operatives, miners, smiths, draymen, and wharf personnel in addition to the occupations I mentioned earlier.[102] Moreover, employers ranged from struggling young businessmen without property or means to railroad presidents. Free blacks hired slaves as well.[103] Slave hiring thus adapted well to both situation and employer.

The sources of slaves for the system were varied and included widows, merchants, estates, and farmers.[104] In the 1850s, however, large-scale suppliers emerged to provide specifically for the urban labor market. These suppliers were typically wealthy planters. Some farmers pooled their labor resources and formed consortiums to supply slaves to urban clients. A group of four farmers in Piedmont Bedford County rented over forty slaves to Lynchburg clients. Similar enterprises, usually family oriented, existed in country districts outside of Lynchburg.[105]

The appearance of middlemen, or agents, was another rationalizing characteristic of urban slave hiring in the 1850s. Prior to the Mexican War such services were rare. Edward N. Dabney, for example, boasted in 1858 that he had been a slave-hiring agent

101. Russell, *North America*, 152. See Robert, *Tobacco Kingdom*, 198; "Forge Wages to Negro a/c," 1850, 1852. See also Buffalo Forge Journal (MS in Weaver-Brady Iron Works and Grist Mill Papers, Alderman Library, University of Virginia), January 13, 1829, and December 31, 1860; 40 BPW 1857–58, "Report of the James River and Kanawha Company," n.p.; 41 BPW 1859–60, "Report of the Virginia Central Railroad Company," 144.
102. Richmond *Daily Dispatch*, January 1, 1853, January 1, 1854, and January 3, 1855.
103. Eighth Census of Virginia: 1860. Slave Schedule, I, IV, V.
104. "Hires of Barbara W. Pettus' Negroes, 1830," Charles W. Dabney to Robert L. Dabney, July 27, 1832, in Dabney Papers; Hiring Bonds, 1843–49 (MS in Tazewell Family Papers, Virginia State Library).
105. Eighth Census of Virginia: 1860. Slave Schedule, I, 244, 322, 326, 327, 328.

for twelve years, one of the oldest in Richmond.[106] The increasing volume of slaves for hire, the inability of many suppliers to make the trip to the city or to remain there to seek employment for their slaves, and the dangers inherent in allowing a slave to roam the city looking for a situation on his own all prompted the development of agencies. Some agents were commission merchants who not only handled their rural clients' produce but their slaves as well. Other agents were slave traders or brokers who added slave hiring as a specialty.[107] By 1860, 52% of the slaves hired in Richmond were hired through an agency. Rent-a-slave services existed in Lynchburg and Norfolk as well.[108] Once again, the arrangement proved equally profitable for urban and rural participants. The agent received his 2½% commission and sought the highest rate of hire for his client.

The pervasive use of the slave hiring system in urban Virginia resulted more from the need for labor than from approbation over the social value of the system. Neither urban nor rural Virginians were satisfied with the system and its effects on the slave. That the system remained virtually unchanged despite grave reservations testified to the general desire for urban growth and economic prosperity. Urbanization generated new, creative roles for slavery.

Although historians continue to disagree whether slave hiring represented a "step toward freedom," or a step backward toward brutality and neglect, scholars and Virginians agreed that urban slave hiring altered the institution of slavery.[109] Free-lancing by slaves in the cities contributed to criticism of the slave-hiring system. Hired slaves, some complained, were without benefit of the master-slave relationship and "its controlling and ameliorating influences." Slaves, some charged, were actually "stipulating their

106. Richmond *Daily Dispatch*, January 1, 1858.
107. N. B. Hill to Mr. Atkinson, February 7, 1855, in James Southgate Papers, Duke University; R. Lewis to A. G. Grinnan, December 29, 1860, in Grinnan Family Papers, Alderman Library, University of Virginia; advertisements in Richmond *Daily Dispatch*, January 1, 1853.
108. Eighth Census of Virginia: 1860. Slave Schedule, IV, II, V.
109. See Starobin, *Industrial Slavery in the Old South*, 128–37; Wade, *Slavery in the Cities*, 38–54; Dew, "Disciplining Slave Ironworkers," 393–418; and Eaton, "Slave Hiring in the Upper South," 663–78.

rights" before entering into a contract with their prospective employer. Essentially, some alleged, the system allowed the slave to "choose his master," and he would select a master who "will grant him the largest license." Bribery or extortion often accompanied the selection process. Moreover, contrary to existing ordinances, slaves found lodging on their own. Their accommodations were usually among the city's free black population, thus effecting a dangerous connection in the view of some Virginians. The upshot of these deviations was to render the slave "insubordinate and vicious" and result in a general "deterioration in morals, in habits, and in health." As one irate farmer near Norfolk stormed, "The hirer may neglect, at his pleasure, to exercise the restraining power with which the master has parted for the year, and yet according to Norfolk law . . . compel the master to pay the penalty of his own neglect of duty."[110]

The solicitude over the hired slave's health was a legitimate concern for masters. The careful wording of hiring bonds in the 1850s indicated indirectly the neglect of the past. Hirers and agents promised to provide "medical attention . . . during sickness and to take every precaution against accidents." A Richmond agent assured a concerned master that his slaves "will be employed in a healthy company, well fed and clothed, and moderately, but regularly worked; and returned at the end of the year."[111] The latter provision for returning the slave to the master was not so obvious as it seemed. The opportunities for escape proved abundant in an urban setting, and legal wrangles constantly embroiled master and hirer.[112] There is evidence that, despite the hiring bond, a few employers balked at paying medical expenses for hired slaves who had been injured or taken ill while under their employ.[113]

110. Richmond *Daily Dispatch*, April 15, 1859; Norfolk *Southern Argus*, November 23, 1858; "Hiring Negroes," *Southern Planter*, XII (1852), 376; Richmond *Whig*, August 27, 1852; Norfolk *Southern Argus*, September 26, 1849; Norfolk *Southern Argus*, November 23, 1858; letter from "A Slave Holder," Norfolk *Southern Argus*, June 7, 1851.

111. Richmond *Daily Dispatch*, January 1, 1854; Henry L. Brooke to John Randolph Tucker, November 29, 1851, in John Randolph Tucker Family Papers, Southern Historical Collection, University of North Carolina.

112. "Hiring Negroes," 376–77.

113. See Hiring Bond, February 7, 1853 (MS in John H. Thomas & Co. Papers, Virginia

The most universal complaint concerning the slave-hiring system centered on the rapid inflation of hiring rates. Considering the labor shortage and the popularity of the hiring system, the high price for hired slave labor was not surprising, but it was aggravating and expensive. The average rate of hire for a prime unskilled male increased from $85 to $175 per year during the fifteen years prior to secession. Skilled laborers commanded $225 or more.[114] Some suggested that, after the fashion of the exchanges, agents had banded together to fix rates of hire, or, worse, that slaves were extorting a portion of the hiring fee in return for their work.[115] The inflated prices for hired slaves prompted some enterprising individuals to purchase slaves for the express purpose of hiring them out.[116]

Virginians, in vain, sought remedies to the alleged abuses and climbing hiring rates of the system. A Norfolk resident suggested lengthening the hiring period from one year to several years. He believed that the extended relationship would have salutary affects on the discipline of both slave and employer. Others recommended city ordinances to prohibit a slave from hiring his own time, thus eliminating a major abuse of the system. Some urged that the master should take a more active and personal interest in the slave-hiring procedure. There were a few suggestions that wages and bonuses should be prohibited by law. Finally, there were numerous opinions on the accountability of master and hirer.[117] All of these suggestions had one feature in common: no city or legislature imposed restrictive measures on the slave-hiring system. A Norfolk ordinance, passed in 1858, in fact codified the practice of a slave hiring his own time, with the only requirement being that

Historical Society); Hiring Bond, September 6, 1847 (MS in Watlington Family Papers, Virginia State Library). See also Bradford, "The Negro Ironworker," 204–06.

114. John N. Tazewell Financial Records, 1846–1860 (MS in Tazewell Family Papers); Buffalo Forge Journal, December 31, 1859; Tredegar Pay Rolls, 1858–60 (MS in Virginia State Library); Richmond *Enquirer*, January 12, 1855; Richmond *Whig*, January 20, 1857.

115. Henry A. McCormick to William Weaver, December 29, 1855, in Weaver-Brady Papers; Richmond *Daily Dispatch*, April 15, 1859.

116. Richmond *Daily Dispatch*, January 10, 1859.

117. Norfolk *Southern Argus*, November 23, 1858; Richmond *Daily Dispatch*, April 15, 1859; Norfolk *Southern Argus*, September 26, 1849; Richmond *Whig*, August 27, 1852; House of Delegates, *House Journal, 1850–51*, 88; "Hiring Negroes," 376–77.

he obtain a license. The law not only ensured a freer flow of the labor supply but increased the city treasury as well.[118]

Slave hiring as an important feature of the urban economy was too important to urban growth and economic prosperity to modify. By 1860 the system was functioning smoothly with agents speeding and rationalizing transactions and suppliers making their operations more efficient as well. It was becoming a big business, not as large as the domestic slave trade, but lucrative enough to sustain a moderate labor flow to large-scale mercantile and industrial operations. Slave hiring was more widespread and versatile than immigrant or female labor, more acceptable than free black labor, and less expensive than purchasing a slave work force.

Slave hiring did not solve urban Virginia's labor problems, though the system ameliorated them to some degree. By 1860 urban Virginians, if they were not complaining about hiring rates, complained about the scarcity of slaves for hire. The alleged abuses stemmed in great part from the fierce competition for the available labor. The rising profitability of agriculture in the Deep South assured the continuation of the domestic slave trade. The agricultural revival in Virginia kept urban slave populations either stable or in decline, though recent scholarship has questioned if this, in fact, indicated a competitive advantage in favor of agriculture. Apparently the slave labor force was undergoing a sifting process as it accommodated itself to urban growth. The unskilled slaves, who were greater in number than the skilled slaves, were remaining on farms, returning to farms from the city, or becoming a part of the domestic slave trade. Urban employers, however, were more successful in bidding for skilled slaves whose labor was particularly valuable for urban growth.[119]

While city dwellers traded slave-labor skills with the countryside, the domestic slave trade continued to compete successfully with all segments of the slave labor supply. Agriculture in the Deep South, one of the most profitable investments in the country, enabled

118. Norfolk *Southern Argus*, August 14, 1858.
119. Claudia D. Goldin, "Urbanization and Slavery: The Issue of Compatibility," in Leo F. Schnore (ed.), *The New Urban History: Quantitative Explorations by American Historians* (Princeton, 1975), 231–46.

planters to outbid Virginians for labor. "As sure as water seeks its level," one planter observed while discussing the labor situation, "so certainly will labor seek its best returns, and money its highest profits."[120] Though slave hiring proved financially rewarding to urban and rural participants, the domestic slave trade was still more attractive.

Slave hiring underscored the versatility and flexibility of the slave and of slavery in a modern urban setting. George Fitzhugh, Virginia's leading proslavery spokesman, perceived the value of slavery to urban society and urged slave labor in factories, internal improvements, and other urban-related enterprises. By the end of the 1850s, urban residents employed slaves in a variety of occupations. The only difficulty connected with urban slave labor was its insufficient supply. Slavery, rather than being an albatross to progress, was an institution that grew more valuable to city dwellers as secession approached. Urban slavery in Virginia, far from weakening the institution, breathed new life into it. Though some Virginians feared that the urban setting debilitated the institution, this feeling was not deep enough to effect a modification of urban slavery. During the sectional crisis, when northern papers attacked slavery daily, any perceived antagonism to the institution's security at home would have provoked a quick and decisive action throughout the state. Since there was no such response, it must be assumed that the benefits of urban slavery to the economy outweighed its dangers to the institution's integrity. If, as a Wheeling journal observed, the survival of slavery was a matter of "dollars and cents," then slavery in Virginia was enjoying robust health.[121]

The amelioration of commercial relationships and the accommodation of labor to the new urban economy represented two significant accomplishments for both urban leaders and their country partners. Commerce and slavery facilitated urban growth and prosperity. While coping with and rationalizing these features of

120. A. A. Campbell, "Capital and Enterprise—the Basis of Agricultural Progress," *Southern Planter*, XX (1860), 36. See also William Calderhead, "How Extensive Was the Boarder State Slave Trade? A New Look," *Civil War History*, XVIII (1972), 55.
121. Fitzhugh, *Sociology*, 87; Wheeling *Daily Intelligencer*, May 28, 1858.

urban society, businessmen developed a sense of their own and their city's identity. Both commerce and slavery presented unique problems to a hopeful urban economy. Entrepreneurs developed solutions and in the process defined their city's needs in relation to the countryside and to other cities. Working together, the city-builders perceived an urban destiny that at once established their cities in the national urban family and reaffirmed their close relationships to the countryside. Even as they worked to erect a new market house or to smooth out the slave hiring relationship, their city grew beyond their capability of dealing with it. Certain features of urban life were becoming too complex and too important for even an energetic coterie of leading merchants, industrialists, and professionals to rationalize.

THE EMERGENCE of local government from the shadows of anonymity was an important indicator of urbanization in mid-nineteenth-century America. Before the era of rapid and sustained urban growth, city governments were ciphers. Mayors possessed few powers beyond that of justice of the peace. City councils met irregularly and passed legislation on important urban issues even more infrequently. Revenues were miniscule, as were expenditures and services. Local government, however, responded vigorously to urban growth, and in turn facilitated the growth process. At a time when organization and association were extending the urban economy, city officialdom became another association concerned with urban destiny. The relationship between business and government organization was not fortuitous. Urban leaders discovered the potential of local government and employed it in two effective ways. First, they viewed government as a catalyst in furthering the economic interests of the city. Second, within the context of sectional conflict and urban rivalry, the resources of government could bestow the attributes of modern urban living to maintain parity with northern cities. In the process of fulfilling these two functions, local government became a central factor in urban growth.

In mid-nineteenth-century urban America, the legislative branch of city government, whether a single council or a council and a board of aldermen, retained the power invested in local government. In Virginia's cities, a mayor and a bicameral legislature shared power. In Norfolk the bicameral system consisted of a select council which the elected "lower house" appointed from their own number. In Alexandria all white adult males elected both houses: an upper house called the board of aldermen and a lower house termed the common council. Bills could originate in both houses, creating a constant and often confusing flow of legislation between the two houses. Wheeling and Petersburg had the same arrangement. Richmond and Lynchburg were exceptions to the bicameral tradition. The capital city had one legislative branch—a city council. All legislative power was vested in that body. It was a large group, composed of eighteen councilmen, or roughly equal to the membership of both houses combined in Norfolk and Alexandria. Lynchburg government was similar with the exception that its council consisted of twelve members—two from each of the six wards.[1]

The mayor, no longer a figurehead, possessed ill-defined powers but could become an inspirational force in urban government, as William Carr Lane, who was mayor of Saint Louis in the 1820s demonstrated. The mayor's role increased from performing judiciary functions presiding over the city court to a more active executive role. By the mid-1850s most urban mayors, including Virginia's, received their offices from the people.[2] They were the only city officials who represented a citywide constituency. Councilmen represented specific wards. By 1852, all six of the designated cities in Virginia had adopted the ward system and elected their councilmen according to these divisions.[3] The ward system developed as a political rationalization of urban growth and tended to diffuse the council's power while the mayor's role increased.

Virginia's cities followed the general trend of direct election of city officers. Democracy, in this case, was a backward step. A growing city meant increased needs and hence a larger bureaucracy. Eventually the ballot became so large that none but the most diligent voter could possibly know the qualifications and positions of all of the individuals running for office. With at least two and in some cases six or seven candidates running for the same office, the ballot must have seemed like a city directory to the voter. The major objective was to maintain sufficient stamina to last until the final

1. Alexandria *Gazette*, January 30, 1853; Norfolk *Southern Argus*, June 26, 1852; Wheeling *Daily Intelligencer*, August 24, 1852. See also Powell, *Old Alexandria*, 161; Lynchburg *Virginian*, April 12, 1852; Richmond *Enquirer*, April 5, 1850; and Horner and Windfree, *Saga of a City*, 118.

2. Wade, *Urban Frontier*, 278; Little, *Richmond*, 292. See also Glaab and Brown, *A History of Urban America*, chap. 7.

3. See Horner and Windfree, *Saga of a City*, 118; Little, *Richmond*; Powell, *Old Alexandria*, 161; and Waring, *Social Statistics of Cities*, 66, 72, 88–89.

name. In Alexandria, for example, the citizens elected the following officers: mayor, aldermen, councilmen, gauger, measurer of wood, measurer of lumber, superintendent of police, superintendent of the gas works, collector of taxes, city attorney, assessors, clerk of the market, auditor, surveyor, and engineers.[4] Further, the annual elections disrupted the continuity of government and created tensions throughout the community. A Richmond city employee observed in 1856 that "we have so much canvassing and electing that one-fourth of our time is devoted to these duties."[5]

Considering the general trend toward efficiency in all aspects of urban life in Virginia in the 1850s, the multiplicity of officers and elections was incongruous. Indeed, after one or two years of the new system, some cities strove to abrogate the suffrage concessions, but the legislature refused to amend their charters accordingly. Richmond's city council devised perhaps the most ingenious scheme for circumventing the electoral procedure. In January 1853, sixteen months after the first experiment with direct elections, the council began appointing city officers with different titles though similar duties to the elected officials. The council proceeded to cut the elected individuals' salaries to a pittance, hoping that no citizens would seek the offices in the coming April elections. The council's motives were undoubtedly selfish in that direct election eroded their patronage power. The elected bureaucracy was also less accountable to the council, thus making it more difficult for council members to enforce directives. The elected officeholders, in effect, formed another branch of government that was virtually autonomous of any other body. The Richmond caper ended quickly, however, as public outcry forced a retraction of the policy. Other cities also wrestled with the dilemma of reconciling democracy with efficiency with similar lack of success.[6] Virginia's urban governments utilized other mechanisms to overcome the instability generated by the electoral system.

4. Alexandria *Gazette*, May 30, 1854. See also, Norfolk *Southern Argus*, June 27, 1856.
5. Quoted in Eaton, *Southern Civilization*, 250.
6. Richmond *Enquirer*, January 15, 1853; Norfolk *American Beacon*, July 28, 1852; Richmond *Whig*, April 4, 1854; and Wheeling *Daily Intelligencer*, December 22, 1853.

Standing committees were the primary vehicles of day-to-day government in urban Virginia. The number of committees increased along with urban growth as citizens channeled their demands into the committees. Turnover on the council was low compared with the rate of change in the elected city bureaucracy. The standing committees were, therefore, as close as a city came to a permanent bureaucracy. In 1853, Alexandria's bicameral city legislature, consisting of the board of aldermen and the common council, included five standing committees in each branch: finance and salaries, streets, lighting, real estate, and public schools. Seven years later the city government had added three new committees: one concerned with claims, another with the poor, and a third with the fire department. Alexandria's committees were the same as those in other Virginia cities, or in any other city for that matter.[7]

The standing committees reflected the concern of city government with urban services. Providing adequate urban services was another method of planning for urban growth. City government played an increasingly active role in this area. As with most other aspects of urban development in Virginia, imitation was important in city government's introduction or expansion of urban services like police and fire protection, water supply, gas lighting, street repairing, charity, and disease control. In providing these services for urban residents, Virginia's city governments sought to duplicate northern systems in order to improve the quality of urban life and enhance the reputation of their city. Equally important, these services were essential to furthering the cities' economic prosperity.

Police protection and crime control were crucial to an orderly city. Crime seemed to accompany urban growth and prosperity. "In the rapid advancement of our city," a Wheeling journal observed, "crime and disorder have kept pace with other progressions." Business leaders viewed crime as disruptive to prosperity. Crime was simply bad business. One disconcerted Wheeling resident observed that it was "not agreeable to the feelings of any

7. Alexandria *Gazette*, January 7, 1853; and March 18, 1860. See Wade, *Urban Frontier*, 273.

person who cherishes city pride, to have it go forth to the world that a condition of things of this character [crime] exists in their midst."[8] The shame of crime was such that the press minimized or excluded mention of the subject from its columns. Any admission appearing in print, therefore, reflected a situation that was considerably worse.

Urban crime consisted mostly of burglary, theft, and assault. Rape and murder were unique enough to arouse more curiosity than wrath. Civic leaders were more concerned about crimes against property, because these were most apt to harm business and create a negative impression abroad. The city-builders' concern stemmed not only from the type of crime, but from its volume and the inability of city authorities to quell the danger to person and possessions. A Lynchburg merchant rejoiced sarcastically in a letter to a friend in the countryside, "Lynchburg has grown more orderly recently. A week has passed without violence or bloodshed." The myth of a low crime rate in southern cities due to the presence of slaves can be dissipated by a daily reading of the "city news" columns, despite the tendency to understate crime. A Norfolk resident charged, "Never was the order of our city in a more deplorable condition. Vice and crime are walking rampant through our streets." A rural resident, commenting on the crime and vice in Richmond, warned his friend who was contemplating a move there, "I shall consider it almost a miracle for a young man without decided religious principle to go unscathed there."[9] The image of the city as crime-ridden and unsafe is not a twentieth-century phenomenon. Citizen's complaints that trickled through to the press attested to the growing concern over the rising crime rate of Virginia's cities.

The unhappiness of citizens over lack of law and order centered on the inadequacy of police protection. Despite the alleged fear of slave revolt, most southern cities, including Virginia's, did not

8. Wheeling *Daily Intelligencer*, December 22, 1852; *Intelligencer,*February 25, 1860.

9. N. H. Campbell to Richard K. Crallé, July 19, 1851, Richard K. Crallé Papers, Alderman Library, University of Virginia; Norfolk *Southern Argus*, June 18, 1850; William L. King to Charles W. Dabney, February 2, 1852, Dabney Papers.

possess a police force. Some cities sent an agglomeration of part-time, nonprofessional, and often reprobate individuals into the streets under the heading *night watch*. This mélange was hardly an effective law-enforcement unit. Complaints of police indifference, drunkenness, brutality, sleeping on duty, and various degrees of criminality came regularly from citizens across the nineteenth-century urban nation.[10] A Norfolk resident complained about his city's night watch, "Our dwellings are fired by the heartless incendiary, and the privacy of our chambers invaded with impunity by the midnight burglar." Four days later a businessman charged that "in the past few weeks there have been a wave of burglaries. Nothing has been done to detect the perpetrators." Six years later, the crime problem evidently had not abated and neither had police ineptness. After a particularly rampant series of robberies and assaults an exasperated resident asked, "Have we any police?"[11]

The city government responded by expanding the police force. The drive for professionalism that had taken root in Cincinnati, Boston, and New York was not yet evident in urban Virginia. Urban dwellers agreed though, that some change was in order. In June 1854, in response to a growing wave of burglaries, Alexandria civic leaders established a private night watch in the business section of the city. When the cold winter months arrived, the private force proved unable to sustain its initial enthusiasm and "propertyholders" reported an increase in crime. In March 1855 the councils of Alexandria appointed a force of twelve night watchmen and named a superintendent. The watch apparently worked well for a few years, but reports filtered back to the councils that the watchmen were less than zealous in their duty. In 1858, the councilmen sought to remedy the situation by exercising greater control over the watch. The councils required the superintendent to issue a monthly report on the number of nights, with specific dates, that

10. See Eaton, *Southern Civilization*, 251; and George C. Rogers, Jr., *Charleston in the Age of the Pinckneys* (Norman, Okla., 1969), 16. See also David Grimsted, "Rioting in the Jacksonian Setting," *American Historical Review*, LXVII (1972), 361–97.

11. Norfolk *Southern Argus*, June 18, 1850; *Argus*, June 22, 1850; *Argus*, January 9, 1856.

individual watchmen were on duty. There were no further complaints prior to secession. Alexandria remained without a day police until after the Civil War.[12]

Police protection was similarly inadequate in other Virginia cities. Wheeling, for example, possessed only a day police composed of six officers. In 1860 the Wheeling City Council rejected a proposal to adopt a night force, fearing that attendant costs would be too much of a strain on an already overworked treasury. Lynchburg established a public night watch in 1850 and neglected law enforcement for the rest of the decade. As a smaller, interior city, Lynchburg was not as victimized by crimes against property as were the eastern cities. Civic leaders organized a private night watch to patrol the business district, but, as in Alexandria, inertia overtook enthusiasm and the watch failed. Norfolk increased its public night watch to twenty men in 1854. Despite the city's continued reputation as a brawling seaport, there were no additions for the rest of the decade. Only Richmond among Virginia's cities organized day and night police. Even in Virginia's largest city, though, the total force of thirty constables and watchmen found it difficult to patrol an entire city.[13]

As if Virginia's cities did not have enough difficulty containing crime and providing efficient police service, juvenile delinquency appeared as a recognized problem for the first time in urban Virginia. City journals complained about "packs of young ruffians" assaulting and robbing "good citizens."[14] Although there is no evidence of organized youth gangs in Virginia's cities, youngsters roamed the streets in groups scavenging, begging, and stealing. Urban Virginians responded to the problem with an enlightened request to their local governments to establish manual training schools as a means of rehabilitating the recreant youths, rather

12. Alexandria *Gazette*, June 8, 1854; December 5, 1854; March 29, 1855; and March 11, 1858.
13. Wheeling *Daily Intelligencer*, July 19, 1854; and February 22, 1860; Christian, *Lynchburg*, 148; Norfolk *Southern Argus*, May 4, 1854; "Commercial and Industrial Cities of the United States: Richmond, Virginia, 1859," *Hunt's*, XL (1859), 51–52.
14. Norfolk *Southern Argus*, June 17, 1851; Richmond *Daily Dispatch*, February 6, 1857.

than incarcerating them in dingy penal institutions. Both Wheeling and Richmond possessed such facilities by 1860.[15]

The amount of police protection afforded to Virginia's cities seemed to be directly proportionate to the concern of the business community over the safety of their residential and business districts. Urban leaders sat on the city councils and were in excellent positions to formulate policies designed to answer their own grievances. Businessmen weighed questions of cost and need to determine the extent of government's involvement in the law-enforcement service. The decision makers could tolerate crime, especially since most of it occurred, as today, in the poorer districts of the city. If civic leaders were paranoid about the presence and mixing of slaves and free blacks, the security forces of Virginia's cities did not reflect that concern. When crime spilled over into more affluent areas, however, considerations of security became uppermost in importance. It is noteworthy that none of the private watches went beyond the boundaries of the business district. The main streets were the avenues of meeting between businessman and client, and therefore, they were a showcase for the city.

City government provided for fire protection in the same haphazard manner in which they oversaw police functions: reliance on private individuals, quasi-public groups, and finally a professional public fire department as part of city government. Fire was a common hazard in nineteenth-century American cities. The risk deepened as prosperity increased. Wooden buildings and primitive fire-fighting equipment could and did destroy whole city blocks. Urban governments, in their perpetual search for a better, more manageable urban environment, sought to remedy the hazard of fire through the passage of regulatory measures designed to inhibit the spread of fire and through the organization of effective fire-fighting forces.

The response of Virginia's cities to the problem of fire was similar to other cities of the time. The basic regulatory act designed to prevent fire in urban Virginia was the prohibition of wooden

15. Richmond *Daily Dispatch*, February 6, 1857; Wheeling *Daily Intelligencer*, January 14, 1858.

buildings from the business district. Alexandria city councils, for example, passed in 1857 an act barring wooden buildings from the major thoroughfares of Duke Street and King Street. Three years later the councilmen amended the act to proscribe wooden construction on adjacent streets as well. Whether these provisions were effective or not is difficult to ascertain. At least there were no reports in Alexandria's papers of any fires of note occurring on the designated streets after 1857. Business considerations again prompted the growth of city government's regulatory powers.[16]

City government did not act with similar alacrity in providing for personnel to fight fires. The fire protection system in urban Virginia consisted of private, nonprofessional companies, or, more appropriately, clubs who competed more against each other than against fires. Local government usually contributed money for equipment and a site for an engine house. Alexandria purchased a lot for the Star Engine Company at a sum of $500. The Wheeling City Council donated $300 worth of hose to the Guards Company and $60 worth to the Rough and Ready Company, as well as a stone wall around the latter's engine house which had been embarrassingly victimized by fire. This spate of civic activity in Wheeling's council chambers resulted from a disastrous fire that had destroyed the wagon factory of a prominent Wheeling citizen. The fire companies had arrived on the scene in due course only to find that their archaic equipment was in such disrepair that they could do virtually nothing to stem the fire's course.[17]

As in the case of police protection, businessmen-politicians seemed to move only when crisis was at their doorstep. In 1858, Wheeling officials abolished appropriations to the private fire companies to counteract declining revenues caused by the Panic of 1857. Several months later, under the heading "Attention Propertyholders," the *Intelligencer* reported that the foundry of I. H. Williams, a councilman, burned to the ground as not a single engine responded. Several fire companies had disbanded, and

16. Alexandria *Gazette*, October 15, 1857. See also Eaton, *Southern Civilization*, 257; and Wade, *Urban Frontier*, 296.

17. Alexandria *Gazette*, January 29, 1855; Wheeling *Daily Intelligencer*, July 12, 1860; and October 10, 1860.

their apparatus was in disarray. Led by councilman Williams, the Wheeling City Council restored the appropriations. Richmond councilmen reacted with similar swiftness when, in the summer of 1853, fire destroyed the Virginia Woolen Mills owned by civic leader Lewis D. Crenshaw and severely damaged booster R. B. Haxall's flour mill. To ensure that the $180,000 loss would not go unheeded, the council donated four fire engines, new hose, and two hook-and-ladder trucks to the volunteer companies.[18]

The introduction of fire insurance helped to solve the businessman's distress if a conflagration victimized his property. Fire insurance supported the regulatory ordinance since only owners of approved structures could secure insurance. In 1850, the seven Richmond fire-fighting brigades organized a fire insurance company. Two years later, the Alexandria fire companies incorporated the Potomac Fire Insurance Company.[19] There is no indication whether insurance helped to curtail the incidence of fires, but at least it provided the victim with a stake for rebuilding and replenishing his inventory.

By 1860 only Richmond possessed a professional fire department. In 1858, the city council abolished the volunteer companies and inaugurated a public, paid department. Other cities in Virginia maintained the semipublic aspect of fire protection. Alexandria, for example, appointed a superintendent with five assistants to oversee the activities of the various volunteer companies.[20] As long as city government was liberal with its financial support, this arrangement was effective in moderating costs and in providing for a modicum of service. The menace of fire remained. Unless a fire destroyed business or prominent residential property, though, equipment would rot, and volunteer companies would trade epithets. Fire protection, like police services, received some direction from city government, but its scope was limited to a portion of the community, and even there its effectiveness was questionable.

18. Wheeling *Daily Intelligencer*, November 13, 1858; and January 5, 1859; Christian, *Richmond*, 179.

19. Eaton, *Southern Civilization*, 257; Powell, *Alexandria*, 49.

20. "Richmond, 1859," *Hunt's*, 61–62; Christian, *Richmond*, 133–35; Alexandria *Gazette*, March 3, 1851.

Street repair was another urban service provided by city government, with once again a decided bias toward the business community. Like fire and police protection, a blend of public and private effort characterized street maintenance as well. No other urban service occupied the city councils' time as much as street repair.[21] A city's streets represented the city's face to the world. Well paved, easily traversed thoroughfares not only facilitated the flow of goods and people but also created a positive impression in the mind of the visitor. "There are few things which operate against a city more than bad streets, and especially when they are the principal ones," observed the Alexandria *Gazette*.[22]

Virginia's cities, entering the competitive milieu of the urban nation, could no more tolerate an unsafe street than a cramped market house. Urban growth not only required an ordering of city life, but also an improvement of the quality of that life. A city with dilapidated streets was unworthy of membership in the urban community. Alexandria's city council responded to the disrepair of King Street, their major business avenue, by levying a special tax on property holders fronting the street at a rate of $1.25 to $1.30 per front foot, depending on value, and by issuing corporate bonds totaling $8,000. The total cost of the repaving project was $13,000. The city completed work in early 1860 and the results were rewarding, at least for one country customer. The visitor recalled that when traveling down King Street in the past "I expected nothing else, than that the wagon would be smashed all to pieces, and the old woman too." He concluded by commending the "marked improvement" in the street's appearance.[23]

The method of arranging for street repair in urban Virginia emphasized the semipublic nature of this urban service. Individuals petitioned the appropriate council committee for street repair or paving—usually done with brick—and the council approved or rejected the request. If the council accepted the petition the committee directed the superintendent of streets in Norfolk, Rich-

21. See Wade, *Urban Frontier*, 282–85.
22. Alexandria *Gazette*, January 26, 1858.
23. *Ibid*., March 8, 1859; letter from "Zekiel Homespun," in *ibid*., April 16, 1860.

mond, Wheeling, and Petersburg, and the superintendent of police in Alexandria and Lynchburg to perform the desired service. The council billed the individual for the price of brick.[24] Since the ability of the property holder to reimburse the city government determined whether the council repaired or paved a particular street or portion of a street, it was obvious that less affluent areas of the city remained mired in mud or choked by dust depending on the season. The only paving project that the city undertook solely at its own expense was the paving of the area around the public market.[25] Norfolk was an exception. City government in the port city paved streets outside the business districts because of the association of unpaved, muddy streets with the frequent diseases that plagued the city.[26] Otherwise, urban government shared costs with private citizens.

Street lighting was another requisite for membership in the urban community as well as a practical facility for dealing with urban growth. Virginia's cities adopted gas lighting enthusiastically and considered its absence a medieval misfortune. "The mere fact that a town is lit with gas," intoned the Lynchburg *Virginian*, "is an assurance to a stranger that, *there* is an intelligent, enterprising, and thrifty people. It is a passport to public confidence and respect, a card to be admitted into the family of well-regulated cities." It appeared as if Lynchburg were transferring the miraculous attributes of the railroad to the gaslight. Lynchburg councilmen were convinced and established the Lynchburg Gas Light Company in 1851.[27]

In January 1851, Richmond became the first Virginia city to receive the benefits of gas lighting. The completion of the Richmond Gas Works culminated an eight-year effort to provide the capital with streetlights. In 1843, Richmond citizens, struggling in a depression and oblivious to the growth of an urban empire to

24. *Ibid.*, June 15, 1854, March 11, 1858; Wheeling *Daily Intelligencer*, May 12, 1858; Horner and Windfree, *Saga of a City*, 118; Thomas, *Confederate State of Richmond*, 19–20. See also Eaton, *Southern Civilization*, 253.

25. Alexandria *Gazette*, August 22, 1850.

26. Norfolk *Southern Argus*, September 9, 1852.

27. Lynchburg *Virginian*, April 21, 1851.

the North, had rejected a proposal for the city to fund a gasworks. The proposal lapsed until 1849, when amidst calls for economic regeneration and urban growth the spirit of the new era revived the idea. Despite incurring a debt of $200,000 to the city, urban leaders believed that the expenditure was necessary and worthwhile. The gasworks was "evidence that Richmond is making herself a worthy metropolis." Efforts by Alexandria civic leader Lewis McKenzie led to the approval of a $50,000 bond issue by the councils in 1850 to introduce gas street lighting into the city. In 1852, Alexandria was "beautifully lit up with gas." By mid-decade six Virginia cities were under the beneficent glow of gaslight and could claim membership in "the family of well-regulated cities."[28]

Except in Wheeling, gas lighting was a public utility. Funding came directly from council appropriations, and administrators of the gasworks received their commissions from the city councils. The city connected gas outlets only upon request and prepayment by those individuals desiring such lighting for their residences, factories, or commercial establishments. Lighting fixtures in the street, however, were erected and maintained at public expense. Streetlights did not extend throughout the city. The government concentrated such apparatus in the more affluent areas of the city. Nevertheless, gas lighting represented an expansion of city government services and an improvement in the quality of urban life.[29]

Pure water was a utility that received little attention from city government in Virginia. All cities had maintained waterworks at least since the late 1830s, but the quality of the water was questionable. Unlike gas lighting or paved streets, water was not a showcase for cities. Cities were more inclined to spend their limited resources on more visible examples of urban modernity. Only Richmond and Alexandria possessed water supplies of good quality beyond the artesian well system. Richmond's endeavor in this area was entirely public and rivaled the systems of cities in the North. City-builders

28. Richmond *Enquirer*, January 31, 1851; Christian, *Richmond*, 146. See also "Richmond, 1859," *Hunt's*, 61–62; Powell, *Alexandria*, 335; and Alexandria *Gazette*, November 22, 1852.

29. See Wheeling *Daily Intelligencer*, January 13, 1860; see also Norfolk *Southern Argus*, November 25, 1950.

in Alexandria operated a waterworks that received a subsidy from the city council.[30] No editorials attacked the water quality or urged its improvement. Virginia's urban residents enjoyed their water boiled and found other potations to satisfy their thirsts.

The indifference of urban government toward an adequate water supply was unusual considering its growing involvement with disease control. Disease, even more so than fire, was a scourge of nineteenth-century cities. While fire destroyed primarily property, the toll of disease was measured in lives. Epidemics transformed bustling cities into ghost towns, optimism into despair, and prosperity into decay and depression. Disease control and health services are usually considered on the periphery of history; yet the deep concern and attention of nineteenth-century urbanites toward disease and its impact on urban growth emphasized its importance in the development of an urban nation.

The health and disease control facilities of southern cities were generally more advanced and more efficient than facilities elsewhere. Disease in southern cities was a constant companion, since killing frosts did not arrive until the late fall in most areas. Southern cities maintained hospitals, established quarantine procedures, organized boards of health, and launched street-cleaning campaigns.[31] If crime was bad business, then disease was anathema. Virginia's cities constantly proclaimed their good health. "The health of our town is excellent," boasted the Lynchburg *Virginian.* "There is not a town in the United States," claimed the Wheeling *Daily Intelligencer*, "where the people enjoy the blessing of health to a greater degree than the residents of Wheeling." The Norfolk *Southern Argus* disagreed: "There is no town as healthy as Norfolk." "There are fewer healthier towns in the United States than Alex-

30. "Commercial and Industrial Cities of the United States: Richmond, Virginia, 1859," *Hunt's*, 61–62; Christian, *Richmond*, 115; Powell, *Alexandria*, 336–37. See also Eaton, *Southern Civilization*, 254.

31. See John Duffy, *Sword of Pestilence: The New Orleans Yellow Fever Epidemic of 1853* (Baton Rouge, 1966); and Joseph I. Waring, "Asiatic Cholera in South Carolina," *Bulletin of the History of Medicine*, XL (1966), 462.

andria," chimed in the *Gazette*. The *Enquirer* upheld Richmond's pride: "Richmond is as healthy as any city in the Union."[32]

A healthful image was essential to a city's prosperity. No farmer wanted to trade cotton or tobacco for yellow fever or cholera. Virginia's cities realized the potential of disease for wrecking their hopes in the competition for trade. In 1850, a southern physician estimated that the cost of disease and death in New Orleans alone totaled $45,000,000 annually in lost business and trade.[33] Cities went so far as to suppress news regarding the existence of an epidemic. The Norfolk *Southern Argus* successfully squelched reports of the devastating yellow fever epidemic of 1855 for six weeks, although rumors had appeared in the Richmond press a month earlier.[34]

The charge by a rival city of the presence of disease, whether true or false, was enough to send editors scurrying to the editorial barricades in defense of their city. In the summer of 1854 Petersburg alleged that cholera existed in Norfolk, causing the *Argus* to retort impatiently, "We say again there is no epidemic disease here. It is not a little singular that newspapers in other cities should continue to make such erroneous statements." A year later Petersburg charged that Richmond had as many cases of yellow fever as Norfolk, which was a false allegation. The *Enquirer,* denying such reports, added bitingly, "We are loath to believe that our neighbors intend us an injustice." The Alexandria *Gazette* defended its city against rumors of disease: "The most gross and exaggerated misstatements are circulated in the upper country relative to the health of this place. We have no cholera—no yellow fever—no ship fever." In responding to a Baltimore story, the *Argus* trotted out letters from seven physicians testifying to Norfolk's good health in 1852. When confronted with the tragic yellow

32. Lynchburg *Virginian*, June 7, 1849; Wheeling *Daily Intelligencer*, April 5, 1858; Norfolk *Southern Argus*, October 19, 1854; Alexandria *Gazette*, May 20, 1851; Richmond *Enquirer*, quoted in Little, *Richmond*, 226.
33. Richmond H. Shryock, *Medicine in America* (Baltimore, 1966), 50.
34. Committee of Physicians, *Report on the Origins of the Yellow Fever in Norfolk during the Summer of 1855* (Richmond, 1857), 26.

fever epidemic of 1855, Norfolk could hardly post denials. After a thorough investigation, though, a blue-ribbon committee issued a clean bill of health to the city, exonerating it from culpability with regard to the onset of the disease. The *Argus* printed the report along with a bitter retort to rival cities: "They [other cities] should blush and retire before the light of *truth,* that discovers not only the origins of the fever, but a reckless, detrimental, and highly censurable disposition on some to fix upon this location, the objectionable and dreaded character of being unhealthful and dangerous."[35]

Being unhealthful was indeed "objectionable and dreaded." Medical knowledge was primitive and a city's populace could rely only on Providence or escape to avoid succumbing to an epidemic once it began. Panic was the most common reaction. Businesses shut down, visitors fled, and farmers took their produce elsewhere. In 1849, the appearance of a handful of cases of cholera in Richmond sent the entire legislature into exile to Fauquier County, over 100 miles from the state capital. In 1855, the mere proximity of Richmond to fever-ridden Norfolk resulted in pleas to remove not only the legislature but the entire apparatus of government permanently to some more healthful location.[36] The serious effect of disease on urban growth and the rational function of community life, however, was placed in sharp and tragic relief by the onslaught of yellow fever upon Norfolk in the summer of 1855.

On June 6, 1855, the steamer *Benjamin Franklin* arrived off Norfolk from the Virgin Islands, where a yellow fever epidemic was raging. Norfolk, like most Atlantic ports, had an established and rigorous quarantine procedure. The *Franklin* remained in quarantine for the required twelve days and then proceeded to tie up in Norfolk for repairs. Norfolk port authorities were unaware that the captain had successfully concealed two cases of the fever. The disease spread to a nearby immigrant shantytown, and from there it took a slow, inexorable course toward the heart of the city. Finally

35. Norfolk *Southern Argus*, August 2, 1854; Richmond *Enquirer*, October 2, 1855; Alexandria *Gazette*, August 12, 1852; Norfolk *Southern Argus*, October 7, 1852; *Argus*, August 1, 1857.

36. Alexandria *Gazette*, June 8, 1849; Lynchburg *Republican*, quoted in Richmond *Enquirer*, October 2, 1855.

breaking a silence of six weeks, the Norfolk Board of Health on July 30 published a statement acknowledging the presence of a yellow fever epidemic in Norfolk.

When the epidemic ended on October 26 at the first frost, nearly ten thousand citizens—two-thirds of the residents of the city—had been afflicted with the disease and more than two thousand had died. The Howard Association, a voluntary charity hastily formed during the epidemic, transformed Norfolk's largest hotel into a hospital which in most cases proved to be a mere way station on the route to the grave. Among those who perished were Mayor Hunter Woodis and more than half of the city's ministers and physicians. The disease left countless orphans. One man, a clergyman, recorded the passing of his wife, daughter, and sister-in-law within six days. By late summer such tragedy was commonplace. In two adjoining houses, thirty-four of thirty-six residents died. During the first week in September, at the height of the pestilence, there were at least eighty deaths a day.

Within a short time, the supply of coffins in the city was exhausted. Ships that had once brought produce to the docks began to bring in hundreds of coffins, and still there were too few. At times survivors buried loved ones in blankets and sometimes they placed them in common graves of forty or more victims. A resident, fortunate to escape the scourge in time, wrote sadly to a friend, "My heart sickens when I think of it. The place where my most sacred interests are located, but a short time ago, full of joy and gladness is now the scene of sorrow and distress. . . . Poor Norfolk, when will it survive the shock!" [37]

The yellow fever epidemic shattered the prosperity of the city. After the official announcement of the epidemic at the end of July, all major Virginia cities as well as several important port cities in other states issued interdicts against trade with Norfolk. The city soon resembled a ghost town: wharves, streets, and business establishments were deserted. The plague wrecked the finances of the Norfolk and Petersburg Railroad, halted the publication of Nor-

37. [?] Rowland to James Southgate, September 5, 1855, James Southgate Papers (Duke University, Durham, N.C.).

folk newspapers, and brought the city's economy to a standstill.

Time, in Norfolk, seemed to date from before or after the "summer of pestilence." Monuments to heroes of the plague, prayers of thanksgiving, and statistics of health reminded citizens of their collective tragedy. The editors of the *Argus*, upon resuming publication of the paper, spoke of a "plague-spirit." In 1859 the paper admitted that the "advancement" of Norfolk was "slow, too slow." The plague had "melted away the population like snow" and had shaken the self-confidence of the city.[38]

The lesson of the Norfolk tragedy to Virginia's cities seemed to be that the best "cure" for an epidemic lay in its prevention. Disease prevention, although orchestrated by the city government, called for a communitywide effort. The primary mechanism of prevention in Virginia's cities was the board of health, a commission composed of physicians and lay visitors appointed by the council. The board's task was to assess health conditions in the various wards, provide recommendations to the city council, and issue periodic bulletins on the residents' health.[39] The health bulletins were more saccharine than accurate. The boards in Virginia, though, never approached the degree of politicization and inefficiency of the New York City Board of Health.[40] Like all nonprofessional, part-time adjuncts of the city government, the local boards of health in urban America could not perform with the vigilence required in an era before the discovery of the germ theory of disease. Nevertheless, the board possessed considerable weight in an urban community, if only because the members were a little less ignorant than the rest of the population as to the etiology of disease.

Local health officials had perceived a relationship between filth and the incidence of disease. In 1848, for example, the Norfolk

38. David R. Goldfield, "Disease and Urban Image: Yellow Fever in Norfolk, 1855," *Virginia Cavalcade*, XXIII (1973), 34–41.

39. Alexandria *Gazette*, June 7, 1849; Richmond *Whig*, June 8, 1849; Wheeling *Daily Intelligencer*, October 11, 1853; Wyndham B. Blanton, *Medicine in Virginia in the Nineteenth Century* (Richmond, 1940), 203.

40. See Alex F. Berba, *Letters on Yellow Fever, Cholera, and Quarantine* (New York, 1852), 20.

Board of Health advised, "Of all preventive means yet discovered, cleanliness is by far the most important." The link between filth and disease motivated city dwellers and local government to direct their efforts toward removing noisome garbage and stagnant pools. Clean streets were an important civic priority for both health and business reasons, though it was often difficult to separate one from the other. In May 1854, amid rumors of an impending attack of cholera, the Richmond *Enquirer* complained that "the nuisance created by kitchen slop thrown into the street is but little calculated to give visitors a favorable impression of the cleanliness of our city, or to promote the comfort and health of citizens." The *Enquirer* suggested that the nearby James River was the proper receptacle for such waste. This would solve the problem of dirty streets while rural downriver residents coped with the consequences. In the meantime, the superintendent of police, the elected city official charged with maintaining the steets, could remove the nuisances.[41]

The Alexandria city government evolved a similar solution to its waste disposal problems, hiring a night scavenger "to remove the contents of any privy, depositing them outside the limits of the Corporation." Evidently, the suburbs outside of Richmond and Alexandria were not quite as fashionable as they are today. When the night scavenger proved unsuccessful, the board of health launched a study of refuse disposal in other cities. Imitation was a common urban phenomenon in nineteenth-century America, and in Alexandria's case it proved rewarding. The board's study recommended that the council implement a plan to station garbage carts in strategic locations so that citizens would use the carts instead of the streets for refuse disposal. The report noted that "in the cities of Philadelphia and Baltimore, this arrangement has been in operation for a series of years and fully accomplished the desired end."[42] The council provided the garbage carts thus placing Alexandria within the modern urban community, at least as far as garbage collection was concerned.

Other communities struggled with the problem of refuse dis-

41. Norfolk *Southern Argus*, December 16, 1848; Richmond *Enquirer*, June 8, 1854.
42. Alexandria *Gazette*, February 16, 1855; *Gazette*, June 23, 1855.

posal with less evident success. The Norfolk Board of Health, an undermanned and overworked organization, complained continuously about inadequate procedures for removing refuse from streets and ditches. In a call for volunteer inspectors, the board suggested that the volunteers "visit every house in town, to see if there is not in and about the premises matter calculated to favor the spread of cholera." The community received the board's proposal with indifference.[43] The era of relying on individual householders to maintain their property was evidently over. The city was growing and becoming more diverse. The reservoir of civic pride was becoming confined to urban leaders and other interested citizens.

Lynchburg leaders confronted the same public apathy in their effort to rid the city's streets of filth and garbage. The railroad brought commerce to town, but the discarded crates and boxes and the spoiled produce strewn about on streets adjacent to the depot indicated that the city was unprepared for this sudden prosperity. A group of merchants complained that the situation was "a monument of disgrace to our city." The Lynchburg *Virginian* urged the city council to "cleanse the gutters of their pestilential contents. . . . It is a matter of pride to a town that its streets be cleanly, and it is equally occasion of shame when they are the reverse."[44] The disinterest with which the city officials greeted these remarks demonstrated that the urban leadership was not monolithic and that disagreement over policy was typical. Some leaders evidently viewed Lynchburg's fine record of healthfulness as proof that preventive measures were superfluous. Perhaps they believed that the city should appropriate funds for railroads and other services where the rewards were more evident.

Stagnant water was another danger to urban health. Intuitively, mid-nineteenth-century urbanites related standing water to the breeding of disease. The Norfolk Board of Health warned that "water should not be allowed to stand in the streets. Evaporation gives off poisonous vapors that cause disease." Once again, health and business combined to elicit government action. As the Norfolk

43. Norfolk *Southern Argus*, December 14, 1848.
44. Lynchburg *Virginian*, September 1, 1854.

Southern Argus implored, "It is of the vast importance to the trade and prosperity of Norfolk, to say nothing of the lives of the people, that the standing pools in our streets should be removed by the appropriate committees of the councils instantly." Norfolk, probably because it was so prone to disease as a low-lying city, made a diligent attempt to fill up marshes, coves, and sunken lots; even if these physical obstacles were not immediately proximate to inhabited areas.[45]

The frustrating aspect of these urban housekeeping measures was that disease came in spite of them. Moreover, the city government was not ubiquitous. It would be decades before a sufficient bureaucracy existed to enforce ordinances that prohibited indiscriminate dumping of waste, for example. City government was not entirely blameless. Alexandria's famed garbage cart law extended only slightly beyond the business district. Two first ward citizens complained irately, "No garbage cart in the South End of the City. The inhabitants of that quarter pour all their slop and kitchen offal into the streets. . . . The First Ward should be exempt from taxation, having none of the *advantages!* of our municipal government." Another citizen, identifying himself as "Health," scoffed, "What a humbug is the 'Garbage Cart' law! In some parts of the city, the garbage cart never goes—never has gone."[46] As with other urban services, the city government's disease-control policy failed to cover poorer, nontaxpaying districts that were precisely the areas of the city most prone to disease. The record of Virginia's urban governments in disease control, however, compared favorably with efforts of northern counterparts.

Disease control created an anomalous situation for urban governments everywhere. Disease was something to be ignored, denied, and suppressed. Yet vigorous prosecution of preventive mechanisms could create the impression that if a city were indeed healthy, these precautions would be unnecessary. Norfolk, after all, possessed the largest and most active disease-control machinery

45. Norfolk *Southern Argus*, August 11, 1854; *Argus*, January 16, 1856; *Argus*, June 4, 1855.
46. Letter from "Two," Alexandria *Gazette*, June 10, 1856; letter from "Health," *Gazette*, April 7, 1856.

between Boston and New Orleans. City government moved through a complex web of business interests and community needs to produce a disease-control policy. Businessmen disliked restrictive quarantine regulations and simultaneously complained about filthy streets. Disease was a fixture of nineteenth-century urban life, and defining and implementing an effective prevention policy was an ongoing dilemma for urban government.

Urban growth, both in area and population, naturally complicated the problem of disease control for urban government and exacerbated other problems as well. Poverty existed in American cities long before the rapid urbanization of the mid-nineteenth century. Urban growth compounded the problem, however, by increasing the number of urban poor at a time when local government funds went toward more glamorous and what many considered to be more necessary urban services such as utilities, crime and disease control, and street repair. Further, though poverty, like disease, was not calculated to enhance a city's image, unlike disease, poverty had little impact on business. Finally, many citizens believed that poverty and immorality were synonymous, so public assistance would be contradictory. It was not surprising, therefore, that relief for the poor received a low priority from urban governments across the nation.[47] It was to the credit of Virginia's city governments however, that they acknowledged the existence of poverty and provided a modicum of relief in conjunction with private endeavors.

Voluntary associations dominated the front ranks of relief for the poor in nineteenth-century urban America, and charitable societies existed in Virginia's cities as well. Civic boosters invariably took the lead in such matters. If poverty could be measured by the extent and number of charity groups, then Norfolk possessed the gravest poverty situation in the state. In 1848 several city-builders, including attorney Tazewell Taylor and banker John G. H. Hatton, formed the Norfolk Association for the Improvement of the Con-

47. See Robert H. Bremner, *From the Depths: The Discovery of Poverty in the United States* (New York, 1956); and Raymond A. Mohl, "Poverty, Pauperism, and Social Order in the Preindustrial American City, 1780–1840," *Social Science Quarterly*, LII (1972), 934–48.

dition of the Poor, utilizing an organization of the same name in New York as a model. The founders of the association viewed relief for the poor in much the same manner as they approached marketing procedures. Organized aid to the poverty stricken was another means of rationalizing urban growth and bringing it in tune with the national urban community. "It has been tried in other cities and has worked well," asserted one member of the Norfolk association. Another spokesman for the association praised the advent of "a systematic plan for the judicious distribution of alms to the poor of our city."[48]

The group divided the city into districts, and its members made visitations to the homes of the poor. In this manner "artful mendicants" could be ferreted out and dropped from the relief rolls. The philosophy of the association was identical to the prevailing paternalism throughout urban America. "*Sound discrimination* then, is the first principle of this Association," proclaimed a member. "It will give to none," he continued, "who will not exhibit evidence of improvement from the aid afforded." The association, whatever its biases, provided the poor of Norfolk with the first year-round assistance program in the city's history. Unfortunately, the association's exertions during the yellow fever epidemic produced its bankruptcy, and for the remainder of the decade it played a limited and sporadic role in Norfolk.[49]

Three organizations shared voluntary relief efforts in Norfolk after 1855: the Dorcas Society, the Humane Society, and the Howard Association. The Dorcas Society was a nonsectarian women's group that had been in existence since 1811. Unlike the Association for the Improvement of the Condition of the Poor, the Dorcas Society operated only in situations of crisis, rather than on a daily basis. This meant that the society's members visited the homes of "the afflicted and suffering," (the hard-core poor consisting primarily of widows) only during the winter months when survival became more difficult with the onset of cold weather. Nevertheless,

48. Norfolk *Southern Argus*, November 27, 1848; and November 29, 1848.

49. *Ibid.*, November 27, 1848. See George D. Armstrong, *The Summer of the Pestilence: A History of the Ravages of the Yellow Fever in Norfolk, Virginia* (Norfolk, 1857), 45, 50, 74.

the women's organization provided clothing and food to the most needy segment of Norfolk's population at a difficult season. The membership included the wives of the civic leaders.[50] The Humane Society was the male counterpart of the Dorcas group. Its major activity was distributing wood to the poor during the winter months. Applicants had to pass standards of worthiness to ensure a warm hearth. Many of the members of the Norfolk Association for the Improvement of the Condition of the Poor lent their time to the Humane Society. John G. H. Hatton, for example, was treasurer of the society.[51]

The Norfolk Howard Association, an organization that had branches in other southern cities, incorporated a wide range of charitable activities under its benevolent charter. The association originated to cope with the massive relief effort required during the yellow fever epidemic of 1855. It performed steadfast, even heroic, services in establishing two hospitals, paying expenses of volunteer physicians from other states, and supplying the salaries for gravediggers. The Howard Association became the repository of donations totaling $157,000 from sympathetic citizens throughout the nation. After the epidemic, the association, led by merchant and civic leader John B. Whitehead and buoyed by funds from brother groups in Baltimore and New Orleans, undertook the functions of the moribund Association for the Improvement of the Condition of the Poor. It remained the major voluntary charity organization in Norfolk up to the time of secession.[52]

Other Virginia cities possessed less elaborate voluntary structures for relieving the poor. Women's charities were common features of relief for the poor in urban Virginia. Richmond's civic leaders established relief houses in the city's wards during the winter months. The houses existed on donations from individuals that seldom totaled more than $300 per year. The managers extended wood and food to "all who would apply for it" without regard for means or the moral terpitude of the supplicant. On the

50. Norfolk *Southern Argus,* January 3, 1856; January 11, 1856; and January 24, 1856.
51. *Ibid.,* December 15, 1854; and January 29, 1857.
52. "Report of the Howard Association of Norfolk," in *ibid.,* December 2, 1857.

other hand, Lynchburg's Dorcas Society carefully scrutinized prospective recipients so that "*none* but the helpless and deserving" should receive charity. Despite such precaution, the directress complained of "an exhausted treasury."[53]

Alexandria's most active voluntary association was the Ladies Benevolent Society. The society, exhibiting more organization than was usual for a temporary operation, followed the administrative procedure developed by the Norfolk Association for the Improvement of the Condition of the Poor. The society divided the city into districts, but unlike the Norfolk association the purpose of this division was to solicit funds to purchase wood and food for distribution to the poor during the coming winter. Wheeling alone of Virginia's cities harbored no continuous organizations to dispense charity, even on a seasonal basis.[54]

Except in Norfolk, voluntary relief for the poor in urban Virginia was seasonal and dependent on the continued generosity of a relatively small proportion of the city's population. In Norfolk only the Howard Association provided permanent relief after 1855. Voluntary associations were neither sufficient nor proficient enough to deal with the growing problem of poverty. Only local government could provide the permanent financial and bureaucratic mechanisms necessary to ameliorate the growing blight of poverty on the urban landscape. Urban government moved slowly and warily into the field of public relief since citywide relief efforts required a public admission of the existence of a poverty problem. Wheeling refused to accede to its existence, preferring instead to attribute "the large number of poor in the streets" to "strangers." Richmond journals rarely mentioned poverty; but in 1855, native son and author John Esten Cooke temporarily abandoned his Revolutionary farces to write *Ellie*, a contemporary novel depicting melodramatically, but nonetheless emphatically, poverty in Richmond.[55] The efforts of city government were understandably di-

53. Richmond *Enquirer*, January 9, 1855. See also Christian, *Richmond*, 146; Lynchburg *Virginian*, May 31, 1849.

54. Alexandria *Gazette*, November 3, 1855; Wheeling *Daily Intelligencer*, May 2, 1859.

55. Wheeling *Daily Intelligencer*, May 2, 1859; Alfred Y. Wolff, Jr., "A Study of the

rected at cooperation with private charitable groups rather than the introduction and maintenance of entire relief programs.

The almshouse was one of the few entirely public poverty institutions in urban Virginia. The Overseers of the Poor, a body appointed by the council that was similar to the board of health, administered the almshouse. Almshouses were essentially workhouses, and living conditions there were primitive. In 1824, Robert Greenhow, president of the Overseers of the Poor in Richmond, observed that the poorhouse was the last resort of those who were poverty-stricken, most of whom preferred even begging in the streets. The almshouse in Richmond also provided out-door relief in the form of wood to over two hundred families. This was a supplement to private charity, however, rather than a significant solution to poverty. In Alexandria the almshouse operated by the Overseers of the Poor recorded only eighteen inmates during the winter of 1854; all but four were immigrants. An Alexandria ordinance required that the overseers collect kitchen offal for the use and "benefit" of the almshouse. The almshouse, though, was the most prominent government effort in the field of relief for the poor in urban Virginia. More than two-thirds of the total expenditure for charitable relief in Alexandria in 1859 went to maintaining and supplying the almshouse.[56]

The budget of the Overseers of the Poor helped to subsidize the Soup House, an urban institution that returned every winter to provide soup, meat, bread, and vegetables to the poor. In Alexandria, as in Richmond and Norfolk, city funds supplied only a portion of the support for the Soup House. A citywide campaign elicited the remainder. Alexandrians were proud of their Soup House and compared it favorably to a similar institution in New York. The Alexandria *Gazette* carried more news about the Soup House than about any other charity. Some objected that the Soup House operated on a haphazard basis without deducing the need

Antebellum Virginia Novel as a Reflection of Virginia Society," (M.A. thesis, University of Virginia, 1965), 82–93.

56. David Rothman, *The Almshouse Experience* (New York, 1971), 1101–04; "Richmond, 1859," *Hunt's*, 64; Alexandria *Gazette*, August 3, 1855; August 21, 1855; and December 15, 1859.

or fitness of the recipient. As a citywide effort, though, the expiation of guilt through giving as well as the food provided to genuinely needy families overcame such demurrers. Besides, urban citizens were not likely to publicly identify themselves as poor, because of the connotations associated with poverty, unless they were in fact poor.[57]

City governments also made periodic supplements to the overseers' budget, or to the poor themselves through the private charities. Lynchburg's city council, for example, donated $300 annually to private societies in addition to the usual $300 that the council gave to the Overseers of the Poor. Norfolk's Humane Society received a gift of $100 from the city council. Relief for the poor had not yet become institutionalized on the public level. The first step had been taken, however, and local government not only acknowledged the existence of poverty, but it began to formulate means to deal with it. In the fall of 1857, the Alexandria *Gazette* urged the city government to undertake a "plan of systematic and judicious charity."[58] In the midst of a depression, however, this was an unrealistic request. At least some Alexandrians recognized that, in a modern city, the government should have responsibility for caring for some of its more unfortunate citizens.

The existence of public relief for the poor indicated that civic leaders were concerned not only with the veneer of urban image, but with improving the quality of life of some of their less visible fellow-citizens. Indeed, it is possible to lump together urban services under the general rubric of urban reform half a century before that movement became the hallmark of the modern city. But this was not all. City-builders in conjunction with their increasingly active government sought also to enlighten their citizens and to provide for a future generation of educated urban inhabitants.

Education at public expense was a relatively new phenomenon in urban Virginia. The urban South generally lagged behind other sections of the country in providing free elementary education for

57. Alexandria *Gazette*, February 10, 1855, January 10, 1856; Richmond *Enquirer*, January 19, 1855; Norfolk *Southern Argus*, January 24, 1857.

58. Lynchburg *Virginian*, February 2, 1853; and February 28, 1855; Norfolk *Southern Argus*, January 28, 1857; Alexandria *Gazette*, October 14, 1857.

its children. The system of higher education was well developed in the South, but, as elsewhere, college remained the province of the affluent.[59] The spirit of the new era generated enthusiasm for public education in the Old Dominion. An educated citizenry was another new weapon in the urban arsenal for the defense of the South. Henry A. Wise, soon to be governor of Virginia, delivered a Fourth of July oration in 1850 on the subject of free schools for all: "The *ends* of our Republic are Liberty, Equality, and Fraternity, and they depend on Popular Education. . . . The people *universally* must be trained alike in Schools of one common education." A Richmond resident, writing in the *Southern Literary Messenger* in 1852, proposed another argument for public education. He urged popular instruction for young women to train them as teachers to replace northerners who were "more or less infected with fanaticism." As with other projects of the new era, there was a sense of urgency in the rhetoric surrounding the subject of education. The Richmond *Enquirer* was emphatic: "The *Public Good* demands that every white boy should be educated." "Free schools should at once be established; educate the people, no matter what it may cost," echoed George Fitzhugh.[60]

Cities were the natural repositories of an education program. They possessed the financial and intellectual resources as well as the concentration of population. Urban leaders looked upon education as another urban service. Public education would help to secure a more orderly urban development by ensuring an enlightened populace. Some urban leaders envisioned a statewide system of public education. The Norfolk *Southern Argus* favored the Wisconsin system where a special fund existed for educational purposes. The interest from the fund maintained a system of common schools. The system had the advantage of relieving local communities of the financial burdens of establishing a free educational system. The Virginia state legislature had established the Literary Fund in 1810, which was a device similar to the Wisconsin

59. See Eaton, *Southern Civilization*, 258.
60. Speech of Henry A. Wise, quoted in Richmond *Enquirer*, September 10, 1850; "The New Constitution," *Southern Literary Messenger*, 118; Richmond *Enquirer*, February 6, 1857; Fitzhugh, *Sociology*, 144.

fund. The money, however, supported the more attractive University of Virginia and the Virginia Military Institute rather than a public school system.[61] In short, a system of public education in urban Virginia depended on the willingness and the ability of local government to fund and to maintain such a system.

By the time of secession, Virginia's cities supported one free school system. The evolution of public schools in Norfolk followed a pattern established in urban areas outside of Virginia. In January 1849, the state legislature amended the Norfolk city charter, granting the councils the power to establish free schools. It was not until the spring of 1855 that councilmen authorized the levy of a capitation tax of two dollars on every white male over twenty-one in order to finance a public school system. Yellow fever interrupted the free school effort, and it was not until January 1856 that the select and common councils established the bureaucracy to administer the new system. The councilmen divided the city into four districts and provided for the popular election of a school commissioner for each district to compose the board of education. The four commissioners would then elect one of their members to the office of Superintendent. Each commissioner would oversee one school in his district. Any white male child between the ages of six and twenty-one was eligible to attend. Following site selection, some construction, and staffing, the system of four free schools opened on September 16, 1858. The citizens of Norfolk responded with such enthusiasm that the rooms set aside for the schools were soon overcrowded and a long waiting list developed. Though other cities talked of the benefits of public education, Norfolk was the only city to initiate a system.[62]

To most Virginians public education meant public higher education. The attitude in Richmond typified urban Virginia's commitment to higher education rather than to a public primary and secondary system. Although a publicly supported Lancastrian School had been educating indigent children successfully since

61. Norfolk *Southern Argus*, November 10, 1853.
62. *Ibid.*, January 29, 1849; May 12, 1855; January 31, 1856; June 15, 1857; and October 13, 1857. See Richmond *Whig*, April 4, 1854; and Wheeling *Daily Intelligencer*, February 1, 1858.

1816, city officials ignored the demand for an expanded primary system and established a woman's college in 1852. The need for southern-trained teachers for the flourishing private school system in the cities prompted the creation of the Richmond Female Institute. Lynchburg ministers began pressing for a public primary school system in that city in 1847. In 1855, however, the city donated $20,000 toward the erection of Lynchburg College.[63] The prestige and urbanity associated with a college proved a more powerful lure than the education of needy youngsters. Education, like other urban services, served only a part of the growing urban community.

While free schools in Norfolk and the colleges in Richmond and Lynchburg educated a future generation of urban Virginians, there was a large mass of adults who never benefitted from formal education. Richmond's famous Night School of the Mechanics Institute filled that void somewhat, but most cities opted for public libraries and lyceums as the means to redeem adults from ignorance. Civic leaders in Wheeling, Richmond, and Alexandria established library associations in the decade prior to the Civil War. The associations were private organizations, not really public libraries in the modern sense. In the usual fashion of urban services, libraries received some financial aid from the city government but relied on members' contributions for the bulk of their budget.[64] Lecture series, though sponsored by private organizations and church groups, were open to the adult public. The Richmond Atheneum was the fine arts center of the city as well as the site for an annual lecture series. Noted British writer William M. Thackeray delivered a series of three lectures at the Atheneum twice during the 1850s. The Richmond Library Association operated the Atheneum and, in 1853, purchased 1,500 books in London for the Atheneum library.[65]

The lecture series and libraries indicated a desire for self-

63. Thomas, *Confederate State of Richmond*, 28–29; Lynchburg *Virginian*, October 1, 1855. See also Horner and Windfree, *Saga of a City*, 44.

64. Wheeling *Daily Intelligencer*, March 8, 1859; Eaton, *Southern Civilization*, 260; Powell, *Alexandria*, 337.

65. Richmond *Daily Dispatch*, July 28, 1857; Christian, *Richmond*, 177.

improvement that characterized a growing urban society. An educated, well-read citizenry was essential for membership in the national urban network. Familiarity with art and music was as important as the ability to quote from the classics. Cities began organizing societies to formally patronize the arts and to support the development of indigenous talent. The Cosmopolitan Art and Literary Association of Wheeling, formed in 1855, provided a free subscription to a magazine and a ticket to a series of art exhibits organized by local artists. The package, including membership dues, cost the patron three dollars a year. The Norfolk Musical Association, organized in 1856 to "cultivate, improve and encourage vocal and instrumental talent in Norfolk," offered scholarships to deserving youths. Just as urban Virginians sought economic independence from northern cities, they hoped to develop their own teachers, writers, artists, and musicians in order to achieve cultural independence.[66]

The attention of citizens to relief for the poor and educational and cultural affairs demonstrated an awareness that the quality of urban life should not be neglected in the headlong rush for growth and prosperity. While civic boosters prayed at its altar, they appreciated the fallibility of progress. Northern cities, which leaders studied avidly, presented vivid examples of the types of decay that could accompany growth and prosperity. Virginia's urban press pointed to the wretched working classes, the depraved criminals, and the filth and disease rampant in northern cities. Just as New York was the model for all that was good about American urban civilization, it was also the exemplar of all that was bad.[67] The editors printed these examples both to reassure their readers of the superiority of Virginia's urban civilization as well as to warn about the dangers inherent in uncontrolled growth. In an effort to maintain a habitable urban environment in the midst of change, urban government and private citizens developed plans to preserve the esthetic features of city life while it was still possible.

66. Wheeling *Daily Intelligencer*, November 14, 1855; Norfolk *Southern Argus*, March 1, 1856.
67. See Richmond *Enquirer*, July 13, 1855; February 20, 1857; and November 11, 1857.

Urban Virginians were aware of the precepts of romantic planning as practiced by landscape architect Frederick Law Olmsted, and of the necessity for open spaces in the urban milieu. They applauded progress yet regretted its incursion into the open environment. In the fall of 1849, the Norfolk *Southern Argus,* under the headline "Progress of Civilization," recorded the passing of two venerable sycamore trees that stood in the center of High Street in neighboring Portsmouth: "Yesterday the axe penetrated those ancient trees—they were doomed to be cut down because they obstructed the track where the railroad is to pass." A Lynchburg resident, attempting to sell the house of a friend who had moved West, urged him to lower his price to effect an immediate sale of his isolated urban homestead because of "the chances of its becoming less desirable by the improvements hereafter to be put up in the neighborhood."[68] While urban Virginians lamented the loss of open spaces, they sought, through their government, to preserve a portion of their diminishing pastoral landscape.

The tree planting campaigns carried on by some urban Virginia governments demonstrated how business and esthetics blended together for mutual advantage. Trees possessed numerous advantages for upwardly mobile cities, as the Alexandria *Gazette* observed in approbation of the city councils' tree planting efforts: "Strangers and visitors to our town notice the improved appearance of many of our streets in consequence of the beautiful shade trees that have, in recent years, been planted along the side walks. Both for health and ornament these trees are worth double the cost of planting and rearing them." Norfolk, whose summer humidity attracted mosquitoes and repulsed people, similarly appreciated the attributes of shade trees. The *Argus* reminded councilmen that "many of our thoroughfares are greatly deficient in a feature which contributes vastly to the beauty and comfort of city life. There is no cool, grateful shade, nor rustling leaves." Wheeling agreed: "Nothing adds to the appearance of a town or city so much as shade trees. Strangers are more readily taken with a place whose streets are

68. Norfolk *Southern Argus*, November 14, 1849; N. H. Campbell to Richard K. Crallé, July 19, 1851, Crallé Papers.

lined with trees."[69] Thus, environment could be utilized for the benefit of business as well as for esthetic purposes.

The establishment of parks was the next logical program after tree planting initiated the city-beautiful campaign. Agitation for New York City's Central Park, begun in 1844 by newspaper editor William Cullen Bryant, awakened urban authorities everywhere to the efficacy of open spaces. By that time, city cemeteries had become the primary recreational facility for urban families who were starved for open spaces and greenery.[70] Visitors to Richmond commented on the commanding vistas of verdant Hollywood Cemetery, which had been established by a group of private citizens, including Joseph R. Anderson, in 1849. Alexandria's Ivy Hill Cemetery achieved similar accolades for its well-planned contributions to relaxation.[71] Such areas, however, could not long withstand the increasing crush of weekend crowds without losing the solemnity for which they were originally designed.

Although Virginia's cities did not come forth with grandiose plans similar to New York's Central Park, they set a realistic, if modest, estimate of their citizens' recreational needs. In the spring of 1851, the Alexandria *Gazette* suggested that the city should acquire "one or two vacant lots or squares" to be transformed into parks. Almost three years later the common council, "impressed by similar action in almost all the cities of the Union," resolved to search for suitable park grounds. A year later, the city located its park land, and the *Gazette* rejoiced that now, as in other cities, "all classes of citizens may enjoy a pleasant walk and breathe fresh air, without cost."[72] Thus, parks, unlike other urban services, were democratic institutions that benefitted all members of the community. In addition to providing respite from the pressures of modern urban life, parks were visual advertisements of a city's modernity and progressive spirit.

69. Alexandria *Gazette*, May 21, 1851; Norfolk *Southern Argus*, May 25, 1855; Wheeling *Daily Intelligencer*, April 3, 1858.

70. John W. Reps, *The Making of Urban America: A History of City Planning in the United States* (Princeton, 1965), 325–47.

71. "Cities of the South—Richmond," *DeBow's Review*, XXVIII (1860), 187–201; Christian, *Richmond*, 163; Powell, *Old Alexandria*, 335.

72. Alexandria *Gazette*, May 21, 1851; January 27, 1854; August 7, 1855.

Norfolk went through similar throes to establish parks for its citizens. Although the Norfolk city government failed to purchase a site for recreational space, the arguments for such action bear repeating because they indicate the existence of a national urban community. Regardless of sectional strife, cities remained aware of activities in other cities and employed similar rhetoric in response to the problems of urban growth. In late summer 1852, the *Argus* recommended that the city councils purchase a lot for the purposes of transforming it into a park: "We have now no enclosure for public resort, except the cemeteries. In other cities and towns there are groves and parks, and pleasant places of resort in the mornings and evenings." Two years later the *Argus* presented two more reasons for the introduction of public parks: "Parks beautify a city and add greatly to its attractions. Towns as well as houses require ventilation with especial regard to health." The editors believed that health and beauty were two qualities that city government should promote. By 1857, however, local government had not responded to the *Argus*'s entreaties. The tone of the editors' arguments became more urgent and still mindful of the example of other cities: "In Norfolk we have sadly neglected to promote those public improvements which take the shape of verdant interspaces in the midst of population. . . . The city would be wise to purchase appropriate areas like New York's Central Park or Boston's Common. A few years hence will see our places of recreation closed up by masses of brick and mortar."[73] The urban environment and vanishing open spaces were a serious concern to urban residents more than a century before the word *ecology* became a part of the nation's popular culture.

The encroaching and expanding city not only felled trees and annihilated flowers and grass, but it threatened the air and water of the city as well. Travelers to Richmond—the state's most industrialized city—began commenting on the haze of tobacco smoke that enveloped the James River's banks. Wheeling's soap factories emitted a stench "you can almost hang your hat upon." In 1854, the Alexandria *Gazette* observed for the first time that the Potomac

73. Norfolk *Southern Argus*, September 7, 1852; May 6, 1854; June 4, 1857.

River near the city was becoming increasingly "brackish." [74] Local authorities duly noted the existence of pollution, but they were inundated by more immediate problems to undertake a serious review of the situation. Besides, truly effective solutions were beyond the capabilities of local government. The mere notice of such environmental considerations, though, was another illustration of the sophisticated and broad-minded outlook of the urban leadership.

The broad interests of urban leaders and their governments, while desirable, proved expensive. The reluctance of Norfolk's city government to provide its citizens with adequate park facilities, for example, probably stemmed more from financial considerations than from indifference. As the list of urban services grew and local government's participation in these services increased accordingly, the expense of rationalizing urban growth and ensuring modernity became burdensome. The need for urban services came at a time when city governments had plunged heavily into financing railroads. The business community, which also directed the course of local government spending, believed that such subscriptions would eventually benefit the entire community. More immediately, however, debts generated more debts until city officials were floating in a sea of red ink. Wheeling, for example, spent $385,000 in 1853; $261,000 of this sum went toward railroad stock subscriptions. Of the $2,000,000 debt hanging over Richmond in 1857, $1,226,000 resulted from internal improvement expenditures.[75] The dilemma for Virginia's urban governments was how to reconcile soaring debt with the increased demands for planned urban growth.

The expenditures of Wheeling over a three-year period illustrates the increased attention that cities accorded to services. Street repair dominated one-third of the expenditures in 1853 (not including railroad subscriptions), with fire and water facilities the next two largest city government expenses. The following year,

---

74. John B. Danforth to Mary A. Atwood, October 14, 1854, John B. Danforth Letter Press Copy Book, Duke University; Wheeling *Daily Intelligencer*, October 13, 1858. See also Richmond *Enquirer*, June 22, 1855; Alexandria *Gazette*, September 26, 1854.

75. Wheeling *Daily Intelligencer*, January 20, 1854; Richmond *Daily Dispatch*, July 28, 1857.

disbursements increased generally. Under the weight of the railroad subscriptions, though, city fathers felt constrained to cut back on urban services though the number of services provided by the city increased. Police and street lighting expenditures appeared for the first time, reflecting the establishment of a day police during the year and the construction of public lamps to accept the gas provided by a private franchise. In 1855, urban expenditures increased again in Wheeling, with urban services accounting for a record $71,456.03. Street repair continued to decline as a percentage of the total outlay, while water and police services registered the largest gains, reflecting the erection of a new waterworks and expansion of the police system. Unfortunately, figures were unavailable for subsequent years. Stable receipts combined with rising expenditures and financial distress after 1857 probably produced a decline in public expenditures, and hence a decline in the quality of urban services in Wheeling.[76]

Richmond's disbursements from available sources for 1856 (expenditures not enumerated) and 1858 revealed that city government outlays almost doubled between the two years. Internal improvements, as in Wheeling, manufactured the heaviest debt. Gas and water services (both were public enterprises in Richmond, and both were new additions to Richmond's budget in the 1850s accounted for the greatest disbursements in urban services.[77] A comparison between the expenditures of Richmond in 1839 and in 1858 reveal both the expanded role of government and the growth of urban services. In the former year, the city spent $40,000 for interest on the public debt; $20,000 for salaries; $9,000 for police protection; $5,000 for fire protection; $5,000 for poor relief; $4,000 for street repair; and $2,000 for public schools and the orphanage asylum. Total expenditures came to $85,000. The small sum expended for street repair and the absence of gas lighting and a waterworks made the following comment by British traveler James Silk Buckingham understandable: "The streets are wretch-

76. Wheeling *Daily Intelligencer*, January 20, 1854; January 12, 1855; January 23, 1856. See also *Intelligencer*, January 16, 1858.
77. Richmond *Enquirer*, March 27, 1857; "Richmond, 1859," *Hunt's*, 64–65.

edly paved, imperfectly drained and never lighted . . . the most dirty, rough, and disagreeable streets to walk on that are to be found perhaps in the Union." [78]

In the 1858 budget, loans accounted for $71,000 (primarily for railroad stock subscription); interest for $125,000; waterworks for $45,000; gasworks for $75,000; street repair for $40,000; improvements in the James River for $3,500; the market house for $2,500; the cemeteries for $3,000; fire protection for $10,000; relief for the poor for $11,000; salaries for city officials (including police) for $40,000; total expenditures: $480,000. Services such as water, gas lighting, cemeteries, the market house, and river improvements did not appear in the previous budget. Some services such as relief for the poor and fire protection, declined as a percentage of the budget, though Richmond still spent more per capita on relief for the poor than New York City did. This decline indicated not only the presence of competing services, but that of the increasingly burdensome debt incurred by Richmond's city government. The role and fiscal power of urban government gained considerably during the two decades. [79]

The galloping debt of urban government in the 1850s reflected the more active role of that government in the affairs of a growing city. As city officials found themselves wading in the mire of debt, they studied and analyzed the system of city finances (perhaps the first time that city government had undertaken such a task) and concluded that citizens must pay for the features of modern urban life. This was not an unusual conclusion, but it proved extremely unpopular. For the first time, city government achieved citywide recognition, although city officials doubtless longed for the anonymity that the limited role of city government had ensured for them prior to the new era.

The property tax was the main source of revenue for Virginia's cities, excluding loans. The rate of taxation on property did not increase as much as rates on other sources of revenue did. In Wheeling, for example, government receipts declined from

78. Eaton, *Southern Civilization*, 251; Buckingham quoted in *Southern Civilization*, 253.
79. "Commercial and Industrial Cities: Richmond, 1859," *Hunt's*, 64–65.

$147,000 in 1854 to $94,000 in 1855, while disbursements were increasing. Although the percentage of property tax contribution to the city treasury rose from 29% in 1854 to 53% in 1855, in actual dollars the amount increased only 12%. The increase in property tax revenue resulted from a rise in property value rather than from an increase in the rate of taxation. For Wheeling and for other cities as well, the property tax was a stable and not an incremental levy.[80] City officials cast about for revenue-producing taxes and budget-trimming procedures. They rarely threatened the property tax, perhaps because it was an imposition on the city-builders from whom they drew their membership and support. Private property, according to the litany of the times, was a sacred instrument in directing and generating sound urban development. A stake in the community was a stake in its future.

Accordingly, cities sought revenues from sources other than real estate. In late 1855, the state legislature allowed Wheeling to levy taxes on the manufacture and sale of liquor. Alexandria's solution to revenue problems during that same year underscored the inviolability of private property in the tax structure. The councils voted to lower the real estate tax rate from $1.10 per $100.00 valuation to $.90. On the other hand, the capitation tax on male inhabitants other than slaves rose from $1.00 to $1.50 and the tax rate on cows increased from $.25 per $100.00 valuation to $.50. The most significant differences in the revenue bill were the new additions: omnibuses, $15.00; boardinghouses, $10.00; biscuit bakers, $20.00; loaf bread bakers, $10.00; horse dealers, $25.00; express agents, $25.00; savings banks, $10.00. These were primarily license fees that served the dual purpose of control and revenue. Three years later the legislature approved a proposal by Alexandria officials to impose an income tax and a paving tax. Some Alexandrians felt lost in the maze of taxable items that seemed to grow geometrically. "Grey Hairs" commented on a recent tax bill by recalling "when I took up the morning's paper before we sat down to breakfast, [I knew] what Corporation taxes I should have to pay, in 5 minutes by the clock. Today I undertook the annual

80. Wheeling *Daily Intelligencer*, January 12, 1855; January 23, 1856.

duty, and before I got through, was peremptorily stopped and asked if I intended to keep the children and servants from their accustomed meal for *an hour* longer than usual. I succumbed—and sighed, on more accounts than one, for *old* Alexandria."[81]

The citizens' reaction to the tax burdens was strong throughout urban Virginia. Richmond residents also yearned for the "good old days" after the council raised taxes and license fees 30% across the board in 1855. A group of irate Richmonders led by James Lyons, city-builder and attorney, held a public demonstration protesting the tax increases. In Alexandria, nonproperty holders voiced vigorous opposition to what they believed to be an unfair tax load. "A Tax Payer" could not see the logic of repaving the major business thoroughfare in Alexandria while city finances were so precarious. Some overtaxed citizens in Wheeling sought enabling legislation from the state to add a second body to the city council "as a check upon the haste, indiscretion, and log-rolling propensities of the council as now organized." In Norfolk a mass meeting protested rising taxes. None of these attempts at citizen pressure was successful immediately. Lynchburg's government was probably the only one to retract its tax package because of significant public outcry. In 1857, the council soothed the powerful mercantile community by reducing merchant's taxes by 40% and the 1% sales tax to ½%. They increased the income tax on lawyers, physicians, and brokers by one-half of 1%. City officials elsewhere pushed forward with their tax programs and argued that it was the only method available to meet their debts.[82]

Citizen unrest prompted a program of general retrenchment that mollified some economy-minded citizens. As a show of good faith, Alexandria's city officials cut the salaries of all officers in half (except for that of the auditor who received a $100 raise presumably because he had to juggle the city's deteriorating finances). Further, the council canceled the $10,000 appropriation promised

81. *Ibid.*, December 3, 1855; Alexandria *Gazette*, April 12, 1855; *Gazette*, June 14, 1856.

82. Richmond *Enquirer*, November 16, 1855; and November 27, 1855; Alexandria *Gazette*, May 22, 1855; and October 1, 1858; Wheeling *Daily Intelligencer*, December 30, 1853; Norfolk *Southern Argus*, June 13, 1860; Lynchburg *Virginian*, May 5, 1857. See Wade, *Urban Frontier*, 280.

to the Piedmont and Potomac Valley Agricultural Society for the purposes of staging a fair in Alexandria in the fall of 1860. As a result, the society was unable to hold its fair and numerous merchants in the city were disappointed. Alexandria's inhabitants however, would rather forgo the fair than do without lights, water, or sufficient police protection. Wheeling, after all, had eliminated subsidies to the voluntary fire companies—a disastrous move, as it turned out. In a gesture of contrition, the Wheeling City Council restored the fire appropriation and reduced the salaries of the city officers. Following the economic turmoil generated by the Panic of 1857, Wheeling threatened to introduce another measure of economy by repudiating its railroad debts. Norfolk officials also threatened to abrogate the city subscription to the mismanaged Seaboard and Roanoke Railroad. Neither city carried through their threats. Norfolk eliminated plans for a modern waterworks instead.[83]

Virginia city governments were not approaching bankruptcy toward the end of the decade, but officials began to rue the extravagance of the early days of the new era. Citizens demanded more and better services yet balked at rising taxes. Moreover, there were indications that the deferential treatment that city government accorded to the business community with respect to urban services was becoming increasingly unpopular with citizens. Inhabitants of one ward in Richmond, for example, threatened secession if services in that section did not attain the level of those in the business district.[84]

The Panic of 1857 compounded the financial distress by tightening the money market. This decreased the cities' borrowing capability and also dealt a blow to their economic bases by throwing mercantile and industrial establishments into financial chaos. The panic severely constricted urban banking capital at a time when urban growth required its expansion. One half of the deposits in New York banks were balances due to out-of-state banks. When banks in Old Dominion cities began to demand these balances to

83. Alexandria *Gazette*, February 25, 1858; August 1, 1860; and October 19, 1860; Wheeling *Daily Intelligencer*, January 16, 1858; March 10, 1858; November 13, 1858; and January 5, 1859; Norfolk *Southern Argus*, January 8, 1852; *Argus*, August 25, 1858.
84. Richmond *Daily Dispatch*, April 8, 1853.

prepare for the coming fall trade, the reckless financial policies of
the New York banks became evident. They suspended payment
because they could not meet demands. Virginia's banks in turn
suspended payment, and urban economies ground to a halt.
Perhaps the most unfortunate result of the panic occurred in its
aftermath. The Virginia legislature, prior to the panic, had been on
the verge of approving a liberal system of branch banking to
increase the amount of capital in the state—a reform that had been
needed badly by urban entrepreneurs. Following the panic, however, prejudice against banks of any form killed the incipient
branch system and shortage of capital became another cross that
the city-builder had to bear.[85] The Alexandria *Gazette* moaned that
"an unusual stringency in monetary affairs, a great falling off in
trade, and a general stagnation in business, all conspire to cast an
unwonted gloom over our whole community.[86]

The bleak financial picture that emerged toward the end of the
1850s could not obscure the rationalization of urban life and the
development of government as an important factor in planning for
urban growth. Urban Virginians lived in a more modern environment and shared the conveniences of urban life with their counterparts elsewhere to a greater extent in 1861 than in 1847. The urban
resident could promenade the well-lit streets of his city's major
thoroughfares at night, fairly confident that the night watch was
somewhere in the shadows, protecting him. If the walker should
carelessly drop a lighted match, local businessmen could rest easy
in the knowledge that the government-subsidized fire department
was ready to answer any emergency in the business district. The
route of the nocturnal perambulator was likely to be well paved and
free of the noisome excreta of urban civilization. While enjoying
the evening breeze free of malodorous aromas now that city fathers
policed and regulated activities in the wharf area, the walker could
congratulate himself that he lived in a city that expressed genuine
concern for the poor, provided or hoped to provide a free educa-

85. Norfolk *Southern Argus*, October 16, 1857; Richmond *Daily Dispatch*, December 7,
1857; Peter Helms Mayo, "Episodes of a Busy Life," (Typescript in Southern Historical
Collection, University of North Carolina); "Banking at the South," *Hunt's*, 312–23.
86. Alexandria *Gazette*, March 25, 1859.

tional system, and possessed an esthetic sense as well. As he returned to his newly constructed house, he passed the railroad depot, silent at this time of night but prepared to carry on the city's business at dawn. "We live in a wondrous age," marveled a Richmond resident, and indeed it was.[87] Urban government expanded to participate in the changes that impressed the walker; not only in personnel and in budget, but in function as well.

As in other commercial cities, business interest often determined the nature and extent of urban services. Virginia cities were not necessarily "private" cities, however. The expansion of local government in the Old Dominion ultimately redounded to the benefit of all city dwellers. In terms of poor relief, education, and open spaces, the benefits were immediate if not extensive. For other services, Virginia's urban leaders, never far apart from the mainstream of their city, had established the precedent of an active government role in city life. As Michael Frisch observed in his study of Springfield, Massachusetts, "As the city grew, the public meaning of government had increased just as significantly as had its implications for private property."[88]

Urban government improved urban life, but it did not transform the city into a paradise with street lights. Some urban streets still made visitors choke from the dust or sink in the mud; disease struck without warning, often violently; taxes were high, and services did not reach much of the population; there was poverty; and blacks, slave or free, lived in a perpetual state of uncertainty. This was not, however, a uniquely Virginian urban situation; it was the urban condition. Civic leaders in urban Virginia coped with growth with available tools. They left problems and remnants of the primitive past to future generations who are still trying to alleviate the negative aspects of urban life.

Virginia's cities strove for identity, modernity, and a place in the urban nation. They attained some of the attributes of urban life and rationalized the flow of information, commerce, and labor to

87. Richmond *Daily Dispatch*, January 3, 1859.
88. Frisch, *Town into City*, 32.

compete better with other cities. Such reordering of life in the city was essential if Virginia was to achieve sectional balance. The organization of the city by civic leaders and their institutions prepared the way for cityhood.

ORGANIZING THE CITY implied the presence of two important indicators of cityhood: an economic superstructure and an urban consciousness. The railroads, factories, and foreign trade triggered
the reordering of urban life. Although the hectic years between the
Mexican and Civil wars left city dwellers little time to intellectualize
about the changes that had occurred, the rationalization of urban
life indicated a developing urban consciousness. Together, the
erection of an economic superstructure and the appearance of a
full-blown civic pride, completed the process of cityhood for antebellum urban Virginians.

Economic progress was the engine of cityhood. Without railroads, factories, and steamers the other measures of cityhood could
not evolve. Virginians built railroads to secure the trade of the
West. Between 1847 and 1861, Virginia constructed more miles of
track than any other state in the Union. In 1847 the state possessed
six railroads and 270 miles of track, ranking her seventh in the
nation in railroad mileage. By 1852, the Old Dominion had doubled her railroads to fourteen and track mileage to 548 miles,
though she still ranked seventh nationally. By 1858, the number of
railroad companies increased to nineteen and the length of track
open, to 1,321 miles, placing Virginia third in the country behind
only New York and Pennsylvania.[1]

Railroad building, like most other aspects of urban growth, involved support from all sectors of the state. If the cities attained
prosperity, the countryside would inevitably prosper as well. A
farmer near Petersburg expressed this mutual interest best:
"Petersburg is our market town; what benefits Petersburg, benefits
the adjoining counties; the more extensive Petersburg's back country is, the more prosperous the back country will be."[2] Without the

1. "Railroads of the United States," *Hunt's*, XXVIII (1853), 110–15; *Hunt's* XLI (1859),
241.
2. "Proceedings of Prince George County Southern Rights Association," in Richmond
Enquirer, December 31, 1850.

recognition of a mutual interest, neither railroads nor prosperity were possible. The railroad was a bridge between countryside and city and a lucrative span at that. Henry Varnum Poor, the nation's leading railroad expert explained, "Railroads . . . are necessary to farming communities in creating a value for their products, in opening a market for them. They explain the rapid growth of cities that are the *termini* of a large number of railroads." The Virginia Board of Public Works echoed Poor's words by predicting that railroads "will enhance by millions the property of the farmer and will restore to the other [the city] her long lost trade."[3]

For rural residents, better access to market was the most favorable aspect of reciprocal trade facilitated by the railroad. Rural industrial proprietors blamed low production on poor transportation to market centers.[4] Country merchants looked forward to expanding their stock and to receiving articles from the now-accessible city in a predictable length of time.[5] Proximity to a market center as a result of improved transportation facilities meant the difference between subsistence and commercial agriculture.[6] One country journal observed that with better access to market the "farmer can go to market without great expense, and sell his flour, corn & c., and bring at city prices whatever he may need for his own consumption. . . . Our farmers have heretofore paid double and treble prices for the transportation of their produce to market."[7]

The farmer would not only pay less for transportation, but with increased volume and prosperity his produce would bring higher prices in the city. A Fredericksburg merchant wrote enthusiastically to a rural friend, after the state legislature chartered a railroad

3. Henry Varnum Poor, "Effect of Railroads on Commercial Cities," *Hunt's*, XXVII (1852), 249; 39 BPW 1855, 889.

4. "Statement Relating to Certain Lead Interests in Virginia, 1853," (MS in Campbell-Preston Papers, Library of Congress); Leesburg *Democratic Mirror*, January 5, 1859; Richmond *Daily Dispatch*, January 18, 1860. See also, Rice, "Coal Mining in the Kanawha Valley," 393–416.

5. Staunton *Vindicator*, quoted in Richmond *Enquirer*, April 4, 1854; Jones, *Railroads*, 45.

6. See Bruce, "Virginia Agricultural Decline," 3–13; John T. Schlebecker, "The World Metropolis and the History of American Agriculture," *Journal of Economic History*, XX (1960), 187–208.

7. Irby, "Notes for Sub-Commissioners Report," i.

to run from that city to a point near the farm of his correspondent, "This will place your section of country within 50 miles of the best grain market in Virginia. The higher character of our flour . . . will enable our millers to pay the highest prices for wheat, and will enable your farmers to deliver in our market at a small expense." A rural journal shared the following observation with its country readers: "The price of all articles of farm produce depends much upon the facilities for transportation to market."[8]

Rural Virginians, impressed with such logic, joined urban residents in the clamor for railroads. Petitions to the legislature and enthusiastic rallies marked the beginning of widespread rural support for rail links to the city. Most important, farmers and country merchants provided significant financial aid for railroads. The financing of the Alexandria, Loudoun, and Hampshire Railroad was typical. Individuals in Alexandria and in the rural counties to be traversed by the road subscribed $250,000; Clarke, Hampshire, and Loudoun Counties, $100,000 each; and the town of Winchester pledged $30,000.[9]

The heaviest financial supporters of railroads were wealthy farm owners or other persons of affluence in their rural neighborhoods. A survey of twenty-six of the largest rural stockholders in four railroad companies revealed that twenty-one were farmers, four were lawyers, and one was a physician. Their median real property holding was $24,000 in 1850, placing them in the top 3% of real estate wealth in Virginia, and their average slaveholding was of plantation size, or twenty-eight.[10] Few wealthy planters failed to have at least several shares of an internal improvement company in their stock portfolios.[11] Nor was rural investment in railroads solely

8. Y. Adkins to James Barbour, March 1, 1853, Barbour Papers; Salem *Weekly Register*, April 3, 1859.

9. "Report of the President of the Alexandria, Loudoun, and Hampshire Railroad Company," in Alexandria *Gazette*, October 22, 1856.

10. Seventh Census of Virginia: 1850. Free Inhabitants I, XVI, XXI; Slave Schedule I, X; Eighth Census of Virginia: 1860. Free Inhabitants XIII, XV, XVIII; Slave Schedule VI, VII; Alexandria *Gazette*, October 23, 1857, September 28; Richmond *Enquirer*, October 25, 1850.

11. See, for example, Jeremiah C. Harris Diary, November 28, 1859; "Inventory and Appraisement of the Estate of William Massie, 1862"; "Meeting of Stockholders of the

a Virginia phenomenon. Planters throughout the Old South contributed heavily to construct railroads to market centers. C. S. Tarpley, a Mississippi planter, was probably the leading railroad proponent in the cotton South. Southern railroads were predominantly local enterprises, much more so than in the North, and rural support was therefore crucial. Rural, especially planter, response demonstrated that southern capital sought enterprises other than land and slaves for investment opportunities. Planters believed that their subscriptions would not only yield dividends, but their land and slaves would increase in value as a result of the railroad.[12]

The countryside's support of urban railroad schemes went beyond financial support. Donations of land, labor, and material accompanied monetary aid. Tobacco planters, for example, formed clubs to act as contractors to build the Richmond and Danville Railroad through rural districts in 1851. They also supplied the slave labor and the necessary wood.[13] This-do-it-yourself railroad building demonstrated the enthusiasm of farmers for the railroad. The Richmond and Danville became one of the state's most prosperous railroads by 1860.

Private investment and aid, however welcome, would not have been sufficient to construct a railroad. Under Virginia's system of mixed enterprise, private subscription usually totaled no more than two-fifths of the company's total capitalization and usually was considerably less. The legislature was responsible for three-fifths of the remaining appropriation.[14] Since rural members dominated the legislature in Virginia, as in other states at that time, the enthusiasm of the countryside had to be transferred to the legislative chambers in Richmond. Usually, this transmission was not difficult since some of the more prolific rural subscribers were members of

Alexandria, Loudoun, and Hampshire Railroad Company," Alexandria *Gazette*, September 8, 1858; and "Annual Meeting of . . . Orange and Alexandria Railroad," *Gazette*, October 23, 1857.

12. Reed, *New Orleans and Railroads*, 88–89; Jones, *Railroads*, 89–97.

13. Richmond *Enquirer*, December 19, 1851; see also, James M. Whittle to Lewis N. Whittle, November 12, 1852, Lewis Neale Whittle Papers; Richmond *Enquirer*, September 2, 1853.

14. See Carter Goodrich, "The Virginia System of Mixed Enterprise: A Study of State Planning of Internal Improvements," *Political Science Quarterly*, LIV (1949), 355–87.

the legislature. Influential country legislators aligned themselves with their urban colleagues and consistently supported major internal improvement legislation. John Rutherfoord, a Piedmont planter, and George Deneale, a country lawyer from the Valley, chaired the Roads and Internal Navigation committees in the House and Senate respectively. They championed major railroad projects emanating from Virginia's cities throughout the 1850s. Hopeful railroad petitioners identified Rutherfoord especially as the key figure in the legislature.[15]

Rural stockholders mingled and interacted with their urban counterparts at stockholders' and directors' meetings, reflecting rural financial participation in railroad building. Company leadership was evenly dispersed among urban and rural residents. Presidencies followed no particular pattern. Two of the most effective and persisting railroad heads were John S. Barbour, a wealthy planter and president of the Orange and Alexandria Railroad; and Lewis McKenzie, an Alexandria merchant and civic leader who was also head of the Alexandria, Loudoun, and Hampshire Railroad.[16] At stockholders' gatherings, usually held in the market city, country subscribers were not only present in good numbers but participated actively and, at times, vociferously in the proceedings to shape company policy.[17] Thus, the railroad not only brought city and country in greater physical proximity to each other, but it also provided opportunities to exchange ideas and to converse on a face-to-face basis.

It is important to recount the role of rural Virginia in railroad construction because it demonstrated that the desire for urban growth was not confined to the city. Indeed, most Virginians perceived urban and rural prosperity as inseparable. Not that city and country were perpetual allies. As with most close relationships,

15. Charles W. Dabney to Robert L. Dabney, March 29, 1853, Dabney Papers; Colin Bass to John McCauley, February 4, 1854, John McCauley Papers, Alderman Library, University of Virginia; Thomas Taylor to John C. Rutherfoord, December 12, 1853, Rutherfoord Papers. See also Richmond *Enquirer*, March 11, 1856; and June 1, 1856.

16. Alexandria *Gazette*, September 23, 1857; "Annual Meeting of . . . Orange and Alexandria Railroad," *Gazette*, October 23, 1857.

17. Jeremiah C. Harris Diary, November 1, 1851; 38 BPW 1853–54, "Report of the President of the Manassas Gap Railroad Company," 291–313.

arguments were sometimes quite rancorous. One of the features of cityhood, in fact, was the growing distinction of urban life from the rural lifestyle. The cooperation of city and country, though, facilitated the urbanization process.

Urban leaders appreciated the role of railroads in fomenting urbanization. "The increase of Richmond," the *Dispatch* explained, "has been owing to a very simple cause—namely, the increase of facilities for getting to market."[18] The facilities the *Dispatch* referred to included the Richmond and Danville Railroad through the tobacco region of Southside Virginia; the Virginia Central Railroad that tapped the wheat and livestock centers in the Piedmont and the Valley; the Richmond and York River Railroad that provided the capital city with access to the Chesapeake fisheries; and the James River and Kanawha Canal that opened Richmond to the coal regions beyond Lynchburg.[19] When the new era began in 1847, only the canal and a small portion of the Virginia Central Railroad existed. Richmond became the most accessible city from anywhere in the state as a result of the railroad connections that had been completed by 1861. The network not only secured a bountiful commerce, it transformed the city into a convention center. The annual state Democratic party convention, for example, usually held in Staunton, shifted to Richmond. As a northwestern Virginia editor noted, Staunton "is the territorial center," but Richmond "is the travelling center."[20]

Alexandria's major connection with the West was the Orange and Alexandria Railroad. The Orange and Alexandria, linked with the Virginia and Tennessee at Lynchburg, formed a continuous railroad to the Mississippi River "commanding the trade of two great sections of the Union, one a great agricultural region, and the other a great commercial region." The Manassas Gap Railroad from Alexandria breached the upper Valley grain, livestock, and coal region. In January 1860, the Orange and Alexandria Railroad was opened to Lynchburg; and the Alexandria, Loudoun, and

18. Richmond *Daily Dispatch*, August 17, 1859.
19. 41 BPW 1860–61, "Report of the Virginia Central Railroad Company," n.p.; and "Railroads," 606; see also, "Richmond, 1859," *Hunt's*, 51–52.
20. Fairmont *True Virginian*, quoted in Richmond *Enquirer*, April 24, 1857.

Hampshire Railroad pushed through to the upper Valley coal-fields. A year later the *Gazette* reviewed the benefits of both railroads to the city and remarked that Alexandria had experienced "the most prosperous year we have had since retrocession." [21] Lynchburg's major work, the Virginia and Tennessee Railroad, opened its full length to Memphis in January 1857, thus connecting that city with the cotton states. [22]

Wheeling, in the northwest corner of Virginia, had better connections with other states than with other sections of Virginia. The Cleveland, Pittsburgh, and Wheeling Railroad allowed the city access to the Great Lakes area; the Baltimore and Ohio, completed to Wheeling in 1853, connected Wheeling with the Chesapeake metropolis; and the Central Ohio Railroad provided service to Cincinnati. [23] Norfolk's railroad lines were more modest but potentially the most remunerative. The financially troubled Norfolk and Petersburg Railroad was Norfolk's only link to the West. From there, the Southside Railroad ran to Lynchburg to connect with the Virginia and Tennessee. After the Civil War, this line was to form the heart of William Mahone's Norfolk and Western Railroad empire. Petersburg's two major links with East and West were the connection with Norfolk and the Southside Railroad to Lynchburg. [24]

The railroad lines emanating from the city and traversing the state represented a prodigious effort of a broad coalition: individuals from farmers to manufacturers, local government, county government, the state, and a small amount of financial support from out of state. Almost all of the work was accomplished in the relatively short span of fourteen years, and almost all of it was a domestic effort. Of the major urban rail lines, only the Norfolk and Petersburg and the Central laid sections of track before 1847. Never had a state constructed so much in so little time. [25]

21. Richmond *Enquirer*, February 19, 1858; Alexandria *Gazette*, January 1, 1861. See also *Gazette*, December 1, 1858.
22. Richmond *Enquirer*, January 27, 1857.
23. Wheeling *Daily Intelligencer*, January 4, 1858.
24. 41 BPW 1860–61, "Railroads," 595–614.
25. See Carter Goodrich, "Internal Improvements Reconsidered," *Journal of Economic History*, XXX (1970), 289–311.

As advertised, the railroad extended the urban commercial empire. Merchants' cards appeared in faraway journals at the other end of the railroad line. Urban leaders predicted that customers from cities with strange but exciting names would soon follow. Alexandria exclaimed in 1860 that the Orange and Alexandria Railroad terminated not in Memphis but in San Francisco, and that Hong Kong would soon be a familiar port of call for produce-laden Alexandria ships.[26] Fanciful, entirely; but every railroad car pulling into urban depots carried dreams as well as goods. There were sufficient amounts of the latter to lend credence to the former. The Virginia Central Railroad, for example, completed to the Valley in 1855, sent 13,842 tons of wheat, corn, and other grains to Richmond and 3,782 tons of tobacco, rye, and oats. By 1857, 22,034 tons and 4,484 tons respectively entered Richmond on the Central's cars. Two years later, the Central became the first Virginia railroad to gross one million dollars in commerce in a year. The Central showered Richmond with 22,794 tons of wheat, corn, and other grains; and 6,794 tons of tobacco, rye, and oats. The upward, or westward, traffic demonstrated that Richmond merchants were not only benefitting from handling farmers' produce, but they also were successful in boosting sales to country customers. Fertilizer, especially guano, was a large item in the upward trade. In 1855 the Central transported 7,248 tons of fertilizer to rural Piedmont and Valley depots; in 1857, the tonnage increased to 12,195 and in 1859 to 12,351.[27] The Virginia and Tennessee Railroad, completed in 1857, exhibited a similar pattern. In 1857 Lynchburg received 20,065 tons of wheat, corn, and other grains, and 7,271,495 tons of livestock. In 1859 the railroad transported 21,382 tons of wheat, corn, and other grains, and 8,232,462 tons of livestock. Manufactured articles in 1857 accounted for 8,647,009 tons westward and 19,829,483 tons into southwest Virginia and Tennessee in 1859.[28]

26. Alexandria *Gazette*, July 11, 1860.
27. 39 BPW 1855–56, "Report of the Virginia Central Railroad Company," 1044–51; 40 BPW 1858–59, "Report of the Virginia Central Railroad Company," 137–62; 41 BPW 1860–61, "Report of the Virginia Central Railroad Company," n.p. See also "Virginia Railroad Earnings," *Hunt's*, XLII (1860), 122.
28. 40 BPW 1858–59, "Report of the Virginia and Tennessee Railroad," 69–113; 41

The crops that were brought into market centers over the railroad established several Virginia cities among the nation's foremost tobacco and wheat markets. In 1851, the first year that tobacco entered Richmond in a measurable quantity over the Central Railroad, the capital inspected 15,678 hogsheads of tobacco. In 1855 the James River Canal and the Central Railroad helped to boost Richmond's tobacco inspections to 29,458 hogsheads. By 1860, the Richmond and Danville Railroad was carrying tobacco from Virginia's most prolific tobacco district. Inspections jumped to 46,633 hogsheads, with 17,481 hogsheads arriving over the tracks of the Richmond and Danville.[29] Tobacco and Richmond became synonymous. "Tobacco in Richmond," a writer in *De Bow's Review* declared, "is in almost every one's mouth, either for mastication, fumigation, inhalation, or discussion."[30] Lynchburg and Petersburg also benefitted from connections to the tobacco region with the Southside Railroad and the James River Canal being the major arteries of tobacco transfer. In 1851, Petersburg and Lynchburg inspected 7,220 and 5,810 hogsheads respectively. By 1855 inspections rose to 13,343 and 9,511 respectively; and by 1860 Petersburg increased its inspections to 17,530 hogsheads and Lynchburg showed a slight rise to 9,801 hogsheads.[31]

The wheat trade, insignificant before the railroad, became the most common item of the staple commerce. Wheat was the primary staple crop of Virginia agriculture. As tobacco culture declined in the early nineteenth century, farmers in Tidewater and later in the Piedmont turned to wheat as a cash crop. By 1860, the Old Dominion was the largest wheat-producing state east of the Appalachians. Wheat, besides providing an excellent alternative to tobacco as a

BPW 1860–61, "Report of the Virginia and Tennessee Railroad," 60–81. See also "Business of the Virginia and Tennessee Railroad," *Hunt's*, XXXV (1856), 241.

29. 39 BPW 1855–56, "Report of the James River and Kanawha Company," 601–19; and "Report of the Virginia Central Railroad Company," 1044–51; "Virginia Tobacco Trade, 1850–51," *Hunt's*, XXV (1851), 735; "Tobacco Trade of Richmond," *Hunt's*, XXXIX (1858), 485–86; "Tobacco Trade of Virginia," *Hunt's*, XLIII (1860), 736–39.

30. "Richmond," *DeBow's Review*, 187.

31. "Virginia Tobacco Trade," *Hunt's*, 735; "Tobacco Trade of Virginia," *Hunt's*, 736–39.

cash crop, obviated importation of this basic food into the state. As Virginia's wheat growers prospered; so did the cities, emphasizing again the bond between city and countryside.[32]

Figures that reveal the magnitude of the movement of wheat from farm to city are unavailable. Since wheat eventually became flour, an accounting of the number of barrels of flour inspected is a reliable alternative to measuring the impact of the wheat trade on Virginia's cities. Between 1819 and 1848 inspection of flour in Richmond fluctuated between 100,000 and 250,000 barrels, going below and above that range only once respectively. By 1852, the barrels of flour inspected increased to over 300,000 and climbed steadily throughout the decade, attaining a high of 613,000 barrels in 1858: nearly a fourfold leap from the figure of a decade earlier.[33] The burgeoning wheat trade reflected the prosperity of Virginia agriculture and the impetus of improved access to market to commercial cultivation.

Testimonials from farmers and comments in the press indicated that improved access to market transformed the countryside as much as the city. Agricultural societies attributed the improvement of livestock, the general availability of fertilizer, and the increased cultivation of wheat to the relative facility of getting to and from the city.[34] Enthusiastic supporters of railroads, of course, were apt to attribute most any change to the presence of the steam locomotive. Nevertheless, the increased property values along railroad routes and the growth in commercial agriculture indicated that access to market was indeed shaping the economic configuration of the hinterland. Richard Irby, a Tidewater farmer and merchant, spoke for numerous grateful rural residents when he averred that the nearby Southside Railroad from Petersburg to Lynchburg was "a

32. Irby, "Notes for Sub-Commissioner's Report," i; Bureau of Census, *Eighth Census: 1860. Agriculture*, II, XXIX; Jones, *Railroads*, 45; Gray, *History of Agriculture*, II, 920–22.
33. "Inspections of Flour at Richmond, Virginia, From 1819 to 1848," *Hunt's*, XXIX (1848), 546; "Virginia Tobacco and Flour Trade," *Hunt's*, XXXI (1854), 600; "Flour Inspections in Virginia," *Hunt's*, XLI (1859), 356.
34. Charles W. Dabney to Robert L. Dabney, March 29, 1853, Dabney Papers; Richmond *Whig*, November 6, 1855; Jones, *Railroads*, 97–100.

great boon to farmers who were prior to this cut off from market for half the year, but now could ship their crops at any time at a cost less than half what it was before the railroad was built."[35]

The bounty from the farm enabled urban Virginia to fulfill another of its major economic objectives: industrial growth. Processing industries still dominated urban manufacturing, but both the quality and quantity of production outstripped most cities in the country and even in the world. By 1860, Richmond was the nation's leading tobacco manufacturing center and among the foremost flour-milling cities.[36] The role of processing industries in Richmond's economy indicated the interrelationship of the economic superstructure in a modern urban setting. Richmond's strategic location in Virginia's wheat belt, its railroad and canal network, and its James River port facilities enabled merchants to attract a prodigious volume of tobacco and wheat. The capital generated by the trade, as well as the sheer volume of it, made large-scale processing industries feasible for enterprising entrepreneurs. Richmond leaders such as James Thomas, Jr., and Lewis D. Crenshaw built tobacco and flour industrial empires in the 1850s. Richmond's manufacturing capability enabled merchants and manufacturers to offer the best prices to prospective customers. Prices for tobacco and wheat in the Richmond market consistently maintained a three-to-five cents per hogshead and per bushel advantage throughout the 1850s.[37] Industry generated more commerce. Reciprocal trade flourished and supportive services from drayage to theaters enjoyed prosperity. The multiplier effect of Richmond's processing industries thus solidified the city's position as the state's primary commercial metropolis.

Richmond's flour and tobacco industries not only achieved fame throughout Virginia's rural population, but throughout the nation as well. James Thomas's tobacco brands found lucrative markets in all sections of the country. Thomas held a virtual monopoly on the

35. Irby, "Recollections."

36. Richmond *Enquirer*, September 30, 1856; "The Tobacco Trade of Richmond," *Hunt's*, XXXVII (1857), 745; Robert, *Tobacco Kingdom*, 182.

37. Peterson, *Historical Study of Prices*, 196; Thomas S. Berry, "The Rise of Flour Milling in Richmond," *Virginia Magazine of History and Biography*, LXXVIII (1970), 388–408.

California tobacco trade. Brands such as "Wedding Cake" and "Eldorado" were particularly popular among serious chewers.[38] Typical of urban leadership, Thomas invested his profits in a wide range of enterprises from banks to the founding of the University of Richmond. Lewis D. Crenshaw was another Richmond industrialist who enhanced Richmond's reputation as a quality manufacturing center. Crenshaw, together with another Richmond civic leader, R. B. Haxall, managed the Gallego mills, reputedly the largest flour milling operation in the country. Just as Thomas's products gained the advantage in California, Crenshaw and the forty-niners arrived simultaneously. Gallego flour possessed a well-earned reputation for durability.[39] Crenshaw, like other entrepreneurs, used his successful business as a springboard to other activities. He purchased a woolen mill in the 1850s and was one of the largest individual stockholders in the James River and Kanawha Canal Company.[40]

Richmond presented the greatest industrial diversity of any city in the South by the time of secession. Of the eighty-seven industries in Richmond, from iron foundries to bookbinderies, tobacco and flour milling combined accounted for nearly 60% of the total sales of manufactured products. The remaining 40% represented a cross-section of American urban industry. Richmond possessed seventy-seven iron-making establishments valued at three and one-half million dollars in 1860, helping the Old Dominion to rank third in the nation in value of iron products.[41] Joseph R. Anderson's Tredegar Iron Works was the most noteworthy iron manufactory in the city. Tredegar employed 1,000 workers in 1860 and produced locomotives and other machinery for a primarily south-

38. J. H. Coghill to James Thomas, Jr., January 13, 1852; Bill of Lading, March 5, 1860; and E. Frankenhall & Co. to James Thomas, Jr., January 5, 1860, James Thomas, Jr., Papers, Duke University.

39. New York *Journal of Commerce*, quoted in Richmond *Enquirer*, November 4, 1853; see also *Enquirer*, September 30, 1856; Berry, "Flour Milling in Richmond," 391.

40. Richmond *Daily Dispatch*, December 8, 1860; Richmond *Enquirer*, October 30, 1857; Butters, *Richmond Directory, 1855*, 61.

41. Bureau of Census, *Eighth Census: 1860. Manufactures*, III, clxxx; Richmond *Daily Dispatch*, August 23, 1860; "Commercial and Industrial Cities: Richmond, 1859," *Hunt's*, 56–59. See also Bruce, *Virginia Iron Manufacture*, 294.

ern market. A brief catalog of ships' manifests and destinations in the spring of 1860 indicated the extent and variety of Anderson's market: schooner bound for Jacksonville, Florida with "railroad wheels, axles, chains, spikes, etc. by JOSEPH R. ANDERSON & CO. of the Tredegar Works"; brig for New Orleans with "steam engines, railroad spikes, etc. by JOS. R. ANDERSON & CO."; schooner for Charleston, South Carolina with "railroad axles and spikes by J. R. ANDERSON & CO."; and schooner for Savannah with "railroad wheels, axles, spikes, etc. by J. R. ANDERSON & CO."[42] Tredegar had not made the South self-sufficient in the manufacture of railroad iron by 1860, but the section's economic dependence on northern and Welsh equipment was less than it was a decade earlier.

New industrial enterprises appeared with increasing frequency as secession approached. In 1860 alone, civic leader Charles Y. Morriss opened a sugar refinery in the capital city that a writer in *Hunt's Merchants' Magazine* applauded as the most mechanized refinery in the nation; Lewis D. Crenshaw invested profits from his successful flour milling enterprise to open the Crenshaw Woolen Manufacturing Company that specialized in clothing for slaves; the Union Manufacturing Company produced sewing machines; and a new branch of the Tredegar works manufactured vulcanized car-springs for railroads.[43] Whatever pastoral remnants Richmond's James River bank possessed were obliterated by 1860. Tobacco factories, flour mills, and iron foundries—modern heralders of the coming industrial age—dominated the shoreline. Tobacco smoke hung over the area in a perpetual cloud. A slightly asphyxiated visitor to the city in 1860 commented that "the atmosphere of Richmond is redolent of tobacco; the tints of the pavements are those of tobacco. One seems to breathe tobacco, to see tobacco, and smell tobacco at every turn. The town is filthy with it." Richmond could well lay claim to being the "Lowell of the South."[44]

Processing industries characterized the industrial economies of other Virginia cities, though heavier industry grew in importance

42. Richmond *Daily Dispatch*, August 23, 1860; *Daily Dispatch*, April 7, 1860.
43. *Ibid.*, December 8, 1860; "Richmond Sugar Refinery," *Hunt's*, XLIV (1861), 244.
44. "Richmond," *DeBow's Review*, 187; Richmond *Daily Dispatch*, September 22, 1859.

during the 1850s. Tobacco and flour manufacturing dominated the industrial output of Lynchburg and Petersburg, though the latter city possessed a locomotive factory by 1860 as well as seven ironworks.[45] Alexandria developed a reputation as a locomotive manufacturing center in the 1850s. The Smith and Perkins Locomotive Works supplied engines for Alexandria's railroad companies as well as for the Baltimore and Ohio Railroad. Richards C. Smith opened the plant in 1850 and completed his first locomotive for the Orange and Alexandria Railroad the following year. Observers commented that his locomotives exhibited "strength, action, and elegance of workmanship."[46] Alexandria also possessed the usual flour-milling enterprises including the Alexandria Steam Flour Company, erected in 1854. It produced an impressive 800 barrels of flour per day. In area, the mill was second only to the Gallego Mills in Richmond.[47] Norfolk's industries were small and few, owing to the absence of effective rail connections. A flour mill and an iron foundry were the only major plants in the city. Specialty industries such as shoes and furniture had moved out of the home and into the factory, but their production did not seriously rival that of northern firms.[48]

Wheeling, next to Richmond, possessed the most impressive industrial credentials in the state by 1860. Because Wheeling was located across the Ohio River from Pittsburgh, it was only natural that she should develop heavy industry. Wheeling's two largest foundries—Crescent and Washington—produced more tons of railroad iron than either Tredegar or James Talbott's Belle Isle Works in Richmond, though none of the iron was in rolling stock. Wheeling specialized in the manufacture of nails. Its six nail factories produced more nails than any other city in the country.

45. Petersburg *Intelligencer*, quoted in Richmond *Enquirer*, September 15, 1854; Frederick Law Olmsted, *Journey in the Seaboard Slave States* (New York, 1856), 57–58; Robert, *Tobacco Kingdom*, 183; Wyatt, "Industry in Ante-Bellum Petersburg," 1–36.

46. Alexandria *Gazette*, November 30, 1853.

47. Alexandria *Virginia Sentinel*, quoted in Richmond *Enquirer*, October 3, 1854. See also Waring, *Social Statistics of Cities*, 57; Carrol H. Quenzel, "The Manufacture of Locomotives and Cars in Alexandria in the 1850s," *Virginia Magazine of History and Biography*, LXII (1954), 181–89.

48. Richmond *Enquirer*, August 27, 1853; Jackson, *Free Negro Labor*, 58.

Wheeling was equally proud of its glass factories, where even today they still produce quality workmanship.[49]

While the factories of urban Virginia were producing everything from flour to nails, vessels at the port cities awaited to distribute them throughout the nation and the world. Direct trade was one of the cornerstones of the new era as the Old Dominion sought to secure economic independence from northern centers of trade, finance, and manufacturing. Virginia's cities not only increased their commercial contacts abroad during the 1850s, but they opened new markets overseas as well. Richmond, as Virginia's commercial and manufacturing center, established a lucrative trade with Brazil, exporting almost $2,000,000 worth of produce (primarily flour) by 1860. Richmond surpassed all other United States ports, including New York, in the South American export trade. Richmond accounted for nearly one-half of all the flour exported directly from major Atlantic ports to South America.[50] The city's tobacco trade encouraged direct exportation to European ports. In 1850 Richmond shipped 6,000 hogsheads of tobacco directly to European ports. Three years later the city exported 10,000 hogsheads. In 1854, exportation of tobacco increased to 14,000 hogsheads, and by 1858 it was over 27,000 hogsheads.[51]

Richmond merchants and manufacturers sought to increase their independence by carrying their products in their own ships. Richmond leaders like miller Lewis D. Crenshaw began a modest shipbuilding program in the mid-1850s.[52] In 1845 Richmond had possessed only four vessels capable of carrying on overseas trade. By 1857 there were nine Richmond-owned ships plying the South American trade alone. New additions to the Richmond fleet included fourteen lighters, five steamboats, and five schooners. This

49. "Railroad Iron in the United States," *Hunt's*, XXXVII (1857), 497; Wheeling *Argus*, quoted in Richmond *Enquirer*, September 16, 1853; Chester D. Hubbard to William Hubbard, May 26, 1859, Hubbard Family Papers, West Virginia University; Alexandria *Gazette*, March 11, 1856.

50. "Exports of Flour to South America," *Hunt's*, XL (1859), 351.

51. "Virginia Tobacco Trade, 1850–51," *Hunt's*, "Virginia Tobacco Trade, 1852–3," *Hunt's*, XXIX (1853), 631; "Virginia Tobacco and Flour Trade," *Hunt's*, "Tobacco Trade of Virginia," *Hunt's*, XL (1859), 343.

52. French, "Biographical Sketches" (Virginia State Library), 749.

nascent commercial armada raised little concern in New York or Boston, but it was an impressive beginning for a city that was not a seacoast port. Confidence brimmed with every ship that was launched. Merchants looked beyond Europe to the new commercial frontier of China and dreamed of Virginia barks gliding majestically into Hong Kong harbor.[53]

The volume of commerce and manufacturing advantages facilitated the direct trade effort in Richmond. Other Virginia cities did not enjoy the capital city's extensive rail network and diverse manufactures. Norfolk and Alexandria, the state's two other major ports, experienced less success in implementing direct trade. They did, however, increase their direct exports in the 1850s over the figures of the previous decade. While Richmond exported $6,000,000 worth of produce in 1859, Norfolk shipped $561,000, Alexandria, $325,000, and Petersburg, $6,000 worth of produce overseas.[54] Emphasizing the importance of railroads in the urban economy, the completion of two rail lines in 1860 afforded Alexandria its best export year since the War of 1812.[55] Richmond, despite possessing fewer natural advantages than either Alexandria or Norfolk, received the benefit of artificial lines of trade.

The economic renaissance in urban Virginia precipitated a period of quantitative growth. Virginia's cities did not experience a great influx of immigrants nor a significant expansion of area. Urbanization was more apparent in economic increments than in physical or population advances; yet the increase of population, territory, and especially of wealth in some cities was sufficient to indicate growth.

Richmond was the state's largest city in 1860, as it had been a decade earlier. The capital city grew by 38.2% in the 1850s to 38,000 inhabitants in 1860. It represented the largest percentage increase in the city's population since the opening decade of the century. Retrocession and railroads rejuvenated Alexandria, and population figures reflected part of the economic good fortune.

53. "Commercial and Industrial Cities: Richmond, 1859," *Hunt's*, 62–63.
54. Richmond *Daily Dispatch*, March 30, 1859. See also Stewart, "Hampton Roads," 48.
55. Alexandria *Gazette*, January 1, 1861.

Population in the city increased from 8,700 in 1850 to 12,700 in 1860 (46.0%): the largest percentage leap since the prosperous colonial period. Petersburg similarly enjoyed a rise in population, though not as sharp a departure from population gains of previous years. In 1860 Petersburg's population was 18,300 which was an advance of 30.7% over the 1850 figure and more than the previous decade's increase, but less than the rise during the 1830s.

Wheeling, whose potential for urban greatness ran aground at Pittsburgh, grew slowly after 1830, gaining between two and four thousand inhabitants each decade. During the 1850s the city's population grew by 23.7% to 14,100 compared with a 54.8% increase a decade earlier. Norfolk's population remained the same during the 1850s, increasing by only three hundred people. In effect this represented a gain in population since two thousand residents died during the yellow fever epidemic of 1855, and hundreds of others were dissuaded from returning or settling in an unhealthy city. Lynchburg was the only city to lose population during the decade, dropping to 6,900—a loss of 13.8% over the 1850 figure.[56] The population gains in urban Virginia were thus relatively unimpressive. The railroads, factories, and ships constructed in the 1850s indicated that enterprise and organization were more significant generators of urban growth than sheer numbers.

Population increases, however modest, altered the physical landscape of the city. The increase in both business and population touched off a building boom in the city to accommodate rising entrepreneurs and newcomers. Renovation also proceeded at a rapid pace as cities put on new raiment to face the urban age. Building construction not only provided necessary dwellings and business establishments, it also signified progress and confidence in the future. "One of the most striking evidences of prosperity," the Lynchburg *Virginian* observed, "is the building of dwellings, factories and storehouses." In the first seven months of 1853, the Alexandria *Gazette* counted the construction of sixty-two new businesses and residences within the city. By 1860 the *Gazette*,

56. Population statistics in Waring, *Social Statistics of Cities*, 55–92.

marveling at the rapid alterations in the city's physiognomy , commented that there had been more building in the city "during the
past ten years than any previous thirty years." Richmond experienced a similar physical transformation during the 1850s. Venerable Richmond chronicler Samuel Mordecai observed in 1860 that
"a few years ago . . . the city was all hills, valleys, and deep ravines."
Progress had removed most of these "barriers to man and horse,"
and houses and stores had replaced the wilderness.[57] The sound of
the trowel and the hammer echoed unceasingly through city streets
accompanying the progress and prosperity of urban growth.

The building effort, though energetic, was insufficient to keep
pace with the growing city. The frequency of households with
boarders was one example of the housing crisis. Workers especially
found it difficult to obtain adequate shelter. In 1860, the *Dispatch*
editors related that they knew "several good mechanics who have
left Richmond because they could not get houses for their families
to live in." Suburbs received the urban overflow. Manchester, a
suburb of Richmond, housed Tredegar workers who were unable
to find lodging in the capital city. The city's first omnibus line,
inaugurated in 1857, provided transportation service for the suburb. By 1860, industries began locating there because of the availability of labor. Metropolitan Richmond grew by 80% in the 1850s,
and some predicted 100,000 inhabitants by 1850. Naylor's Hill, a
suburb of Alexandria for which population figures are unavailable,
grew during the decade "from a few straggling tenements into a
collection of dwellings and shops that are more than a village, and
contains a population greater than many country towns."[58] The
countryside surrounding the city generally grew and prospered.
Except for Petersburg's Dinwiddie County, all counties gained
population at a greater rate than their major cities.[59] Urban growth
and prosperity ramified throughout the region.

The physical expansion of the city accelerated the process of

57. Lynchburg *Virginian*, October 2, 1852; Alexandria *Gazette*, August 5, 1853, May 3,
1860; Mordecai, *Richmond in By-Gone Days*, 76–77.
58. Richmond *Daily Dispatch*, July 14, 1860; and September 11, 1860; Alexandria *Gazette*,
September 14, 1860.
59. Bureau of Census, *Seventh Census: 1850*, 257; *Eighth Census: 1860. Population*, I, 518.

differentiation. Devices such as the ward system, city directories, street labeling, and house numbering rationalized growth and attested to the existence of a differentiated city. By 1860, Richmond included an identifiable industrial district along the James River and a business district along Main and Franklin streets. Residences were becoming differentiated from commercial establishments. The Richmond city directory for 1855 acknowledged this new feature of urban life by printing both residential and business addresses for the first time. By 1860 Virginia's cities possessed well-defined business and residential districts.

Differentiation also occurred in the Richmond economy. Industries were moving out of the home and into factories along the James. Corporations such as railroads, ironworks, and processing plants required large work forces. The distinction between employer and employee became sharper. Skilled craftsmen became less important to the urban economy. The number of types of occupations increased statewide from 215 in 1850 to 306 in 1860. Most of the new occupations were urban related, such as architect, commission merchant, gas maker, milkman, newsman, nurse, packer, and undertaker. The proliferation of occupations indicated the increasing specialization of the urban economy. Further, the number of workers employed in urban-related activities was advancing at a more rapid rate than rural employment. The number of clerks increased from 2,967 to 5,134 (73.0%), and the number of factory hands from 230 to 1,567 (581.3%). Between 1850 and 1860 the number of farmers, including farm laborers, rose from 106,807 to 139,476 (30.6%). Considering the new settlements in western Virginia in the 1850s, agricultural prosperity, and the breaking up of large farm units, the advance of urban-related employment is more impressive. Although other cities in Virginia did not undergo the process of differentiation to the extent experienced by Richmond, the movement toward a segregated metropolis was evident.[60]

Expansion of the city placed greater stress on the organization

60. Bureau of Census, *Seventh Census: 1850*, 272; *Eighth Census: 1860. Population*, I, 524–25.

and application of urban services, though the ward system provided a convenient framework. Growth made the city less familiar
and less convenient. It was not coincidental that associational activity soared as the city became more diverse. If a businessman no
longer knew everyone he met on the street, though, he could fret
over the growing anonymity of his city while he thumbed through
new accounts and counted his rising profits.

Growth was indeed profitable. The per capita wealth of urban
Virginia reflected not only the prosperity of the cities but the
confidence of the citizens in their city's future. Accurate figures are
available only for Richmond, Lynchburg, and Norfolk; but even
these figures are revealing. The per capita valuation in Lynchburg
was $1,623.31 in 1859 (slaves are included as personal property).
Only New Bedford, Massachusetts, possessed a higher per capita
wealth in 1859. The third wealthiest city in the nation was
Richmond with a per capita wealth of $1,593.42. Boston's figure
was $1,543.77, while New York City was further down the list at
$779.29. Norfolk, despite the crushing blow of yellow fever, had
rebounded sufficiently by 1859 to have a per capita wealth of
$923.10. The 1859 figures represented a significant increase over
per capita wealth in 1850—greater than the increase in either New
York or Boston. In 1850 the valuation in Richmond was a modest
$801.30; in Lynchburg, $793.15; and in Norfolk, $417.00. New
York and Boston registered a per capita wealth in 1850 of $706.15
and $1,296.93, respectively.[61] The analysis of the Richmond ran-
dom sample provided an indication of the relative prosperity of the
city's population. The figures of per capita wealth confirm the fact
that Virginia's white city dwellers were generally more prosperous
than the rest of the urban nation.

Cityhood is not only measured quantitatively, it is felt. The
railroads, factories, and export cargoes added wealth, area, and
population to urban Virginia. Economic prosperity also generated

61. Campbell County Land Book, 1850, 1859 (Virginia State Library); "Progress of
Boston in Wealth, Population, Etc.," *Hunt's*, XXV (1851), 628; "Real and Personal Property
in New York City," *Hunt's*, XXV (1851), 226; "City Population and Valuation," *Hunt's*,
XXXIX (1858), 518; "Commercial and Industrial Cities: Richmond, 1859," *Hunt's*, XL
(1859), 66.

an urban consciousness. The creation of an urban identity was an inevitable outcome of growth. Civic leaders created their own organizations, their own methods of relaying and deciphering pertinent information, their own labor system, and they developed their own services to and improvements of urban life. They could not have accomplished the ordering of a modern city without urban pride. Cities exhibited this consciousness or pride in three other manifestations that were all calculated to further growth and prosperity. Urban rivalry, the articulation of unique economic needs in a national economy, and a growing estrangement from the countryside indicated that city dwellers were conscious of their environment as a distinct entity.

Urban growth was a contest. It had to be. Every city could not sprout huge populations, the wealth of the Seven Cities of Cibola, and a limitless commerce. People, wealth, and commerce were finite. Urban Virginians were aware enough of the world around them to appreciate that success embodied wealth and power. Failure meant oblivion and subserviency. In a sectional context, failure meant perpetual bondage to northern urban economic power. The urban North was the ultimate enemy to urban Virginians. The lure of prosperity, though, often mitigated sectional considerations: enemies lurked below the Potomac as well. Charleston, Savannah, Memphis, and New Orleans were equally dangerous rivals threatening to usurp a trade that Virginia's cities hoped to capture for themselves. Civic leaders trusted in-state adventurers after the commercial Golden Fleece even less. Intrastate adversaries were potentially more dangerous than rivals beyond state borders. Pride as well as logic demanded that hegemony in the region or even in the nation could not be attained until leadership within Virginia was secure.

Urban rivalry was a common phenomenon of the mid-nineteenth century as cities fought each other for trade and prosperity. Urban growth and urban rivalry were inextricably entwined: Chicago's successful rivalry with Saint Louis and Cincinnati ensured that city's position as the most populous and most prosperous city west of New York. Pittsburgh's triumph over Wheeling, Louisville's hegemony over Lexington, Kansas City's victory against Leavenworth, and the success of Houston over Galveston signified regional supremacy and growth for the victors and a more modest profile for the losers. The bonanza that awaited successful combatants and the failure and humiliation that dogged some victims provided sufficient examples to guarantee that the contest would be waged in earnest. Cities did not hesitate to borrow from each other, but they could easily turn on their models with a vengeance.[62]

Urban rivalry was more intense in Virginia than it would have ordinarily been in other states for three reasons. First, Virginia's cities, with the exception of Wheeling, awoke to the promise of modern urban life simultaneously. This meant that they had to construct their economic superstructure with a finite amount of state and local capital. Second, urban Virginia discovered that during their somnolence cities elsewhere had undertaken the task of city-building. There was much catching up to do. The imminency of the sectional crisis as well as the hardening trade circuits precluded dawdling. Urgency generated impatience and eventually rancor. Finally, Virginia's cities were fairly similar in population, wealth, and prospects. Richmond was the most important city in the state, but its advantages were not overwhelming.

Urban Virginians were aware that the special circumstances that surrounded their thrust for commercial empire and cityhood were conducive to bitter rivalry. They warned each other that division meant defeat for all. A Richmond resident asserted that "a feeling of jealousy between rival localities is the cause of the slow development of resources." In a more apocalyptic tone, the *Dispatch* claimed that "the absence of union will change a garden into a desert. . . . Virginia . . . shall be destined to weakness, impoverishment and insignificance by the suicidal jealousies of her own people."[63] These were apt phrases. As urban Virginians viewed the

62. See Wyatt W. Belcher, *The Economic Rivalry Between Saint Louis and Chicago, 1850–1880* (New York, 1947); Charles N. Glaab, *Kansas City and the Railroads*; Wade, *Urban Frontier*; and Wheeler, *To Wear a City's Crown*.

63. Richmond *Enquirer*, October 3, 1854; Richmond *Daily Dispatch*, January 17, 1854.

urban nation, however, competition, not unity, was the prevailing key to success in America.

It was not surprising that with the mystique surrounding the railroad's regenerative powers, the most acrimonious rivalry raged over internal improvements. The focus of the debate was the state legislature. The legislature not only chartered companies but provided substantial capital as well. Urban strategy centered on persuading legislators to part with the state's money for the best scheme. There were three strategies employed by Virginia's cities and their representatives to secure appropriations. All of the maneuvers tended to exacerbate interurban animosity. The bitterness, in turn, sharpened urban identity and civic pride.

The first strategy centered on arousing the sympathy of the legislators. The petitioning city depicted itself as the most needy and neglected applicant in the state and its sated rivals as undeserving of consideration. A Fredericksburg railroad promoter wrote to delegate John Rutherfoord, seeking the latter's support for the Fredericksburg and Gordonsville Railroad: "We have been injured very much by other internal improvements and this bill is but a simple act of justice to enable us to keep our place with our neighbors." One Alexandrian, exercised over Richmond's opposition to the Orange and Alexandria Railroad, fired off an open letter to the Richmond press admitting that he was "somewhat astonished that cities which are already *well provided for* should attempt to oppose so great an improvement." Alexandria, recently retroceded to the Old Dominion, itself became the target of attackers. Rivals claimed that money for the interloper was not as judicious as support for cities whose loyalty to Virginia was unquestioned. After Alexandria delegates successfully opposed a Fredericksburg railroad scheme, the latter town reminded lawmakers that "from the time when she was taken in by Virginia—or rather when Virginia was *taken in* by her—she has not ceased to cry *give, give*." Wheeling, away in the northwest corner of the state, received similar verbal abuse whenever she threatened the projects of eastern cities. Wheeling was "the spoiled child of Virginia." Railroads from that city would ultimately benefit the "free-soil city of Pittsburgh," or that "den of Fanny Wrightism and queen of abolition cities, the city of *Cleveland in the State of Ohio!*" [64]

When it came to feeling slighted, Norfolk was probably most vocal in relating her feelings to the legislature. Between 1849 and 1856, Norfolk residents hurled steady invectives at lawmakers for alleged favoritism to other cities and the neglect of Norfolk. A review of the rhetoric revealed the frustration that came with defeat. In the spring of 1849, after the legislature voted down appropriations to a Norfolk railroad, several citizens called for secession from Virginia and annexation to North Carolina. One Norfolk resident declared crudely but forcefully, "I go in for hitchin' teams with the Old North State, for it has long been my notion that Virginia cares little for Norfolk. Huzza for North Carolina and annexation!" A year later and after another railroad defeat, one editor complained, "When Norfolk comes forward to ask the smallest favor, though it be as clearly just and equitable as others she invariably gets the cold shoulder." As a remedy to this continued spurning, the editor raised again the idea of secession. In 1852, the assembly still had not satisfied the city's demands, and the same editor expressed his and his city's anguish: "While the interests of all other cities . . . are fully considered, those of her only seaport have been entirely overlooked and disregarded. . . . We will not quietly submit to such wholesale injustice. To us the alternative will be to submit to galling, degrading and hopeless oppression, or take refuge in revolution." [65] It was the rhetoric of the fire-eater, and the cause was equally consuming.

The sense of urgency that accompanied the quest for commerce added to Norfolk's anger. When Richmond and Petersburg journals urged patience and calm, Norfolk retorted, "We are admonished to 'bide our time'; yes, indeed, our hour will come, but if we are treated with neglect and contempt while the division of all the available funds is going on, what are we to expect as residuary

64. John Seddon to John Rutherfoord, February 22, 1853, in Rutherfoord Papers; Richmond *Enquirer*, January 21, 1853; Fredericksburg *News*, quoted in Alexandria *Gazette*, January 26, 1854; Richmond *Daily Dispatch*, January 19, 1853.

65. Norfolk *Southern Argus*, April 25, 1849; Norfolk and Portsmouth *Herald*, March 15, 1850; and February 3, 1852.

legatee after the entire estate is distributed?" During the next three years Norfolk began receiving state appropriations. In 1856, however, the legislature rejected an extension of the city's only link westward, the Norfolk and Petersburg Railroad. The *Argus* launched its most effusive flow of vitriol against the legislators to date. It reflected both the bitterness of urban rivalry within the state and the fear of failure. The editorial also indicated a perception in Norfolk that the sectionalism engulfing the nation had a poisonous parallel in Virginia.

Are the Senators insane? Have they determined that a "Mason & Dixon's line" shall be drawn through the State of Virginia, South of Richmond, and North of Norfolk—that Norfolk shall be kept in perpetual bondage below this line, while the privileges of crossing it, and tapping the improvements South of it shall be cordially extended to Richmond, Alexandria, and all places North of it, that they may desire to rival our poor legislature-tyrannized port? [66]

The technique of arousing pity for oneself and animosity toward a rival was not as successful as a more positive strategy. Urban leaders discovered that professing disinterest and arguing on the merits of their project for *all* cities was more rewarding. As the legislature assembled for the 1857–58 session, the Alexandria *Gazette* hoped that it "will not suffer the important lines of improvement to be suspended or ruined" in view of the financial uncertainty around the nation. The *Gazette* recommended two "important lines of improvement," both of which were Alexandria projects. Richmond offered the Covington and Ohio Railroad to the legislators and urged that "it is all important that local rivalries and conflicting interests should at once be buried to consummate this grand enterprise." On another occasion, five members of the Richmond Board of Trade memorialized, "The Covington and Ohio Railroad is a great State work inferior to none in importance and ought to be completed by the State with as little delay as possible." Lynchburg, however, disagreed with Richmond's interpretation of state interest and urged the state to fund the James River and Kanawha Canal for the same reasons.[67]

66. Norfolk and Portsmouth *Herald*, February 17, 1852; Norfolk *Southern Argus*, March 13, 1856.
67. Alexandria *Gazette*, September 24, 1857; Richmond *Whig*, July 18, 1851; Richmond

The third strategy employed by Virginia's cities to influence legislators wrapped civic leaders in the mantle of patriotism. The arguments related the cataclysm that would occur if a city outside Virginia should achieve the desired link to the West before a native city could enter the contest. Because of the Old Dominion's proximity to the Baltimore and Ohio Railroad, it was a common tactic to drag the specter of Baltimore's commercial supremacy before the legislature. Baltimore was not so much the target as the means to undermine the claims of some other city in the Old Dominion. Alexandria and Wheeling were nearest to the Baltimore and Ohio Railroad. The two cities were therefore most vulnerable to the Baltimore bugaboo. One Richmonder reminded the legislature that its $700,000 appropriation to the Central Railroad could be wasted if that body connected Alexandria with the Central: "Thus the city of Baltimore will be put in competition with our own cities for the Western trade." The correspondent urged instead the extension of the Central to the Ohio River. A Wheeling railroad request prompted the *Dispatch* to ask the legislators if they were "willing to see the last dollar of that immense western commerce . . . go to swell the coffers of an insatiable neighbor [Baltimore]?" On another occasion, under the headline "Shall Wheeling Sell out the Covington and Ohio Railroad?" the *Enquirer* urged the legislature not to be "deceived" and "surrender the keys that secure to her own commerce the garnered wealth of the great West." [68]

As the sectional conflict worsened during the mid-1850s, civic leaders utilized stronger rhetoric to warn lawmakers of schemes destined to benefit Baltimore. Richmond, for example, cautioned the assembly, "Our Legislature should not give away the State to Baltimore, a Northern city, having no sympathy with us." Alexandria, taking the offensive, sought to block a Richmond project: "Our citizens cannot but view with alarm a scheme calculated to divert the long sought trade from their city and railroad to Balti-

---

Board of Trade, *Proceedings of the Internal Improvements Convention Held at White Sulphur Springs* (Richmond, 1855), 8; Lynchburg *Virginian*, December 8, 1859.

68. Letter from "An Observer," Richmond *Enquirer*, February 27, 1852; Richmond *Daily Dispatch*, January 18, 1853; Richmond *Enquirer*, March 16, 1860.

more, a foreign city." By 1860, the issue of defense was a common concern in Virginia. The *Dispatch* captured the feeling well in a plea to lawmakers: "This road [Richmond and Lynchburg Railroad] ought to be built as a means of self-defense and protection for Richmond and Virginia. The question is not one between Richmond and any Virginia city. It is between Richmond, the most prosperous and powerful commercial community in the State, and Baltimore and other Northern cities."[69]

The state legislature sifted through the arguments—valid, pompous, or overstated, and almost always self-serving—in a charged atmosphere. The provisions of the new constitution compounded the tension in the legislature. Biennial sessions forced a mountain of bills, each with its own urgency, upon the harried lawmakers. Two years was a long time to lick wounds and to fret over disappointments. In these circumstances, alliances formed and broke apart with regularity, shifting with each bill. Subterfuge and machination characterized debate over internal improvement. Tempers and, occasionally, violence flared. The stakes were high, and the delegates and senators played each bill accordingly.

The tension in the legislature increased by the middle of the decade. With each railroad, turnpike, and canal connection, cities attracted country districts into their commercial orbits and hence into support of their projects. The support of rural sections in the legislature was formidable. Norfolk's poor communications with even her immediate back-country, for example, placed that city at a disadvantage in debate. Dr. Francis Mallory, a Norfolk city-builder and member of the house of delegates, complained to his colleagues that "we [Norfolk] have had to contend against opposition from almost every section of the State. Richmond, Petersburg, Lynchburg, and Alexandria are sustained by Counties trading to them which make common cause with their interests. But with Norfolk it has been far otherwise . . . located on brimy waters that separate us from all other parts of the State."[70]

69. Richmond *Daily Dispatch*, February 2, 1853; Alexandria *Gazette*, December 21, 1857; Richmond *Daily Dispatch*, April 10, 1860.
70. Speech of Dr. Francis Mallory in Virginia House of Delegates, February 11, 1854, quoted in Norfolk *American Beacon*, March 15, 1854.

Tributary towns would sometimes join their market center's rhetorical barrage on the legislature. Charlottesville, on the line of Richmond's Central Railroad, commented on a competing Alexandria railroad project, "There is no road in the State which will do so little good to Virginia." Abingdon, a potential Richmond customer, touted the state capital over Norfolk, describing the former as "an emporium of Virginia and the South." A Clarke County newspaper betrayed a lack of familiarity with the state's railroad system as well as partisanship toward Alexandria, its market center, by remonstrating legislators, "The leading roads *all* happen to lay down there and [look] to Norfolk as a terminus." [71] Appropriations, not necessarily reality, were the goals of Virginia's cities and their respective supporters. The legislature, rushed as it was, could barely separate truth from bluster, and the rhetoric of rural supporters only added to the chorus of confusion.

Temporary alliances and bargains allowed the legislature to function with something resembling efficiency. Such jockeying and behind-the-scenes maneuvering are characteristic of any deliberative body. They were carried on in especial earnest in antebellum Virginia. A city's future prosperity and growth often rested on a particular appropriation. The alliances forged by cities and their allies were temporary and sometimes difficult to maintain if a group of delegates received a better offer from a rival city. In debate, partners sometimes had to be reminded of their pledges. When Lynchburg delegates appeared to oppose the extension of the Richmond and Danville Railroad, supporters of that project recollected the backing they had given Lynchburg "when that city was struggling for the Virginia and Tennessee Road." Lynchburg fell into line and the legislature appropriated the funds. [72]

Another temporary alliance proved incapable of holding together, with drastic consequences. When the Central Railroad Company first petitioned the legislature in 1851, its major

71. Charlottesville *Advocate*, quoted in Richmond *Daily Dispatch*, September 16, 1853; Abingdon *Democrat*, June 21, 1856; Clarke County *Journal*, quoted in Alexandria *Gazette*, December 21, 1857.
72. "Proceedings of the Virginia House of Delegates, February 3, 1850," in Richmond *Daily Dispatch*, February 10, 1860.

advocates—delegates from Richmond, the Valley, and a group of counties near the Ohio River—consummated an alliance with southwestern delegates based on the backing that the Central's supporters had given to the Virginia and Tennessee Railroad during the previous session. During the debate it became apparent that southwestern members were going to renege on their bargain and vote against the Central. Barbs turned into insults and shortly there was "a pugilistic passage at arms" between several members.[73] Fisticuffs were rare in the staid legislature. The incident demonstrated the bitterness of urban rivalry as well as the ephemeral quality of partnership. Party affiliation where internal improvement legislation was concerned was irrelevant in Virginia, as it was in other states. Whatever discipline party membership developed in other issues was totally subservient to self-interest on the matter of railroads. This state of affairs tended to lessen predictability and to increase tensions in the legislature.[74]

For city leaders the moral of legislative proceedings was to be vigilant. Rivals could be and probably were eroding hard-won support. There was a paranoia in some of the expressions of urban rivalry. Norfolk's almost hysterical diatribe against the legislature was one example. Comments from other cities, however, indicated that this state of mind was widespread. Once again, the rhetoric of sectionalism blended well into Virginia urban rivalry. Hostility against the North transformed into hostility against each other. "A severe struggle has yet to take place between Alexandria on the one hand," predicted the Richmond *Whig* in 1850, "and Richmond, Petersburg, and Norfolk on the other, to determine which section shall enjoy the benefits of the internal improvements." Two years later an anxious Richmond resident shifted Norfolk to the enemy camp: "Richmond is now between two counteracting influences calculated to draw from her very much of the trade on which her

73. Richmond *Whig*, February 4, 1851. For other evidence of debate generated by the fragility of legislative alliances, see Charles W. Dabney to Robert L. Dabney, March 29, 1853, April 13, 1854, in Dabney Papers; Charles W. Russell to John Imboden, September 16, 1852, in John Imboden Papers, Alderman Library, University of Virginia.

74. See Richmond *Enquirer*, March 29, 1850. See also, Carter Goodrich, "Local Government Planning of Internal Improvements," *Political Science Quarterly*, LXIV (1951), 411–45.

future prosperity depends. *Alexandria* and *Norfolk* are fast sapping her life blood." Lynchburg similarly felt surrounded by a voracious rival: "Citizens of Richmond want to cut off the trade of this town on every side.[75]

Whatever effect these dour declarations of doom might have had on the legislature, they were calculated to incite the local citizenry to action. In the contest for urban growth, a large, united army was an important asset. Civic leaders, by urging all city dwellers to join the fray, spread urban pride throughout the community. The widely read urban press functioned once again as the medium for the message of action. Charles Dimmock, a Richmond city-builder, used the *Enquirer* as a forum to urge his fellow citizens to subscribe freely to the Richmond and Danville Railroad in 1850. If support was not forthcoming, Dimmock warned, and Alexandria connected with Lynchburg, "we may see the bright visions of the future passing away from us, and the promised fruits turning to ashes on our lips." Toward the end of the decade, Richmond leaders recounted to citizens the benefits derived from communication with North Carolina, and concluded, "Would a Northern city need more arguments? She [Richmond] is beset on every hand with rivals who are working openly and covertly to drain her of every stream of trade that flows towards her." Despite the propensity to see enemies lurking in every boxcar, Richmonders rejected a proposed subscription to the railroad. A year later a subscription to the Richmond and Lynchburg Railroad secured the approval of the voters who evidently heeded the *Dispatch*'s warning this time: "Is she [Richmond] willing that others shall secure not only the cotton, but every other kind of trade, and sink herself into a grass-grown, one-horse suburb of the Northern cities!"[76]

The fear of becoming a "grass-grown, one-horse suburb"—and there were numerous examples of that in mid-nineteenth-century America to lend realism to the metaphor—was a prime motivating force behind urban rivalry. Rivalry dominated debate on internal

75. Richmond *Whig*, November 5, 1850; Richmond *Enquirer*, February 1, 1852; Lynchburg *Virginian*, November 8, 1847.
76. Richmond *Enquirer*, Quoted in Alexandria *Gazette*, September, 1850; Richmond *Daily Dispatch*, February 14, 1859, February 21, 1859; *Dispatch*, August 11, 1860.

improvements because success and railroads were closely connected in the new urban age. Railroads, though an important link in the economic chain, were part of a larger program for growth and prosperity. Virginia's cities contested each other on other economic fronts. The verbal thrusts and parries revealed a civic pride that sometimes approached vanity.

Urban Virginians battled for customers as they had for railroads. The plans for urban growth initiated by civic leaders enabled the press to advertise the commercial benefits of the city. Since wheat and tobacco were the two primary market commodities in antebellum Virginia, most of the rivalry centered around demonstrating which city provided the best prices and accommodations for these staples. In 1855, Richmond claimed that ordinary wheat at $2.45 a bushel was the highest price offered in forty years, and that this made Richmond "as good a market for breadstuffs as our farmers can find anywhere." Lynchburg and Alexandria challenged Richmond's declaration by citing wheat prices in their own cities.[77]

Richmond's superiority in the tobacco trade drew sharper fire from urban rivals. The Lynchburg *Republican*, noting the purchase of a lot of tobacco by a local manufacturer, issued the following declaration: "We have no doubt this is the highest price ever obtained for the weed in the State, if not in the country. Richmond is no where in comparison with Lynchburg as a tobacco market." The *Enquirer* replied by pointing out the differences between a lot of tobacco and a hogshead and concluded, "When our friends in Lynchburg chronicle the selling of *hogsheads* at *as high* a price as has been recently paid in this city for *crops* of tobacco, we shall be pleased to admit that Lynchburg *equals* Richmond as a tobacco market." Petersburg and Clarksville joined Lynchburg in verbally challenging Richmond's hegemony as a tobacco market. Petersburg claimed "superiority over all other markets," and little Clarksville boldly asserted that "we rank as high as any tobacco market of the State." Richmond dismissed Petersburg as premature—"ahead

77. Richmond *Enquirer*, April 10, 1855. See also Alexandria *Gazette*, November 30, 1852; and July 30, 1858; and Lynchburg *Virginian*, April 28, 1851.

of the music"—and observed wryly that Clarksville buyers sold their tobacco in Richmond at a profit.[78]

Despite the quiet confidence of Richmond, Lynchburg proclaimed victory in the tobacco market war in 1856: "Lynchburg is triumphant—'Big Richmond' and 'Little Petersburg' beaten out of sight—completely vanquished. Send on your tobacco, ye planters of the Tidewater region—the Piedmont, the Valley, and the Old North State—send your crops right here to Lynchburg, if you want to get the very tip top of the market." Three weeks later, Lynchburg reiterated its claim: "It is a fact now settled that beyond a doubt Lynchburg is the best market for the sale of fine manufacturing tobacco in the world." The *Enquirer* countered by reprinting an article from the Danville *Register* that deprecated Lynchburg as a tobacco market.[79] Although Lynchburg's declarations were more bravado than fact, they were expressions of confident cityhood, similar to the claims of other protoempire cities around the nation at the time.

When boasts proved ineffectual in deflating either Richmond's prices or civic ego, rivals attributed Richmond's advantages to fraud and corporate collusion. Lynchburg charged that Richmond's reputation as a wheat center was built at the expense of Lynchburg. When Richmond inspectors reinspected Lynchburg flour for trans-shipment, Lynchburgers alleged, they removed the Lynchburg brand and replaced it with Richmond's imprimatur. Alexandria and Fredericksburg claimed that Richmond employed its vast rail network to gouge lines to competing cities. Specifically, they asserted that Richmond's Central Railroad charged exorbitant freight rates for guano at the Central's junction with the Orange and Alexandria Railroad. Valley farmers purchased their guano from Richmond because freight rates from there were considerably cheaper. Thus, although Alexandria's initial price for the

78. Lynchburg *Republican*, quoted in Richmond *Enquirer*, May 27, 1851; Petersburg *South-Side Democrat*, quoted in *Enquirer*, May 21, 1852; Clarksville *Tobacco Plant*, quoted in *ibid.*, May 30, 1854.
79. Lynchburg *Virginian*, June 12, 1856; and July 2, 1856; Danville *Register*, quoted in Richmond *Enquirer*, October 6, 1857.

fertilizer was cheaper than Richmond's, farmers secured guano in Richmond because the higher freight rate from Alexandria resulted in a higher final price.[80]

The bitterest economic rivalry occurred between Richmond and Norfolk. Richmond-Norfolk animosity dated from the beginning of the century when the youthful capital on the James challenged the commercial superiority of the state's venerable seaport. The battle waxed in earnest in the 1850s as both cities sought to inaugurate direct trade with Europe.[81] "The denizens of Richmond seem particularly anxious," the *Argus* scoffed, "in defiance of nature and the laws of trade, to make their city the great commercial emporium of Virginia. This ambition on the part of our metropolitan sister has seriously retarded the prosperity of those towns whose position entitle them to the fostering care of the State." The *Enquirer* found the *Argus*'s tirade unfortunate: "It was hoped that the time had arrived when Virginia could unite upon a line of packets between the James River and Europe without the least feeling of rivalry." A statewide direct trade convention in the fall of 1851 adjourned abruptly after Richmond and Norfolk delegates accused each other of attempting to rig the convention. In 1857, with the battle still at a draw, the *Argus* regretted the stalemate and observed, "New York has New York City, Pennsylvania has Philadelphia, Maryland her Baltimore, Louisiana her New Orleans, Alabama her Mobile; Virginia has neglected her only seaport and cherished those towns incapable of becoming marts of extensive trade."[82] Virginia was still groping for a compromise when the war came.

Urban rivalry forced each city to define itself and its interests not merely as a reflection of the surrounding countryside, but as a distinct entity. The ferocity of the rivalry stemmed, in part, from the fact that the definitions were remarkably the same. As cities

80. Lynchburg *Virginian*, April 28, 1851; Alexandria *Gazette*, April 8, 1854; and September 22, 1858.

81. See Peter C. Stewart, "Railroads and Urban Rivalries in Antebellum Eastern Virginia," *Virginia Magazine of History and Biography*, LXXXI (1973), 3–22.

82. Norfolk *Southern Argus*, quoted in Richmond *Enquirer*, September 30, 1851; Richmond *Enquirer*, September 19, 1851; Norfolk *Southern Argus*, November 24, 1857.

battled in the legislature and in the press, they were becoming more similar to each other and northern urban models than to the rural countryside. Urban Virginians developed urban needs as they grew to cityhood. Civic leaders, with their associations and their expanding government, attempted to answer these needs. Some solutions, though, were beyond the purview of even the most energetic group of boosters. The hard-pressed state legislature again became the battleground for urban interests. This time, however, warring cities buried their epithets to explain their distinctiveness to the lawmakers. In the process, they became more distinct and more aware of their cityhood.

The railroads, factories, and export trade broadened the economic contacts of urban Virginia. Commercial intercourse with northern cities convinced civic leaders that urban Virginians were fighting for commercial rights with a blunderbuss while their northern competitors were using Kentucky rifles. Associations and local government helped to lift urban Virginia from the economic Stone Age, but they needed help from the state. Leaders saw repeal of a merchants' sales tax law as the first step in legislative aid. When the state legislature passed a sales tax to help relieve its burdened finances, Virginia's cities closed ranks and petitioned heatedly for redress.

State taxation in Virginia was a simple matter. In 1857, the year the legislature inaugurated the sales tax, the farmer paid forty cents on every one hundred dollars' value of his land, the manufacturer paid forty cents on every hundred dollars' value of capital invested or used in his business, and the property holder remitted forty cents on every hundred dollars' value of personal property. These taxes were not unusual; in fact Virginia had one of the lowest rates of taxation in the country. Merchants, however, did not escape so easily. The revenue bill required the merchant to pay first a license fee for the privilege of doing business and second a sales tax. The merchant paid six times as much in taxes as any other individual, which came to an average of about two dollars and fifty-six cents on every one hundred dollars worth of sales. The Richmond Board of Trade believed that a tax on sales would limit profit and would therefore curtail growth. Alexandria and Norfolk expressed indignation at the tax and termed it an "onerous burden."[83] The legislature pointed to similar levies on merchants in other states, and the taxes remained.

When the legislature convened for the 1859-60 session, finances were still in a precarious condition and John Brown's Raid had thrown the state into a turmoil. Despite vigorous urban opposition, the lawmakers levied a 1% sales tax on goods not imported or manufactured in Virginia. The object of the bill was to encourage the wholesale merchant to import directly into the state and the retail merchant to buy in Virginia cities. This was a laudable goal, but one that was counter to the general pattern of trade. It meant that produce from out-of-state farmers, for example, was subject to the tax. Since Virginia's cities looked to expand their commercial empire, this bit of economic isolationism was, in the words of Thomas Sweeney, a Wheeling city-builder, "a disaster."[84]

The case presented by urban leaders against the levy indicated three things about the state of urban consciousness in Virginia's cities. First, the arguments demonstrated a sophisticated awareness of the mechanisms of a national economy of which urban Virginia had become a part. Second, the urban rhetoric revealed that leaders still viewed the sectional crisis in an economic framework. Finally, the debate betrayed a condescension toward the rural lawmakers who could not see beyond their local market centers to a national economic network. Mentally, urban Virginians were light years away from 1847.

Norfolk, never a city to show deference toward the legislature, began the urban assault. At a meeting of the Norfolk Merchants and Mechanics Exchange to protest the tax, civic leaders composed a memorial and fired it off to the legislature. The merchants predicted that the tax would "prostrate the commerce of our city. . . . *Norfolk will be Commercially ruined.*" The *Argus* agreed with the merchants and again raised the possibility of secession. The result

83. Richmond Board of Trade, *Address to the Merchants of Virginia* (Richmond, 1857); Alexandria *Gazette*, quoted in Norfolk *Southern Argus*, December 6, 1857. See also Wheeling *Daily Intelligencer*, February 10, 1858.

84. Wheeling *Daily Intelligencer*, March 15, 1860.

of the tax, the *Argus* believed, would be to permanently destroy the quest for economic equality with the North: "The contest between the merchants of Virginia and the merchants of New York, Philadelphia, or Baltimore is now very unequal. . . . The merchants of those cities can sell for the farmers of Virginia at lower charges, and to them at lower prices than the over-taxed merchants of their own State. The anti-commercial policy of Virginia alone . . . has prevented the growth of her cities."[85]

Richmond merchants also analyzed the tax measure thoroughly and presented the legislature with a number of odious ramifications. They emphasized, as had Norfolk merchants, the competitive disadvantages incurred by the business community as a result of the tax. In New York, they argued, there was no tax on merchants' licenses. Further, New York merchants paid a percent tax on their actual capital. In Virginia, merchants paid license fees and their taxes were calculated on sales rather than on capital. "Thus," the merchants reasoned, "a man with an actual capital of $10,000 who may, by his superior energy, sell twice as many goods as another with $15,000 capital, pays twice as much into the State Treasury." Such taxation, they continued, dampened incentive. The memorial included a comparative study of taxation in Baltimore and in Richmond. The study found that the tax burden on Richmond merchants was nine times as great. Further, one-third of the wholesale merchants in Richmond did not clear 1% net on goods sold, so the tax would eliminate profit entirely. The *Enquirer* supported the merchants' cause and added that the tax was "ruinous . . . to the commercial interests of Virginia."[86]

The legislature minimized the effect of the tax and in doing so indicated a general ignorance of the principles operating in a national economy. Lawmakers suggested that Virginia's merchants should allow customers to absorb the tax by raising retail prices. The Richmond memorial countered by predicting that customers would circumvent both the tax and the merchants by shopping at

85. "Proceedings of the Merchant's and Mechanic's Exchange," in Norfolk *Southern Argus*, March 17, 1860; *Argus*, March 21, 1860.
86. "Memorial of the Merchants of Richmond to the Virginia General Assembly," in Richmond *Daily Dispatch*, March 17, 1860; Richmond *Enquirer*, March 23, 1860.

Baltimore, Philadelphia, or Cincinnati where taxes, and hence prices, were lower. The legislature also alleged that the tax would encourage direct trade and home manufactures by placing a tariff on out-of-state goods. Urban growth and economic independence would inevitably result. As Richmond merchants noted, however, until the cities developed a sufficient manufacturing capability, the tax served to drive customers to northern cities and thus reduced capital formation in local industry. The tax would therefore derail urban prosperity and make competition with northern cities exceedingly difficult. The legislature, persuaded by both logic and pressure, repealed the 1% tax a week after Richmond merchants presented their memorial.[87]

Urban Virginians attacked other economic inequities that prevented them from competing with northern rivals on a basis of equality. Just as businessmen developed mechanisms to secure the free flow of commerce, they sought also to remove the trammels surrounding the movement of capital. The tax on private credit was one obstacle to capital formation. Petitioners complained to the legislature that every time money "turned over" it was subject to the tax. For example, if A loaned money to B, who loaned the same to C, each person was liable for the tax. Since banks held tight reins on lending, the tax tended to restrict the flow of capital. This placed a burden on the small businessman who was most likely to be a third-party borrower.[88]

Urban Virginians also attacked the state usury laws on similar grounds. The state, by setting a maximum interest rate, forced excess capital out of state where usury laws were lenient or nonexistent. A Richmond merchant claimed that there was "at least $10,000,000 of Richmond capital employed on the streets of New York—driven hence by our absurd State Legislation and usury laws . . . and at least $30,000,000 of Virginia capital employed in New York, Philadelphia, New Orleans, and Mobile."[89] The ban on

87. "Memorial of the Merchants of Richmond," Richmond *Daily Dispatch*, March 17, 1860; *Dispatch*, March 26, 1860.
88. Richmond *Enquirer*, April 9, 1858.
89. *Ibid*., September 18, 1857. See also Lynchburg *Virginian*, March 23, 1857; and Norfolk *Southern Argus*, December 7, 1848.

mortgage loans was another measure that restricted capital accumulation. A potential borrower could not establish his real property as collateral to the loan. In an agricultural community, real estate was synonymous with a person's vocation. In the city, real estate was "merely a spot to dwell upon or whereon to conduct business." Thus, in the city, real estate yielded only rents and beyond that was dormant capital unless the businessmen could pledge it for loans. Prejudice against mortgage loans "is an anti-commercial prejudice and deprives men in cities of the best of resources."[90]

The banking system was perhaps the greatest frustration to city residents seeking large amounts of capital for their various projects. Virginia's banking system consisted of three large state banks whose headquarters were in Richmond with branches in each of the cities. There were no independent or "free" banks.[91] Admittedly, free banks had been unreliable in the past. A growing urban economy, though, required a great deal more capital than three tightly monitored state banks could pump into the economy. The large issues of state bonds for internal improvements and the subscriptions made by private individuals to railroads added to the stringency of capital. In 1851, the banking capital of Virginia (with 1,400,000 inhabitants) was $9,913,100, while that of Massachusetts (with 994,000 people) was $38,645,000.[92]

The diverse investment opportunities in Richmond made the capital shortage especially acute in that city. The *Enquirer* urged the legislature to pass a general charter (free banking) law similar to New York's law. Four years later in 1855, the *Enquirer* pressed its case again: "We need twice as much currency now as we did eight years ago. The growth of our towns and cities and the increase of the price of town property has doubled in eight years. By the free use of capital and credit, New York and London tax a prostrate world." George Fitzhugh also regretted that a restrictive currency in Virginia limited investments in industry: "In a growing and

90. Richmond *Daily Dispatch*, April 10, 1860.
91. See "Regulations of Banking in Virginia," *Hunt's*, XXXVII (1857), 721–22.
92. Richmond *Enquirer*, March 14, 1851.

improving State, its [currency's] capacity for expansion is one of its greatest recommendations. . . . The increase of currency . . . gives rise to new pursuits of industry and new investments of capital which are profitable"[93] The Panic of 1857 and the collapse of several New York banks, however, dispelled any notion the legislature might have entertained with respect to liberalizing its banking system.[94]

Cities fought the strictures placed on capital by the legislature in vain. The legislature lavished considerable funds on railroads that aided urban growth. These projects, though, were also rural measures; so support in the legislature was easier to obtain. Many rural lawmakers did not comprehend the new urban needs or the national urban competition. Further, the memory of the financial insecurities of the 1830s and 1840s coupled with the large expenditures of the 1850s produced an unwillingness to break completely with conservative financial policy. Urban leaders translated the lawmakers' caution into narrow-mindedness and grumbled the eternal rhetoric of cities against rural-dominated legislatures. The Richmond Board of Trade claimed that state financial policies "seriously tend to dwarf the growth of cities and towns of the State." The Wheeling *Daily Intelligencer* reached a similar conclusion: "The members of our legislature have always represented an agricultural sentiment, and that sentiment . . . has been always hostile to the interests of the merchants and tradesmen."[95] It was at once an expression of isolation from rural Virginia and a declaration of urban uniqueness.

Cityhood implied a philosophical separation from the countryside. As city and country developed intimate commercial, social, and financial relations, they were growing apart. The urban consciousness exhibited in the appeals to the legislature was one manifestation of this division. Urban questioning of the Jeffersonian

93. *Ibid.*, March 14, 1851; and September 11, 1855; Fitzhugh, *Sociology*, 127. See also Alexandria *Gazette*, March 13, 1856.

94. See Message of Governor Henry A. Wise to the Virginia General Assembly, quoted in Richmond *Daily Dispatch*, December 8, 1857.

95. Board of Trade, *Address to the Merchants*, 7; Wheeling *Daily Intelligencer*, February 10, 1858.

emphasis on agriculture was another signal of cityhood. The Alexandria *Gazette* summarized a general urban feeling by the end of the 1850s: "No people can be successful, prosperous and independent, who mainly rely upon the production of the soil." George Fitzhugh decried official favoritism to agriculture and warned that "exclusive agriculture has depressed and impoverished the South."[96] As cities came to define and to articulate different needs, their identity with agriculture and with rural problems in general declined.

The tariff created a strain in urban-rural relations. Though urban Virginians were not solidly behind a higher tariff (neither were New Yorkers, for that matter) sentiment for protection was increasing. In 1858 and 1859, after the economic downturn convinced many urbanites that home manufacturing was the best method for avoiding such financial calamities; Richmond, Alexandria, and Wheeling journals published letters advocating protection. As the Wheeling *Daily Intelligencer* reasoned, "We want a tariff sufficiently high to protect the manufacturer so that he may receive a just reward for his labor, and every class of society, and every branch of business will feel the impulse."[97] George Fitzhugh, who wrote volumes on the perils of free trade, reasoned that "free trade doctrines, not slavery, have made the South agricultural and dependent."[98] Most Virginians, urban and rural, were probably wary of expressing preference for the tariff because of its entanglement with the sectional debate. The willingness of respected journals to feature letters supporting the tariff was an indication of the distinctive urban mind.

The growing estrangement of cities from their immediate rural neighbors provided another indication of the philosophical separateness of the city. As cities developed distinctive needs, residents preferred, even demanded, their own representatives in the legislature. The days were gone when a county resident could speak for a city. When Lynchburg's delegate (a county resident) voted against

96. Alexandria *Gazette*, December 16, 1859; Fitzhugh, *Sociology*, 87.
97. Wheeling *Daily Intelligencer*, February 14, 1859. See also Alexandria *Gazette*, October 4, 1858; and Richmond *Whig*, December 13, 1850.
98. Fitzhugh, *Sociology*, 87.

a railroad connection between that city and Alexandria, Lynch-burgers fumed and pledged to send a Lynchburg man to Rich-mond. In the next election, they were successful. Smaller urban areas expressed similar interests. A Danville resident complained to a friend in Richmond, "I find no one who, if elected, would be calculated to reflect or to represent the interests of the people of Danville. Pannill is a candidate, also Thomas T. Jones; both backed and supported by the Court House crowd. . . . I think our city is entitled to *one*." When a county farmer won the House of Delegates seat for the Norfolk district in 1859, the *Argus* cried, "And now when our vital interests are to be represented in the Legislature we get a stranger." [99]

Country residents were aware of the development of an urban civilization and of the divergent interests of town and country. Organizing merchants and manufacturers and the vocal combination of urban lobbyists produced an uneasiness in rural districts. The intimate merchant-farmer relationship still held, but the merchant very likely had more clients, larger overhead, increased inventory, and wider contacts. There was less time for personal handling of each detail of each customer's business. Charges of fraud and collusion continued to pepper urban merchants. Perhaps the most frequent accusation was that urban wholesalers adulterated guano. The Virginia State Agricultural Society charged in a petition to the legislature that Richmond inspectors were in league with merchants to defraud the farmer.[100] High prices, a perennial consumer complaint, enraged farmers who believed prosperity and inflation were not cause and effect. A "Friend from the Country" complained that Norfolk merchants "wanted 20% profit on their purchases while other cities' merchants are contented with 10%." Dissatisfaction with new marketing procedures and organizations convinced the farmer that the

99. Lynchburg *Virginian*, quoted in Petersburg *South-Side Democrat*, February 3, 1854; George W. Woodruf to William T. Sutherlin, March 24, 1861, in William T. Sutherlin Papers, Southern Historical Collection, University of North Carolina; Norfolk *Southern Argus*, May 27, 1859.

100. "The Inspection Laws," *Southern Planter*, XVI (1856), 80–88. See also Alexandria *Gazette*, December 1, 1856; and Richmond *Enquirer*, November 10, 1854.

merchants' interests were not his own. The *Enquirer* pondered aloud whether Virginia's farmers considered the city "inimical to their interests."[101] Such merchant-farmer bickering is timeless and reflected, in part, the closer business ties between city and country. Nevertheless, the complaints revealed that rural Virginians did not perceive urban and rural interests as identical.

The growing philosophical distinctiveness of the city was more alarming to rural Virginians than alleged fraud or price fixing. As early as 1851 the *Enquirer* noted "a wide distinction between the people of Richmond and the people of the country." Other Virginians observed this distinction as well. John Randolph Tucker, a farmer, wrote to an aspiring politician, "If Politics be your object, flee a city, the most tainted and corrupted air for pure political aspirations. You may expect the oak to grow in the dark cells of the Penitentiary, but never hope to see the pure and honest politician thrive in the heated and putrid atmosphere in which alone can flourish the political rabble of the city." Charles W. Dabney, railroad promoter and farmer, viewed the State Agricultural Fair in Richmond as an event for "the trapping of country gulls." On another occasion, Dabney questioned the materialism that seemed to grip modern city life: "I can conceive of a prayer meeting in an engine house; of one in an Exchange, in a Bank parlor, or Broker's shop—I cannot." John Rutherfoord, a longtime urban supporter, wondered privately if "Virginia was becoming from year to year, more imbued with the spirit of the Yankees." The *Dispatch* responded to these accusations by agreeing that "there is a great amount of vice in cities," but only, the writer argued, "because there is a great amount of humanity. The country is not without vice. There is probably more scandal and gossiping in a small town in twenty-four hours than there has been in London or New York for the last one-hundred years."[102]

101. Letter from "A Friend from the Country," in Norfolk *Southern Argus*, December 19, 1857; Richmond *Enquirer*, September 30, 1856.

102. Richmond *Enquirer*, August 25, 1851; John Randolph Tucker to Muscoe R. H. Garnett, July 24, 1848, in Mercer Papers; Charles W. Dabney to Robert L. Dabney, January 31, 1855, in Dabney Papers; Charles W. Dabney to Robert L. Dabney, May 11, 1858; John Rutherfoord to Benjamin Johnson Barbour, June 27, 1855, in James Barbour Papers; Richmond *Daily Dispatch*, October 18, 1859.

Antiurban sentiment was not, of course, indigenous to Virginia. Americans were ambivalent toward their cities. Indeed, some of the more vociferous critics of modern urban life were urban residents themselves. Expressions of disdain for urban life in Virginia were neither unique to that area nor peculiar to that period. Characterizations of the city as corrupt, sinful, and materialistic did not so much signify that the city possessed these aspects in fact as they indicated that individuals, regardless of where they lived, perceived the city as distinctive.

Urban Virginia was cosmopolitan as it was distinctive. Civic leaders moved in fast company with contacts around the nation and even the world. They became less insular. The solutions to problems of growth and the definition of urban economic needs indicated an awareness and an understanding of the urban nation. Leaders studied and borrowed selectively from other cities. By 1860 their cities were members of the national urban community. The credentials of Virginia's cities were impeccable: the most extensive railroad network in the South; the foremost tobacco manufacturing centers in the nation in Lynchburg and Richmond; the leading export center to South America in Richmond; respectable heavy industry in Wheeling and Richmond; a revival of trade and general prosperity in two previously moribund seaports, Norfolk and Alexandria; and the development of the physical and philosophical trappings of modern urban life. Virginia cities resembled northern cities more than their surrounding countryside. Urban Virginia had attained cityhood.

The urbanization of antebellum Virginia might have occurred between 1847 and 1861 regardless of the sectional crisis. Other cities had developed and would develop quite independently of national issues; yet the simultaneous growth of sectionalism and of cities seems too compelling to dismiss as coincidence. The rhetoric of the urban leadership and their economic policies embodied a greater goal than local aggrandizement. While the quantitative and qualitative changes in urban life accounted for growth, the urban response to sectionalism reinforced and provided an important rationale for urban development. The attainment of cityhood occurred within the context of an urbanizing and a dividing nation. It was within that framework that urban Virginians faced some agonizing decisions about their future.

IF URBAN VIRGINIANS in 1861 could spare a moment from their ledgers and forges to look out upon their James River, the scene would have confirmed their personal success. Factories, railyards, and wharves replaced retreating wheat and corn fields. The slow cadence of the James, unpreturbed by its boisterous new neighbors, masked a torrent of activity on its shores. The river was no longer a watery country highway that carried an occasional hogshead or a lonely traveler. It was a cosmopolitan thoroughfare of commerce, opening its winding pathways to the urban nation. Others had come from distant places not to admire its beauty but to share its wealth.

Virginia's city dwellers looked beyond an urban nation to an urban world. They dreamed of a day when "our grandsons will be . . . commercial potentates, and our granddaughters will wear diamonds in their shoes, and take wedding trips in mammouth steamers plying direct between Norfolk and Utopia."[1] While urban Virginians looked to future greatness, the realities of a national economy threatened to engulf their present. In a section where ironies grew like cotton in black soil, it was Virginia's irony that urban growth and prosperity resulted in greater dependence on northern cities rather than in the hoped-for economic independence. The dream of a commercial empire and of sectional equality foundered on the cold laws of trade. Urbanization and economic independence, so closely connected in the minds of Virginians, became just as disparate. Urban Virginia's success in joining an urban nation resulted in her ultimate failure.

Two factors militated against the ultimate victory of urban Virginia in the contest for economic wealth and sectional equality: timing and the centralization of trade in northeastern cities. Geographer Peter G. Goheen observed that timing was a key to mid-nineteenth-century urban growth. Cities had to synchronize inter-

1. Norfolk *Southern Argus*, March 21, 1857.

nal improvements, industries, and export commerce in order to secure urban success.[2] Virginia's cities possessed the basic structures of urban economic parity, but they were in various stages of development by 1861. The lure of national politics, the lethargy and stagnation generated by a prolonged agricultural depression, and the relative calm of sectional politics prior to the Mexican War had inhibited southern cities in general, and Virginia's cities in particular, from advancing toward economic parity with cities elsewhere. Virginia's cities, like other southern cities, initiated their programs for growth and prosperity in the late 1840s and early 1850s. In a little more than a decade (one which included a mild depression) the complete resurrection of Virginia's cities through internal improvements, industry, and export trade was unlikely.

While the Old Dominion's urban centers moved slowly beneath a narcotizing shroud of inaction and depression, northern cities had already developed the requisites for urban economic leadership. At the very moment that Richmond, Alexandria, Norfolk, Petersburg, Lynchburg, and Wheeling were charting new directions for themselves, northern cities were completing their economic superstructures. By 1850 three developments had occurred in northern cities that proved fateful for urban Virginia. First, transportation lines from the northeast had forged an inexorable commercial link between the Ohio River Valley and the cities of the northeast. Trade still went down the Mississippi to New Orleans, but the trend of commerce was unmistakably away from the Crescent City to more northerly routes. Second, the early development of industry in northeastern cities enabled those markets to establish a lucrative reciprocal trade with hinterland merchants and farmers. As a result, northeastern urban merchants were able to offer customers the highest prices for their produce and a variety of wares and goods at relatively low prices in return. Finally, by 1850 New York was well established as the nation's foremost import-export center.

2. Goheen, "Industrialization and the Growth of Cities," 49–65. See also James A. Ward, "A New Look at Antebellum Southern Railroad Development," *Journal of Southern History*, XXXIX (1973), 409–20.

The rise of the port of New York was a combination of luck and enterprise. New York's Black Ball Line was the first company to sail to Europe on a regular basis following the War of 1812. The factors, the warehouses, and the financial machinery grew with the trade. By the time the Erie Canal opened in 1825, New York was already solidifying its position as the port of the nation. If, as economist Douglass C. North has contended, a national economy had developed by 1860, then New York was the hub of this economy. Just as transportation lines and manufacturing and export capabilities worked in an almost self-generating fashion to elevate Richmond as a regional center of trade, so too New York became the national market center. Any alteration of the pattern of trade, especially as late as 1850, would have been a difficult if not an impossible task.[3]

Virginia's cities experienced difficulties in attempting to develop an economic superstructure in little more than a decade. The task required the telescoping of a generation of development into half that time. The projects of the new era, impressive as they were, lay in various stages of incompletion. Internal improvements failed to achieve their destinations. All but one of the four commercial sectors designated by the board of public works in 1851 were unfinished. Only the southwestern commercial sector, with the Virginia and Tennessee Railroad providing Lynchburg with direct access to Memphis, developed as planned. In the southern commercial sector, the Richmond and Danville Railroad was the only improvement of note in the area. Norfolk's connections with Southside Virginia and North Carolina remained poor. The central commercial sector did not include any completed projects. The serpentine Central Railroad had penetrated the Valley at Staunton but had proceeded only slightly beyond that town by 1861. The calamitous James River and Kanawha Canal ran beyond Lynchburg but was 100 miles from its ultimate terminus, Covington. The Covington and Ohio Railroad—the "keystone of the arch"—

3. See North, *Economic Growth*, 193–94; Cochran, "Business Revolution," 1449–66; and Schmidt, "Internal Commerce," 798–822.

existed only on the maps of the Virginia Board of Public Works. The northwestern trade empire remained illusory.[4]

It was not surprising that such an elaborate network remained far from fruition only a decade after the board of public works first formulated the sectors. Nevertheless, the haste attending construction of this system generated a number of evils that decelerated progress. The problems that arose were not indigenous to Virginia but were magnified by the pressure of time. Railroads and canal companies were the first modern corporations. Since there were no precedents, a lack of trained leadership plagued internal improvement companies. Intricate finances baffled even the most well-intentioned executives. A writer in *Hunt's* in 1856 referred to railroad directors as "hurrying, half-informed, poorly-paid, and slightly interested." Directors were "chosen for their personal wealth, influence, or respectable standing in society." When lawyer John Y. Mason assumed the presidency of the James River and Kanawha Canal Company, his close friend congratulated him and added, "It [the presidency] will give you pocket money and will not interfere with your practice.[5]

Given this type of leadership, the antics of some Virginia internal improvement companies as well as a growing anxiety over corporate behavior among some civic leaders was understandable. The Central Railroad directorship charged the highest freight rates in the country and wondered why business took other routes.[6] In another characteristic display of business acumen the Central executives hired an engineer to construct a tunnel, failed to supply him with bricks, and fired him for procrastination.[7] The directors

4. 41 BPW 1860–61, "Railroads," 595–614; BPW, *Report on Turnpikes and Canals, 1860–61* (Richmond, 1861), 267; see also, Elizabeth Dabney Coleman, "The Story of the Virginia Central Railroad, 1850–1860" (Ph.D. dissertation, University of Virginia, 1957), 177, 180.

5. "Railroad Management in the United States," *Hunt's*, XXXIV (1856), 685; "Railroads and their Future," *Hunt's*, XXXVIII (1858), 185; Beverly Tucker to John Y. Mason, May 18, 1849, in John Y. Mason Papers, Southern Historical Collection, University of North Carolina.

6. "Comparative Fares of Railroads in the United States," *Hunt's*, XVIII (1848), 97–98; "Railroad Fares in Virginia," *Hunt's*, XXX (1854), 251.

7. Richmond *Enquirer*, July 28, 1857.

of the Hempfield and Marietta Railroad, a small branch leading westward from Wheeling, tacitly condoned the taking of timber from farms adjacent to the route. Farmers retaliated by tearing up the track. On another occasion workers walked off the construction site when the directors failed to pay them. Finally, a Wheeling newspaper accused the president of embezzling the quarter-of-a-million-dollar subscription appropriated by the city.[8]

The leadership of the James River and Kanawha Canal Company, referred to by one stockholder as "the worst in this union," had several accomplices in their romp through mismanagement.[9] The company seemed to ingest millions in state appropriations with only meager results. When a legislative committee attempted to launch an investigation in 1851, the company refused to cooperate, then relented, but a report never appeared. Faced with declining business as a consequence of competition from the faster and more reliable Virginia and Tennessee Railroad, the directors raised tolls and lost more business. As a result, the company was unable to pay interest on its debt, and the state rescued it. In 1860, the state converted its debt into capital stock in order to resume construction of the delayed and nearly bankrupt enterprise. When the Civil War intervened, stockholders were considering unloading the company on the French, which would have been a fittingly bizarre climax to its ill-starred past.[10]

Lawmakers participated in the company's profligate ways. The legislature lavished funds on the project throughout the decade. Some Virginians seemed mystically obsessed with the idea of a direct water line to the Ohio River. George Washington first proposed the idea in 1794, but work did not begin until the early 1830s. Long after the canal (and canals in general) had ceased to be the most effective mode of transportation, appropriations continued to pour forth from the legislature. By 1861, nearly one-third of Vir-

8. Wheeling *Daily Intelligencer*, January 11, 1858.
9. E. M. Cabell to John Y. Mason, October 30, 1849, in Mason Papers.
10. Richmond *Daily Dispatch*, March 6, 1855, April 4, 1860, September 6, 1860; Richmond *Enquirer*, February 7, 1851, December 16, 1853; "James River and Kanawha Canal," *Hunt's*, XLII (1860), 369.

ginia's state debt of $33,000,000 was generated by subsidies to the James River and Kanawha Canal Company.[11]

The state's improvident financial policy with regard to the canal resembled similar extravagance in Michigan, Pennsylvania, and Massachusetts.[12] Though Virginia never seriously considered repudiation before the Civil War, debt funding became a central issue in state politics during and after the Reconstruction era.[13] In the antebellum period, the state hardly set an example of frugality for internal improvement companies to follow. The legislature not only failed to deal intelligently with the state's finances, but railroad entrepreneurs, shrewd in financial transactions if bungling in management, used several artifices to dupe the state out of appropriations.

In 1852, for example, the legislature subscribed on behalf of the state three-fifths of the capital of the Southside Railroad Company. A year later the company directors appeared before the lawmakers and sadly related that they had been unable to raise the remaining two-fifths of the total capitalization. They appealed successfully for the remainder of the capital from the state, offering as security a mortgage on the property purchased by the original three-fifths appropriation. The state thus had a lien on its own property. Available evidence indicated that these appeals were common and that the legislature acquiesced under the threat that the promoters would abandon the project altogether.[14] In the race for economic parity such an occurrence would be unfortunate. Further, lawmakers were stockholders too. The legislature, overworked by the

11. Bureau of Census, *Tenth Census: 1880. Valuation, Taxation, and Public Indebtedness*, VII, 555.

12. See Oscar Handlin and Mary F. Handlin, *Commonwealth: A Study of the Role of Government in the American Economy, Massachusetts, 1774–1861* (New York, 1947); Louis Hartz, *Economic Policy and Democratic Thought: Pennsylvania, 1776–1860* (Cambridge, Mass., 1948); and Robert J. Parks, *Democracy's Railroads: Public Enterprise in Jacksonian Michigan* (New York, 1972).

13. See Allen W. Moger, *Virginia: Bourbonism to Byrd, 1870–1925* (Charlottesville, Va., 1968); and Raymond H. Pulley, *Old Virginia Restored: An Interpretation of the Progressive Impulse, 1870–1930* (Charlottesville, Va., 1968).

14. Richmond *Enquirer*, February 11, 1853. See also C. D. Whittle to Lewis N. Whittle, March 25, 1854, in Whittle Papers; and Ambler, *Sectionalism*, 313–17.

short biennial sessions and pressured by conflicting and heated debate, usually took the line of least resistance and appropriated funds without regard to system.

The directors were also successful in dealing with stockholders. Annual stockholders' reports invariably apologized for the dividend drought but added that present sacrifice meant future riches. To increase credibility, the directors presented the precarious condition of company finances as due to causes beyond the control of the leadership: "The embarrassed condition of the company's finances," caused by "severe commercial revulsions" or "unusual financial difficulties throughout the country"; lack of progress due to "the very high price of iron, provisions, and labor"; and "the peculiar financial condition makes private subscription for construction absolutely hopeless." [15]

Civic leaders, themselves stockholders, lost their initial enchantment with internal improvements as misuse of financial resources became evident. The endless cornucopia of funds from city subscribers subsided toward the end of the decade. Revenue problems and increased urban services contributed to the reluctance of cities to fund railroad projects. A general antipathy toward company policies solidified resistance to further financial aid. Rate differentials were especially irksome to urban businessmen and their rural customers. Norfolk complained that the Roanoke Valley Railroad charged higher freight rates for the short haul from nearby Portsmouth to Weldon, North Carolina, than for the longer haul from Weldon to New York City via Petersburg. Norfolk merchants charged that the city subscribed $200,000 on the agreement that freight rates would be the same, regardless of distance. In the meantime, the tobacco crop went to Petersburg and ultimately to New York. [16]

Negligence was another accusation leveled by cities at their rail-

15. 39 BPW 1855–56, "Report of the Virginia and Tennessee Railroad Company," 763; 40 BPW 1857–58, "Report of the Virginia Central Railroad Company," 119; 39 BPW 1855–56, "Report of the Virginia Central Railroad Company," 1024; 38 BPW 1853–54, "Report of the Virginia Central Railroad Company," 530; 36 BPW 1850–51, "Report of the Virginia Central Railroad Company," 125.

16. Norfolk *Southern Argus*, May 17, 1855.

roads. Alexandrians, for example, alleged that the Orange and Alexandria Railroad abused and detained produce, thereby damaging commercial relations between city merchants and Piedmont customers. The *Gazette* wondered aloud, "What did we vote our money for?"[17] Cities expressed their disgust by refusing to vote new appropriations, by placing severe restrictions on railroad rights of way in the city, and by passing ordinances requiring railroads to maintain their depots and property adjacent to tracks.[18] Railroads and cities were no longer synonymous. As one Alexandria leader averred, "If we do not look sharp, after all our debts and taxes, we may find . . . the Railroad interest perfectly indifferent to the prosperity of Alexandria, to say the least of it."[19] Such a climate was not propitious for extensive railroad development.

Companies defended themselves by pleading penury. Many of their complaints were legitimate. The Old Dominion's roads were not smashing financial successes in part because of the problem of synchronization of economic activities. Virginia's railroads, characteristic of most southern internal improvements, were too dependent on crops. The traffic from urban terminuses was insufficient to alleviate financial distress caused by crop failures. The Old Dominion's roads generally forwarded twice as much tonnage to market centers as they took away, even in years of crop shortfalls. A depressed director reported the unhappy effects of crop failures to Manassas Gap Railroad stockholders: "Manassas has no relief from the extremes of the seasons which attack localities."[20] Toward the end of the decade, as urban manufacturing and the variety of wares increased in cities, this disparity narrowed. The Virginia Central

17. Alexandria *Gazette*, July 4, 1857.
18. *Ibid.*, November 6, 1855; and August 1, 1860; Richmond *Daily Examiner*, March 12, 1861; Speech of Charles Bruce in Virginia Senate, February 16, 1858, quoted in Richmond *Enquirer*, April 9, 1858.
19. Letter from "A.B.C.," Alexandria *Gazette*, May 10, 1856.
20. "Annual Meeting of the Stockholders of the Manassas Gap Railroad Company," in *ibid.*, October 22, 1858. See also "Meeting of the Stockholders of the Alexandria, Loudoun, and Hampshire Railroad Company," in *ibid.*, September 8, 1858; 40 BPW 1857–58, "Report of the Manassas Gap Railroad Company," 223; 41 BPW 1859–60, "Report of the Virginia and Tennessee Railroad," 59.

Railroad, for example, sent one-and-one-half times as much tonnage to Richmond as it received from that city in the last two years before secession. The Central had averaged consistently twice as much during the early and mid-1850s.[21]

The uneven development of industry accounted in large part for the imbalanced trade of the railroads. It illustrated the difficulty of synchronizing different segments of the economy in a short time period. The iron foundries of Wheeling, the Perkins and Smith Locomotive Works in Alexandria, and the Tredegar and Belle Isle works in Richmond manufactured railroad iron, parts, and stock. The rapid construction of southern and especially Virginia railroads, however, easily outstripped the capacity of nascent urban industry. Consequently, Virginia's railroads still had to rely on the North and Wales for the remainder of their railroad iron.[22] A committee appointed by the presidents of several railroad companies in 1860 estimated that despite the presence of local suppliers, Virginia railroads exported $1,000,000 annually for railroad iron. The committee recommended that the railroad companies pool their financial resources and establish a factory in Richmond devoted exclusively to railroad iron. The Civil War intervened before the railroad executives could consider the measure.[23]

The problems of poor linkages between internal improvements and urban industry affected the processing establishments. Unless transportation lines provided a significant volume of produce for urban processing plants, these industries would become, at best, operational on a seasonal basis only. At worst, they might close their doors. William F. Fowle, one of Alexandria's most prominent civic leaders, invested heavily in an extensive flour mill in that city. Fowle anticipated a continuous flow of wheat from the hinterland over the Manassas Gap and the Orange and Alexandria Railroads. Crop failures and preference for higher prices at Richmond resulted in only a relatively small amount of wheat at Alexandria depots.

21. 41 BPW 1859–60, "Report of the Virginia Central Railroad," 107–8.
22. H. W. Vandegrift to Bush and Lobdell Co., August 28, 1860, in Bush and Lobdell Co. Papers, Alderman Library, University of Virginia; Richmond *Enquirer*, October 15, 1858; 35 BPW 1850, "Report of the Virginia and Tennessee Railroad Company," 151.
23. Richmond *Daily Dispatch*, March 26, 1860.

Fowle, considerably wiser and poorer, admitted that "I have lost a fortune by it. It was too large for the back country." In a related problem, railroads could, at times, be too generous in discharging their duties as commercial carriers. Alexandria and Richmond faced the difficulty throughout the decade of having too much produce and too few vessels to freight them to appropriate ports. As the president of the Virginia and Tennessee Railroad observed accurately, "Railroads and canals may strive for tonnage . . . without success, unless they are properly sustained by commercial arrangements at terminal points."[24]

The meshing of economic gears is an extended process that only the most successful urban economies achieve. For Virginia's cities, developing a system where railroads disgorged volumes of produce onto waiting vessels and returned laden with manufactured products for the interior was unrealistic given the short amount of time from the inception of the economic programs. Whether Virginia's cities could ever hope for a synchronized economy was problematical. The national economy probably precluded such a possibility. Urban Virginia's increasing participation in the national economy was the second obstacle militating against fulfillment of the cities' and the state's economic dreams.

The peripatetic mind of George Fitzhugh effectively summarized the effect of the national economy, centered in the urban northeast, on Virginia's cities: "Trade very easily effects now what conquest did formerly." The centralization of commerce at the port of New York was probably the single most important event in the creation of a national economy in mid-nineteenth-century America. The proximity of manufacturing and the presence of financial and commercial expertise helped to make New York the focal point of the national economy. It was the railroad, however, that guaranteed New York's position at the head of the national economy. Economist Paul H. Cootner, who generally has underplayed the impact of the railroad on economic growth, admitted

24. Alexandria *Gazette*, April 6, 1857; and February 29, 1860; *Gazette*, May 8, 1856; Richmond *Daily Dispatch*, April 7, 1860; 40 BPW 1857–58, "Report of the Virginia and Tennessee Railroad Company," 68.

that railroads "began to revolutionize trade patterns" in the 1850s.[25]

The railroad helped to solidify a west-to-northeast pattern of trade, and the South lost the contest for the West. The belated southern railroad-building effort of the 1850s merely served to feed the northeastern centers of trade. The railroad facilitiated the northern economic "conquest." Railroads, Fitzhugh observed aptly, "usually impoverish the interior and create immense wealth in the seaboard towns." Thus, as the railroad brought Natchez closer to New Orleans, and Demopolis nearer to Mobile, it eliminated the need for the middleman, or middle cities in this case, and provided the farmer and country merchants with better prices and facilities in the metropolis. Natchez and Demopolis were reduced to way stations rather than market centers.[26]

The Virginia tobacco trade illustrated the centralization of commerce abetted by improved access to market. In 1852 Richmond conducted 46% of Virginia's tobacco inspections; in 1856, 57%; and in 1860, 61% of all tobacco inspected went through Richmond. The losers in this trend were the interior markets; towns like Farmville and Clarksville that subscribed heavily to railroads hoping to buy prosperity but instead sealing their respective fates as failures in the commercial contest. The completion of the Southside Railroad and the Richmond and Danville Railroad in the mid-fifties resulted in a decline of the tobacco trade for these two towns. In 1852 Farmville and Clarksville accounted for 12% of Virginia's tobacco inspections; in 1856, 6%; and in 1860, 5%. Petersburg and Lynchburg, cities rather than towns, fared only a little better. In 1852, Petersburg's inspections amounted to 20% of Virginia's total; in 1856, 24%; and in 1860, 23%. Lynchburg inspected 21% of Virginia's tobacco in 1852; 13% in 1856, and 12% in 1860.[27] Richmond's tobacco bonanza triggered a series of linkages like the development of manufacturing facilities, the construction

25. Fitzhugh, *Sociology*, 203; Paul H. Cootner, "The Role of the Railroads in U.S. Economic Growth." *Journal of Economic History*, XXIII (1963), 499.

26. Fitzhugh, *Sociology*, 142. See also Reed, *New Orleans and Railroads*.

27. "Virginia Tobacco Trade," *Hunt's*, 631; "Tobacco Trade of Virginia," *Hunt's*, 343; XLII (1860), 356.

of warehouses, and the supply of credit that secured the city's dominance over the tobacco trade to an even greater extent. The promise of railroads turned sour for other cities.

What was happening on a regional scale began to occur on a national scale. A writer for *Hunt's* in 1857 observed that "more tobacco is inspected in Richmond than perhaps in any one place in the United States."[28] Richmond led the nation in inspections, but not in final sales. The absence of economic linkages such as a fleet of local vessels, factoring and financial facilities, and extensive domestic and overseas wholesale contacts sent the tobacco northward. Northern railroads and ships sped the produce of Virginia's farms to urban centers like Philadelphia and New York. Nearly two-thirds of the unprocessed tobacco leaving Richmond wharves and depots went to northern cities. More significant, almost all (95%) of the chewing and smoking tobacco manufactured in Richmond was shipped to northern cities, primarily to New York. The Empire City then either reexported the tobacco to Europe or distributed it over excellent rail facilities throughout the country.[29]

The situation was even more frustrating for Richmond because southern merchants were among the buyers of Virginia-manufactured tobacco in New York. The Empire City's commercial tentacles thus grasped what should have been a natural trade relationship for Richmond tobacco manufacturers.[30] The tobacco smoke rising from the prosperous factories along the James River symbolized progress for the city and riches for the North. Between 1839 and 1859 the volume of tobacco processed through Richmond's factories quadrupled; so did coastwise exports to Baltimore, Philadelphia, New York, and Boston.[31] The *Enquirer*, sur-

28. "The Tobacco Trade of Richmond," *ibid.*, 745.
29. "Import of Virginia Tobacco into the Port of New York," *ibid.*, XX (1849), 219; "The Tobacco Trade," *ibid.*, XXVI (1852), 358–59; "Tobacco Trade and Inspections at New York," *ibid.*, XXX (1854), 354–55; "Direct Exports of Tobacco from Richmond," *ibid.*, XXXVI (1852), 89; "Tobacco Trade of Virginia," *ibid.*, 736–39.
30. Greene, Heath and Allen to William T. Sutherlin, January 21, 1860, in Sutherlin Papers, Connolly and Adams to James Thomas, Jr., October 6, 1855, in Thomas Papers; Fisher and Co. to James Thomas, Jr., March 15, 1860, in Beale-Davis Papers, Alderman Library, University of Virginia. See also Robert, *Tobacco Kingdom*, 224–25.
31. "Tobacco Trade of Virginia," *Hunt's*, 736–39.

veying the national economy in 1856, observed sadly, "It is now a well established theory of political economy that the centre of trade robs the extremities of their . . . independence as well as of their wealth.[32]

The tobacco trade typified the closer commercial relationship between Virginia and northern cities. Alexandria, and especially Norfolk, revived as seaports primarily because of the eagerness of northern urban merchants to accept and redistribute their produce. Norfolk became known as the "Atlantic Garden" during the 1850s. The city's economy was synonymous with the coastwise trade. Norfolk was New York's market garden. A favorable climate, proximity to a seaport, and a vigorous scientific agriculture movement provided the impetus for market garden cultivation in the vicinity of Norfolk. Transplanted New Jersey farmers took advantage of these conditions as well as the renewed interest in commerce and began cultivating fruits and vegetables in the mid-1840s. In 1858, the most active trading year for Norfolk before the Civil War, the fruit and vegetable trade accounted for $450,000 of the $535,000 total value of goods shipped coastwise.[33]

The "truck trade," as contemporaries called it, was especially busy between Norfolk and two ports to the North: Baltimore and New York. These two market centers received $419,000, or 93% of the truck trade.[34] Fruits and vegetables were not ideal articles for direct export, and Norfolk's export commerce, therefore, was meager. In the Chesapeake port's best export year—1858—it sent directly abroad only $20,000 worth of goods; $19,000 of the total value consisting of staves. Cotton was the only staple on the list of exports. At 252 bales, however, Norfolk's cotton trade evoked little concern from New Orleans and Mobile.[35] Norfolk's fine harbor thus served primarily as a funnel for northern merchants.

Norfolk benefitted from the market garden commerce as well.

32. Richmond *Daily Dispatch*, February 3, 1860.
33. Waring, *Social Statistics of Cities*, 66; Stewart, "Hampton Roads," 43–44; "Vegetable and Truck Trade of Norfolk, Virginia," *Hunt's*, XXXIX (1858), 733.
34. "Vegetable and Truck Trade of Norfolk," *Hunt's*, 733. See also Richmond *Enquirer*, January 28, 1853.
35. "Vegetable and Truck Trade of Norfolk," *Hunt's*, 733; Stewart, "Hampton Roads," 160–62.

Not only did it provide a base for the city's economy, but it transformed a languid countryside into small, profitable fruit and vegetable farms. The *Argus* announced with authority that "all that is required to make a fortune on a small farm near Norfolk—now that we are supplying the tables of the hotels and private houses of the northern cities with fruit and vegetables—is a small capital, industry, and some knowledge of the way of cultivating the soil to the best advantage." The *Argus* pointed to a Mr. P. H. Whitehurst who "recently shipped one thousand baskets of strawberries to New York." On another occasion, under the headline "Virginia Feeding the North," the *Argus* related the story of one farmer who shipped 300 bushels of peanuts weekly to New York, and who had sent over the course of five months, 20,000 bushels of dried apples to the Empire City. A Norfolk merchant boasted that he was shipping 6,000 to 8,000 bunches of radishes to Baltimore daily; a colleague stated that he supplied the New York market with 600 barrels of sweet potatoes a week. One Norfolk resident estimated that his city's trade with northern markets exceeded in value the tobacco manufactured by Richmond.[36] The coastwise trade, in short, was a big business.

Alexandria, Virginia's third port city, also developed firm links with northern cities during the 1850s. Rail connections to the northern Piedmont and upper Valley regions of the Old Dominion enabled Alexandria to secure a portion of the wheat trade. Though the 91,000 bushels it received in 1859—the city's best trade year —paled before Richmond's annual receipt of 500,000 bushels, Alexandria was the second largest wheat exporting center in the state.[37] Since little of the wheat was milled in the city, merchants shipped most of it northward for processing and re-export. Alexandria's direct export statistics were more anemic than Norfolk's. The Potomac River port did not possess a large-volume

36. Norfolk *Southern Argus*, quoted in "Garden Farms in Virginia," *American Agriculturist*, XIII (1854), 166; Norfolk *Southern Argus*, quoted in Richmond *Enquirer*, May 2, 1854; Norfolk *Southern Argus*, May 1, 1851. See also "The Profits of Market Garden Farms," *Southern Planter*, XVII (1857), 756–57.
37. "Flour Inspections in Virginia," *Hunt's*, 356.

trade, such as staves in Norfolk or flour in Richmond, and, as a result, direct ocean commerce was not feasible.[38]

Coastwise trade statistics alone did not completely reflect the intimate commercial connections between northern and Virginia cities. Merchant's day books were constant reminders of the inter-relationship between urban markets. Stuart C. Hoffer, an Alexandria merchant, shipped all of the wheat he received from various clients to H. C. Newman & Co. of New York. Hoffer evidently found the Orange and Alexandria and the Manassas Gap Railroads very helpful in his business, since all entries included freight charges from one or the other of these carriers. Hoffer's westbound trade consisted primarily of organic fertilizers that he received from Baltimore. New York and Baltimore merchants appreciated Mr. Hoffer's railroads as well.[39]

Northern cities attempted to formalize what was becoming a lucrative trade with urban Virginia. In 1854, for example, Baltimore merchants established a triweekly steamer service to Alexandria "as the trade between Alexandria and Baltimore is rapidly increasing." Five years later, New York inaugurated a similar line. The *Gazette* promised that goods unloaded from New York vessels would be "promptly" placed on railroads and sped to "any point." Norfolk's market garden trade brought prompt response from Baltimore and Philadelphia as those two cities began operating regularly scheduled runs in 1851. New York established a service to Norfolk in 1858. The *Argus* readily acknowledged New York as "the great commercial centre of the continent" and quietly abandoned its desires for direct trade with Europe.[40]

Sixteen of the twenty-one vessels owned by Richmond in 1859 belonged to regular lines between Richmond and the ports of New York and Boston. The New York and Boston services ran semi-weekly and, noted a writer in *Hunt's*, traveled "with full freights both ways." Philadelphia and Baltimore merchants competed for

38. Richmond *Daily Dispatch*, March 30, 1859.
39. See entries from November 16, 1859 to March 13, 1861 in Stuart C. Hoffer Day Book (MS in Alderman Library, University of Virginia).
40. Alexandria *Gazette*, March 15, 1854; *Gazette*, August 1, 1859; Norfolk *Southern Argus*, May 1, 1851; *Argus*, September 3, 1858.

the Richmond market as well. Baltimore operated three steamers semiweekly as did the Philadelphia line.[41] As the nation prepared for the final throes of sectionalism, urban Virginia and the urban North were locked in an ever-tightening economic embrace.

The embrace effectively suffocated urban Virginia's dream of direct trade with Europe. Direct export statistics reflected the centralization of the national economy at the port of New York (see tables 34 and 35). In 1815 New York exported 19.2% of the nation's total value of exports. Richmond and Norfolk combined accounted for 11.5%. By 1840 New York's supremacy as a trade center was more evident, as was the decline of Richmond and Norfolk. In that year, New York exported 25.8% of the nation's total value of exports, and the two Virginia cities only 3.0%. In 1860, despite a considerably more prosperous economy, Richmond and Norfolk together accounted for a paltry 1.3%, compared with 36.2% for New York. The Virginia export figures were no less embarrassing than the statistics for Boston, Philadelphia, and Baltimore in 1860: 4.3%, 1.3%, and 2.3%, respectively. The centralization of trade knew no sectional boundaries.

The centripetal force of the national economy not only inhibited direct trade in urban Virginia but hampered industrial development as well. New York dominated the import trade, capturing 68.5% of the nation's total value of imports in 1860 (see tables 36 and 37). Boston was the nearest competitor at 11.3%, while Richmond and Norfolk managed less than .1%. New York's prominence as an import center meant that manufactured articles from abroad would be in the most abundant quantities and at the cheapest prices. Further, New York's reputation as a distribution center ensured that city a healthy influx of domestic manufactures from the growing industrial centers of the northeast. Even factories near Boston preferred to send their wares to New York for the best marketing.[42] Consequently, Virginia merchants characteristically bypassed local manufacturers in favor of procuring

41. "Commercial and Industrial Cities: Richmond, 1859," *Hunt's*, 62; Richmond *Enquirer*, October 30, 1857.
42. "The Removal of Commerce from Boston to New York," *Hunt's*, XXX (1854), 391.

Table 34 Share of Total Value of Exports of Principal Ports, 1815–1860 (in Millions of Dollars)

Year	Total Value	New York	Other Northern Ports (Boston, Philadelphia)	Southern Ports (Savannah, Richmond–Norfolk, New Orleans, Baltimore, Charleston, Mobile)
1815	$ 52	$ 10	$ 9	$ 26
		19.2%	17.3%	50.0%
1820	69	13	16	31
		18.8	23.2	44.9
1825	99	35	22	35
		35.4	22.2	35.4
1830	73	19	11	33
		26.0	15.1	45.2
1835	121	30	13	71
		24.8	10.7	58.7
1840	132	34	16	71
		25.8	12.1	53.8
1845	114	36	13	56
		31.6	11.4	49.1
1850	151	52	14	75
		34.4	9.3	49.7
1855	275	113	34	102
		41.1	12.4	37.1
1860	400	145	22	198
		36.2	5.5	49.5

SOURCE: U.S. Secretary of the Treasury, *Reports on Commerce and Navigation, 1815–1860*.
NOTE: Percentages are state totals, but each port selected monopolized its state's import export trade. The percentages do not add up to 100% because several minor ports were omitted.

Table 35 Share of Total Value of Exports of Individual Ports, 1815–1860 (in Millions of Dollars)

Year	Boston	Phila- delphia	New Orleans	Balti- more	Charles- ton	Mobile	Savan- nah	Richmond– Norfolk
1815	$ 5	$ 4	$ 5	$ 5	$ 6	....	$ 4	$ 6
	9.6%	7.7%	9.6%	9.6%	11.5%	....	7.7%	11.5%
1835	10	3	36	3	11	7	8	6
	8.3	2.5	29.8	2.5	9.1	5.8	6.6	5.0
1840	10	6	34	5	10	12	6	4
	7.6	4.5	25.8	3.8	7.6	9.1	4.5	3.0
1860	17	5	107	9	21	38	18	5
	4.3	1.3	26.8	2.3	5.3	9.5	4.5	1.3

SOURCE: U.S. Secretary of the Treasury, *Reports on Commerce and Navigation, 1815–1860*.

products that had established reputations for quality and price in New York. Lack of home patronage retarded investment in domestic manufactures.

As sectional animosity increased, so did southern patronage of northern distributors of manufactured goods. Business evidently was a more powerful attraction than philosophy was a repulsion. It was, after all, a materialistic age, and growth and progress occupied thoughts and conversation. An Alexandria resident visiting New York in 1860 observed more southern merchants in that city than ever before. He concluded, "Southern people, despite of everything said and done, buy where *they think* they can get the best assortment, and purchase at the *cheapest* rates." Nor were Virginia's urban merchants clandestine about their northern economic predilections. The Alexandria *Gazette* boasted in 1855, "Our merchants have returned from the North with excellent stocks of goods which they are selling at very reduced rates." Even hinterland towns advertised northern wares eagerly. A Bristol merchant displayed "a large supply of Northern-made furniture." The Boston *Post* reported that one Richmond mercantile concern spent $400,000 in 1850 for shoes manufactured in Boston. The *Post* also

Table 36 Share of Total Value of Imports of Principal Ports, 1821–1860 (in Millions of Dollars)

Year	Total Value	New York	Other Northern Ports	Southern Ports
1821	$ 62	$ 23	$ 22	$ 11
		37.1%	35.5%	17.7%
1825	96	49	30	9
		51.0	31.3	9.4
1830	70	35	18	12
		50.0	25.7	17.1
1835	149	88	31	23
		59.1	20.8	15.4
1840	107	60	24	16
		56.1	22.4	15.0
1845	117	70	30	11
		59.9	25.6	9.4
1850	178	111	42	17
		62.4	23.6	9.6
1855	261	164	60	20
		62.9	23.0	7.7
1860	362	248	55	33
		68.5	15.2	9.1

SOURCE: U.S. Secretary of the Treasury, *Reports on Commerce and Navigation, 1821–1860.*
NOTE: Import data not available prior to 1821.

estimated that Virginians paid $500,000 for northern brooms in that year.[43] Consumers in urban Virginia equated quality with northern origin, and local merchants readily obliged their tastes.

Some urban residents, especially manufacturers and southern patriots, objected to the emphasis that local merchants placed on northern products. The Richmond *Dispatch* complained that while there were a number of nurseries in the vicinity of the city, "Virginia farmers prefer sending to the North and paying from thirty to sixty percent more for young trees and scions, to buying them at

43. Letter from "Linsey-Woolsey" to Alexandria *Gazette*, March 6, 1860; *Gazette*, March 31, 1855; Bristol *Virginia and Tennessee News*, June 10, 1859; Edward Ingle, *Southern Sidelights* (New York, 1896), 127.

Table 37 Share of Total Value of Imports of Individual Cities, 1821–1860 (in Millions of Dollars)

Year	Boston	Phila- delphia	New Orleans	Balti- more	Charles- ton	Mobile*	Savan- nah*	Richmond– Norfolk*
1821	$14	$ 8	$ 3	$4	$3	....	$1	....
	22.6%	12.9%	4.8%	6.5%	4.8%	....	1.6%	....
1835	19	12	17	5	1			
	12.8	8.1	11.4	3.4	.7	....	....	....
1840	16	8	10	4	2			
	15.0	7.5	9.3	3.7	1.9	....	....	....
1860	41	14	22	9	1			
	11.3	3.9	6.1	2.5	.3	....	....	....

SOURCE: U.S. Secretary of the Treasury, *Reports on Commerce and Navigation, 1821–1860.*
*Less than .1% share of the total import trade.

their own doors." A Lynchburg railroad executive charged that Richmond and Norfolk were "mere way stations to Philadelphia, New York, and Boston." Roger A. Pryor, a fire-eating Richmond journalist, took a similar view: "We are *literally* hewers of wood and drawers of water." A Wheeling editor noted that while the Richmond *Enquirer* urged southern economic independence, it was advertising simultaneously for northern patronage in New York papers. Struggling urban industries such as publishing enterprises suffered from the general penchant for northern items. At the height of "Bleeding Kansas," the Richmond *Whig* remarked, "The best chance now of getting a Southern book sold, is to manage to secure the favourable notice of the Northern press, and then the South buys it. Our magazines and periodicals languish for support." [44]

Heavy patronage of northern cities was common throughout the South up until the firing on Fort Sumter. A textile mill owner in Augusta, Georgia, complained that southern consumers invariably preferred northern goods over home products. South Carolina

44. Richmond *Daily Dispatch*, August 25, 1859; 40 BPW 1857–58, "Report of the Virginia and Tennessee Railroad Company," 68–69; Richmond *South*, April 9, 1857; Wheeling *Daily Intelligencer*, January 27, 1860; Richmond *Whig*, quoted in Frederick Law Olmsted, *The Cotton Kingdom* (Rev. ed.; New York, 1962), 591.

industrialist William Gregg noted ironically that his textile products were "more popular in New York and Philadelphia than at home." In frustration and for profit, some southern industrialists pirated northern brand names and marketed their goods as such. Perhaps the ultimate in dependence on northern cities was the fact that the Virginia State Seal was engraved in Philadelphia.[45] The pre-eminence of northern market centers in the national economy was too powerful for southern cities to overcome. Unable to beat the urban North, the urban South joined their brethren above the Mason-Dixon Line.

The economic fate of urban Virginia depended on the extent of its trade with northern cities. The degree of economic interrelationship varied, however. Norfolk's commerce relied almost entirely on what the *Argus* called the "intimate connection" with northern ports. Toward the end of the decade, Norfolk merchants were seeking closer, more regular commercial ties with New York: "We must connect ourselves intimately with New York," the *Argus* advised. Isolated from the staple region, and viewing ports to the South more as rivals than as trading partners, Norfolk cast her lot with northern cities. Alexandria possessed better rail connections than Norfolk, but the Baltimore and Ohio Railroad circumscribed its hinterland. Civic leaders hoped that the recent connection with the Virginia and Tennessee Railroad would diversify the city's trade. In 1860 it was too early to discern any modification in the pattern of dependence on northern markets. Wheeling, in the words of one Richmond editor, was "lost to Virginia." The Baltimore and Ohio Railroad, completed to the Ohio River city in 1853, directed Wheeling trade to Baltimore and Philadelphia. Wheeling never had much commercial contact with market centers in the eastern portion of the Old Dominion. Residents were more comfortable in dealing with northern cities.[46] As one Wheeling mer-

45. Griffin, "Origins of the Industrial Revolution in Georgia," 370; quoted in Eaton, *Growth of Southern Civilization*, 227; George W. Munford to William Wagner, February 4, 1857, Executive Letter Book, 1856-1860 (MS in Virginia State Library).

46. Norfolk *Southern Argus*, September 3, 1858; Alexandria *Gazette*, April 3, 1860; Richmond *Daily Dispatch*, January 28, 1853; Wheeling *Daily Intelligencer*, August 17, 1853; and January 1, 1858. See also Henry T. Shanks, *The Secession Movement in Virginia* (Richmond, 1934), 7; Richard O. Curry, "A Reappraisal of Statehood Politics in West

chant wrote, "The God of Nature made us a part of Pennsylvania, while the surveyor made us a part of Virginia."[47]

Richmond enjoyed the most diverse commercial network in the state. The capital city was in the process of developing contacts in the Gulf states to inaugurate a cotton trade. Meanwhile, Richmond's heavy industries secured numerous southern clients during the 1850s. The foundation of the city's economy, however, remained in the processing industries and in the commerce that supplied those industries. In turn, northern cities transformed tobacco and flour into profits for Richmond's merchants and manufacturers. Lynchburg and Petersburg were not as involved, at least directly, in the national economy as were other Virginia cities. The two interior cities functioned as regional market centers. Lynchburg had commercial relations with the Gulf states through Memphis, the western terminus of the Virginia and Tennessee Railroad. Nevertheless, the wheat, tobacco, and cotton that Lynchburg and Petersburg received eventually found its way to northern cities through Alexandria, Norfolk, or, more likely, Richmond.[48]

The Virginia urban economy was not, of course, merely a stream of commerce northward. The reciprocal trade in which manufactured products, capital, and even expertise went southward completed the economic interrelationship of urban Virginia and the northeastern cities. The trade, however, was not a mutually dependent connection. For northern market centers like New York, the trade with urban Virginia and the urban South, for that matter, amounted to only a part of the national economy. The western trade was expanding at a greater rate than the commerce with the South. Further, urban centers such as Chicago, Cincinnati, and Saint Louis in the western heartland provided northern cities with an extensive market for imported and domestic manufactures.

The ability of northern market centers to push a transportation network westward in order to secure the trade of that region made

Virginia," *Journal of Southern History*, XXVIII (1962), 414–15; Boughter, "Internal Improvements," 275–81.

47. Quoted in James C. McGregor, *The Disruption of Virginia* (New York, 1922), 85.

48. See Richmond *Daily Dispatch*, April 9, 1859. See also speech of Charles Bruce in the Virginia Senate, quoted in Richmond *Enquirer*, April 9, 1858.

the Civil War economically feasible for the North. The shock of losing the southern market was significant. A wartime boom and the western bounty, however, eventually covered economic losses and then some. For urban Virginia, the only hope of retaining its newly won prosperity as the Civil War approached was to remain within the national economy as a northern tributary or to somehow reconstruct the web of relationships and assume an important economic position with the Deep South. After John Brown's Raid on Harper's Ferry in October 1859 the question of the role of urban Virginia in an urban nation dominated the Virginia sectional debate.

Although the participants on both sides of the question referred to a wide range of arguments to support their positions, the economic argument achieved the greatest prominence. Following the Mexican War, some Virginians had defined their state's and their section's power in economic terms. Release from commercial vassalage and economic independence would not only restore Virginia to her accustomed preeminence, it would also save the Union by making it a Union of equals. The Old Dominion's cities received particular attention because the economic supremacy of northern cities was largely responsible for northern wealth and political power. The sectional debate, having begun on an urban-economic theme, would logically reach a climax in the same framework.

The city and economic progress touched virtually every phase of antebellum American life. Town promoters on the urban frontier dreamed of great cosmopolitan centers rising from the dust overnight. Existing towns hoped to blossom into cities. Urban civilization represented wealth, power, and culture to these nascent metropolises. Their leaders sought to grasp the opportunity for personal fortune while guiding their communities to greatness. Farmers also shared in these dreams, watching their crops grow with their market center. Prosperity and urban growth intertwined with each other and with the national economy. Urban Virginians living in such a society in the 1840s and 1850s naturally viewed local and national events within the context of their impact on their cities' economic growth. Since urban growth depended on the role a particular city played in the national economy, discussion about that role became the focal point of debate.

Following John Brown's Raid and the ensuing deterioration in sectional relations, Virginians emphasized the themes of economic independence that had characterized their rhetoric after the Mexican War. The Central Southern Rights Association, a Richmond group headed by merchant and civic leader Daniel H. London, stated, "Commercial independence of the North is the first great object in looking about for the means of remedy and redress." The association emphasized that this was not a call for secession, but rather the only method to "restore a just sense of constitutional obligation and honor." In the event of secession, such a program would "place ourselves in better condition to stand the shock of dissolution." The specific features of southern economic independence were familiar: "encouragement of domestic manufactures; completion of important lines of internal improvements; and direct trade abroad." The Richmond *Enquirer* reiterated a familiar theme: "We should have large cities, a flourishing commerce and manufactures, abundant roads, and a direct trade with Europe. . . . These are indispensable to our independence."[49] The *Enquirer* wrote not only of economic independence, but of independence in general. The two had become identical in the urban Virginian mind.

Virginians still understood the importance of western trade in the northern juggernaut, and its role in elevating northern cities, and hence the North to its position of wealth and power. "There is the great West lying behind our Alleghenies," related secretary of the commonwealth George W. Munford. "We must separate her from the North. . . . Then we shall be able to build up our cities, to erect our own manufactories . . . to carry our own commerce in our own ships, and let them know there is a Virginia." Charles W. Russell of Wheeling urged the legislature in May 1860 to bind the West to the South "with hooks of steel, to secure our indepen-

49. "Memorial of the Central Southern Rights Association of Virginia to the General Assembly," in Richmond *Enquirer*, December 23, 1859; Richmond *Enquirer*, December 9, 1859.

dence."[50] It was a familiar theme: wealth, recognition, and urban growth—all to be secured by the western trade.

In the statewide feeling of revulsion toward the North that came in the wake of John Brown, some Virginians favored more immediate economic action. Nonintercourse, a popular topic in the late 1840s and early 1850s, was revived as a means to hurt the North's pocketbook and to force the South to produce and trade for itself as well. By mid-decade, however, cessation of commercial relations with the North was "a Utopian scheme" that would quickly impoverish not only urban Virginia but the entire state as well.[51] With this in mind, proponents of nonintercourse focused attention on a voluntary campaign to bar northern manufactured goods from Virginia market centers. Edmund Ruffin paraded in homespun, and urban journals preached the "greater encouragement of Home Manufactures"; but when the legislature moved to place a license tax on merchants dealing in northern goods, the roar from the mercantile community reverberated throughout the state.[52] The failure of the home manufacture movement before it began emphasized not only the degree of northern intrusion into urban Virginia, but the difficulty of implementing economic policies aimed at independence within a national economy. At the end of the decade some urban Virginians had abandoned their lofty goals to work for greater prosperity within the confines of the national economy.

The rhetoric of economic independence that flowed in torrents after the raid on Harper's Ferry indicated that Virginians were aware that their efforts to achieve that independence remained short of fulfillment. Internal improvement lines extended westward, but not far enough; industries processed crops at an impressive pace and turned out railroad iron and nails more than any other southern cities, but they lagged far behind the manufactur-

50. Speech of George W. Munford, quoted in Richmond *Enquirer*, January 10, 1860; Charles W. Russell to R. M. T. Hunter, May 13, 1860, in Ambler (ed.), *Correspondence of Robert M. T. Hunter*, 326.

51. Richmond *Enquirer*, January 29, 1856.

52. See Petersburg *Intelligencer*, quoted in Alexandria *Gazette*, December 3, 1859; Speech of John T. Anderson in House of Delegates, March 7, 1860, quoted in Richmond *Enquirer*, March 23, 1860.

ing complexes of the northeast; and cities plied a direct trade throughout the western hemisphere but failed to expand exports to Europe. The gains since the Mexican War were sufficient to bestow prosperity on Virginia's farm and cities, but they fell considerably short of generating an economy that was competitive with northern cities. Few civic leaders deluded themselves or their fellow citizens into believing that economic parity with the North was an established fact by 1861. Most Virginians, urban and rural alike, still held out hope that a successful commercial empire would eventually be established in the Old Dominion. With the Union crumbling about them, Virginians had to decide with which section their dreams would most likely come true.

The dilemma facing urban Virginia following Lincoln's election was indeed profound. For more than a decade Virginia's cities had experienced an unprecedented era of growth and prosperity. In the process they each had developed an economic superstructure, an active civic elite, extensive urban and commercial services, and an identity as a modern city. The result of these urban changes was the cities' participation in a national economy and inclusion in the developing network of modern cities. Northern cities were accomplices in both of these developments. The connections with the urban North were thus not only economic but philosophical as well. On the other hand, urban Virginians were aware of their secondary position in the national economy. They might have more promising prospects in a regional economy where already they were having an influence. Further, there was also an emotional bond with southern states that in some ways exceeded the recently forged philosophical union with northern cities.

Caught between the economic and philosophical ties of both sections, urban Virginians urged caution. The Richmond *Daily Dispatch* wrote of "calmly awaiting events," the Lynchburg *Virginian* stated flatly that "the election of Lincoln is not sufficient cause for a dissolution of the Union," and Alexandria and Wheeling presses advised their citizens to act cautiously.[53] The conservative stance of urban Virginia reflected not only a love for the Union, but

53. Richmond *Daily Dispatch*, November 9, 1860; Lynchburg *Virginian*, November 22,

a great indecision as to where to go. As a Christiansburg editor stated, "Will Virginia join the Northern Union or the Southern Union—that is the True Issue." The Richmond *Daily Dispatch* recorded the same question: "The question before us is not Union or disunion, but which will we join, North or South." Throughout the Old Dominion, city or countryside, "each man [had] his own way of 'saving the Union' or dissolving it."[54]

Some Virginians, rural and urban alike, believed that the best opportunity for urban growth and economic equality existed in union with the North, or at the very least with the slaveholding and nonslaveholding border states. The commercial ties with the North were extensive, and cessation would be ruinous to the entire state. William L. Goggin, a small-town lawyer from the Valley and delegate to the secession convention posed a simple question to his fellow delegates: "Are you to be told that your wheat and tobacco . . . cannot enter the ports of Boston, Philadelphia or New York, because we have made them aliens and strangers to us?"[55] The outcome would be, Goggin implied, economic disaster.

Advocates of a northern union argued also that the economy of the cotton South was basically inimical to Virginia. William C. Rives, a railroad promoter and urban booster, claimed that the Old Dominion's nascent industrial enterprises would be jeopardized by the free-trade doctrines espoused by leaders of the southern confederacy: "Could there be an act of more suicidal rashness than for Virginia to place herself in a situation in which 'king cotton,' by undisputed preponderance in the councils of a separate Southern Confederacy, would be enabled to throw her ports wide open to the free and indiscriminate admission of the manufactures and productions of foreign countries?" In December 1860, the Wheeling *Daily Intelligencer* argued against secession along similar lines, though with more earthiness: "A pretty figure a city like ours would

1860; see also Alexandria *Gazette*, February 9, 1861; and Wheeling *Daily Intelligencer*, November 28, 1860.

54. Christiansburg *New Star*, April 13, 1861; Richmond *Daily Dispatch*, February 22, 1861; *Daily Dispatch*, January 10, 1861.

55. Speech of William L. Goggin in the Virginia State Convention, February 26, 1861, quoted in Richmond *Enquirer*, February 28, 1861.

cut in a Cotton Confederacy whose motto would be cheap niggers and free trade. We would be a one-horse cow pasture in a year or two."[56] For Wheeling, a city with industrial ambitions, a southern match would be ill-conceived from the start.

Alexandrians also viewed the free-trade proclivities of the Deep South with alarm. An Alexandria civic leader and delegate feared that the courting of France and England by the southern confederacy, if successful, would doom processing industries throughout the state. Another Alexandrian reasoned, four days before the opening of the convention, that since "the South has no commerce on which to levy a tariff, Virginia, if she joins this confederacy, will have the honor of bearing the lion's share of taxes, since she has a larger representation than any of the other slave States." Besides, the Alexandrian added, there would be "no tariff to protect her [Virginia's] manufactures." The *Gazette* properly summarized the sentiment of the city's business community when it asked rhetorically, "Who can contemplate Virginia as the tail of a Southern Confederacy, standing as a guard, and playing patrol for 'King Cotton'?"[57] Some Virginians were unwilling to submerge the economic identity of their cities and state in favor of other cities and states regardless of ideological similarities.

The wary attitude of urban Virginians toward competition from Deep South cities underlay some of the arguments against the influence of cotton on economic policy. Norfolk merchants, of course, viewed their city as the natural distribution point for northern products. Charleston, Savannah, and Chattanooga—all with better rail connections northward—were the major obstacles to the fulfillment of Norfolk's revised plans for a place in the national economy.[58] Resentment of southern urban rivals appeared in the annual review of the Southern Commercial Convention by the urban press. The journals termed these assemblages "a ridiculous

56. William C. Rives, *Letter from the Hon. William C. Rives to a Friend on the Important Questions of the Day* (Richmond, 1860), 15; Wheeling *Daily Intelligencer*, December 27, 1860.

57. Speech of George W. Brent in the Virginia State Convention, March 8, 1861, quoted in Alexandria *Gazette*, March 18, 1861; Letter from "Junius" to Alexandria *Gazette*, February 9, 1861; Alexandria *Gazette*, December 15, 1860.

58. Norfolk *Southern Argus*, September 3, 1858.

spectacle," "a humbug," "a failure," "silliest humbug of the season," and "an abortion."[59] Urban Virginians were annoyed at the politicization of the conventions. As the Alexandria *Gazette* asserted: "What we in the South want is *deeds*, not *words*."[60]

More important, Virginia schemes were not only ignored but opposed at the gatherings. At the 1857 convention in Knoxville, A. Dudley Mann, a Norfolk merchant, presented a plan for the initiation of direct trade from Norfolk to Europe. The delegates rejected it "upon the ground that it should come to no other than a cotton port."[61] The annual discussion of a southern route for the Pacific railroad was another disconcerting feature of the conclaves. A southern route, considerably below Virginia, would seriously inhibit urban and commercial expansion in the state.[62] The most alarming discussions of the conventions, as far as Virginia was concerned, centered on the reopening of the African slave trade. As long as the Deep South remained within the Union, Virginians could dismiss such a prospect as "a distraction." When secession became a reality, the Richmond *Enquirer* wondered aloud whether "the South of the Northern confederacy would not be far more preferable for her than the North of a Southern confederacy."[63]

Opponents of secession hammered home the dangers of the reopening of the African slave trade. The domestic slave trade was a multi-million-dollar enterprise for the Old Dominion in which urban and rural residents shared equally. A serious diminution of the capital generated by the trade would have ramifications throughout the state's economy, severely limiting investment capital, depressing the agricultural sector, and hampering urban growth. Ultimately the institution of slavery itself—the labor force of urban growth—would be destroyed. George W. Brent, delegate from Alexandria to the state secession convention, reasoned

59. *Ibid.*, April 18, 1854; Richmond *Whig*, November 29, 1850; Wheeling *Daily Intelligencer*, May 13, 1858.

60. Alexandria *Gazette*, August 31, 1852.

61. Norfolk *Southern Argus*, August 20, 1857.

62. *Ibid.*, April 18, 1854. See also Jere W. Roberson, "The South and the Pacific Railroad, 1845–1855," *Western Historical Quarterly*, V (1974), 163–86.

63. Richmond *Enquirer*, May 25, 1858.

shortly after Lincoln's inauguration, "I regard secession as the
doom of slavery within the Border States. Why would the people of
the South go to Virginia and purchase negroes for $1500 when the
same could be procured on the coast of Congo and Guinea for
$200?" Samuel McDowell Moore, a lawyer and delegate from
Lexington in the Valley, believed that revival of the African slave
trade was a logical extension of Deep South policy: "Our interest is
that slaves should be sold as high as possible. Their policy, then, will
be to re-open the African slave-trade."[64]

Even if the Deep South should not decide to revive the African
slave trade, Virginians feared that slavery would suffer severely
within a southern confederacy. Brent of Alexandria believed that
slavery would rapidly deteriorate as a result of secession: "Secession . . . will have the tendency to promote increased facilities for
escape on the part of our negroes. The owner, conscious of the
insecurity of his property, will be anxious to put it in a place of
safety and security. The increased price of cotton and the negro
will cause the removal of slaves from the Border States." Brent
predicted that northerners and immigrants—both groups who
were hostile to slavery—would fill the labor vacuum created by the
rapid exodus of slaves and accelerate further the disappearance of
slavery. Thomas M. Branch, a Petersburg merchant and civic
leader as well as a delegate from that city to the secession convention, agreed with Brent's logic: "If you value a negro in Virginia to
be working on a plantation here, according to the value of a negro
in Mississippi you must at once see that you lose all the negroes.
They will be taken into those States where they can be worked more
profitably." The precipitous departure of the slave population
would have a serious impact on Virginia's economy, especially that
of the cities. The loss of slaves would also affect the state's tax base.
Merchants and manufacturers as well as farmers would "have to
pay away a very large proportion of the forty millions of dollars
now due by the State."[65]

64. Speech of George W. Brent in the Virginia State Convention, March 8, 1861, quoted
in Alexandria *Gazette*, March 18, 1861; Speech of Samuel McDowell Moore in the Virginia
State Convention, February 25, 1861, quoted in Richmond *Enquirer*, February 26, 1861.
65. Speech of George W. Brent in the Virginia State Convention, March 8, 1861, quoted

The upshot of these arguments was that, as William C. Rives observed, "Slavery is better protected in the Northern Confederacy." If slavery were a major factor precipitating sectional conflict, this comment was ironic in the extreme. The view becomes more plausible, though, when it is understood that slavery for many Virginians was not as much an ideological issue as a part of a larger economic question. Those who believed that slavery was most secure with the North were really saying that the economic benefits generated by slave labor would be protected best in a society that relied primarily on free labor. When William C. Rives states that "the question of slavery has not the power to override other considerations in deciding the new affinites and relations of the States," he was summarizing the experience of more than a decade of urban growth and participation in the national economy.[66] The "new affinities and relations of the States" that Rives referred to resulted from Virginia's connections with northern market centers, the hub of the national economy. Slavery became a consideration within the framework of these "new affinities."

Although most Virginians agreed that these "new affinities" were crucial in determining the state's role in or out of the Union, there was disagreement as to what these relations signified for Virginia's cities in particular and for the state's economy in general. Those favoring secession emphasized the economic benefits that would accrue to urban Virginia if the Old Dominion should secede. A writer in De Bow's Review promised that Richmond would "become one of the great, if not, the greatest city of the Southern Union." George W. Randolph, a Richmond attorney and delegate to the Virginia State Convention of 1861, argued that the South represented a greater potential market for the Old Dominion's manufactures than the North: "If we wish to become a manufacturing State, it will be an extraordinary policy for us to unite ourselves with a people who produce vastly more than they consume, and to decline a union with States who will take everything we produce."

in Alexandria *Gazette*, March 18, 1861; Speech of Thomas M. Branch in the Virginia State Convention, March 18, 1861, quoted in Richmond *Enquirer*, March 19, 1861.
    66. Rives, *Letter from William C. Rives*, 15, 13.

Tredegar's Joseph R. Anderson, eyeing a southern monopoly for his products, agreed that urban Virginia's manufacturing prowess would ensure command of the southern market.[67]

As for Virginia's commerce, the Richmond *Daily Dispatch* argued that the demand for the Old Dominion's staples had existed in the southern states all along but went to New York for redistribution. Secession would allow urban Virginia to market the staples directly to southern consumers. The *Dispatch* prophesied that this "will produce a revolution in commerce." The *Enquirer* depicted the alternative to the "revolution in commerce": "If Virginia remains where she is . . . her manufactured tobacco and clothes will find no sale within the Gulf States, while leaf tobacco and wool are admitted free in the North."[68]

Secessionists stressed the dependence of the South on northern cities. They argued that secession would end commercial vassalage and inaugurate a new economic era for southern cities. The Charleston *Mercury* articulated the hopes of many urban southerners when it observed, "There are no people in the Southern States who will gain so certainly by a dissolution of the Union as the merchants and mechanics of our cities. At present, Norfolk, Charleston, Savannah, and Mobile are but suburbs of New York, Philadelphia, and Boston. . . . Break up our union with the North—let Southern cities resume their natural commerce—and what a mighty change will come over the prospects of our cities." In dissolving the Union, the *Mercury* hoped to dissolve the national economy, extricate southern cities from its grasp, and begin anew. Indeed, some Virginians, well aware of the shock to the economy in the event of cessation of trade with the North, welcomed disunion as an opportunity to fulfill their economic programs outside the confines of the national economy. The Richmond *Enquirer* called for the creation of a southern national economy with Virginia, released from dependence, at its head.

    67. "Cities of the South: Richmond," *DeBow's Review*, 187; Speech of George W. Randolph in the Virginia State Convention, March 23, 1861, quoted in Richmond *Enquirer*, April 8, 1861; "Richmond," *DeBow's Review*, 190.
    68. Richmond *Daily Dispatch*, January 28, 1861; Richmond *Enquirer*, March 23, 1861.

We shall be compelled to multiply our industrial and intellectual pursuits, to carry on our own commerce and navigation in our own ships, to make our own clothes, our own wines, silks, brandies, and, in fine, to manufacture for ourselves and almost to be a world within ourselves. We must write our own books, have our own schools and colleges presided over by southern teachers, have our own fashions, our own costume, our own dialect, and our own thought. We must cease to be cosmopolitan, imitative and dependent, and become national, original, and independent.[69]

The *Enquirer's* panegyric, almost a plea, was the ultimate expression for the creation of a distinct (or ethnic) southern identity. It was prayer to exorcise a generation of national economic development that had witnessed southern cities like Virginia's rise to prosperity and modernity, yet simultaneously sink into dependence. The cost of this dependence in dollars and cents was enormous. Richmond merchant and civic leader Daniel H. London estimated that Richmond alone lost $1,250,000 on the tobacco shipped to foreign countries from New York. London calculated that the total value of Richmond's manufactured tobacco was $12,500,000 in 1859. Virtually all of it went to New York and other northern ports for redistribution and reexport abroad. Commissions, guarantees, and freights amounted to 10% of the total value of the tobacco. London's statistics concerning the wheat trade (wheat was Virginia's other staple) were even more disheartening. London estimated that the loss on wheat, using the same costs as in the tobacco trade, amounted to $1,760,000. Thus Virginia, for want of direct trade, paid northern cities annually a tribute of $3,010,000 for the privilege of marketing its staples. A southern confederacy, London argued, would allow Virginia's cities to develop their own direct-trade outlets and marketing facilities.[70]

Secessionists also claimed that while the southern confederacy promised economic freedom, the Union portended increasing dependence. Under Republican policies the state and her cities would suffer economic privation. The Republican Party platform was probably the first in American history that recognized the existence

69. Charleston *Mercury*, quoted in New York *Herald*, November 4, 1860; Richmond *Enquirer*, August 29, 1956.
70. Speech of Daniel H. London to the General Assembly, January 5, 1860, quoted in Richmond *Enquirer*, January 13, 1860.

of a national economy and sought to conform economic policy to it. The platform was a bold document that presaged an active role by the federal government in fomenting the maturation of the national economy. It seemed likely to spokesmen for disunion that the national government would wield its wealth and patronage for the benefit of northern cities and states.[71]

The Republican party's control over patronage was a powerful economic weapon, secessionists believed. Before the era of civil service, the federal government was a vast patronage mill. As population and wealth burgeoned in the decades before the Civil War, the patronage power increased vastly. Virtually every corner of the union came under the scrutiny of federal patronage. Virginia's lieutenant governor, John Randolph Tucker, in a speech delivered in 1851 and reprinted eight years later, noted that the creation of a national economy had not only consolidated commerce but government as well. He warned of the dangers of patronage in the hands of an increasingly powerful executive: "patronage is the greatest element in political power in modern times, and has almost superceded the use of the sword." In 1856 the *Enquirer* related how this expansive power would be utilized in the control of a Republican executive: "Mr. Fremont's election will exclude the South from the dispensation of 50 or 60 millions of the common revenue and in the granting of numerous lucrative contracts." William C. Rives, a Unionist, also feared the federal patronage power concerning contracts. The government would award these contracts, Rives alleged, "from the sole consideration of the number of voters of the preferred party."[72]

The federal government had grown wealthy. Since wealth and power were synonymous, the parceling out of funds was bound to have an impressive economic effect. Federal expenditures amounted to $80,000,000 annually prior to Lincoln's election. There was every indication that this sum would increase under the economic nationalism of a Republican administration. Seces-

71. See Foner, "The Causes of the American Civil War," 213.
72. John Randolph Tucker, *An Address Delivered before the Society of Alumni of the University of Virginia* (Richmond, 1851), 29–30; Richmond *Enquirer*, October 7, 1856; Speech of William C. Rives in Richmond, May 3, 1859, quoted in Richmond *Whig*, May 6, 1859.

sionists at the state convention were deeply concerned that Republicans would handle these expenditures in a partisan manner.[73] As William M. Tredway, a Danville attorney, declared on the floor of the convention, the crucial problem for the South, even more important than slavery, was "the money question" and how Republicans would handle it. In an age of materialism it was indeed an appropriate question. "Politicians of the North," Tredway concluded, "do not care so much about your slaves as they do about riding into power on the strength of the agitation of the slavery question and clutching the spoils of office."[74]

To supporters of the southern confederacy, the "spoils of office" included not only individual appointments, but the division of federal funds as well. The control and partisan distribution of federal patronage in the forms of offices and wealth would be only the beginning of Republican party efforts to depress southern economic and hence political power. Even prior to Lincoln's election many Virginians felt that the federal government had been less than even-handed in bestowing economic benefits upon the state and its cities. In January 1860, Daniel H. London catalogued some of the federal economic indignities over the years: first, claimed the Richmond merchant, the federal government paid out $300,000 annually to the citizens of New England for catching cod fish, "a vocation," London added, "in which the people of Virginia have no interest." Second, there were the navigation laws that prohibited foreign vessels from engaging in the coasting trade, thus "benefitting the ship-owners of the Northern States." Finally, the reciprocity treaty with Canada, passed in 1857, allowed wheat and breadstuffs to enter the United States freely, depreciating and excluding Virginia wheat.[75]

With a past record that was discriminatory, secessionists felt the role of the federal government under Republican leadership

73. Speech of Jeremiah Morton in Virginia State Convention, February 28, 1861, quoted in Richmond *Enquirer*, March 2, 1861.

74. Speech of William M. Tredway in the Virginia State Convention, April 1, 1861, quoted in Richmond *Enquirer*, May 21, 1861.

75. Speech of Daniel H. London to the Virginia General Assembly, January 5, 1860, quoted in Richmond *Enquirer*, January 13, 1860. See also Russel, "Southern Secessionists Per Se," 77–78.

would be even more exclusive. Control of patronage and a desire to maintain northern economic supremacy would leave Virginia's economy in a stagnant condition. The Richmond *Examiner*, in April 1861, contended that "should Virginia remain in the Union . . . the whole patronage and power of the Federal Government will be wielded to prevent the attainment of either direct trade or the completion of the James River and Ohio Canal."[76] The *Examiner* did not specify the exact course the federal government would take in attaining these objectives, but the editors and a portion of the readership accepted the fact that the Republican leadership would go to any lengths to maintain the economic dominance of its section.

One of the ways in which the Republicans could maintain the North's power was through the construction of a transcontinental railroad. As Unionists feared that the southern confederacy would build a railroad to the Pacific Coast through the Deep South, advocates of southern unity believed there was more imminent danger of the federal government, under Republican control, building a Pacific Railroad along a northern route. Indeed, Republicans had discussed this measure openly, almost from the party's inception. The *Enquirer* estimated that the project would require at least sixty million dollars. The Richmond journal believed that the government would raise the money through a discriminatory tax structure featuring a prohibitive tariff.[77] By the time the Virginia State Convention assembled on February 13, 1861, the prophesied tariff had become reality. The Morrill Tariff generated consternation among Virginia merchants, and one called it "a bill by which it is intended to plunder the South." If equality was "the cornerstone . . . of American liberty" as one Norfolk resident put it, then the Union under partisan Republican domination was doomed.[78]

With measures like the Morrill Tariff foreshadowing an aggressive economic policy, the institution of slavery seemed as threat-

76. Richmond *Examiner*, April 12, 1861.
77. Richmond *Enquirer*, January 28, 1859.
78. Richmond *Daily Dispatch*, February 22, 1861; Norfolk *Southern Argus*, December 22, 1861.

ened as the Old Dominion's economy. A planter near Richmond predicted that "under the pretext of regulating commerce between the States, the right to transport slaves from one State to another is forbidden."[79] Since the domestic slave trade was undoubtedly interstate commerce, the possibility of shutting off the trade was a real and frightful prospect for Virginians who were dependent on it. Further, secessionists asserted that the Republicans' avowed policy to prohibit slavery in the territories would have serious ramifications for the viability of the domestic slave traffic. Also, with slavery moribund in Delaware and declining in Maryland and Kentucky, the Old Dominion faced the prospect of becoming surrounded by free states. Some feared that by remaining in the Union, slave property would be unsafe, and large slaveholders—the heaviest cultivators of tobacco and wheat—would remove to the Deep South thereby crippling the state's economy.[80] Finally, there were a few, Edmund Ruffin included, who believed that the Republicans would emancipate slaves through the use of force. Personal liberty laws and John Brown's Raid indicated that the potential existed for armed intervention.[81]

Neither side—unionists nor secessionists—displayed logic that was sufficiently compelling to undercut the other. Their arguments contradicted each other. Unionists claimed that Virginia's economic future would be served best within the national economy, despite dependence on northern market centers. The Deep South, they averred, was antithetical to her economic programs. Supporters of the southern confederacy, on the other hand, were certain that the Old Dominion's cities could perform the functions of New York on a regional basis. Besides, the Republicans' power of patronage and access to the federal treasury suggested that Virginia's interests would not be appreciated within the Union. There was a similar divergence of opinion concerning slavery. Opponents of secession

79. Speech of Willoughby Newton in Virginia House of Delegates, January 12, 1860, quoted in Richmond *Enquirer*, January 17, 1860.

80. Robert B. Davis to Wilbur F. Davis, March 8, 1861, in Beale-Davis Family Papers; Richmond *Enquirer*, February 26, 1861.

81. Edmund Ruffin, *Toward Independence: October 1856–April 1861* (Baton Rouge, 1972), 463–64, 478–79, Vol. I in William Kauffman Scarborough (ed.), *The Diary of Edmund Ruffin* (Baton Rouge, 1972).

believed that both the institution and the domestic slave trade were safer in the Union than outside it. Spokesmen for the southern confederacy advocated the opposite viewpoint, fearing that the Republicans, despite disclaimers from party leaders, sought to destroy or at least to weaken both slavery and the domestic slave trade.

A polarization of viewpoints deadlocked the secession convention. It droned on for more than two months without deciding anything except that it was not yet ready to decide. The protracted convention debates and the growing list of seceded states produced severe economic dislocation in Virginia, especially in the cities. The banks in Virginia cities suspended specie payments in mid-November, following the lead of northern banks shaken by the disruption of commercial intercourse between the North and the Deep South.[82] By the end of December, the Orange and Alexandria Railroad defaulted on its debts, unable to meet its obligations due to "the deranged condition of the business of the country."[83] Other internal improvement companies suffered heavy losses, and farmers withheld their crops waiting for higher prices and a break in the crisis.[84]

The economic situation worsened with the New Year. With each passing month, the hard-won growth and prosperity seemed to be sinking in a morass of unpaid bills and empty account books. By January, according to one source, "thousands of good men" lapsed into bankruptcy, unable to obtain capital to pay debts and unable to carry on business because of a dearth of customers.[85] By Lincoln's inauguration in early March, hundreds of city and country merchants boarded up their shops, unemployment became chronic,

82. Alexandria *Gazette*, November 23, 1860; Richmond *Daily Dispatch*, November 22, 1860; Wheeling *Daily Intelligencer*, November 23, 1860.
83. James H. Reid [Treasurer of the Orange and Alexandria Railroad] to George Lobdell, December 28, 1860, in Bush and Lobdell Papers. See also Angus J. Johnston, II, *Virginia Railroads in the Civil War* (Chapel Hill, 1961), 6–15.
84. H. N. Wallace to James L. Kemper, March 26, 1861, in James L. Kemper Papers, Alderman Library, University of Virginia; Angus R. Blakey to Beverly R. Wellford, December 3, 1860, in White, Wellford, Taliaferro, Marshall Papers, Southern Historical Collection, University of North Carolina; BPW, *Report on Turnpikes and Canals, 1860–61*, 74–75.
85. F. H. Mays to James L. Kemper, January 14, 1861, in Kemper Papers.

and men roamed the city streets bewildered, poor, hungry, and anxious to lay blame for their predicament.[86] By April a rump convention had assembled in Richmond, and violence seemed imminent. When Lincoln called on Governor John Letcher for troops to quell the insurrection in South Carolina, the decision in favor of secession was in fact made for the convention, and the delegates passed the ordinance by a vote of eighty-eight to fifty-five on April 17, 1861.[87] Although the people of the state elected a predominantly Unionist convention in January, the economic downturn that threatened the decade of urban growth and progress helped to shift public opinion against the Unionist cause long before Lincoln's call for troops. As northern banks suspended, as northern factors and financiers (themselves hard pressed) called in notes held by Virginians, and as Virginia's wharves grew quiet and empty, the North became the obvious target of discontent. The crisis demonstrated the interrelationship of Virginia and northern economies.

There were actually two votes on a secession ordinance: one rejected on April 4, and one approved on April 17. It is interesting to chart the votes on these two ordinances, if only to speculate on the influences that moved each delegate to cast his vote in a particular way. The vote on the April 4 resolution, introduced by Richmond railroad executive Lewis E. Harvie, was a truer expression of delegate preferences than the April 17 vote which ratified what was, in effect, a fait accompli. Beset by threats of violence, economic collapse, and the impossible idea of sending Virginia troops against a sister state, the delegates' frame of mind on April 17 was more likely motivated by fear or resignation than by reason. Eyewitnesses who described the chaos within and without the convention hall support this view.[88] Rather than discard the results of the April 17 vote, however, I shall give it less emphasis in this study.

Two generalizations emerge from a cursory glance at the dele-

86. Richmond *Examiner*, March 21, 1861; Shanks, *Secession Movement*, 200.
87. Virginia State Library, *Journals and Papers of the Virginia State Convention of 1861* (3 vols.; Richmond, 1966), I, 10–11 (Journal of the Secret Session).
88. See John B. Jones, *A Rebel War Clerk's Diary at the Confederate States Capital* (2 vols.; Philadelphia, 1866), I, 15, 20.

gates and their votes. First, slaveholding had little to do with determining an individual's vote: the largest slaveholder in the convention, John Coles Bruce of Halifax County, was a staunch Unionist until the end. He voted against the April 4 ordinance. Bowing to pressure from constituents, he recorded his vote in favor of secession on April 17. Of the total number of delegates voting on the first resolution, 93 were slaveholders and 42 were nonslaveholders. Fifty-nine slaveholders (63.4%) and 31 nonslaveholders (73.8%) formed the majority in rejecting Harvie's resolution by a margin of two to one (90 to 45). There was no significant difference in the voting pattern of slaveholder and nonslaveholder. In the less reliable April 17 vote, 102 slaveholders voted and 41 nonslaveholders cast their ballots. Seventy-one slaveholders (69.6%) and 17 nonslaveholders (41.5%) supported the secession ordinance. Although there was a substantial difference between the two groups on the April 17 ordinance, even there the figures were not lopsided. Most slaveholders represented Tidewater and Piedmont staple districts which were hardest hit by the depression and closest to other southern states. Many of the nonslaveholders resided in western districts which were less affected by economic failure and more proximate to northern states. Thus, factors other than slaveholding may have influenced votes.

The second interesting aspect to the two secession votes was that the voting patterns of urban delegates did not diverge significantly from the patterns of nonurban delegates. The urban vote on the April 4 ordinance was four delegates in favor and six opposed (with two abstentions). On April 17, there were seven urban votes in favor of the ordinance, and five against. This was a slightly narrower margin than the convention vote, but nevertheless a representative shift in favor of secession.[89]

The configuration of the urban vote deserves further analysis because it implied what the rhetoric of the convention made explicit: the role of a particular city in the national economy influenced its delegate's viewpoints on the sectional crisis. Wheeling possessed the strongest economic connections with the North,

89. VSL, *Virginia State Convention*, I, 31–32.

especially after the completion of the Baltimore and Ohio Railroad in 1853. The *Intelligencer* estimated that in 1860 Wheeling carried on three-quarters of its business with the free states. Her merchants would consider it a disaster to be "cut off from Ohio, Indiana, and Illinois markets." [90] More than once during the 1850s Wheeling's residents expressed a desire for annexation to Pennsylvania or Ohio. Wheeling's two delegates to the state convention were Sherrard Clemens and Chester D. Hubbard. Clemens, a Wheeling lawyer who had been educated in Pennsylvania, received a serious wound in 1859 as a result of a duel with O. Jennings Wise, a co-editor of the Richmond *Enquirer*. Clemens was absent for the April 4 vote but limped into the convention hall to record his vote against secession on April 17. Chester D. Hubbard was a wealthy lumber dealer in Wheeling. Following the pattern of prominent Wheeling residents, Hubbard had received a northern education at Wesleyan University in Connecticut. Prior to his service at the state convention, Hubbard was a typical civic leader: member of the city council, president of the Bank of Wheeling, proprietor of an iron foundry, and a member of the house of delegates from 1852 to 1853. Hubbard voted against secession on both occasions.

Norfolk, at the other end of the commonwealth from Wheeling, developed a lucrative trade with northern cities during the 1850s. The city possessed a small hinterland with few ties to southern commerce, although she did have impending rail connections with the cotton states. Both Norfolk delegates (one actually lived in Portsmouth, just across the river) were representative of the city's leadership. George Blow, Jr., educated in Virginia,, practiced law in the city. He campaigned for the state convention as a Unionist and was easily elected. Blow voted against secession on April 4, but he supported the April 17 ordinance. James G. Holladay, also elected as a Unionist, practiced law in Norfolk's sister city. He was deeply involved in charity and civic affairs and served heroically during the 1855 yellow fever epidemic. Absent on April 4, Holladay voted against disunion on April 17. Norfolk County's representative, William White, also voted against the April 17 ordinance.

90. Wheeling *Daily Intelligencer*, November 28, 1860.

Richmond's economy was the most diverse in the state. The city's merchants and manufacturers depended on northerners to market their flour and tobacco. Richmond's extensive rail network, however, brought produce from neighboring southern states, thereby developing a southern clientele for the city's merchants. Iron manufacturers like Joseph R. Anderson and James M. Talbott found their best and only market in the Deep South. Citizens reflected the commercial connections to both regions by electing two Unionists, one secessionist, and one who was somewhere in between. William H. Macfarland was one of Richmond's wealthiest and most active civic leaders. He was president of both the Farmer's Bank of Richmond and the Richmond and Petersburg Railroad. In addition to his business affairs, Macfarland was active in church and charitable organizations. He was a Unionist who voted against Harvie's resolution on April 4, but he joined the majority in approving the ordinance of secession on April 17. Marmaduke Johnson, who at thirty-five was among the younger members of the convention, received a Virginia education and rapidly became one of the city's leading criminal lawyers. Richmonders elected Johnson as a Unionist, though he disclaimed the label, preferring to call himself a moderate. Johnson, like Macfarland, opposed the April 4 resolution but supported the April 17 ordinance. George W. Randolph, Richmond's third delegate to the convention, came from a prominent Virginia family. He graduated from the University of Virginia and settled in Richmond to practice law. He voted in favor of secession on both April 4 and April 17. The fourth Richmonder at the convention was Williams C. Wickham, who actually represented Henrico County. Wickham, an attorney and railroad executive in Richmond, was a staunch Unionist. He opposed both ordinances.

Alexandria, like Wheeling, Norfolk, and Richmond, carried on a prosperous trade with northern cities. By 1861, however, Alexandria merchants were hoping that the recently completed railroad connections with Lynchburg might bring about a diversity of trading partners by opening the southwest to Alexandria. An added problem faced by Alexandrians as the Union crumbled about them, was their geographical proximity to the North. Secession could be dangerous for a city in such a precarious location. George W. Brent, the lone delegate from the city, represented Alexandria's interests ably at the state convention. Brent, raised and educated in the Old Dominion, had recently (1853) moved to Alexandria from Warrenton. Although residing in the city for only seven years prior to his election to the convention, Brent had earned an outstanding reputation as a lawyer and civic leader. Brent voted against secession on April 4 and again on April 17.

Petersburg and Lynchburg were the two cities in the Old Dominion with the strongest economic ties to the South. Direct-trade contact between them and the North was unusual. Petersburg and Lynchburg merchants carried a considerable amount of northern wares in their inventories, but the articles invariably came through Richmond. On the other hand, the proximity to the Virginia and North Carolina tobacco fields and Lynchburg's rail connections with Memphis and the cotton South ensured a more direct relationship with southern states. Thomas Branch, elected as a Unionist from Petersburg, was the city's leading merchant. A former mayor and city councilman, Branch was also president of the local bank. Economic setback and "instructions from constituents," persuaded Branch to drop his Unionist stance by the end of March. He voted in favor of both secession ordinances. James Boisseau represented Dinwiddie County in the convention, but he resided near Petersburg; so it is appropriate to note that he too recorded two positive votes on secession. Lynchburg sent two delegates to the convention, though technically they represented Campbell County of which Lynchburg was a part. John M. Speed came to Lynchburg following graduation from William and Mary College. He was a lawyer, active in the city's economic progress, and president of the Farmer's Bank of Lynchburg. The county elected him as a "moderate Unionist," though Speed soon shed whatever Unionist sympathies he had. He supported both secession ordinances. Charles R. Slaughter, educated in the state, was, like Speed, a lawyer and also a bank president, and like Speed represented the county as a "moderate Unionist." He opposed secession on April 4 but supported it on April 17.[91]

The impact of a city's role on the national economy is difficult to measure quantitatively. Not only would values have to be assigned subjectively to denote a city's commercial ties to the North and the South, but all delegates would have to be included in any tabulation. A correlation employing only twelve cases would be meaningless. Nevertheless, it seems logical to assume that if delegates discussed the relative economic merits of a southern or northern union, such considerations weighed equally as prominently in the voting, especially on the April 4 ordinance. Finally, it was perhaps more than coincidence that the voting pattern of the urban delegates conformed to expectations if a city's relationship in the national economy were indeed the only variable operating on the delegates' votes.

The delegates representing urban Virginia were typically civic leaders who were immersed in the economic destinies of their cities. Wheeling, completely removed from the southern commercial orbit, sent two delegates who, when they were present, cast their votes against secession. Norfolk, whose coastwise trade with the North was the foundation of its prosperity, yet whose plans included a livelier trade with the Deep South, had two delegates who cast two of three votes (one delegate was absent) against secession. Richmond, with varied commercial ties, elected four delegates who cast three of four votes against the April 4 resolution, and three of four votes supporting secession on April 17. Alexandria possessed an economy similar to Norfolk's, and its delegate opposed secession on both occasions. Petersburg and Lynchburg, victims to some degree of a regional economic centralization at Richmond, had more developed relations with the South. The two cities sent three delegates who cast five of their six votes in support of union with the southern confederacy.

As urban Virginia prepared for war, the citizens could not of

91. William H. Gaines, Jr., *Biographical Register of Members: Virginia State Convention of 1861* (Richmond, 1969).

course know that a decade of economic progress would end under
the crush of northern artillery. The war buried the last vestiges of
hope for economic independence and sectional equality which
were foreign ideals in an integrated national economy. Urban
growth, though, was measured not only in material terms. It also
generated an active leadership, an array of commercial and urban
services, a useful labor system, and an indomitable urban spirit.
Civil war may have quieted these aspects of cityhood in the Old
Dominion, but it did not extinguish them. The New South demonstrated the resiliency of modern urban life in Virginia's cities—a
lifestyle that had been forged in the Old South.

Historian Eric Foner has stated that the Civil War was a struggle
for the future of the nation as each side fought to preserve its own
way of life.[92] The nature of the South's "way of life" remains
unclear. For Virginia's cities, the verdict of the war was that a
national economy centered in the northeastern cities would forge
an urban nation. Virginia and the South would have to find their
place in the context of northeastern economic supremacy—a place
which Virginia's cities had begun to assume before the war. Soon,
the credo of commercial and industrial enterprise and of urban
growth and prosperity would echo through the very heartland of
the South. The paeans to cities and genuflections to factories were
familiar rituals to Virginia's urban leaders. They were present at
the birth of a new era. Their response to sectionalism in the Old
South helped to develop a new South, as they renewed their quest
to become simply "other Americans" rather than distinctly southerners.[93]

92. Foner, "Causes of the American Civil War," 213.
93. See Grady McWhiney, *Southerners and Other Americans* (New York, 1973).

Epilogue: The Renewed South

W. J. CASH first submitted the thesis that continuity rather than difference marked the transition between the Old South and the New South. The Civil War was thus an interruption in southern development rather than the beginning of a fundamental reordering of southern society. Recent studies of race and of the southern character have confirmed Cash's intuitive judgment about his homeland.[1] The view persists, however, that the Old South and the New South were as distinct and different as the labels *Old* and *New* imply. The Civil War, according to this view, was both regional holocaust and catharsis. The result was the birth of a new nation complete with new ideology and sense of purpose. The New South Creed was a major part of the ideology. The creed was the section's response to a new sectional relationship with the North following the war.[2] It might be worthwhile, therefore, to analyze the continuity, if any, between that response and the response of the Old South to a different sectional situation nearly two decades earlier.

The view that plantation slavery and planters themselves monopolized the Old South stage has been a major obstacle to depicting the history of the South as continuous. David Potter, for example, posited the following dilemma for the South in 1865. Southerners, he wrote, "could not bear either to abandon the patterns of the Old South, or to forego the material gains of modern America."[3] The implication, of course, was that the "patterns of the Old South" were antagonistic to the "material gains of modern America." The idea of a primitive, backward Old South became an important reference point in discussions concerning the New South. Thus, the pastoral, premodern ideal of the antebellum South began any interpretation of the postwar South.

Paul M. Gaston, whose provocative and brilliant distillation of

1. See Pete Daniel, *The Shadow of Slavery: Peonage in the South, 1901–1969* (Urbana, Ill., 1972); Tindall, "Beyond the Mainstream," 3–18.
2. Paul M. Gaston, *The New South Creed: A Study in Southern Mythmaking* (New York, 1970).
3. David Potter quoted in Gaston, *New South Creed*, 10.

the mind of the New South has added significantly to our understanding of the postwar era, approached his subject from the same assumptions as Potter. Gaston cited the three "intertwining economic and social interests" of the Old South: staple crop agriculture, planter aristocracy, and slavery that "frustrated industrial urban developments capable of undermining their foundations."[4] There are two difficulties with this statement. First, it implies a monolithic antebellum South. Gaston's triumvirate did not dominate the mountain regions, the pine barrens, and even the Tidewater areas of the Upper South by 1860. Gaston ignored Virginia's urban civilization, not to mention Louisville, Memphis, New Orleans, Mobile, Savannah, and Charleston. Second, the statement suggests that the three dominant patterns of the Old South civilization (assuming for the moment that they were dominant) were antithetical to industrial and urban growth. For one thing, much of the South's industry, as in the North, existed in pastoral surroundings. Further, planters invested heavily and enthusiastically in manufacturing enterprises. Finally, if it were not for staple crop agriculture, southern cities would have been, at the most, roadside hamlets.

Building on assumptions that have questionable validity, Gaston presented the New South as a new departure for southerners. The postwar era for the South was a sort of coming out of their premodern shell, or, as Gaston called it, the "cotton curtain."[5] With the development of a national economy by 1860, this type of isolation would have been impossible, as Virginia's cities demonstrated. Using northern cities both as models and as trading partners, Virginia's cities were in closer contact with the North than at any other time in the nation's history. Although the Old South cities talked bravely about economic independence, they were farther from that goal in 1860 than in 1840. Southern planters were also more aware of and more concerned with goings on in London and New York than at any other time.

Gaston's viewpoint found some support among southerners

4. Gaston, *New South Creed*, 20.
5. *Ibid.*, 21.

after the war. Former Confederate general Benjamin Harvey Hill, for example, declared after the war that the South was at the crossroads when "one civilization abruptly ends and another begins." Such a declaration was understandable considering the natural desire to start anew and to forget the past, especially the defeat. In 1858, a Virginia lawmaker, referring to a pending railroad appropriation, observed that the subscription would mark a turning point for the state and would determine "for good or evil, its future character and destiny."[6] This, of course, did not mean that "one civilization" was abruptly ending and another just as magically beginning. It indicated rather, the proclivity of all contemporaries, particularly politicians, to employ phrases such as "turning point" and "crossroads" to add greater significance to their words and deeds. Governor Joseph Johnson of Virginia, for example, referred to the "new era" of economic resurgence in three of his five annual reports to the people from 1851 to 1855.[7]

There is sufficient supporting evidence in antebellum Virginia to suggest that the prewar period was indeed a "new era" and that a "progressive spirit" had overtaken the lethargy of the past.[8] The sudden blossoming of railroads, urban and commercial services, civic leadership, and urban spirit were more concrete indications of progress and change than political rhetoric was. New South leaders, as Gaston pointed out, acknowledged their debt to antebellum pioneers who first made urbanization, railroads, and industrialization important aspects of southern economic thought. Richard Hathaway Edmonds, whose *Manufacturers' Record* was a major New South oracle, repeatedly lavished praise on his antebellum economic forebears. Edmonds wrote that leaders in the 1840s and 1850s laid the foundation for the basic programs of the New South. Not only was such a bow to the past good public relations, it was also a perceptive reading of the economic genesis of the New South Creed. Edmonds allowed that his contemporaries were "too prone to believe that the Old South was a non-progressive, pastoral coun-

6. Benjamen Harvey Hill, quoted *ibid.*, 34; Richmond *Enquirer*, February 16, 1858.
7. See Virginia House of Delegates, Annual Messages of the Governor, *House of Delegates Report* (Richmond, 1851–1855).
8. Charlestown *Spirit of Jefferson*, September 30, 1851.

try." The New South, according to Edmonds, was merely "taking up the unfinished work of the Old South so rudely interrupted by the shock of war." On another occasion Edmonds stated succinctly, "The South of today is no novel creation; it is an evolution." Gaston presented other New South spokesmen who similarly stressed the continuity between the two Souths—Old and New. In 1893, educator Amory Dwight Mayo declared that the New South was "the Old South asserting herself under a new dispensation." Nine years later, Joseph G. Brown discarded the label "New South" for a more accurate one, "Renewed South."[9]

The renewed South bore striking similarity to its antebellum progenitor. Sectionalism again played a significant role in determining and defining the parameters of New South policy. Sectional reconciliation was a basic tenet of the New South Creed. Through economic regeneration, the postwar South would achieve equality and hence sectional amity with the North. In the 1850s George Fitzhugh predicted similarly that commercial relations would be the new foundation for sectional unity. John Randolph Tucker, a Virginia political leader and contemporary of Fitzhugh's, agreed that "commercial interests are the strongest cements of political union." The New South was thus continuing an antebellum pattern: viewing sectional alignments in economic terms. Just as the Virginia Board of Public Works in 1851 believed railroads and direct trade would "secure our political independence," so New South spokesmen asserted that the South's perpetual colonial status would be obliterated by implementation of a full slate of economic remedies.[10]

New South prophets consciously imitated northern urban leadership in devising their programs for industry, railroads, and education. The echoes of J. D. B. De Bow, a founding father of the renewed South, resounded throughout the rhetoric of his postwar followers. In 1847, De Bow had rallied his countrymen: "we must

9. Richmond Hathaway Edmonds, quoted in Gaston, *New South Creed*, 163, 164; Amory Dwight Mayo, quoted in *New South Creed*, 101; Joseph G. Brown, quoted in *New South Creed*, 165.

10. See Fitzhugh, *Sociology*, 203; John Randolph Tucker to M. R. H. Garnett, January 1, 1846, in Mercer Papers; 36 BPW 1851, viii.

meet our Northern competitors upon their own ground and with corresponding weapons." Several years later when De Bow analyzed Norfolk's prospects as a major commercial entrepôt he asked, "Can Virginia accomplish as much for the South as New York has done for the North?"[11] Characteristically, as New South leaders carefully planned their programs for sectional reconciliation, they looked once again to their section's cities as the centers of economic progress.

Cities were the repositories of industry and population; the keys to the regeneration of the renewed South. Richard Hathaway Edmonds emphasized consistently the need for heavy manufacturing and the growth of large urban centers.[12] J. D. B. De Bow supported urban and industrial development as he had done so often before the war. In 1867 De Bow wrote, in rhetoric reminiscent of his prewar campaigns, "We have got to go to manufacturing to save ourselves." Before the war, De Bow had commented in a similar vein, "No country that produces raw materials only can be prosperous." A Mobile journal advised, even earlier, that "the subject of manufactures at the South should claim the first attention." Finally, New South leaders saw the efficacy of cities as great population centers. Population meant power and prosperity. In antebellum Virginia, the Norfolk *Southern Argus* expressed a similar view: "Even before capital, the great desideratum of every community is population." George Fitzhugh, one of antebellum urban Virginia's leading spokesmen, summarized the role of cities as population and manufacturing centers: "They afford respectable occupations in the mechanic arts, manufactures, and the professions. . . . They sustain good schools. . . . They furnish places and opportunities for association and rational enjoyment."[13]

The specific aspects of the New South program thus first

11. "Contests for the Trade of the Mississippi Valley," 98; "Foreign Trade of Virginia and the South," 502.

12. Gaston, *New South Creed*, 50, 64–69.

13. *DeBow's Review*, quoted *ibid.*, 25; *DeBow's Review*, quoted in "Southern Patronage to Southern Industry," *Southern Planter*, XXI (1861), 160; Mobile *Register and Journal*, February 20, 1845, quoted in Miller, "Pratt's Industrial Urbanism," 6; Gaston *New South Creed*, 25; Norfolk *Southern Argus*, February 17, 1852; Fitzhugh, *Sociology*, 136.

achieved circulation during the decade and a half before the Civil War. George Fitzhugh, whom Gaston stated "lauded a stratified agrarian society," set forth the New South economic policy in *Sociology for the South*: "The South must vary and multiply her pursuits, consume her crops at home, increase her population, build up cities, towns, and villages, establish more schools and colleges, educate the poor, construct internal improvements, [and] carry on her own commerce." [14] Edmonds, Henry W. Grady, Daniel A. Tompkins, or other prominent leaders of the postwar era could not have stated the region's postwar goals any better.

The Readjuster movement in postwar Virginia embodied the continuity between the economic philosophies of Fitzhugh and of Grady. The Readjusters formed an urban-rural coalition with a vigorous urban leadership. Their programs bore a strong resemblance to the projects promoted by the antebellum urban elite: the encouragement of immigration, capital investment, manufacturing, and economic growth in general. The similarity was not surprising considering that Readjuster leaders like William Lamb of Norfolk, John S. Wise of Richmond, and William Mahone of several cities had served fruitful apprenticeships in the urban workshops of prewar Virginia. They viewed funding as an onerous fetter to economic and urban growth, much as they chafed under the currency restrictions of an earlier regime. The possibility of the New South lay for the Readjusters in the fulfillment of the dreams of the Old South. [15]

The differences between the Readjusters and their Conservative opponents were distinctions of degree rather than of kind. Though there is some disagreement among historians as to the Funders' commitment to the dreams of antebellum urban Virginia, they at least paid lip service to industrial capitalism, internal improvements, and urban growth. City dwellers dominated their leadership, and the Conservative's policies, such as railroad development and the abolition of state tobacco inspection, favored the urban

14. Fitzhugh, *Sociology*, 158.
15. James T. Moore, *Two Paths to the New South: The Virginia Debt Controversy, 1870–1883* (Lexington, Ky., 1974), 53, 85, 87.

mercantile class. The "two paths to the New South" in postwar Virginia seemed to stem from the same antebellum branch.[16]

New South leaders not only espoused similar goals as the prewar economic activists, they followed their predecessors' tradition of warning fellow southerners about the dangers of looking backward. Do not become mesmerized by the glories of the past nor lured by the attractions of political power, were common warnings issued by New South activists.[17] In 1886, New South prophet Henry W. Grady assured members of the New England Society in New York that the South has "sowed towns and cities in the place of theories, and put business above politics." More than a generation earlier, the Richmond *Daily Dispatch* had informed a much less select group that "a new and brighter era is evidently at hand. . . . The man of business is substituted for the political theorist." A writer in the *Southern Literary Messenger* advised antebellum southerners to be "more occupied in personal interests than in public affairs."[18]

Not only politics but overweaning concern with the glorious past—whether battles or statesmen—vexed civic leaders in both the prewar and the postwar South. Postwar spokesmen had the additional task of guarding against the use of the Confederate flag and assorted memorabilia as a cocoon against reality and economic progress. As one Virginian urged in 1854, the South must close its ears "to the lullaby song of self-glorification."[19] The past, of course, was not to be totally denied, just as interest in politics could not be expunged from any American. Both Old and New South leaders asked that southerners place both the past and politics in their proper perspectives without dominating the truly important objectives of economic progress.

The medium for both the goals and the warnings articulated by

16. Maddex, *The Virginia Conservatives*, xii, 69, 276. *Cf.* Moore, *Two Paths to the New South*, 38–44.

17. Gaston, *New South Creed*, 19.

18. Henry W. Grady, quoted *ibid.*, 86; Richmond *Daily Dispatch*, October 31, 1854; John Y. Mason, "Letter to D. H. London, Esq. on a Line of Steamers to Europe, Southern Literary Messanger, XVIII (1852), 590.

19. Gaston, *New South Creed*, 31, 86; Van Zandt, *Claims of Virginia*, 18.

New South activists was the press. The printed word, effectively utilized by antebellum leaders, became the sword of New South commanders. It was not surprising that the major spokesmen for the postwar economic effort were closely associated with a major newspaper or magazine. Just as James A. Cowardin and William F. Ritchie utilized their columns to further the "new era" in antebellum Richmond, so too New South editors played a leading role in promoting the regeneration of their section. Henry W. Grady joined the Atlanta *Constitution* in 1876 after several years as a newspaperman in the North. The *Constitution* and Atlanta became the symbols of New South progress, literally rising from the ashes of defeat. The newspaper provided Grady with a daily forum for his ebullient philosophy. Walter Hines Page, another prominent figure in Gaston's pantheon of New South leaders, edited a newspaper in his native North Carolina. Henry Watterson was a newspaper editor most of his adult life. In his early twenties he had assumed the editorship of a Civil War propaganda sheet, *The Rebel*. After the war he became editor of the Nashville *Banner* and, subsequently, the Louisville *Courier*. The latter paper, along with Grady's *Constitution*, were probably the two most widely read and influential journals in the South.[20]

Richard Hathaway Edmonds's *Manufacturers' Record*, established in Baltimore in 1881, was the only major publication entirely dominated by New South philosophy and figures. By 1870 *De Bow's Review* had ceased publication. After De Bow's death in 1867, Virginia urban booster William M. Burwell became editor. Despite his valiant efforts, the *Review* succumbed to financial difficulties shortly thereafter. De Bow and his *Review* were the primary drumbeaters of cities, industry, and internal improvements in the late antebellum South. De Bow used his magazine to apprise southerners of the benefits of urban growth and economic diversification, to illuminate examples of southern enterprise and success, and to occasionally chastise his neighbors for lagging spirit and energy—two qualities that he himself never seemed to lack. Edmonds's publication filled a vacuum left by the departure of the *Review*. The

20. Gaston, *New South Creed*, 48, 51, 53.

New South required a regional journal to outline goals and to announce advances. Edmonds used, or as some critics have claimed, abused statistics the way other journalists used words. For a section suffering from a crisis of confidence, the *Record* served a purpose. Edmonds ignored or glossed over the failures of the New South Creed. Nevertheless, by serving as a regional forum for statistics and philosophy, the *Record* followed the well-worn path that *De Bow's Review* had cleared in the antebellum era.[21]

The rhetoric of the New South journals exhibited the same enthusiasm and exaggeration that characterized the antebellum urban press. A writer in *De Bow's Review*, following the war, predicted that the ravaged South would develop its resources and make "Ninevah, Babylon, Rome, and Britain sink into insignificance." In 1869, the Richmond *Whig* returned to a familiar prewar refrain by touting Richmond as the South's leading manufacturing city—a proposal considerably more realistic than the statement in the *Review*. Edmonds was perhaps the most adept at transforming a cliché into a rallying cry. Virginia, a frequent exemplar of Edmonds's statistical flights became not the Mother of Presidents, but the "mother of millionaires." Antebellum journalists frequently matched and even exceeded New South predictions. In 1852, the Richmond *Enquirer* maintained that Virginia's railroad network combined with direct trade "will make Virginia the 'Excelsior State of the Union.'" In another rhetorical comparison the Salem *Register* dreamed of Richmond as the Manchester and Norfolk as the Venice of America.[22] These predictions were not quite as provocative as comparisons with Ninevah and Babylon, but the point was the same: the programs for economic progress would ensure greatness for the South and her cities in the nation and in the world.

Recognition and acceptance were important to the New South. Postwar journals displayed their cities and section as much for outsiders as for each other. The taint of backwardness; defeat; and,

21. *Ibid.*, 51, 59, 79.
22. *DeBow's Review*, quoted *ibid.*, 24; Richmond *Whig*, quoted *ibid.*, 31; Richard Hathaway Edmonds, quoted *ibid.*, 79; Richmond *Enquirer*, November 23, 1852; Salem *Weekly Register*, October 1, 1858.

above all, slavery held fast for decades after Appomattox. New South spokesmen unanimously denounced the "peculiar institution." They also portrayed contemporary race relations in a positive, harmonious framework. The South was right on race. The South's desire to handle the race issue without outside interference was another motive for declaring racial harmony. The Old South, of course, expressed a similar wish. The New South dealt with the black as southerners had before the War. Slavery was gone, but the subservient, degrading condition of the black remained. All indications pointed to the fact that the New South attempted to approximate the master-slave relationship as closely as possible.[23]

The continuity of race relations in southern history is not a new theme; U. B. Phillips emphasized it in a celebrated essay nearly fifty years ago.[24] Southerners sought the normalization of race relations following the war for a number of reasons, not the least of which was economic. The centrality of black labor to economic progress was an important aspect of race relations. Slave labor, in the cities and on the plantations, was essential to the economic development of urban centers and of commercial agriculture. Emancipation brought freedom of mobility, if nothing else, to the blacks. The slave codes became the Black Codes. Debt peonage, the chain gang, and convict lease were urban Old South labor devices that enjoyed extensive popularity in the New South. The goals of the codes and of the labor systems were the same in either era: to restrict mobility and to provide a reliable labor force. Although the New South leaders spoke of European immigration as much if not more than antebellum civic leaders, black men and women provided the sinews for economic regeneration. Richard Hathaway Edmonds recognized the value and the necessity of black labor and extolled the virtue and reliability of blacks in factories and on railroads. Thus, although blacks were no longer slaves, their ability and versatility, demonstrated in the antebellum era, made them an equally if not a more valuable work force in the postwar era.[25]

23. Gaston, *New South Creed*, 7.
24. U. B. Phillips, "The Central Theme of Southern History," *American Historical Review*, XXXIV (1928), 30–43.
25. Gaston, *New South Creed*, 147; Berlin, *Slaves Without Masters*, 224, 382; William

Leaders of the renewed South emphasized the same programs, sought the same goals, employed identical tactics, and adhered to similar views on race as had antebellum civic leaders. The commonality between the pre- and postwar South, as seen through the New South Creed, was understandable. Rapid urbanization, industrialization, and corporate enterprise—the basic features of postwar American life—all appeared before the Civil War. Whether the war accelerated or retarded these trends is immaterial here. It is important to note that they existed and that Appomattox neither marked the beginning or the end of a significant era in American history—North or South.

For the New South, the unfortunate aspect of the continuity of American history was the continued and increasing dominance of northern cities in the national economy. Spokesmen for the New South confronted the same dilemma as their prewar brethren: how to create an independent economy within a national economy based on interrelationships. The rush to imitate and to trade with the North irked ante- and postbellum southerners alike. George Fitzhugh pleaded, "We must build centres of trade, of thought, and fashion at home . . . where young men may learn to admire their homes, not to despise them." But the very book in which Fitzhugh wrote this admonition was published in New York. Several years after the war, former Confederate general Daniel Harvey Hill hoped for southern economic independence and complained that the South was dependent on the North "for everything from a lucifer match to a columbiad, from a pin to a railroad engine." [26]

Other southerners recognized that it was impossible to fulfill either Fitzhugh's or Hill's desires without becoming indistinguishable from the enemy itself. Edward A. Pollard, editor of the Richmond *Examiner*, which was an excellent vantage point from which to view the efforts of progressive civic leaders to attain economic independence, scoffed at such windmill tilting and warned of a loss of southern identity: "The danger is that they [southerners] will

Cohen, "Negro Involuntary Servitude in the South, 1865–1940: A Preliminary Analysis," *Journal of Southern History*, XLII (1976), 31–60.

   26. Fitzhugh, *Cannibals All!*, 59; Daniel Harvey Hill, quoted in Gaston, *New South Creed*, 31.

lose their literature, their former habits of thought, their intellectual self-assertion, while they are too intent upon recovering the mere material prosperity."[27] It was an impossible order for New South leaders to fulfill. They had to maintain the integrity and identity of their section and simultaneously secure its economic independence. They had to achieve independence by following the example of northern cities and by encouraging urban growth, population, railroads, and factories. This magic would be performed in a section bankrupted by war.

The New South failed. The section could not achieve economic independence without heroic sacrifices and further impoverishment, and it could not attain a modicum of prosperity without assuming a dependent position in the national economy. Gaston, in assessing the New South leaders and their Hobson's choice, emphasized the "relative lateness" of the movement compared with the North.[28] Thus, timing played an important role in frustrating the dreams of economic independence in the New South, as it had in the Old South. The irony, as Gaston correctly discerned, was that the New South Creed led the South to an unequal economic relationship with the North without significantly improving the section's economy.[29] Virginia's civic leaders achieved modest urban growth, prosperity, and an urban identity; though they were further away from their goal of economic independence and sectional equilibrium in 1860 than at the beginning of their crusade.

The failure of the New South Creed was only temporary. Today the northeast has grudgingly relinquished its dominance over the national economy for a more integrated and equal relationship. Southern cities, like their counterparts more than a century ago, are still the cauldrons of change for their section. The urban South has pioneered in race relations, education, and economic progress. Southern cities are not only regional leaders but in some areas like architecture (Atlanta's John Portman), urban growth (Houston and Dallas, Texas), and even race relations (the increasing political

27. Edward A. Pollard, quoted in Gaston, *New South Creed*, 156.
28. Gaston, *New South Creed*, 206.
29. *Ibid.*, 189.

and economic power of blacks in all major southern cities), they are setting national examples. The importance of the urban South today is another example of the continuity of southern history. The hopes of antebellum Virginia resided in urban factories, on the boards of trade, and in city streets. Perhaps cities in other states had a similar impact on their state and ultimately their section. Such a proposal is worth study. It is time to place the magnolias on Main Street and to develop an urban view of southern history.

Appendices

Crosstabulation and the Computer   A

A CROSSTABULATION is a joint frequency distribution of cases according to two or more variables. Crosstabulation is a common method of analysis in the social sciences. The researcher can crosstabulate interval variables like real property holding and nominal variables like occupation where the researcher supplies the number code. The chi-square statistic is a test of significance for the joint frequency distributions. The contingency coefficient is a measure of association between pairs of variables within the joint frequency tables. The *Statistical Package for the Social Sciences* (SPSS) provided a ready-made computer program for crosstabulation as well as for simpler and more complex statistical procedures.[1] The SPSS manual is a readable, easily understood guide to statistics and to packaged computer programs. For someone who once viewed numbers as adversaries rather than as research assistants, I did not find SPSS threatening. To the contrary, I discovered that SPSS was an effective liaison between myself and the computer, an IBM 370/158.

The SPSS-packaged programs for crosstabulation are CROSSTABS and FASTABS. I chose to work with the former because there is less card preparation and there is no requirement that the lowest and highest values of each variable be known. The output on the CROSSTABS program includes the frequency distribution, the row percentage, column percentage, and total percentage. The program also includes a full complement of significance tests and measures of association: chi square, Cramer's V, contingency coefficient, Kendall's Tau B, Kendall's Tau C, gamma, and Somer's D. In the interests of clarity as well as because of the nature of the study, I suppressed the row percentage and all significance tests and association measures except for the chi square and contingency coefficient statistics.

1. Norman Nie, Dale H. Bent, and C. Hadlai Hull, *Statistical Package for the Social Sciences* (New York, 1970), 115–29.

Appendix A

The CROSSTABS program is desirable because it is flexible. One variable, for example may have as many as 250 values. The maximum number of dimensions for crosstabulations is ten. Thus, two-way distributions may blossom into tables where the control variables are stacked eight deep. This arrangement, though, would be rare for the historian. A more likely calculation is a three-dimensional table. For example, a crosstabulation for occupation by persistence by slaveholding would generate a tabular distribution for occupation and persistence with slaveholding as the control variable. Both the chi square and the contingency coefficient would, of course, reflect the presence of the control variable.

The CROSSTABS program is a fast and relatively simple method of determining relationships between interval and nominal variables. Hand calculating the chi square and contingency coefficient is a lengthy and complex (at least for me) task. A widely used guide to statistical procedures recommends a desk calculator as a necessary adjunct to computerless computation.[2] The SPSS programs are part of most university computer libraries, and the job control cards that tell the computer which SPSS program to set in motion are either prepunched or written out for easy keypunching. Finally, most SPSS programs have the virtue of being quick; and in the computer world, time literally means money. The total run charges for all of my crosstabulations was $4.03. In short, the SPSS system is a valuable research assistant for the historian who is engaged in quantitative analysis.

The following tables (38-57) offer comparisons between the sample persisters and the elite persisters (1850-60), employing the crosstabulation technique.

---

2. Charles M. Dollar and Richard J. Jensen, *Historian's Guide to Statistics: Quantitative Analysis and Historical Research* (New York, 1971), 80.

Table 38 Persistence by Occupation of Richmond Study Groups, 1850

Count Column % Total %	Unlisted	Unskilled and Semiskilled	Middling[a]	Proprietors[b]	Total
Transiency	74	25	82	26	207
	69.2	51.0	51.9	22.0	
	17.1	5.8	19.0	6.0	
Priority or Persistence	28	23	58	51	160
	26.2	46.9	36.7	43.2	
	6.5	5.3	13.4	11.8	
Permanence	5	1	18	41	65
	4.7	2.0	11.4	34.7	
	1.2	0.2	4.2	9.5	
Column	107	49	158	118	432
TOTAL	24.8	11.3	36.6	27.3	100.0

Sample and leadership groups are combined here.
NOTES: Chi square = 78.12444 with 6 degrees of freedom.
Significance = 0.0000.
Contingency coefficient = 0.39134.
[a]Includes petty proprietors, skilled, clerical and sales, and semiprofessionals.
[b]Includes professionals.

Appendix A

Table 39 Persistence by Age of Richmond Study Groups

Count Column % Total %	17–32	33+	Total
Transiency	89 61.4 20.9	116 41.3 27.2	205
Priority or Persistence	51 35.2 12.0	107 38.1 25.1	158
Permanence	5 3.4 1.2	58 20.6 13.6	63
Column	145	281	426
TOTAL	34.0	66.0	100.0

NOTES: Chi square = 27.36241 with 2 degrees of freedom.
Significance = 0.0000.
Contingency coefficient = 0.24567.

Table 40 Persistence by Real Property of Richmond Study Groups

Count Column % Total %	No Real Property	$25–6500	$6501 +	Total
Transiency	181 60.1 41.8	21 28.0 4.8	5 8.8 1.2	207
Priority or Persistence	100 33.2 23.1	40 53.3 9.2	20 35.1 4.6	160
Permanence	20 6.6 4.6	14 18.7 3.2	32 56.1 7.4	66
Column	301	75	57	433
TOTAL	69.5	17.3	13.2	100.0

NOTES: Chi square = 118.24565 with 4 degrees of freedom.
Significance = 0.0.
Contingency coefficient = 0.46315.

Appendix A

Table 41 Persistence by Marital Status of Richmond Study Groups

Count Column % Total %	Unmarried	Married	Widow or Widower	Total
Transiency	48	105	38	191
	57.8	41.0	55.9	
	11.8	25.8	9.3	
Priority or	33	97	24	154
Persistence	39.8	37.9	35.3	
	8.1	23.8	5.9	
Permanence	2	54	6	62
	2.4	21.1	8.8	
	0.5	13.3	1.5	
Column	83	256	68	407
TOTAL	20.4	62.9	16.7	100.0

Table 42 Persistence by Age of Wives of Richmond Study Groups

Count Column % Total %	17–29	20–38	39+	Total
Transiency	51	33	21	105
	51.5	42.9	26.3	
	19.9	12.9	8.2	
Priority or	39	25	33	97
Persistence	39.4	32.5	41.3	
	15.2	9.8	12.9	
Permanence	9	19	26	54
	9.1	24.7	32.5	
	3.5	7.4	10.2	
Column	99	77	80	256
TOTAL	38.7	30.1	31.3	100.0

NOTES: Chi square = 20.03613 with 4 degrees of freedom.
Significance = 0.0005.
Contingency coefficient = 0.26942.

Appendix A

Table 43 Persistence by Number of Children of Richmond Study Groups

Count Column % Total %	No Children	1–2	3+	Total
Transiency	89 54.9 20.6	64 49.2 14.8	54 38.3 12.5	207
Priority or Persistence	61 37.7 14.1	51 39.2 11.8	48 34.0 11.1	160
Permanence	12 7.4 2.8	15 11.5 3.5	39 27.7 9.0	66
Column	162	130	141	433
TOTAL	37.4	30.0	32.6	100.0

NOTES: Chi square = 26.93005 with 4 degrees of freedom.
Significance = 0.0000.
Contingency coefficient = 0.24198.

Table 44 Persistence by Age of Youngest Child of Richmond Study Groups

Count Column % Total %	1–3	4+	Total
Transiency	62	56	118
	43.4	43.8	
	22.9	20.7	
Priority or	52	47	99
Persistence	36.4	36.7	
	19.2	17.3	
Permanence	29	25	54
	20.3	19.5	
	10.7	9.2	
Column	143	128	271
TOTAL	52.8	47.2	100.0

NOTES: Chi square = 0.02372 with 2 degrees of freedom.
Significance = 0.9882.
Contingency coefficient = 0.00936.

Table 45 Persistence by Age of Eldest Child of Richmond Study Groups

Count Column % Total %	1–8	9–16	17+	Total
Transiency	55 51.4 20.3	37 43.5 13.7	26 32.9 9.6	118
Priority or Persistence	42 39.3 15.5	28 32.9 10.3	29 36.7 10.7	99
Permanence	10 9.3 3.7	20 23.5 7.4	24 30.4 8.9	54
Column	107	85	79	271
TOTAL	39.5	31.4	29.2	100.0

NOTES: Chi square = 14.98339 with 4 degrees of freedom.
Significance = 0.0047.
Contingency coefficient = 0.22889.

Table 46 Persistence by Boarders of Richmond Study Groups, 1850

Count Column % Total %	No Boarders	Boarders	Total
Transiency	114	93	207
	52.8	42.9	
	26.3	21.5	
Priority or	69	91	160
Persistence	31.9	41.9	
	15.9	21.0	
Permanence	33	33	66
	15.3	15.2	
	7.6	7.6	
Column	216	217	433
TOTAL:	49.9	50.1	100.0

NOTES: Chi square = 5.15315 with 2 degrees of freedom.
Significance = 0.0760.
Contingency coefficient = 0.10845.

Appendix A

Table 47 Persistence by Relative Boarders of Richmond Study Groups, 1850

Count Column % Total %	No Relative Boarders	Relative Boarders	Total
Transiency	194 49.0 44.8	13 35.1 3.0	207
Priority or Persistence	142 35.9 32.8	18 48.6 4.2	160
Permanence	60 15.2 13.9	6 16.2 1.4	66
Column	396	37	433
TOTAL	91.5	8.5	100.0

NOTES: Chi square = 2.88190 with 2 degrees of freedom.
Significance = 0.2367.
Contingency coefficient = 0.08131.

Table 48 Persistence by Occupational Boarders of Richmond Study Groups, 1850

Count Column % Total %	No Occupational Boarders	Occupational Boarders	Total
Transiency	197 50.0 45.5	10 25.6 2.3	207
Priority or Persistence	140 35.5 32.3	20 51.3 4.6	160
Permanence	57 14.5 13.2	9 23.1 2.1	66
Column	394	39	433
TOTAL	91.0	9.0	100.0

NOTES: Chi square = 8.51255 with 2 degrees of freedom.
Significance = 0.0142.
Contingency coefficient = 0.13885.

Table 49 Persistence by Servant Boarders of Richmond Study Groups, 1850

Count Column % Total %	No Servant Boarders	Servant Boarders	Total
Transiency	199 50.3 46.0	8 21.6 1.8	207
Priority or Persistence	142 35.9 32.8	18 48.6 4.2	160
Permanence	55 13.9 12.7	11 29.7 2.5	66
Column	396	37	433
TOTAL	91.5	8.5	100.0

NOTES: Chi square = 12.87098 with 2 degrees of freedom.
Significance = 0.0016.
Contingency coefficient = 0.16990.

Table 50 Persistence by Family Boarders of Richmond Study Groups, 1850

Count Column % Total %	No Family Boarders	Family Boarders	Total
Transiency	179 47.6 41.3	28 49.1 6.5	207
Priority or Persistence	139 37.0 32.1	21 36.8 4.8	160
Permanence	58 15.4 13.4	8 14.0 1.8	66
Column	376	57	433
TOTAL	86.8	13.2	100.0

NOTES: Chi square = 0.08680 with 2 degrees of freedom.
Significance = 0.9575.
Contingency coefficient = 0.01416.

Table 51 Persistence by Unknown Boarders of Richmond Study Groups, 1850

Count Column % Total %	No Unknown Boarders	Unknown Boarders	Total
Transiency	153 47.4 35.3	54 49.1 12.5	207
Priority or Persistence	116 35.9 26.8	44 40.0 10.2	160
Permanence	54 16.7 12.5	12 10.9 2.8	66
Column	323	110	433
TOTAL	74.6	25.4	100.0

NOTES: Chi square = 2.23848 with 2 degrees of freedom.
Significance = 0.3265.
Contingency coefficient = 0.07172.

Table 52 Persistence by Slaves Owned by Richmond Study Groups, 1850

Count Column % Total %	No Slaves	Slave Owners	Total
Transiency	155 67.4 35.8	52 25.6 12.0	207
Priority or Persistence	64 27.8 14.8	96 47.3 22.2	160
Permanence	11 4.8 2.5	55 27.1 12.7	66
Column	230	203	433
TOTAL	53.1	46.9	100.0

NOTES: Chi square = 85.63385 with 2 degrees of freedom.
Significance = 0.0000.
Contingency coefficient = 0.40634.

Appendix A

Table 53 Persistence by Male Slaves Owned by Richmond Study Groups, 1850

Count Column % Total %	No Male Slaves	Male Slave Owners	Total
Transiency	183 59.8 42.3	24 18.9 5.5	207
Priority or Persistence	101 33.0 23.3	59 46.5 13.6	160
Permanence	22 7.2 5.1	44 34.6 10.2	66
Column	306	127	433
TOTAL	70.7	29.3	100.0

NOTES: Chi square = 80.19623 with 2 degrees of freedom.
Significance = 0.0000.
Contingency coefficient = 0.39531.

Table 54 Persistence by Female Slaves Owned by Richmond Study Groups, 1850

Count Column % Total %	No Female Slaves	Female Slave Owners	Total
Transiency	160 64.8 37.0	47 25.3 10.9	207
Priority or Persistence	72 29.1 16.6	88 47.3 20.3	160
Permanence	15 6.1 3.5	51 27.4 11.8	66
Column	247	186	433
TOTAL	57.0	43.0	100.0

NOTES: Chi square = 75.83383 with 2 degrees of freedom.
Significance = 0.0000.
Contingency coefficient = 0.38605.

Table 55 Persistence by Race of Richmond Study Groups, 1850

Count Column % Total %	White	Black	Mulatto	Total
Transiency	167	31	9	207
	45.3	73.8	40.9	
	38.6	7.2	2.1	
Priority or	138	10	12	160
Persistence	37.4	23.8	54.5	
	31.9	2.3	2.8	
Permanence	64	1	1	66
	17.3	2.4	4.5	
	14.8	0.2	0.2	
Column	369	42	22	433
TOTAL	85.2	9.7	5.1	100.0

NOTES: Chi square = 17.76575 with 4 degrees of freedom.
Significance = 0.0014.
Contingency coefficient = 0.19853.

Table 56 Persistence by Sex of Richmond Study Groups

Count Column % Total %	Male	Female	Total
Transiency	147	60	207
	43.0	65.9	
	33.9	13.9	
Priority or	132	28	160
Persistence	38.6	30.8	
	30.5	6.5	
Permanence	63	3	66
	18.4	3.3	
	14.5	0.7	
Column	342	91	433
TOTAL	79.0	21.0	100.0

NOTES: Chi square = 19.89807 with 2 degrees of freedom.
Significance = 0.0000.
Contingency coefficient = 0.20961.

Table 57 Persistence by Nativity of Richmond Study Groups, 1850

Count Column % Total %	Virginia	Southern States	Northern States	Foreign- Born	Total
Transiency	145	8	12	41	206
	46.5	40.0	46.2	55.4	
	33.6	1.9	2.8	9.5	
Priority or	116	9	8	27	160
Persistence	37.2	45.0	30.8	36.5	
	26.9	2.1	1.9	6.3	
Permanence	51	3	6	6	66
	16.3	15.0	23.1	8.1	
	11.8	0.7	1.4	1.4	
Column	312	20	26	74	432
TOTAL	72.2	4.6	6.0	171.	100.0

NOTES: Chi square = 5.66641 with 6 degrees of freedom.
Significance = 0.4616.
Contingency coefficient = 0.11378.

Virginia's Urban Leaders and Their Associational Activity

B

RICHMOND

Maximum Activists (10)

Joseph R. Anderson
David J. Burr
James A. Cowardin
Hugh W. Fry
Larkin W. Glazebrook
Richard O. Haskins
R. B. Haxall
William H. Macfarland
Gustavus A. Myers
David J. Saunders

Moderate Activists (25)

William C. Allen
Thomas P. August
James Bosher
William F. Butler
Henry C. Cabell
James Caskie
John H. Claiborne
James C. Crane
Lewis D. Crenshaw
Charles Dimmock
Lewis E. Harvie
William H. Haxall
Roscoe B. Heath
Nathaniel B. Hill
William B. Isaacs
John Jones
Horace L. Kent
John J. London
Joseph Mayo
Robert A. Mayo
Bernard Peyton

Thomas R. Price
Archibald Thomas
James Thomas, Jr.
Charles T. Wortham

Minimum Activists (30)

Joseph M. Carrington
John S. Caskie
Isaac Davenport, Jr.
Samuel D. Denoon
Charles Ellis
Thomas T. Giles
John N. Gordon
Peachy R. Grattan
Fleming Griffin
R. W. Hughes
George N. Johnson
Daniel H. London
James Lyons
Robert H. Maury
Charles S. Mills
Charles Y. Morriss
William Palmer
Samuel M. Price
John Purcell
Henry W. Quarles
William H. Richardson
William F. Ritchie
Wyndham Robertson
Charles J. Sinton
Robert Stannard
G. B. Stovall
Bacon Tait
James M. Talbott
John E. Womble
Edwin Wortham

NORFOLK

Maximum Activists (10)

John E. Doyle
William I. Hardy
William T. Harrison
John G. H. Hatton
Henry Irwin
Henry B. Readon
Charles Reid
John Tunis
John B. Whitehead
Josiah Wills

Moderate Activists (28)

George F. Anderson
Joseph T. Allyn
James E. Barry
Alexander Bell
George W. Bluford
Samuel Borum
James Cornick
William Dey
George W. Farant
William H. Hunter
James H. Johnston
N.C. King
William W. Lamb
Andrew B. McClean
Francis Mallory
Seth March
Aaron Milhado
Myer Myers
Edmund C. Robinson
William W. Sharp
Charles H. Shield

William H. Smith
Frederick W. Southgate
Joseph R. Spratley
Tazewell Taylor
Thomas D. Toy
William Ward
Nathan C. Whitehead

Minimum Activists (18)

Kadar Biggs
Robert W. Bowden
Thomas G. Broughton, Sr.
Ryland Capps
Solomon Cherry
Thomas J. Corprew
William Denby, Sr.
James Gordon
William P. Griffiths
William T. Hendren
Abram F. Leonard
Charles Rowland
James A. Saunders
Samuel T. Sawyer
Simon S. Stubbs
William H. Turner
John Williams
Hunter Woodis

ALEXANDRIA

Maximum Activists (10)

James A. English
George D. Fowle
William H. Fowle
William Gregory
Robert Jamieson
Lewis McKenzie
William N. McVeigh
Robert H. Miller
Stephen Shinn
Francis L. Smith

Moderate Activists (19)

George Bryan
William G. Cazenove
Henry Daingerfield
John B. Daingerfield
William Fowle
Anthony Grover
James Green
Benjamin Hallowell
David Hume
Phineas Janney
Cassius F. Lee
James H. McVeigh

Hugh C. Smith
Charles C. Smoot
George H. Smoot
Charles F. Suttle
George I. Thomas
Robert G. Violett
J. J. Wheat

Minimum Activists (15)

Robert Brockett
Lewis A. Cazenove
Joseph Eaches
Daniel F. Hooe
William D. Massey
William L. Powell
Henry L. Simpson
Richards C. Smith
Thomas W. Smith
Edgar Snowden
Lawrence B. Taylor
Peter G. Uhler
William Veitch
Benjamin Waters
George K. Witmer

Classification of Occupations   C

1. UNSKILLED AND MENIAL SERVICE

Laborer
Factory Hand
Washerwoman

2. SEMISKILLED SERVICE

Dressmaker
Public Guard
Barber (also 3, 4)
Watchman
City Police
Butcher (also 3, 7)
Boatman
Dining Room Servant
Night Watch

3. PETTY PROPRIETORS, MANAGERS, AND OFFICIALS *(Owning less than $1000 in real property)*

Merchant (also 7)[1]
Hotel Keeper (also 7)
Trader (also 7)
Livery Stable Owner
Overseer
Auctioneer
Brewer (also 7)
Eating House Owner (also 7)
Contractor (also 7)
Furniture Dealer (also 7)
Soda Manufacturer (also 7)

Categories are from Knights, *Plain People of Boston*, Appendix E. Occupations from the three leadership study groups and Richmond random sample. Specific occupations are listed according to the frequency encountered.

1. As Edward Pessen has noted, "There are merchants and there are merchants." Knights' occupational categories, by adding an economic dimension, allows both greater flexibility and accuracy in classifying the sometimes ambiguous occupational designations offered by the manuscript census.

Manufacturer of Nails (also 7)
Undertaker (also 7)
Bookseller (also 7)
Plough Maker (also 7)
Stockbroker (also 7)
Customshouse Collector (also 7)

4. SKILLED

Carpenter (also 7, 3)[2]
Blacksmith (also 7, 3)
Shoemaker (also 7)
Tailor (also 7, 3)
Machinist (also 3, 7)
Cabinetmaker (also 3, 7)
Painter (also 3, 7)
Founder (also 3, 7)
Saddler (also 3, 7)
Bricklayer (also 3, 7)
Baker (also 3, 7)
Watchmaker (also 3, 7)
Wigmaker (also 3, 7)
Engineer
Finisher
Builder (also 7)
Confectioner (also 3, 7)
Locksmith (also 3, 7)
Printer (also 3, 7)
Coach Maker (also 3, 7)
Upholsterer (also 3, 7)
Ship Chandler
Stonemason (also 3, 7)
Paper Hanger
Moulder (also 3, 7)
Piano Tuner

5. CLERICAL AND SALES

Clerk
Agent and Collector

2. Occupational categories in parentheses are listed according to frequency encountered in the 1850 manuscript census, not according to socioeconomic status. Thus, most carpenters were skilled, some were proprietors, and only a few were petty proprietors.

Salesman
Bank Cashier
Bookkeeper

6. SEMIPROFESSIONAL

Musician

7. PROPRIETORS, MANAGERS, AND OFFICIALS *(Owning more than $1000 in real property)*

Postmaster
Railroad Superintendent (also 3)
City Chamberlain
Sheriff
Iron Manufacturer
Banker
Railroad President
Mayor
Shipmaster
Plasterer (also 3, 7)
Cooper
Gun Smith (also 3, 7)
Tanner (also 3, 7)

8. PROFESSIONAL

Lawyer
Druggist
Editor
Minister
Dentist
Teacher
Insurance Company President

9. MISCELLANEOUS AND UNKNOWN

No Occupation Listed
Woman as Head of Household
Gentleman

Bibliography

Manuscript Collections

DUKE UNIVERSITY

Danforth, John B. Letter Press Copy Book.
Harris, Jeremiah C. Diaries.
Loveland, Julia L. N. Journal.
Massie, William. Notebooks
Rutherfoord, John Coles. Papers.
Southgate, James. Papers.
Thomas, James, Jr. Papers.

LIBRARY OF CONGRESS

Campell-Preston Papers

NATIONAL ARCHIVES

U.S. Bureau of Census, Seventh Census of Virginia: 1850. Free Inhabitants MSS
    and Slave Schedules
U.S. Bureau of Census, Eighth Census of Virginia: 1860. Free Inhabitants MSS
    and Slave Schedules

UNIVERSITY OF NORTH CAROLINA, SOUTHERN HISTORICAL COLLECTION

Dabney, Charles W. Papers.
Mason, John Y. Papers.
Mayo, Peter Helms. "Episodes of a Busy Life."
Mordecai Family. Papers.
Sutherlin, William T. Papers.
Tucker, John Randolph. Family Papers.
Whittle, Lewis Neale. Papers.

UNIVERSITY OF VIRGINIA, ALDERMAN LIBRARY

Barbour, James. Papers.
Beale-Davis Family Papers.
Bush & Lobdell Co. Papers.
Crallé, Richard K. Papers.
Gilliam. Family Papers.
Grinnan. Family Papers.
Harris-Brady. Papers.
Hoffer, Stuart C. Day Book.

Bibliography

Hubard. Family Papers.
Hunter, R. M. T. Papers.
Imboden, John. Papers.
Irby, Richard. Papers.
Kemper, James L. Papers.
McCauley, John. Papers.
Omohundro Brothers. Papers.
Weaver-Brady Iron Works and Grist Mill. Papers.
Woods-Belmont. Farm Journals.

WEST VIRGINIA UNIVERSITY

Hubbard. Family Papers.

VIRGINIA HISTORICAL SOCIETY

Central Southern Rights Association of Virginia. Records.
Rutherfoord, John Coles. Diary.
John H. Thomas & Co., Papers.

VIRGINIA STATE LIBRARY

Cabell, Nathaniel F. Papers.
Campbell County Land Books, 1850, 1859.
Executive Letter Book, 1856–1860.
French, S. Bassett. "Biographical Sketches."
Mercer, Charles F. Papers.
Tazewell. Family Papers.
Tredegar. Journal.
Tredegar. Payrolls.
Watlington. Family Papers.

PUBLISHED COLLECTIONS

Ambler, Charles H., ed. *Correspondence of Robert M. T. Hunter, 1826–1876, in Annual Report of the American Historical Association*, 1916, Washington, D.C., 1918, Vol. II.
Scarborough, William Kauffman, ed. *The Diary of Edmund Ruffin*, Vol. I, *Toward Independence: October, 1856–April, 1861*, Baton Rouge, 1972.

Government Documents

U.S. Bureau of Census. *Compendium of the Seventh Census: 1850*. Washington, D.C., 1851.
———. *Compendium of the Eighth Census: 1860. Population*. Vol. I. Washington, D.C., 1861.

———. *Compendium of the Eighth Census: 1860. Manufactures.* Vol. II. Washington, D.C., 1861.

———. *Compendium of the Eighth Census: 1860. Agriculture.* Vol. III. Washington, D.C., 1861.

———. *Compendium of the Eighth Census: 1860. Mortality and Miscellaneous.* Vol. IV. Washington, D.C., 1861.

———. *Compendium of the Tenth Census: 1880. Valuation, Taxation, and Public Indebtedness.* Vol. VII. Washington, D.C., 1881.

———. *Historical Statistics of the United States: Colonial Times to 1957.* Washington, D.C., 1960.

U.S. Secretary of the Treasury, *Reports on Commerce and Navigation, 1815–1860.*

Virginia. *Journals of the House of Delegates,* 1850–1861.

Virginia Board of Public Works. *Annual Reports,* 1850–1860–61.

———. *Report on Turnpikes and Canals,* 1860–61. Richmond, 1861.

Virginia House of Delegates. *Document Number 1,* 1859–60. Richmond, 1860.

———. *Document Number 1,* 1861. Richmond, 1861.

———. *Document Number 3,* 1861. Richmond, 1861.

Virginia State Library. *Journal and Papers of the Virginia State Convention of 1861.* 3 vols. Richmond, 1966.

Newspapers

Abingdon *Democrat,* 1856.
Alexandria *Gazette,* 1847–1861.
Alexandria *Virginia Sentinnel,* 1853.
Bristol *Virginia and Tennessee News,* 1859.
Charleston *Courier,* 1836.
Charlestown *Spirit of Jefferson,* 1851.
Christiansburg *New Star,* 1861.
Danville *Appeal,* 1860.
Fincastle *Democrat,* 1847.
Leesburg *Democratic Mirror,* 1859.
Lynchburg *Virginian,* 1847–1861.
Norfolk *American Beacon,* 1851–1854.
Norfolk *Day Book,* 1857.
Norfolk and Portsmouth *Herald,* 1850, 1852, 1854.
Norfolk *Southern Argus,* 1847–1861.
Petersburg *South-Side Democrat,* 1854.
Portsmouth *Daily Pilot,* 1850.
Richmond *Daily Dispatch,* 1851–1861.
Richmond *Daily Examiner,* 1861.
Richmond *Enquirer,* 1847–1861.
Richmond *South,* 1857.

Bibliography

Richmond *Whig*, 1847–1861.
Salem *Weekly Register*, 1855, 1858, 1859, 1860.
Wheeling *Daily Intelligencer*, 1852–1861.

Contemporary Books and Pamphlets

Armstrong, George D. *The Summer of the Pestilence: A History of the Ravages of the Yellow Fever in Norfolk, Virginia*. Norfolk, 1857.
Berba, Alex F. *Letters on Yellow Fever, Cholera, and Quarantine*. New York, 1852.
Boyd, John. *Boyd's Washington and Georgetown Directory, 1860*. Washington, D.C., 1860.
Butters, James. *Butters' Richmond Directory, 1855*. Richmond, 1855.
Committee of Physicians. *Report on the Origins of the Yellow Fever in Norfolk During the Summer of 1855*. Richmond, 1857.
Fitzhugh, George, *Cannibals All! or, Slaves without Masters*. New York, 1857.
———. *Sociology for the South; or, the Failure of Free Society*. New York, 1854.
Forrest, William S. *The Norfolk Directory for 1851–52*. Norfolk, 1851.
Hildreth, Richard. *Despotism in America: An Inquiry into the Nature, Results, and Legal Basis of the Slave-Holding System in the United States*. Boston, 1854.
Howison, William R. *Virginia: Her History and Resources*. New York, 1848.
Hundley, Daniel R. *Social Relations in Our Southern States*. New York, 1860.
Johnston, James F. W. *Notes on North America; Agricultural, Economical and Social*. 2 vols. Boston, 1851.
Jones, B. M. *Railroads: Considered in Regard to their Effects upon the Value of Land in Increasing Production, Cheapening Transportation, Preventing Emigration and Investments for Capital*. Richmond, 1860.
Jones, John B. *A Rebel War Clerk's Diary at the Confederate States Capital*. 2 vols. Philadelphia, 1866.
Little, John P. *Richmond: The Capital of Virginia*. Richmond, 1851.
Mordecai, Samuel. *Virginia, Especially Richmond in By-gone Days: Being Reminiscences and Last Words of an Old Citizen*. Richmond, 1860.
Montague, William L. *Richmond Directory and Business Advertiser for 1852*. Baltimore, 1852.
Olmsted, Frederick Law. *The Cotton Kingdom*. Rev. ed. New York, 1962.
———. *Journey in the Seaboard Slave States*. New York, 1856.
Richmond Board of Trade. *Address to the Merchants of Virginia*. Richmond, 1857.
———. *Proceedings of the Internal Improvements Convention Held at White Sulphur Springs*. Richmond, 1855.
Rives, William C. *Letter from the Hon. William C. Rives to a Friend on the Important Questions of the Day*. Richmond, 1860.
Russell, Robert. *North America: Its Agriculture and Climate*. Edinburgh, 1857.
Scott, John [Barbarossa]. *The Lost Principle; or, The Sectional Equilibrium: How It was Created—How Destroyed—How It May be Restored*. Richmond, 1860.

Tucker, John Randolph. *An Address Delivered before the Society of Alumni of the University of Virginia*. Richmond, 1851.
Van Zandt, Reverend A. B. *The Claims of Virginia upon Her Educated Sons*. Petersburg, 1854.

Articles in Contemporary Periodical Publications

"Bank Capital of Cities in the United States." *Hunt's Merchants' Magazine*, XVIII (1848), 326.
"Banking at the South with Reference to New York City." *Hunt's Merchants' Magazine*, XLII (March, 1860), 312–23.
Barbour, Benjamin Johnson. "Address to the Literary Societies of Virginia Military Institute." *Southern Literary Messenger*, XX (1854), 513–28.
Burwell, William M. "Virginia Commercial Convention." *DeBow's Review*, XII (1852), 30–41.
"Business of the Virginia and Tennessee Railroad." *Hunt's Merchants' Magazine*, XXXV (1856), 241.
Campbell, A. A. "Capital and Enterprise—the Basis of Agricultural Progress." *Southern Planter*, XX (1860), 36.
Carter, Hill. "Address Delivered before the Virginia Central Agricultural Society." *Southern Planter*, XX (1860), 272.
"Cheap Virginia Lands." *American Agriculturist*, X (1851), 192.
"Cities of the South—Richmond." *DeBow's Review*, XXVIII (1860), 187–201.
"City Population and Valuation." *Hunt's Merchants' Magazine*, XXXIX (1858), 518.
"Commercial Agriculture and Intellectual Independence of the South." *DeBow's Review*, XXIX (1860), 466–88.
"Commercial and Industrial Cities of the United States: Richmond, Virginia, 1859." *Hunt's Merchants' Magazine*, XL (1859), 54–66.
"Comparative Fares of Railroads in the United States." *Hunt's Merchants' Magazine*, XVIII (1848), 97–98.
"Contests for the Trade of the Mississippi Valley." *DeBow's Review*, III (1847), 98.
"Direct Exports of Tobacco from Richmond." *Hunt's Merchants' Magazine*, XXXVI (1857), 89.
"Exports of Flour to South America." *Hunt's Merchants' Magazine*, XL (1859), 351.
"First Annual Show of the Virginia State Agricultural Society." *American Agriculturist*, XXII (1853), 136.
"Flour Inspections in Virginia." *Hunt's Merchants' Magazine*, XLI (1859), 356.
"Foreign Trade of Virginia and the South." *DeBow's Review*, XIII (1852), 493–503.
"Garden Farms in Virginia." *American Agriculturist*, XIII (1854), 166.
"Hiring Negroes." *Southern Planter*, XII (1852), 376.
Howison, William R. "Virginia: Her History and Resources." *Hunt's Merchants' Magazine*, XXI (1849), 185, 187.

Bibliography

"Import of Virginia Tobacco into the Port of New York." *Hunt's Merchants' Magazine*, XX (1849), 219.

"The Inspection Laws." *Southern Planter*, XVI (1856), 80–88.

"Inspections of Flour at Richmond, Virginia, From 1819 to 1848." *Hunt's Merchants' Magazine*, XXIX (1848), 546.

"Iron Ore in Virginia for Iron Manufactures." *Hunt's Merchants' Magazine*, XXXI (1854), 768.

"James River and Kanawha Canal." *Hunt's Merchants' Magazine*, XLII (1860), 369.

Mason, John Y. "Letter to D.H. London, Esq. on a Line of Steamers to Europe." *Southern Literary Messenger*, XVIII (1852), 588–92.

Meldahl, E. "Letter for the *American Agriculturist*." *American Agriculturist*, XIII (1854), 345.

"Moral View of Railroads." *Hunt's Merchants' Magazine*, XXVII (1852), 173.

"Northern Agency for the Sale of Land." *Southern Planter*, X (1850), 17–19.

Poor, Henry Varnum. "Effect of Railroads on Commercial Cities." *Hunt's Merchants' Magazine*, XXVII (1852), 249.

"The Profits of Market Garden Farms." *Southern Planter*, XVII (1857), 756–57.

"Progress of Boston in Wealth, Population, Etc." *Hunt's Merchants' Magazine*, XXV (1851), 628.

"Progress of the Population in the United States." *Hunt's Merchants' Magazine*, XXXII (1855), 191–95.

"Railroad Iron in the United States." *Hunt's Merchants' Magazine*, XXXVII (1857), 497.

"Railroad Management in the United States." *Hunt's Merchants' Magazine*, XXXIV (1856), 685.

"Railroads and their Future." *Hunt's Merchants' Magazine*, XXXVIII (1858), 185.

"Railroad Fares in Virginia." *Hunt's Merchants' Magazine*, XX (1854), 251.

"Railroads of the United States." *Hunt's Merchants' Magazine*, XXVIII (1853), 110–115.

"Railroads of the United States." *Hunt's Merchants' Magazine*, XLI (1859), 241.

"Real and Personal Property in New York City." *Hunt's Merchants' Magazine*, XXV (1851), 226.

"Regulations of Banking in Virginia." *Hunt's Merchants' Magazine*, XXXVII (1857), 721–22.

"The Removal of Commerce from Boston to New York." *Hunt's Merchants' Magazine*, XXX (1854), 39a.

"Report of the Virginia State Agricultural Society." *Southern Planter*, XX (1860), 756.

"Richmond, Virginia." *Hunt's Merchants' Magazine*, XX (1849), 52–55.

"Richmond Sugar Refinery." *Hunt's Merchants, Magazine*, XLIV (1861), 244.

Ruffin, Edmund. "The Effects of High Prices of Slaves." *Southern Planter*, XIX (1859), 472–77.

S. "The New Constitution." *Southern Literary Messenger*, XVIII (1852), 116–22.

"Southern Patronage to Southern Industry." *Southern Planter*, XXI (1861), 160.

Sumner, Charles. "Influence of Railroads." *Hunt's Merchants' Magazine*, XXVI (1852), 506–507.

"The Tobacco Trade." *Hunt's Merchants' Magazine*, XXVI (1852), 358–59.

"Tobacco Trade and Inspections at New York." *Hunt's Merchants' Magazine*, XXX (1854), 354–55.

"The Tobacco Trade of Richmond." *Hunt's Merchants' Magazine*, XXXVII (1857), 745.

"Tobacco Trade of Richmond." *Hunt's Merchants' Magazine*, XXXIX (1858), 485–86.

"Tobacco Trade of Virginia." *Hunt's Merchants' Magazine*, XL (1859), 343.

"Tobacco Trade of Virginia." *Hunt's Merchants' Magazine*, XLIII (1860), 736–39.

"Vegetable and Truck Trade of Norfolk, Virginia." *Hunt's Merchants' Magazine*, XXXIX (1858), 733.

"Virginia Iron and Steel." *American Railroad Journal*, XX (1847), 593–94.

"Virginia Railroad Earnings." *Hunt's Merchants' Magazine*, XLII (1860), 122.

"Virginia State Agricultural Convention." *Southern Planter*, XII (1852), 81–82.

"Virginia Tobacco and Flour Trade." *Hunt's Merchants' Magazine*, XXXI (1854), 600.

"Virginia Tobacco Trade, 1850–51." *Hunt's Merchants' Magazine*, XXV (1851), 735.

"Virginia Tobacco Trade, 1852–53." *Hunt's Merchants' Magazine*, XXIX (1853), 631.

"White Girls in Tobacco Factories." *Hunt's Merchants' Magazine*, XL (1859), 522–23.

Secondary Works

BOOKS

Albion, Robert G. *The Rise of New York Port [1815–1860]*. New York, 1939.

Ambler, Charles H. *Sectionalism in Virginia, 1776–1861*. Glendale, Cal., 1910.

Bancroft, Frederic. *Slave-Trading in the Old South*. Baltimore, 1931.

Belcher, Wyatt W. *The Economic Rivalry Between Saint Louis and Chicago, 1850–1880*. New York, 1947.

Berlin, Ira. *Slaves without Masters: The Free Negro in the Antebellum South*. New York, 1974.

Blanton, Wyndham B. *Medicine in Virginia in the Nineteenth Century*. Richmond, 1940.

Bremner, Robert. *From the Depths: The Discovery of Poverty in the United States*. New York, 1956.

Brownell, Blaine. A. and David R. Goldfield. *The City in Southern History: The Growth of Urban Civilization in the South*, Port Washington, N.Y., 1976.

Bibliography

Bruce, Kathleen. *Virginia Iron Manufacture in the Slave Era, 1800–1860*. New York, 1931.

Cappon, Lester J. *Virginia Newspapers, 1821–1935*. New York, 1936.

Cash, W. J. *The Mind of the South*. New York, 1941.

Christian, W. Asbury. *Lynchburg and Its People*. Lynchburg, 1900.

———. *Richmond: Her Past and Present*. Richmond, 1912.

Conzen, Michael P. *Frontier Farming in an Urban Shadow*. Madison, Wisc., 1971.

Craven, Avery O. *Soil Exhaustion as a Factor in the Agricultural History of Virginia and Maryland*. Urbana, Ill., 1926.

Dahl, Robert A. *Who Governs: Democracy and Power in an American City*. New Haven, 1961.

Daniel, Pete. *The Shadow of Slavery: Peonage in the South, 1901–1969*. Urbana, Ill., 1972.

Dew, Charles B. *Ironmaker to the Confederacy: Joseph R. Anderson and the Tredegar Iron Works*. New Haven, 1966.

Dodd, Donald B., and Wynelle S. Dodd. *Historical Statistics of the South, 1790–1970*. University, Ala., 1973.

Duffy, John. *Sword of Pestilence: The New Orleans Yellow Fever Epidemic of 1853*. Baton Rouge, 1966.

Dunaway, Wayland F. *History of the James River and Kanawha Company*. New York, 1922.

Dykstra, Robert R. *The Cattle Towns*. New York, 1968.

Eaton, Clement. *The Growth of Southern Civilization, 1790–1860*. New York, 1961.

Evans, Eli N. *The Provincials: A Personal History of Jews in the South*. New York, 1973.

Fogel, Robert W., and Stanley L. Engerman. *Time on the Cross: The Economics of American Negro Slavery*. Boston, 1974.

Foner, Eric. *Free Soil, Free Labor, Free Men: The Ideology of the Republican Party Before the Civil War*. New York, 1970.

Frisch, Michael H. "The Community Elite and the Emergence of Urban Politics: Springfield, Massachusetts, 1840–1880." In Stephen Thernstrom, and Richard Sennett, eds. *Nineteenth-Century Cities: Essays in the New Urban History*. New Haven, 1969, 277–96.

———. *Town into City: Springfield, Massachusetts and the Meaning of Community, 1840–1860*. Cambridge, Mass., 1972.

Gaines, William H., Jr. *Biographical Register of Members: Virginia State Convention of 1861*. Richmond, 1969.

Gaston, Paul M. *The New South Creed: A Study in Southern Mythmaking*. New York, 1970.

Genovese, Eugene D. *The Political Economy of Slavery*. New York, 1965.

———. *The World the Slaveholders Made: Two Essays in Interpretation*. New York, 1969.

Gilchrist, David T., ed. *The Growth of the Seaport Cities, 1790–1825*. Charlottesville, Va., 1967.

Glaab, Charles N. *Kansas City and the Railroads*. Madison, Wisc., 1962.

Glaab, Charles N., and A. Theodore Brown. *A History of Urban America*. New York, 1967.

Goldin, Claudia D. "Urbanization and Slavery: The Issue of Compatibility." In Leo F. Schnore, ed. *The New Urban History: Quantitative Explorations by American Historians*. Princeton, 1975, 231–46.

Gray, Lewis C. *History of Agriculture in the Southern United States*. Washington, D.C., 1933.

Green, Fletcher. *The Role of the Yankee in the Old South*. Athens, Ga., 1972.

Griffen, Clyde. "Workers Divided: The Effect of Craft and Ethnic Differences in Poughkeepsie, New York, 1850–1880." In Stephen Thernstrom and Richard Sennett, eds. *Nineteenth-Century Cities: Essays in the New Urban History*. New Haven, 1969, 49–97.

Handlin, Oscar and Handlin, Mary F. *Commonwealth: A Study of the Role of Government in the American Economy, Massachusetts, 1774–1861*. New York, 1947.

Hartz, Louis. *Economic Policy and Democratic Thought: Pennsylvania, 1776–1860*. Cambridge, Mass., 1948.

Horner, John V., and P. B. Windfree, Jr., eds. *The Saga of a City: Lynchburg, Virginia, 1786–1936*. Lynchburg, 1936.

Ingle, Edward. *Southern Sidelights*. New York, 1896.

Jackson, Luther P. *Free Negro Labor and Property Holding in Virginia, 1830–1860*. New York, 1942.

James, D. Clayton. *Antebellum Natchez*. Baton Rouge, 1968.

Johnston, Angus J., II. *Virginia Railroads in the Civil War*. Chapel Hill, 1961.

Katz, Michael B. "Social Structure in Hamilton, Ontario." In Stephen Thernstrom, and Richard Sennett, eds. *Nineteenth-Century Cities: Essays in the New Urban History*. New Haven, 1969, 209–44.

Katzman, David. *Before the Ghetto: Black Detroit in the Nineteenth Century*. Urbana, Ill., 1973.

King, Joseph L., Jr. *Dr. George William Bagby: A Study of Virginia Literature, 1850–1880*. New York, 1927.

Knights, Peter R. *The Plain People of Boston, 1830–1860: A Study in City Growth*. New York, 1971.

Lebergott, Stanley. "Wage Trends, 1800–1900." In *Trends in the American Economy in the Nineteenth-Century*. Princeton, 1960, 462–63.

Litwack, Leon F. *North of Slavery: The Negroes in the Free States, 1790–1860*. Chicago, 1961.

Maddex, Jack P., Jr. *The Virginia Conservatives, 1867–1879: A Study in Reconstruction Politics*. Chapel Hill, 1970.

McComb, David G. *Houston: The Bayou City*. Austin, 1969.

McGregor, James C. *The Disruption of Virginia*. New York, 1922.

McWhiney, Grady. *Southerners and Other Americans*. New York, 1973.

Bibliography

Moger, Allen W. *Virginia: Bourbonism to Byrd, 1870–1925*. Charlottesville, Va., 1968.

Moore, James T. *Two Paths to the New South: The Virginia Debt Controversy, 1870–1883*. Lexington, Ky., 1974.

Niehaus, Earl F. *The Irish in New Orleans, 1800–1860*. Baton Rouge, 1965.

North, Douglass C. *The Economic Growth of the United States, 1790–1860*. New York, 1961.

Owsley, Frank L. *Plain Folk of the Old South*. Baton Rouge, 1950.

Parks, Robert J. *Democracy's Railroads: Public Enterprise in Jacksonian Michigan*. New York, 1972.

Peterson, Arthur G. *Historical Study of Prices Received by Producers of Farm Products in Virginia, 1801–1927*. Virginia Agricultural Experiment Station at Virginia Polytechnic Institute, Technical Bulletin, No. 37, Blacksburg, Va., 1929.

Powell, Mary G. *The History of Old Alexandria, Virginia*. Richmond, 1928.

Pulley, Raymond H. *Old Virginia Restored: An Interpretation of the Progressive Impulse, 1870–1930*. Charlottesville, Va., 1968.

Reed, Merl E. *New Orleans and the Railroads: The Struggle for Commercial Empire*. Baton Rouge, 1966.

Reps, John W. *The Making of Urban America: a History of City Planning in the United States*. Princeton, 1965.

Robert, Joseph C. *The Tobacco Kingdom: Plantations, Market and Factory in Virginia and North Carolina, 1800–1860*. Durham, N.C., 1938.

Rogers, George C., Jr. *Charleston in the Age of the Pinckneys*. Norman, Okla., 1969.

Rothman, David, ed. *The Almshouse Experience*. New York, 1971.

Rubin, Julius. *Canal or Railroad: Imitation and Innovation in Response to the Erie Canal in Philadelphia, Baltimore, and Boston*. Philadelphia, 1961.

Russel, Robert R. "Southern Secessionists Per Se and the Crisis of 1850." In Robert R. Russel, ed. *Critical Studies in Antebellum Sectionalism*. Westport, Conn., 1972, 75–86.

Shanks, Henry T. *The Secession Movement in Virginia*. Richmond, 1934.

Shryock, Richard H. *Medicine in America*. Baltimore, 1966.

Skipper, Otis C. *J. D. B. DeBow: Magazinist of the Old South*. Athens, Ga., 1958.

Starobin, Robert S. *Industrial Slavery in the Old South*. New York, 1969.

Still, Bayrd. *Urban America: A History with Documents*. Boston, 1974.

Taylor, George Rogers. *The Transportation Revolution, 1815–1860*. New York, 1951.

Taylor, William R. *Cavalier and Yankee: The Old South and American National Character*. New York, 1961.

Thomas, Emory M. *The Confederate State of Richmond*. Austin, 1971.

Wade, Richard C. "An Agenda for Urban History." In George A. Billias, and Gerald N. Grob, eds. *American History: Retrospect and Prospect*. New York, 1971. Pp. 367–98.

————. *Slavery in the Cities: The South, 1820–1860*. New York, 1964.

————. *The Urban Frontier: The Rise of Western Cities, 1790–1830*. Cambridge, Mass., 1959.

Waring, George E. *Report on the Social Statistics of Cities: Part II, the Southern and Western States*. Washington, D.C., 1887.

Warner, Sam Bass, Jr. *The Private City: Philadelphia in Three Periods of Its Growth*. Philadelphia, 1968.

Wertenbaker, Thomas Jefferson. *Norfolk, Historic Southern Port*. Durham, 1931.

Wheeler, Kenneth W. *To Wear a City's Crown: The Beginnings of Urban Growth in Texas*. Cambridge, Mass., 1968.

White, Morton, and Lucia White. *The Intellectual versus the City: From Thomas Jefferson to Frank Lloyd Wright*, Cambridge, Mass., 1962.

Williamson, Chilton. *American Suffrage: From Property to Democracy, 1760–1860*. Princeton, 1960.

Woodman, Harold D., ed. *Slavery and the Southern Economy: Sources and Readings*. New York, 1966.

PERIODICAL ARTICLES

Abbott, Carl. "Civic Pride in Chicago, 1844–1860." *Journal of the Illinois State Historical Society*, LXIII (1970), 399–421.

Barrows, Robert G. "The Manuscript Federal Census: Source for a 'New' Local History." *Indiana Magazine of History*, LXIX (1973), 181–92.

Bateman, Fred, James Foust, and Thomas Weiss. "The Participation of Planters in Manufacturing in the Antebellum South." *Agricultural History*, XLVIII (1974), 277–97.

Bellamy, Donnie D. "Free Blacks in Antebellum Missouri, 1820–1860." *Missouri Historical Review*, LXVII (1973), 198–225.

Berry, Thomas S. "The Rise of Flour Milling in Richmond." *Virginia Magazine of History and Biography*, LXXVIII (1970), 388–408.

Bozeman, Theodore Dwight. "Joseph LeConte: Organic Science and a 'Sociology for the South.'" *Journal of Southern History*, XXXIX (1973), 565–82.

Bradford, S. Sydney. "The Negro Ironworker in Ante Bellum Virginia." *Journal of Southern History*, XXV (1959), 194–206.

Brown, Richard D. "The Emergence of Urban Society in Rural Massachusetts, 1760–1820." *Journal of American History*, LXI (1974), 29–51.

Brownell, Blaine A. "Urbanization in the South: A Unique Experience?" *Mississippi Quarterly*. XXVI (1973), 105–20.

Bruce, Kathleen. "Virginia Agricultural Decline to 1860: A Fallacy." *Agricultural History*, VI (1932), 3–13.

Calderhead, William. "How Extensive Was the Border State Slave Trade? A New Look." *Civil War History*, XVIII (1972), 42–55.

Cochran, Thomas C. "The Business Revolution." *American Historical Review*, LXXIX (1974), 1449–66.

Bibliography

Cohen, Hennig. Review of Grady McWhiney, *Southerners and Other Americans.* *American Historical Review*, LXXIX (1974), 582–83.

Cohen, William. "Negro Involuntary Servitude in the South, 1865–1940: A Preliminary Analysis." *Journal of Southern History*, XLII (1976), 31–60.

Cootner, Paul H. "The Role of the Railroads in U.S. Economic Growth," *Journal of Economic History*, XXIII (1963), 477–521.

Curry, Leonard P. "Urbanization and Urbanism in the Old South: A Comparative View." *Journal of Southern History*, XL (1974), 43–60.

Curry, Richard O. "A Reappraisal of Statehood Politics in West Virginia," *Journal of Southern History.* XXVIII (1962), 403–21.

Dew, Charles B. "Disciplining Slave Ironworkers in the Antebellum South: Coercion, Conciliation, and Accommodation." *American Historical Review*, LXXIX (1974), 393–418.

Dorsett, Lyle W., and Arthur H. Shaffer. "Was the Antebellum South Antiurban? A Suggestion." *Journal of Southern History*, XXXVIII (1972), 93–100.

Eaton, Clement, "Slave-Hiring in the Upper South: A Step Toward Freedom." *Mississippi Valley Historical Review*, XLVI (1960), 663–78.

Engerman, Stanley L. "A Reconsideration of Southern Economic Growth, 1770–1860." *Agricultural History*, XLIX (1975), 343–61.

Foner, Eric. "The Causes of the Civil War: Recent Interpretations and New Directions." *Civil War History*, XX (1974), 197–214.

Glazer, Walter S. "Participation and Power—Voluntary Associations and the Functional Organization of Cincinnati in 1840." *Historical Methods Newsletter*, V (1972), 151–68.

Goldfield, David R. "Disease and Urban Image: Yellow Fever in Norfolk, 1855." *Virginia Cavalcade*, XXIII (1973), 34–41.

———. "Urban-Rural Relations in the Old South: The Example of Virginia." *Journal of Urban History*, II (1976).

Goheen, Peter G. "Industrialization and the Growth of Cities in Nineteenth-Century America." *American Studies*, XIV (1973), 49–65.

Goodrich, Carter. "Internal Improvements Reconsidered." *Journal of Economic History*, XXX (1970), 289–311.

———. "Local Government Planning of Internal Improvements." *Political Science Quarterly*, LXIV (1951), 411–45.

———. "The Virginia System of Mixed Enterprise: A Study of State Planning of Internal Improvements." *Political Science Quarterly*, LIV (1949), 355–87.

Griffen, Clyde. "Occupational Mobility in Nineteenth-Century America." *Journal of Social History*, V (1972), 310–30.

Griffin, Richard W. "The Origins of the Industrial Revolution in Georgia: Cotton Textiles, 1810–1865." *Georgia Historical Quarterly*, XLII (1958), 355–75.

Grimsted, David. "Rioting in the Jacksonian Setting." *American Historical Review*, LXVII (April, 1972), 361–97.

Gutman, Herbert G. "The World Two Cliometricians Made: A Review Essay of F + E = T/C." *Journal of Negro History*, LX (1975), 101.

Hackney, Sheldon. "The South as a Counterculture." *American Scholar*, XLII (1973), 283–93.

Hareven, Tamara K. "The Historical Study of the Family in Urban Society." *Journal of Urban History*, I (1975), 259–65.

Hite, James C., and Ellen J. Hall. "The Reactionary Evolution of Economic Thought in Antebellum Virginia." *Virginia Magazine of History and Biography*, LXXX (1972), 476–88.

Hunter, Robert F. "The Turnpike Movement in Virginia, 1816–1860." *Virginia Magazine of History and Biography*, LXIX (1961), 278–89.

Jaher, Frederic C. "Nineteenth-Century Elites in Boston and New York." *Journal of Social History*, VI (1972), 32–77.

Knight, J. Stephen, Jr. "Discontent, Disunity, and Dissent in the Antebellum South: Virginia as a Test Case, 1844–1846." *Virginia Magazine of History and Biography*, LXXVIII (1970), 437–50.

Lewis, Clifford M. "The Wheeling Suspension Bridge." *West Virginia History*, XXXIII (1972), 203–33.

Luraghi, Raimondo. "The Civil War and the Modernization of American Society." *Civil War History*, XVIII (1972), 230–49.

Lurie, Jonathan. "Private Associations, Internal Regulation and Progressivism: The Chicago Board of Trade, 1880–1923, as a Case Study." *American Journal of Legal History*, XVI (1972), 215–38.

McCaughey, Robert A. "From Town to City: Boston in the 1820's." *Political Science Quarterly*, LXXXVIII (1973), 191–213.

McQuade, Walter. "Spring in Virginia: An Appreciation." *New York Times*, February 11, 1973.

Miller, Randall. "Daniel Pratt's Industrial Urbanism: The Cotton Mill Town in Antebellum Alabama." *Alabama Historical Quarterly*, XXXIV (1972), 5–35.

Modell, John, and Tamara Hareven. "Urbanization and the Malleable Household: Examination of Boarding and Lodging in American Families." *Journal of Marriage and the Family*, XXXV (1973), 467–79.

Mohl, Raymond A. "Poverty, Pauperism, and Social Order in the Preindustrial American City, 1780-1840." *Social Science Quarterly*, LII (1972), 934–48.

O'Brien, Michael C. "C. Vann Woodward and the Burden of Southern Liberalism." *American Historical Review*, LXXVIII (1973), 589–604.

Olsen, Otto, "Historians and the Extent of Slave Ownership in the Southern United States." *Civil War History*, XVIII (1972), 101–16.

Owsley, Frank L. "The Fundamental Causes of the Civil War: Egocentric Sectionalism." *Journal of Southern History*, VII (1941), 3–18.

————, and Harriet C. Owsley. "The Economic Basis of Society in the Late Antebellum South." *Journal of Southern History*, VI (1940), 24–26.

Bibliography

Pessen, Edward. "The Egalitarian Myth and the American Social Reality: Wealth, Mobility, and Equality in the 'Era of the Common Man.' " *American Historical Review*, LXXVI (1971), 989–1034.

———. "Who Governed the Nation's Cities in the 'Era of the Common Man.' " *Political Science Quarterly*, LXXXVII (1972), 591–614.

Phillips, U. B. "The Central Theme of Southern History." *American Historical Review*, XXXIV (1928), 30–43.

Quenzel, Carrol H. "The Manufacture of Locomotives and Cars in Alexandria in the 1850s." *Virginia Magazine of History and Biography*, LXII (1954), 181–89.

Rice, Otis K. "Coal Mining in the Kanawha Valley to 1861: A View of Industrialization in the Old South." *Journal of Southern History*, XXXI (1965), 393–416.

Roberson, Jere W. "The South and the Pacific Railroad, 1845–1855." *Western Historical Quarterly*, V (1974), 163–86.

Rogers, A. A. "Constitutional Democracy in Antebellum Virginia." *William and Mary Quarterly*, 2nd Series; XVI (1936), 399–407.

Rubin, Julius. "The Limits of Agricultural Progress in the Nineteenth-Century South." *Agricultural History*, XLIX (1975), 362–73.

Schlebecker, John T. "The World Metropolis and the History of American Agriculture." *Journal of Economic History*, XX (1960), 187–208.

Schmidt, Louis B. "Internal Commerce and the Development of the National Economy Before 1860." *Journal of Political Economy*, XLII (1939), 798–822.

Schnell, J. Christopher, and Katherine B. Clinton. "The New West: Themes in Nineteenth-Century Urban Promotion, 1815–1880." *Bulletin of the Missouri Historical Society*, XXX (1974), 75–88.

———, and Patrick E. McLear. "Why the Cities Grew: A Historiographical Essay on Western Urban Growth, 1850–1880." *Bulletin of the Missouri Historical Society*, XXVII (1972), 162–77.

Scott, Anne Firor. "Women's Perspective on the Patriarchy in the 1850s." *Journal of American History*, LXI (1974), 52–64.

Smiley, David L. "The Quest for a Central Theme in Southern History." *South Atlantic Quarterly*, LXII (1972), 307–25.

Stewart, Peter C. "Railroads and Urban Rivalries in Antebellum Eastern Virginia." *Virginia Magazine of History and Biography*, LXXXI (1973), 3–22.

Stone, Lawrence. "Prosopography." *Daedalus*, C (1971), 46–89.

Tindall, George B. "Beyond the Mainstream: The Ethnic Southerners." *Journal of Southern History*, XL (1974), 3–18.

Ward, James A. "A New Look at Antebellum Southern Railroad Development." *Journal of Southern History*, XXXIX (1973), 409–20.

Waring, Joseph I. "Asiatic Cholera in South Carolina." *Bulletin of the History of Medicine*, XL (October, 1966).

Warner, Sam Bass, Jr. "If All the World Were Philadelphia: A Scaffolding for Urban History, 1774–1930." *American Historical Review*, LXXIV (1968), 26–43.

Welter, Rush. "The Frontier West as Image of American Society." *Pacific Northwest Quarterly*, LXII (1961), 1–6.

Wyatt, Edward A., IV. "Rise of Industry in Antebellum Petersburg." *William and Mary Quarterly*, 2nd Series; XVII (1937), 1–36.

UNPUBLISHED MATERIALS

Boughter, Isaac F. "Internal Improvements in Northwestern Virginia: A Study of State Policy Prior to the Civil War." Ph.D. dissertation, University of Pittsburgh, 1930.

Clark, Malcolm C. "The First Quarter-Century of the Richmond and Danville Railroad, 1847–1871." M. A. thesis, George Washington University, 1959.

Coleman, Elizabeth Dabney. "The Story of the Virginia Central Railroad, 1850–1860." Ph.D. dissertation, University of Virginia, 1957.

Penn, Sydney. "Agricultural Organization in Ante-Bellum Virginia." M. S. thesis, University of Virginia, 1935.

Stewart, Peter C. "The Commercial History of Hampton Roads, Virginia, 1815–1860." Ph.D. dissertation, University of Virginia, 1967.

Wolff, Alfred Y., Jr. "A Study of the Antebellum Virginia Novel as a Reflection of Virginia Society." M. A. thesis, University of Virginia, 1965.

Index

Agriculture: revival in 1850s, xvii; railroads and, xx, 9, 182–84, 191–92; southern cities and, xxvi; depression of, 1; Virginia State Agricultural Society, 97–98; fairs, 98–100; and opposition to commodity exchanges, 114, 116–17; and opposition to short term credits, 117; and demand for labor, 136; wheat cultivation, 190–91; exclusive emphasis on, 221; inspection procedures in, 222; market gardening, 238–39

Alexandria: history of, 19; geographic advantages of, 19–20; railroad subscriptions in, 21; characteristics of leadership in, 54–59; commerce and industry in, 106–107, 112–14, 117; need for theater in, 108; city council structure, 139, 142; police services, 144–45; fire protection, 147–48; street repair in, 149; street lighting in, 151; waste disposal in, 157, 159; Ladies Benevolent Society, 163; Overseers of the Poor, 164; importance of trees in, 170; Ivy Hill Cemetery, 171; need for parks in, 171; pollution of Potomac, 172–73; taxes in, 176–77; retrenchment in, 177–78; and railroads, 187–89, 204, 206, 213–14, 233; locomotive industry in, 195; flour millery in, 195; export trade in, 197; population increase in, 198; construction boom in, 198; suburban growth in, 199; coastwise trade, 239, 240; commercial ties with New York, 243; trade pattern in, 246, 269; economic opposition to secession in, 253, 268

Anderson, Joseph R., 32, 193–94

Associations: for promotion of business, 111–12; for commodity exchanges, 113; for poor relief, 160–63; urbanization and, 201

Baltimore: urban Virginia's objections to, 207–208; and steamer line to Virginia, 240–41

Banking: and Panic of 1857, 178–79; as obstacle to urban growth, 219–20; suspension of, 264

Blow, George, Jr., 266

Board of Public Works: internal improvement plan of, 22–24; and incomplete commercial sectors, 228–29

Boisseau, James, 268

Branch, Thomas M., 255, 268

Brent, George W., 254–55, 268

Brown, Joseph G., 274

Burwell, William M., 24, 278

Cash, W. J., xi, 271

City council, 139–42

Civil War, xxvi–xxviii, 270–71

Clemens, Sherrard, 266

Commercial conventions, southern, 253–54

Constitution of 1851, p. 27

Convict lease, 126

Cowardin, James A., 33–101

Crenshaw, Lewis D., 192–93, 194, 196

Crime: in Virginia cities, 142–44; impact on urban image, 143; against property, 143–44; juvenile, 145–46. See also Police

Dahl, Robert A., 60

De Bow, J. D. B., xxiii, xxiv, 274–75

Dimmock, Charles, 211

Directories, 109

Disease: costs of, 153, 155; and fear of epidemic, 153; and impact of epidemic, 155–56. See also Health

Edmonds, Richard Hathaway, 273–74, 275, 278–79

Education: vocational, 123; demands for public system of, 166; and sectionalism, 166; urban environment conducive to, 166; Literary Fund, 166–67; commitment to higher, 167–68; adult, 168–69

Export trade: European, 11, 196–97; dependence on northern ports, 12, 238; decline in, 12; impact on domestic trade, 12; and coastwise trade, 12, 238–41; and

Index

local capital formation, 13; and sectionalism, 13; and manufacturing, 14, 15; Norfolk conventions on, 25; and South American, 196; and railroads, 197, 235; failure to develop, 241

Family relations: among Richmond leaders, 43–48; importance of, 43–44; among Norfolk leaders, 53–54; comparisons of, 54, 59, 66–67; among Alexandria leaders, 56, 59; among Richmond household heads, 66–68, 88

Financial administration, urban: and increasing debt of local governments, 173–75; budgets, 174–75; taxes, 175–77; citizen complaints about, 176–77; retrenchment, 177–78; and service levels, 178

Fire protection: and fire hazards, 146, 148; regulations, 147; business considerations in providing, 147; volunteer companies for, 147–48; professionalization of, 148

Fitzhugh, George: and southern urban growth, xviii, xxiii, 275; and railroad building, 9; and peonage plan for free black labor, 128–29; and urban slavery, 137; and public education, 166; and easy money, 219–20; and diversified economy, 221, 276

Foner, Eric, 270

Fowle, George D., 56

Free blacks: in Richmond, 63–68; and population increase, 127; threatened removal of, 127; as important labor force, 128, 130; selective enforcement of laws against, 129

Frisch, Michael, 180

Fry, Hugh W., 33

Gallego flour, 193

Gaston, Paul M., 271–72, 273, 282

Genovese, Eugene, xi

Geographic determinism, 19–21

Glazer, Walter S., 32, 34, 40, 41

Grady, Henry W., 277, 278

Griffen, Clyde, 36, 40, 43, 64

Harvie, Lewis E., 264

Haxall, R. B., 33–34, 193

Health: importance to urban image, 152–53; boards of, 156; cleanliness and, 157; waste disposal, 157–58; drainage, 158–59; selective application of regulations, 159–60

Hill, Benjamin Harvey, 273

Hill, Daniel Harvey, 281

Holladay, James G., 266

Hotels, 107–108

Howard Association, 155, 162

Hubbard, Chester D., 266

Hundley, Daniel R., xxii

Immigration, European, 125

Immigration, northern, 124

Irwin, Henry, 51

James River and Kanawha Canal: importance to Richmond, 24, 187; labor requirements, 119; slave hiring on, 132; poor management of, 228, 229, 230; debts of, 230–31; support by legislature of, 231

John Brown's Raid, 248–50

Johnson, Marmaduke, 267

Katz, Michael B., 60

Knights, Peter R., 34, 64

Labor shortage, 119, 122, 123

Leadership: studies in, 29; characteristics of, 30; definition of, 31; and urbanization, 60–61

London, Daniel H., 249, 258, 260

Luraghi, Raimondo, xi

Lynchburg: history of, 19; urban press of, 102; tobacco warehouse in, 106; Norvell House Hotel, 108; city directory, 110; city council structure, 140; crime in, 143; night watch in, 145; street lighting in, 150; waste disposal in, 158; Dorcas Society, 163; and relief societies, 165; and higher education, 168; and Lynchburg College, 168; taxes, 177; and commerce from railroads, 189; as tobacco market, 190; population decline in, 198; per capita wealth of, 201; rivalry over railroads, 211; challenges Richmond as tobacco and wheat market, 212–13; demands own legislator, 221–22; trade pattern of, 247; impact of trade pattern on secession vote, 268, 269

Macfarland, William H., 267

McKenzie, Lewis, 56–57, 186

McVeigh, William M., 56
Mallory, Francis, 208
Manufacturers' Record, 273, 278–79
Manufacturing: in Old South, xiv–xv; relation to urbanization, xv; and sectionalism, 13; low volume in Virginia, 14;
and tariff, 14; processing industries, 14,
192–95; impact on agriculture, 14; impact on railroads, 14, 233; and export
trade, 14, 15; labor requirements, 119;
multiplier effect of, 192; diversification
in, 193; employment in, 193; and heavy
industry, 193–95; in Northeast, 227;
linkages with internal improvements,
234; southern preference for northern,
246; and home manufacture movement,
250; in New South, 275
Market facilities, 105, 106
Mayo, Amory Dwight, 274
Mayor: extension of powers, 139–40; direct
election, 140–41
Moore, Samuel McDowell, 255
Morriss, Charles Y., 194

National economy: centered at New York,
227–28, 235–36; inclusion of Virginia
cities in, 251; opposition to, 244–45, 250,
257; Republicans' recognition of, 258–
59; influence on secession vote, 269; in
New South, 281
Native-born residents: among Richmond's
leaders, 41; comparative rates, 41, 53, 58,
65; among Norfolk leaders, 53; among
Alexandria leaders, 58; amomg Richmond household heads, 65
New South Creed: similarity with Old
South, 274–75, 281; dangers of, 281–82;
revival of, 282
New York City: as foremost import-export
center, 227; origins of economic supremacy, 228; centralization of commerce at,
235–36, 241; importance of railroads to,
235–36; establishment of steamer lines to
Virginia, 240–41; increased southern
patronage of, 243, 245–46; objections to
dependence on, 244–45
Norfolk: depression in, 2; history of,
17–18; geographic advantages of, 19–20;
and railroad subscription, 21; and European trade efforts, 26, 241; characteristics of leadership in, 48–54; *Southern Argus*, 101; iron market house, 106; hotel

facilities, 107; city directory, 109; board
of trade, 113; corn exchange, 114; vocational education in, 123; women in counting rooms, 126; slave hiring ordinance,
135; crime in, 143; night watch in, 144–
45; street paving policy, 150; 1855 yellow
fever epidemic, 154–56; waste disposal
in, 158; drainage in, 158–59; Association
for the Improvement of the Condition of
the Poor, 160–61; Dorcas Society, 161–
62; Howard Association, 162; government donations to private poor relief
societies, 165; public school system, 167;
Musical Association, 169; trees in, 170;
parks in, 172; citizen complaints against
taxes, 177; as small industrial base, 195;
export trade, 197; population increase,
198; per capita wealth in, 201; rivalry
over railroads, 205–206, 208; rivalry with
Richmond over export trade, 214; opposes merchants' sales tax, 216–17; and
conflict over railroad freight rates, 232;
as "Atlantic Garden," 238; and coastwise
trade, 238–39, 246; impact of trade patterns on secession vote, 266, 269

Occupation: among Richmond leaders,
34–36; comparative figures, 34–36, 50,
55, 61; among Norfolk leaders, 48–50;
among Alexandria leaders, 54–55;
among Richmond household heads,
61–62, 63; strength of difference between Richmond household heads and
leaders, 68, 88; growth of urban occupations, 200
Old South: distinctiveness, xxviii;
similarities to other sections, xxviii; as
rural-dominated, 271, 272; and New
South Creed, 274–75, 281
Omnibus service, 199

Panic of 1857, 115, 117, 178–79
Parks, 171–72
Persistence and priority: among Richmond's leaders, 40–41; comparative
rates, 40, 53, 58, 64; among Norfolk
leaders, 52–53; among Alexandria leaders, 58; among Richmond household
heads, 64–65; and economic profile of
Richmond persisters, 88–91; relative
mobility of Richmond persisters, 91–94
Petersburg: depression in, 2; history of, 18;

Index

city council structure, 139; railroad network, 188; as tobacco market, 190; population increase, 198; trade pattern of, 247; impact of trade pattern on secession vote, 268, 269

Police: night watch by, 144; inadequacy of, 144–45; business concern about, 145–46. *See also* Crime

Pollard, Edward A., 281–82

Pollution, 172–73, 194

Poor relief: public attitude toward, 160, 163; organized private, 160–63; seasonal, 161–63; public charity, 164–65

Potter, David, 271

Press: functions of, xxi, 100; urban journalism, 100–102; circulation in countryside, 103, 104; as urban image maker, 103; as advertising medium, 104–105; as initiator of programs, 211; role in New South, 278–79

Property ownership: among Richmond leaders, 36–38; among Norfolk leaders, 52; comparative figures, 52, 57, 62; among Alexandria leaders, 57; among Richmond household heads, 62, 63; strength of difference between Richmond household heads and leaders, 88

Race relations, 280

Railroads: rural investment in, xvi, xvii, 184–85; impact on agriculture, xx, 9, 182–84, 191–92; and national economy, xx; benefits to urban merchants, 9; and sectionalism, 10; state investment in, 10–11, 185–86, 231; Richmond and Danville R.R., 10–11, 185, 187, 190, 228; and manufacturing, 14, 233; Virginia and Tennessee R.R., 24, 187, 189; Covington and Ohio R.R., 24, 207; Virginia Central R.R., 24, 189, 207, 213, 229, 233; benefits to Virginia cities, 24–25, 187–91; labor requirements, 119; slave hiring on, 132; urban investment in, 173; urban disenchantment with, 178, 232; mileage, 182; urban-rural management of, 186; Orange and Alexandria R.R., 187, 189, 233, 263; Manassas Gap R.R., 187; Alexandria, Loudoun, and Hampshire R.R., 187–88; Baltimore and Ohio R.R., 188, 207, 246; Norfolk and Petersburg, 188; Southside R.R., 190, 231; and export trade, 197, 235; and defense, 208; rate-

gouging charged, 213; northern network of, 227; and patterns of trade, 227, 236–37, 240; unfinished network of, 228; poor management of, 229–30; financial problems of, 230, 231–34; reliance on foreign suppliers, 234; and New York City, 235–36; transcontinental, 261

Randolph, George W., 267

Randolph, Thomas Mann, 5

Readjuster movement, 276

Reid, Charles, 51–52

Richmond: depression in, 2; history of, 17; geographic advantages of, 19–20; railroad subscription, 21; characteristics of leadership in, 31–48; characteristics of general population and leadership in, 61–94; community of interests between household heads and leaders, 95–96; support of agriculture, 98–100; *Daily Dispatch*, 101; hotel facilities, 107; city directory, 109; board of trade, 112, 215–16; tobacco exchange, 114–16; Virginia Mechanics' Institute, 123, 168; immigrants in labor force, 125; slave hiring agencies in, 133; city council structure, 140; election of city officers, 141; police service, 145; juvenile institutions, 146; fire protection, 148; street lighting in, 150–51; waterworks, 152; waste disposal in, 157; private poor relief in, 162; and Overseers of the Poor, 164; higher education in, 167–68; and Richmond Female Institute, 168; adult education in, 168; and Richmond Atheneum, 168; and Hollywood Cemetery, 171; debt of, 173; budgets of, 174–75; citizen complaints against taxes, 177; differential service levels, 178; railroad network, 187; and commerce from railroads, 189; as tobacco market, 190, 212–13; flour inspections in, 191; as tobacco manufacturing center, 192–93, 194; as flour milling center, 193; other industries in, 193; iron industry in, 193–94; as "Lowell of the South," 194; and Brazil flour trade, 196; and European tobacco trade, 196; shipbuilding in, 196; population increase, 197; physical transformation of, 199; suburban growth of, 199; emergence of business district in, 200; emergence of residential district in, 200; per capita wealth in, 201; and rivalry over railroads, 206, 207, 210, 211; railroad policy, 211; as wheat market, 212; and rivalry with Norfolk over export trade, 214; opposes merchants' sales tax, 216, 217, 218; capital shortage in, 219–20; centralization of tobacco and flour trade at, 236; dependence on northern markets, 237–38; coastwise trade of, 240; export trade of, 241; diverse commercial ties of, 247; economic prospects in the Confederacy, 256–57; and impact of trade patterns on secession vote, 267, 269

Rivalry, urban: and urban consciousness, 202, 214–15; and fear of economic failure, 202, 211; southern, 202, 253; in mid-nineteenth-century America, 202–203; reasons for bitterness of, 203; and railroads, 204–11; state legislature as forum for, 204–10; and southern nationalism, 207–208; rural supporters of, 208–209; over rural customers, 212–14; over export trade, 214

Rives, William C., 256, 259
Robertson, Wyndham, 5
Rural ideal, xv–xvi, xxvi
Russell, Robert, 131

Sales tax repeal, 215–18
Secession convention, 263–69
Secession crisis: choices for urban Virginia, 248, 251, 252; nonintercourse suggested, 250; caution after Lincoln's election, 251; commercial arguments against secession, 252–54; African slave trade issue, 254–56; economic arguments for secession, 256–61; benefits of secession to cities, 257; financial tribute to North, 258; economic policies of Republican party, 258–59; fear of federal government's economic power, 259–62

Segregation: spatial, xx, 200; economic, xx, 200
Sellers, Charles G., xxviii
Slaughter, Charles R., 268
Slave hiring: history of, 130–31; flexibility of, 131, 136, 137; increase during 1850s, 131; types of employment suited for, 132; sources of slaves for, 132; agents for, 132–33; complaints about, 133–34; rates of hire, 135; suggested remedies for, 135

Slaveholding: in Old South, xxvii–xxviii, 38; among Richmond leaders, 38–40; among Norfolk leaders, 50; comparative figures, 50, 57, 62; among Alexandria leaders, 57–58; among Richmond household heads, 62, 63; and secession convention, 265

Slavery: compatibility of with city, xxvii, 137; as cause of depression, 4; and rising prices for slaves, 122; and shortage of slaves, 123; and slave hiring, 130–37; and slave occupations in city, 136; and African slave trade, 254–56; and secession debate, 256; use of federal power against, 262

Slave trade: profits from, 120; extent of, 121; labor drain as result of, 121, 136–37
Smith, Richards C., 195
Southern Rights Association: purpose, 25; advocates economic independence, 249
Speed, John M., 268
Street lighting, 150, 151
Street repair, 149–50
Suburban growth, 199

Taxation: merchants' sales tax, 215–18; tax on private credit, 218
Taylor, George Rogers, xx
Thomas, James, Jr., 192–93
Tredegar Iron Works, 32, 131, 193–94
Tredway, William M., 260
Trees: impact on urban image, 170; tree planting campaigns, 170–71
Tucker, John Randolph, 259, 274

Urban consciousness: indicator of urban growth, xxii, 202; manifestations of, 202–224
Urban growth: in Old South, xi–xiv; and sectionalism, xvii–xviii, xxii–xxv, xxix, 16, 224–25, 248–49; in United States, xviii–xix; indicators of, xix–xxii; and leadership, xxi; and imitation, 9; population, 197–98; physical, 198–200; importance of timing to, 226–28, 282
Urban-rural conflict: on taxation, 216, 217; on mortgage loans, 218–19; on general financial policies, 220; and urban consciousness, 220–21; and political representatives, 221–22; and inspection procedures, 222; philosophical distinctions of, 223

Index

Usury laws, 218–19

Virginia: sections of, xxix–xxx; slavery in, xxix, 121; depression in, 1; intrastate sectionalism in, 2–3; fixation on past, 3, 4, 277; political impotence, 3–4, 5–6; fixation on politics, 5, 6, 277; fear of northern economic power, 6–7; fear of federal government, 7–8; importance of economic growth to, 9; locational advantages, 20; importance of education to, 166; taxation in, 215–18

Wade, Richard C., xxii
Water, 151
Western trade: importance to South, xxiv, xxv, 249–50; and northern cities, xxv, 247–48; and New Orleans, xxv; and New York City, xxv, 235–36, 247; and sectionalism, xxv
Wheeling: depression in, 2; history of, 18; railroad subscription, 21; urban press, 102; *Daily Intelligencer*, 102; iron market house, 106; city directory, 109; board of trade, 113; short-term credit arrangements, 117; city council structure, 140; crime in, 142–43; night watch in, 145; juvenile institutions in, 146; volunteer fire companies, 147–48; Cosmopolitan Arts and Literary Association, 169; trees, 170; air pollution in, 172; debt of, 173; expenditures of, 173–74; taxes, 176; railroad network, 188; iron foundries, 195; nail manufacturing, 195; glass factories, 196; population increase, 198; rivalry over railroads, 204–205; ties to northern markets, 246–47, 269; economic opposition to secession, 252–53, 266
White, William, 266
Wickham, Williams C., 267
Wise, Henry A., 4, 166
Women: property ownership in Richmond, 63; slaveholding in Richmond, 63; persistence and priority in Richmond, 64; nativity of Richmond, 65; family relations of Richmond, 67–68; in factories, 125–26